HUMAN
DEVELOPMENT
IN AN
URBAN
AGE

HUMAN
DEVELOPMENT
IN AN
URBAN
AGE

THERON ALEXANDER

Temple University

Prentice-Hall, Inc.
Englewood Cliffs, New Jersey

Library of Congress Cataloging in Publication Data

ALEXANDER, THERON
    Human development in an urban age.

    Includes bibliographies.
    1. Man—Influence of environment.   2. Personality
and culture.   3. Social problems.   I. Title.   [DNLM:
1. Psychology, Social.   2. Social behavior.
3. Socialization.   4. Urbanization.   HM 251 A378h
1973]
HM206.A42   155.9′2   73-506
ISBN 0-13-444786-7

HM
206
·A42

© 1973 by Prentice-Hall, Inc.
Englewood Cliffs, New Jersey

Printed in the United States of America

10   9   8   7   6   5   4   3   2   1

Prentice-Hall International, Inc., London
Prentice-Hall of Australia, Pty. Ltd., Sydney
Prentice-Hall of Canada, Ltd., Toronto
Prentice-Hall of India Private Limited, New Delhi
Prentice-Hall of Japan, Inc., Tokyo

CONTENTS

v

Part II

SOCIALIZATION   45

Part III

INTELLIGENCE, LANGUAGE, AND CREATIVITY

Chapter 5

The Foundations of Response

Part IV

EMOTIONS, MOTIVATION,
AND LEARNING   163

Chapter 8

Human Emotions   165

Chapter 12

Individual Autonomy in Urban Society 272

A NOTE
FROM THE AUTHOR

It may be of value to describe some origins of the direction of this book. At the beginning of the writing, I was involved in an extensive research activity associated with the Federal program for Head Start. As director of one of the regional research centers set up throughout the United States, I was able to gain a perspective on the social change created by the program not only from my own research but from the research of others in centers across the nation. Extensive work was being done throughout the country in order to better understand the problems of the "disadvantaged." The studies included data from the parents as well as the children. This information provided a view of family life in both urban and rural areas.

During the writing, I visited the major countries of Europe to observe a range of human development programs. Seeing these programs maintained by universities, governments, and private organizations had considerable influence. I was able to use the experience in viewing our own educational efforts.

While a member of a Department of Pediatrics faculty at a midwest university, I participated in a program for children from poverty backgrounds as well as in research projects with those who had various physical problems. I worked, too, in a clinical setting with adults who saw in their own lives the difficulties growing out of relationships in their environmental context. It became very clear to me that it was quite in error to perceive all of an individual's problems in development as internal, as a personal failure to adequately deal with the environment. External social conditions, too, had a bearing. Undoubtedly, my view of human development has grown in part out of my study in several of the social and biological sciences under the Committee on Human Development at the University of Chicago and from experience as a faculty member in Colleges of Liberal Arts, Medicine, and Education.

Recent exchanges with students in a large urban university with its problems as part of a great population complex has brought immediacy to my awareness of the need for a different perspective of developmental psychology today. During four years of work on the book, the theme of bringing together developmental principles and social conditions in contemporary society has become of even greater importance to me.

To be even more personal, I must tell you that while writing the book, I could look from my office window across the city to a great bridge spanning the river into another state, a continuation of Megalopolis. In between lay block after block of deteriorated housing with all the hopelessness such conditions bring. As evening would come, lights in the great buildings and the parkways leading to the museums and cultural centers of the city changed the scene into one of beauty, pleasure, and hope.

I could see, too, just before complete darkness, the area of the city where the old buildings, dating back to the founding of the nation, seemed to bring amidst the noise of the rush hour traffic a serenity of years long past, of a less hurried life style. Although the old government buildings are now only a minute island in the vastness of Megalopolis, nevertheless they exert an influence on the present; they frequently attract protest groups who seem to feel that symbolically some inspiration or direction can be gained from their place in history.

Regardless of where one is in our society today, a view of human development seems to demand that the conditions of the society be seen as an important factor in the course of events in any individual's life. We can see, I believe, that elements of modern society hold promise of both despair and hope. The perspective outlined in this book, I trust, will lead toward the latter.

PREFACE

How can fundamental principles of human development be made relevant to the new modes of living in contemporary society? How can they help prepare the individual to live in a rapidly changing soicety? This book seeks to answer these questions first, by discussing the fundamental principles usually covered in texts on human development under such topics as socialization, intelligence, learning, language, creativity, emotions, motivation, and control of behavior; and second, by discussing the relationship of the individual to society, to its structures and social processes now undergoing accelerating change.

The book differs from others in the field in three ways: (1) it takes a view of development in which modern man is seen in a life space as part of the ecological system of the earth; (2) it relates human development to conditions of urban and modern society and emphasizes the consequences of social change; and (3) it provides a relevant approach by emphasizing the fact that development principles ought to be perceived as directly related to social conditions.

While relating development to conditions in society and dealing with the current problems of young people with the "system," the book lays a foundation by utilizing current theory and research. It emphasizes principles and is not tied directly to a time. Thus it can provide a basis for a realistic understanding of human development in a modern society.

The material is organized according to subject matter rather than chronological age, but the age periods are covered within topics whenever age differences are significant.

The organization of the book is in five parts. The early chapters emphasize topics currently recognized as basic to the field. In the later chapters, the basic topics are related to social conditions in modern society. This approach is new in the developmental field; in the past little effort has been made in texts to relate developmental experience to social conditions and issues.

Part I (Environment and Man) begins with a foundation for the concept of man in his life space, a limited environment. It also deals with the development of cities, urban regions, and man's modification of the environment.

Part II (Socialization) deals with the preparation of the individual for life in an urban society. This part covers the development of life styles and cultural differences characteristic of the urban age.

Part III (Intelligence, Language, and Creativity) covers development as related to these three topics. The concern over the issue of genetic and cultural influences is included.

In the discussion of emotions and motivation, Part IV (Emotions, Motivation, and Learning) theories and research findings are stressed.

Part V (The Individual and Society) reflects a new emphasis in the field of human development by including topics on the control of behavior, youth's discontent with modern society, the development of radical thought, the problems of authority and autonomy, and the exercise of power in modern times.

Thus, this book includes fundamental information about research findings and theories available in the field today, but it does more. It seeks to relate these findings and principles to the end goal of the developmental and socialization experience, that is, the individual's assumption of an adult role in modern society.

Developmental psychology more than any other area of social science ought to be concerned with the *results* of the developmental experience. Yet, we in the field all too often have been so much preoccupied with stages or processes, research strategies, and theoretical controversy that we have neglected the essential task of relating the developmental experience to social conditions and the destiny of youth in society.

This book therefore makes an effort to deal both with the processes of learning and with the significance of the context of the environment. The approach reflects a convergence of views of the developing person as one who learns by responding to the influences of the environment and as one who selects and influences the context of the environment. Special emphasis on the context of experience is made in the latter part of the book. This attention reflects a merging of theoretical constructs drawn from developmental psychology and from sociological and anthropological frameworks.

At no time in history have so many youth turned away from the teaching of their fathers and the culture. Anyone now reading this book can find within hearing the troubled voices, not only of youth, but of their parents, of social agents, and those in the educational system.

This book only begins to respond to these voices because it is not a book dealing with problems but a text on human development. It does, nevertheless take a first step toward putting the standard textbook topics in a perspective of the social conditions that youth encounter in society. It also tries to present some of the issues that these conditions pose for the socialization process.

HUMAN
DEVELOPMENT
IN AN
URBAN
AGE

ENVIRONMENT AND MAN

The study of human development should concern not only the process of learning and the way the individual responds or changes during the developmental years but also the influence of the environmental context in which learning takes place. This context includes the physical or natural features of the land—the valleys, mountains, and rivers—and artificial features such as buildings and cities. The context also includes the social structures that surround, aid, or constrain each individual.

The essential purpose of Part I is to describe the characteristics of the environment and life space in which the individual develops. Subsequently, the *process* of human development is taken into account, that is, the way the individual learns to respond to the environment. The study of individual response should include both the individual's reactions to stimuli and his own initiation of action. Initiation of action by the individual sets in motion a cycle of interaction in which the environment changes the person and the person changes the environment. All too often in the study of human development the context in which the learning takes place has been overshadowed by emphasis on the process of learning. Both must be taken into account.

The significance of the physical environment for man has been brought into new awareness during a period when technology and increased population are threatening an environment that earlier seemed to draw on endless resources. Now the rivers, forests, air, and oceans have been adversely affected. In recent years it has been recognized, too, that the use of land and space has psychological aspects that cannot be ignored. The psychological significance not only of space and buildings but also of social organizations is now perceived as important in the study of human development.

Just as the importance of life space features is increasingly apparent, so is the importance of social structures and their functions. The family, the educational system, religious organizations, government, and economic units all affect the child's learning and influence his development of a life style that will characterize his future role in society. Some of the influences of the social structures in the life space are beneficial and create a dynamic and highly satisfactory way of life, while others have an adverse effect on development and behavior.

As the society changes, more and more decisions about trends and directions must be made. Thoughtful decisions can prevent unfavorable conditions that may prove to be irrevocable. As individual influence on a complex society is minimal, however, and methods of social change are not clearly visible, revolutionary means have become widespread throughout the world. There seems to be as much resort to violence to bring change as ever. It is therefore easily recognized that if social change is to come about without traumatic results for large numbers of people, education and training during the developmental years must receive more attention. Early experiences should prepare youth to cope with the conditions of the urban age.

ECOLOGY
AND
HUMAN
DEVELOPMENT

1

In 1623, late in the rule of King James I of England, John Donne, Dean of St. Paul's Cathedral, described man's dependent relationship to his environment in words that are poignant and still appropriate: "No man is an island, entire of itself; every man is a piece of the continent, a part of the main. . . ." [1] The description was written at the time of the first successful voyages of the East India Company and the establishment of the colonies in Virginia, heralding the expansion of living space far to the west in the New World. In the following years, the East India Company was greatly extended, William Penn received the grant of Pennsylvania, the Dutch began to settle New York, and the basic foundations were laid for the extension of the British Empire. In the next three hundred years man's environment changed more than it had in all the preceding thousands of years of the world's history.

To understand man's psychological reactions to such great social change, it is necessary to understand the facts and influences of human development in the process of interacting with the environment.

In modern times the study of man's relationship to his environment includes a vast panorama of facts and ideas which has been described

---

[1] *Devotions upon Emergent Occasions,* Meditation XVII.

by the word *ecology*. The term refers to the interpretation and explanation of the relationships among all living things. *Human ecology* has in recent years become an identifiable area of study dealing with man's relationships with his environment, although it has not yet become a discipline. It is more a point of view than a discipline, a view that draws information and ideas from a number of disciplines: psychology, biology, geography, anthropology, sociology, health science, economics, and political science.

At first the concept of human ecology was largely based on biological principles such as biological individuality. At the beginning of human life, meiosis (random genetic exchange) brings about biological individuality. Body structure, physiology, rate of growth, life span, and some aspects of behavior are determined in this process. Biological foundations are related not only to cycles of short duration, such as changes that may take place in body temperature during a 24-hour period, but also to the overall progression of growth, maturity, aging, and death. During this biological progression an organism directs behavior to finding situations in which stress is reduced and physical conditions are most favorable. Man, for example, prefers certain places for each of his activities; he seeks different areas for rest (bedroom or wilderness retreat), for work (small shop or large corporation), for food procurement, for recreation and other activities.

Certain conditions on the earth influence man's behavior, particularly in reference to food and its availability. His body requires the nutritional constituents of proteins, fats, carbohydrates, minerals, and water; in obtaining these constituents and using them for life processes man becomes part of a symbiotic relationship with other species dependent upon the same habitat conditions. Greater numbers of people have settled in the temperate zone and in areas of the earth where food crops can be cultivated and where animals can be more available for food than in less favored areas. Even in the desirable areas, man has increased the fertility of the earth and learned to control species of life that interfere with his use of the resources in the environment. He has also changed the physical environment merely by his presence in large numbers and by forming vast population complexes.

The natural environment influences man's behavior through changes in temperature, humidity, pressure, and oxygen. Most of the conditions on the earth are within man's tolerance range, because he is capable of coping with extreme variations. Some environmental conditions such as hurricanes, tidal waves, earthquakes, and volcanic eruptions can be traumatic occurrences, but these conditions have relatively little effect on the total human population on the earth.

Man as a biological organism does not persist in biologically instigated behavior alone but fulfills his needs and progresses through his biological timetable in communal activity and social relationships. Although his community is biotic, it is also cultural. A description of man's environmental interaction includes observation of the effects of natural environment on him as well as the influences of the social organizations he has created.

MAN AND HIS ENVIRONMENT

At the beginning of his life, the infant's interaction with the environment is limited by the limits of his biological capabilities, but upon developing his own locomotion the child begins to expand his environment. As years pass he extends its reaches to his own yard, his block, and eventually school and beyond. In the developmental years a hierarchy of influences exists in the environment of the child, and some factors are more significant than others. Interaction with his mother, for example, is more significant for him than interaction with a sibling. His own house and yard as he begins to explore the world on his own are more significant than the yards of neighbors or friends.

The study of the individual's interaction with the environment can be approached from several points of view. Theoretical concepts in such a complex problem require some organization of observation in order to deal with the necessary abstractions and symbolism with some degree of practicality. A human being, like any other organism, is an object in space; he is surrounded by a milieu with which he interacts. This milieu is limited both by the power of stimuli to arouse the individual and by his capacity to respond. Everyone is enclosed in a life space that is variously influenced by characteristics of the space beyond, but also his capacity and learned response pattern. If a person is not aware of some of the stimuli surrounding him and they elicit no response, those stimuli cannot be of significance to him; in this sense the environment consists of what is perceived. The processes of developing spatial perception determine to some extent the way each individual fashions his environment; eventually "reality" comes to be what is seen as reality. And yet response to the environment is influenced by experience, for example, by reward and punishment, by learned discriminations, and by generalizations that result from observing which events follow certain responses.

Certain theoretical positions have been taken on the basis of these principles; points from these theories relevant to the concept of man in interaction with his environment will be presented here.

Concepts of the Life Space—The Limited Environment

Lewin's Meaning of the Life Space. The theoretical ideas of Kurt Lewin (1936) about the life space have been of much interest to social scientists. Lewin defined *life space* as all the facts that determine the individual's behavior at a given time. But as Baldwin (1967) points out, Lewin limited life space to only those facts relevant to the behavior being observed or taking place. Lewin did not believe that past events directly influenced the life space. However, in his theory, past events can influence behavior through representatives in the situation. Facts of particular relevance to the student of behavior are those which directly influence the contemporary behavior of persons.

In defining the life space, Lewin used a concept of needs, for example, hunger. As he found it necessary to broaden the concept beyond basic biological needs, he expanded his ideas into a "need system" that involved the idea of tension. Lewin believed that tension exists when a need remains unfulfilled. In his need system some areas of the environment have a *positive valence,* that is, they contain conditions in which the need could be satisfied. For Lewin, all significant influences of the environment have positive valences that indicate opportunity for the individual to fulfill his needs. The significant aspects of the environment are determined in part by an environmental *filter.* For example, if the child's perception of food is determined by the mother as she makes selections and places food on the table, her selection becomes a filter for the child.

Although Lewinian theory seeks to explain the individual's relationships to the environment, the theory is difficult to apply to everyday behavior, particularly in the determination of facts of the environment. The concept of life space is useful, as an individual's surroundings have much to do with determining his development and behavior. The concept is practical, too, in that it allows the student of behavior to limit his search for significant forces to those which immediately and currently surround the individual.

Piaget's Conception of Space. Another influential theorist is Piaget, who dealt with the environment in his studies of the child's conception of space. Piaget (with Inhelder, 1948) sought to explain progression of spatial concepts with age. Piaget's explanation of the development of spatial concepts grew out of his theory of intelligence. According to the theory, the child's awareness of proximity, enclosures, and boundaries is the beginning of understanding of spatial relationships. While the young child can distinguish between two geometrical forms such as a triangle and a square, he cannot conceptualize the qualities of each until he acquires further understanding and can perform more complex intellectual operations. Piaget maintains "It is also quite obvious that the perception of space involves a gradual construction and certainly does not exist ready-made at the outset of mental development (Piaget and Inhelder, 1948)." Further, Piaget believes that the individual's conception of space is best understood by studying the development of cognition.

According to Piaget's theory, the child proceeds through successive stages as he becomes aware of the environment. For Piaget, equilibrium is the primary goal of the organism in interaction with the environment. This equilibrium is attained through the two basic processes of assimilation and accommodation. *Assimilation* is a term used for the process in which the individual adapts the environment to himself. .

He tries to control the environmental effect, or he seeks to modify it in ways that allow him to fulfill his needs. *Accommodation* is the term applied to the process by which the individual adjusts to the environment and alters response capabilities in order to deal with environmental requirements. These terms have biological roots. It can be said that assimilation indicates that the individual adapts and copes with the situation that he confronts. For example, food is altered in digestion to make its constituents.useful in body functioning. In accommodation, the individual changes himself in order to adapt. If a new food is introduced, the digestive system may change in order to accommodate to the different diet. In different cultures human beings have accommodated to vastly different diets.

Piaget's interest in cognitive development and his explanation of the process are the essence of his theory. His description of developmental periods has varied over the years, but usually his approach is divided into five phases: (1) the Sensorimotor Phase, (2) the Preconceptual Phase, (3) the Intuitive Thought Phase, (4) the Concrete Operations Phase, and (5) the Formal Operations Phase. In the Sensorimotor Phase lasting from birth to two years, the infant moves from reflexive behavior (the first stage) to the beginnings of "mental operation." By the end of this phase, the child shows awareness of the permanency of objects and is able to differentiate among them or their qualities. He also begins to understand that he can cause or initiate action. Evidence of a beginning of what is called the *conservation of substance* is encountered. When an object is pulled behind a screen from the child's line of vision, he will continue to look for it. If a small block is placed on the child's lap, and the experimenter puts his hand over it, the child will raise the hand and grasp the block. Then if the experimenter slowly takes the block away from the child and, while the child watches, puts it under a rug some distance away and again places his hand in the child's lap, the child will lift the experimenter's hand and look for the block beneath it. Piaget sees this as a conflict between repetition of previously successful (but no longer appropriate) behavior and the acquisition of new appropriate behavior patterns.

Piaget illustrated *perceptual constancy* by placing a ring in his right hand and showing it to an 18-month-old child. When he closed his hand over the ring, the child opened his hand to find the ring. Then he placed the ring in his left hand and pressed it against his right hand and extended both closed hands to the child. The child opened the left hand and could not find the ring. On the next trial, the child looked in the left hand and then in the right to find it. Later, Piaget put the ring in his hand, put his hand into a beret, and then extended his closed hand to the child. It took several trials for the child to find the ring in the beret rather than in either hand.

The environment, then, acquires its significance for the child in stages of learning and development, according to Piaget. The child's awareness of his life space grows in complexity from the phase in which specific

objects have little meaning (when the child's understanding of his surroundings and their significance to him is quite limited) to the phase in
which he can deal with the environment on a symbolic level (when the
environment continues in his awareness on the basis of symbols).

Freud's Idea of Perceptual Experience. Sigmund Freud also contributed to this topic. The idea of the *unconscious* developed by Freud is
important for any discussion of the individual's relationship to the
environment. As the child grows, he learns to perceive stimuli through
the sense organs; but if, through memory, feelings of pain are associated
with certain stimuli, he seeks to avoid perceptual experiences associated
with them. According to Freud, an individual can avoid admitting these
perceptions to consciousness. The feelings remain in the unconscious
area of the personality although they continue to influence behavior.
Perceptions of stimuli associated with pleasure are more likely to be
admitted to consciousness. Individuals tend to be consciously aware of
things desired or things that hold positive emotional significance. The
more something is wanted, the more often associated ideas reach consciousness.

While ideas are constantly moving into consciousness, their origin
and their control of behavior may be hidden in the unconscious, because
the psychological functioning of the person depends upon the flow of
ideas into consciousness. As the child develops, the ideas that enter his
consciousness come under control of the *ego,* which relates behavior to
perceived reality. In this way ideas become controlled by reality and
logic; the child's behavior becomes increasingly adaptive. At first the
child operates according to the pleasure principle and tries not to think
about unpleasant stimuli; his behavior becomes more adaptive than it
was earlier, because he may now avoid harm.

Certain defenses distort the process whereby ideas reach consciousness
and make it possible for the individual to avoid anxiety. Baldwin (1967)
suggests that such defense mechanisms may develop into a cognitive style
that influences the individual's entire interaction with the environment.
If so, the environment is to a considerable extent determined by the individual. As he comes to perceive environment as the result of pleasantness or unpleasantness, he may learn to exclude the parts of it that
brought pain in the past. What is admitted to consciousness is that
which he believes to be safe, pleasant, or rewarding. The extent to which
behavior is so governed has been a source of controversy.

Stimulus-response Theory and Environmental Awareness. Still another
approach to the interaction of the individual with his life space is provided by *stimulus-response theory.* This approach consists of several contributing theoretical entities, although the foundation of the approach
stems from the behavioristic concepts of John B. Watson. He maintained
that those who study human behavior should be concerned only with its
overt and observable aspects. Investigators adhering to the theory avoid
such terms as consciousness, thoughts, and feelings. The theory has been
espoused by those who believe that behavior should be understood

through laboratory experimentation, and many of its principles have been worked out in experiments with animals.

In building the theory, much attention has been given to the problems of social learning, and the work of Dollard and Miller (1950), Sears (1951), and Bandura and Walters (1963) is of particular importance. According to their view, the child acquires adult behavior patterns during the developmental years through reinforcement. In addition to the general principles of conditioning, the theory includes the principles of stimulus discrimination and stimulus generalization. *Discrimination* between two stimuli can be furthered in behavior by reinforcing or rewarding the response to one but not the other. Not only experimental animals in the laboratory can be taught in this way, but also children. *Stimulus generalization* means that a response associated with one stimulus tends also to occur in association with other stimuli similar to that original stimulus. A child learns, for example, that his pet dog acts in certain ways, and he comes to expect other dogs to act similarly.

One of the conclusions that can be reached in relating the stimulus-response theory to the interaction of the individual with the environment is that responses to specific aspects of the environment can be reinforced when they occur. Thus, the environment can be said to modify and shape the behavior of the individual (Skinner, 1971).

These four theoretical positions are examples of views explaining the development of the individual's response to significant forces surrounding him. These ideas can assist thinking about the individual in relation to the environment.

The Nature of Man and His Capacity to Adapt

Man's ability to live in various climatic changes depends on the physiological mechanisms in his body and, to a considerable extent, on his behavior. Through behavior he can control changes in climate that immediately surround his body. His behavior, which depends on his intellectual processes, is more important in coping with extremes than his body's capability for physiological and adaptive change. In adaptation man has found that his physiological mechanisms apparently have been better able to deal with external cold than with external heat. It is easier, through behavior, to regulate and moderate the body's heat loss in external cold than to deal with heat eliminating problems in hot climates (Fox, 1965).

The Influence of Climate. Some conditions about the world, where excessive heat or excessive cold occur, diminish activity and cause biological strain as man tries to adapt to such extreme conditions. The negative effects of climate reveal themselves in people's expressions about pain and the prevalence of disease and death. Where conditions are favorable, the population enjoys health, energy, and efficiency, as well as high productivity in both manufacturing and agricultural activities. In the North Temperate Zone, human energy, at least as measured by manufacturing productivity, is highest in October and November. Periods of highest and lowest energy, as indicated by such activity, vary according to climatic zones. In Scandinavia the summer seems to be the season of best health, as indicated by the low incidence of illness, whereas in the Mediterranean, winter is the best time of year. These observations suggest that man's strength and activity, and even mental activity, are at their best within a specific range of climatic conditions (Olgyay, 1963). Outside this range, man's efficiency and well-being are reduced, and he is more susceptible to various forms of stress and disease than in moderate climates. Thus, adaptability to the constituents of the environment—light, sound, climatic conditions, space, and terrain—influences in various ways the physical and psychological effects of man's struggle for biological equilibrium.

Maintenance of Body Temperature. If climate can be dealt with to leave energy available after coping with climatic disadvantages, productivity and cultural achievement can be increased. In all activities man's body temperature must be maintained very near 98.6° Fahrenheit, despite the fact that in some parts of the world the environmental temperature may fall as low as 90° below zero as in Siberia or rise to 130° as in the Sahara Desert. Extremes may bring about continuing conditions of altered body processes. Adaptation to temperature can be found in a number of places. Natives of southern Chile, for example, have been found to have higher metabolic rates than Europeans.

Men in climates of severe cold have several ways to keep themselves warm. In addition to covering themselves with animal skins, Eskimos eat whale and seal, foods that contain large quantities of fat. By eating such food they themselves accumulate a reserve of fat underneath their skins. Thus, men living in a cold climate adapt physically in ways similar to the animals of the area (Lebon, 1966). Men living in warmer climates show a preference for vegetarian diets and seek to avoid animal fats.

In the moderate climate zones, at elevations not higher than 1,000 feet above sea level, the temperature range of comfort for people doing light work while wearing the usual amount of indoor clothing is between 70° and 82°, with a relative humidity between about 20% and 50%. Comfort gradually tapers off within this temperature range as the humidity approaches 80%.

In order for the body to maintain its normal temperature in warm climates, blood vessels expand to increase the flow of blood to the skin, taking heat from the interior of the body to the surface (Viessman, 1966). Perspiration allows heat to escape in the form of water vapor. The body cannot continue such a physiological adaptation indefinitely without developing deficits. After about a 12% loss of fluids because of overheating, the skin and respiration can no longer deal with heat; then body temperature rises until the overheated condition becomes lethal. Similarly in cold climates, if the temperature in the environment of the body drops extensively, the blood vessels next to the skin constrict to keep the warm blood away from the surface of the body and thus conserve heat. The body surface then becomes cool and does not give off heat to the environment. Further heat loss can be reduced by covering the body with clothing. If the body still cannot maintain its temperature balance, the condition also becomes lethal. The maintenance of a normal and safe body temperature is possible only within a certain range and under certain conditions.

Part of the temperature-balancing process comes from oxidation of food. Oxidation keeps the body temperature above the temperature of a cold environment. But the balance between the metabolic release of heat and environmental temperature is complicated by the diurnal variation of body processes (or variation in even greater cycles). Body efficiency varies with the task of coping with waste heat from internal combustion; only an estimated 20% or 25% of man's combustion energy can be invested in work. In other words, efficiency of the human organism in terms of effective activity is comparatively low. As long as the waste heat can be lost appropriately, the body functions within its effective range; but within this range, as body processes change in a cyclic manner, the bodily capacity for effective performance rises and falls. Mammals particularly have difficulty with external heat because their effective performance can take place only within a small range of temperature variation (Mills, 1963).

Temperature and Mental Functioning. In the investigation of the effect of temperature on efficiency and activity, experiments with rats have indicated that the ones that lived in rooms at 55° Fahrenheit were more efficient in learning a maze than those living in rooms at 75° and were much more efficient than those that had lived in rooms at 92°. The rats from cooler temperatures also retained their learning much better than did the ones from the warmer temperatures (Hellmer, 1943).

The influence of warm temperatures upon human mental performance is not clearly established, however. A study found that young male adults subjected to a high ambient temperature (125.6° F.) improved their performance on tasks involving simple reaction time, as well as on certain mental tasks such as the addition of two-digit numbers (Lovingood, *et al.,* 1967). The work at the higher temperatures was better than that of a control group working at normal temperatures with less than 60% humidity. However, the subjects had received a period of acclimatization to the higher temperatures before the testing, at least seven hours of exposure to exercise in the same high temperature later used in the test situation. Another study found that young male adults who preferred summer temperatures had higher blood pressures than those who preferred winter temperatures (Driver, 1964). The investigator concluded that generally those who prefer warm temperatures maintain a reasonably high blood pressure and a tolerance of heat and that those who prefer winter have a less efficient cardiovascular system and a dislike of heat. Individual differences thus make it difficult to draw conclusions about ideal conditions for working. Much more study of the efficiency of human performance under carefully controlled experimental conditions is needed, but evidence now available shows that conditions of both heat and cold can affect man's efficiency (Carlson and Hsieh, 1965).

Because the brain has a high combustion rate and high heat production, a moderate difficulty in dealing with heat apparently affects the central nervous system and the brain before other parts of the body, even though reasonable efficiency of physical activities still continues. Sudden changes in environmental temperatures also affect heat production, even though the body tries to compensate by the movement of blood to or away from the skin.

Prolonged external heat or cold affects the adaptive change in the body, and extremes of temperature cause physical and mental activity to decline. In children, if external conditions cause a low combustion rate in the cells of the body, even though sufficient food is available, growth may be slowed or stopped, puberty delayed, and resistance to infection impaired.

Functioning and Nutrition. Other conditions in the environment affect human activities and well-being. An indirect factor in man's successful functioning is the availability in the environment of proper nutrients as well as climatic conditions which allow them to be produced. It has been established that adequate human nutrition must include essential amino acids as part of the protein content if human beings are to thrive. Growth and the ability to cope with infectious agents are reduced if the diet does not contain adequate protein. Sunlight in sufficient quantity is another factor in vitality, because the amount of light affects body processes. The hemoglobin in the blood of Norwegians, for example, is considerably greater in the summer than during the winter (Mills, 1963).

Man's interaction with others in his social structures and society is the foundation for the development of a life style, but it should be kept in mind that his physical characteristics are realities that must be perceived as fundamental to behavior.

FUNDAMENTALS OF
ENVIRONMENTAL INTERACTION

The environment includes not only the natural environment but features influenced or created by the activities of man. Environmental features which have been changed in some way are called the artificial environment; but a clear distinction between the natural environment and the artificial environment is not easily made, as basically all the elements man has to work with come from the natural environment. Interaction between man and various environmental characteristics involves a system that is part of the ecology of the earth. To some extent man's body adapts to environmental characteristics, but he must change the environment for further adaptation. By combining his physical adaptability with his capacity to change features of the environment, he has been able to live under wide-ranging conditions across the world.

An important form of man's effort is directed toward the use of space, the areas of the environment (Wheaton, 1967). How he uses space is dependent upon cultural rules and his socialization experience within the family. This experience in turn is much affected by the sociocultural conditions under which the family lives.

The Use of Space

An important facet of man's use of the environment is his organization of it into territories. These territories influence behavior from one location to another since territorial transactions with elaborate cultural rules are associated with such parcels. The kinds of divisions and accompanying rules affect the character of each man's life space.

Shelter in the Life Space. Shelter for protection from adverse conditions is a primary way of fulfilling the need for comfort; through many kinds of shelter man extensively modifies his environment. Through buildings and in other ways he searches diligently for ways to reduce the stress of climatic conditions. Present-day technological advances now make possible the creation of an artificial environment and balanced shelters that fulfill most of his biological needs. Through technical means it is possible to achieve control of air temperature, radiation, air movement, and humidity—major climatic elements that influence human behavior. Other climatic influences of somewhat less concern are solar radiation, evaporation effects, and the velocity of the wind. The last still is of significance for comfort balance within many modern shelters. Windbreaks, both natural and artificial, can serve in temperature moderation. In addition to the major elements of the climate, attention is given to microclimatic characteristics, the results of minute climates existing side by side at ground level. These vary with changes of just a few feet in elevation, and their effects can be seen in the melting of snow on slopes while the ground nearby remains covered.

In selecting advantageous locations for shelters, exposure to light is important; the best locations are inclined surfaces that are exposed to greater amounts of radiation in underheated periods and less radiation at overheated times. Orientation of the shelter somewhat to the east and south often will secure a balanced heat distribution. Sites part way up the slope located in the south-southeast direction offer the most desirable habitation. As technology increases, shelters of the future will not be as dependent on natural light and cooling or warming breezes as they have been in the past (Olgyay, 1963).

One of man's outstanding achievements is the grouping of shelters into cities; such grouping is an indication of the complexity and accomplishment of a civilization (Forrester, 1969). In creating shelters in cities, two elements are important, *mass* and *space*. Some architects suggest that too much concern is shown for mass and not enough for space, because space is particularly important in achieving esthetic satisfaction in daily life (Bacon, 1967). Historically, since the time of the early Greek architects, space itself has been valued. The Greeks set aside specific spaces for spirits. Early Islamic architecture was characterized by four minarets about a mosque, which created a cube of space with a dramatic effect. Modern architects have tried to show life as a flow of experiences, with shelters and buildings of a city as a part of that flow. Buildings are designed with a recession of planes to provide scale for form beyond. An archway, for example, placed beyond another archway gives a feeling of movement by providing depth. Architectural use of space, then, means a continuity of experiences created through the use of spatial forms as part of a culture or society.

Human Sectors. To properly use space in the city Doxiadis (1963) has suggested the use of the concept of the *human sector.* In such an area, human needs are held paramount. Settlements planned on the basis of sectors are about a mile and a half long and less in width; residents can walk from 20 to 30 minutes to reach jobs, theaters, markets, and the like. The cultural centers, too, are within a sector and ideally no more than a half-mile from any resident within the sector. Houses and buildings are constructed on a human scale. Automobiles can enter a sector but cannot pass through; they can move rapidly around, however. The main center of the sector is exclusively for pedestrians. Each sector is as self-contained as possible, including institutions as well as a transportation system. Some sectors are covered in order to provide an optimal climate.

Public and Private Space. Other city planners have approached the use of space differently. City space, for example, is divided into six hierarchical categories. The first, *urban-public,* includes the publicly owned facilities such as roads and parks. The second category, *urban-semipublic,* includes areas of public use for government and institutional facilities, such as city halls and courts, as well as service stations and theaters. The third category, *group-public,* refers to areas of joint access between private and public groups. The fourth category, *group-private,* includes those components under public control but used for private interests, such as playgrounds and community gardens. The fifth category, *family-private,* consists of space controlled by a single family, their areas for private activities and entertainment. The sixth category, *individual-private,* refers to very personal space, such as the room of one person. The most important point among the urban domains is the junction between the residential realm of the *family-private* category and the larger environment, the *group-public.* This junction can be considered the link between the dwelling and the city. A buffer is important where the private domain borders on the public domain. In this concept of the use of space, hierarchies within both the public and the private domain are preserved. As a person moves toward the private domain he has a series of opportunities for withdrawal, until finally he enters his own room (Chermayeff and Alexander, 1963).

As man becomes more dependent upon an environment that is modified in various ways, consideration for individual satisfaction in the use of space is more important. It is necessary to know not only about the content of the stimulus field of the *life space,* but also how the individual becomes aware of the field, the effect of personal characteristics on functioning, and the symbolic meanings assigned to that field. Further, the concept of the *city* is changing. In modern and urban society it is increasingly difficult to describe the city as one space and the country as another space opposed to the city. The city flows outward away from the central business district through suburbs, and although it sometimes narrows and is less concentrated, it characteristically becomes dense again. Thus life styles spread further and further by virtue of transportation and quick communication.

The Urban Space. Life styles of the people in modern America tend to be similar, with similar tools, techniques, objects, and ideas. Consequently the concept of a rural-urban dichotomy is less and less tenable. Because the increase in urbanization is a result of technological and organizational change, the distinction between *urban* and *rural* is valid not so much in terms of space, but in terms of a high degree of technology and organization as against a low degree of technology and organization. As modern cities are large systems of social and technological complexity, it is likely that they will produce a new type of society in the future (Eldredge, 1967).

Large concentrations of population about the world will probably come to be similar to the great American city complex on the east coast, beginning in Maine and extending along the Old Post Road to Norfolk, Virginia (Webber and Webber, 1967). This area is the living space of some 40,000,000 people; it contains the major financial, educational, and industrial centers of the world. It also contains a great traffic volume over superhighways, bridges, and high-speed train lines. The lives of people in such interurban areas are not directly related to one town, but dependent on a whole region. The concept of the town consisting of industries, stores, business, and homes is changing as such towns cease to exist. People flow into a city and are part of it for a time and then flow outward again to areas a considerable distance away from "center city." The city itself has a circadian rhythm.

The term *urbanization* refers to technological and organizational methods and activity, in addition to the physical forms of buildings or specific types of space. Density of population does not necessarily mean urbanization as, for example, certain large congregations of people in oriental cities demonstrate. But low population densities in the vast areas surrounding a megalopolis do not indicate a lack of urbanization, at least to the extent that urbanization refers to human qualities.

The medieval concept of a city within a wall with a defined organization and a spatial allocation has little similarity to a modern city. Just as space and organization are no longer entirely appropriate terms for defining a city, other more complex and variable factors are subsumed under the term urbanization. For there is some unity even in megalopolis; behavioral patterns have some similarity over widespread living areas, and equivalent life styles are increasingly characteristic of all American society (Webber, 1968).

In many cities, bridges make it possible for people to cross into another city, perhaps into another state, within a few minutes; people from one city crossing the bridge to work pass people going to work in the other. In such instances, influences affecting the well-being of one city also affect the well-being of the other. Hence, organization and living patterns of the people transcend these earlier geographical and political differences. Life styles are to this extent factors in reorganizing political, social, economic, and geographical systems.

The pattern of the city state is again in prospect as the city has become a region as large as some states. New terms to describe these areas of human activity have been developed, for example, the word *community* frequently refers to cities, states, and suburbs bound together in an urban region. In parts of such regions, however, the village green and town square all too often have been replaced by shopping plazas and highway strips of stores, motels, stands, junkyards, and billboards. The natural features of the environment, the beauty of the rivers and valleys, have not been preserved.

Sociocultural Differences in the Use of Space

The use of space by people is much more complex than the geographical measurement of distance, particularly when social, economic, political, cultural, and psychological concerns are taken into account. The use of space involves not just distance and time, but also values.

The Intellectual Elite and Space. Some see the population in industrial societies as divided into two groups, the *intellectual elite* and the *working class,* and these groups as differing in their use of space (Webber and Webber, 1967). The ideas of these authors about stratification in society are described here but theoretical and practical descriptions are very complex and will be dealt with in different ways subsequently. Coleman and Neugarten (1971) point out that social scientists in the early part of the century perceived the structure of this society as consisting of five classes with the classes being distinguished primarily by occupation and income. Since the beginning of the century the upper class has remained about 1% of the population; the upper middle has increased from 5% to 10% and the lower middle from 26% to 32%; the working class has decreased from 42% to 39%; and the lower class has decreased from 26% to 18%. These authors warn, however, that social classes should not be seen as *real* entities but as concepts. They also warn about seeing prestige, reputation, and patterns of informal participation as continuing to have the same relation to income, occupation, and education as they did in the early part of the century. Class lines, they believe, are becoming blurred in American society. The Webbers see two main divisions, nevertheless.

The *intellectual elite* is seen as including university professors, business and governmental executives, scientists in research and industrial organizations, editors, and those in the arts. The primary characteristic of these people is their orientation toward performance in their work and the way in which they define intellectual and scientific problems. Their performance, based on standards of the group, often disregards geographical distance and maintains communication with colleagues over the world through journals, books, mail, telephones, and commercial transportation. Each belongs to organizations that are given professional loyalties.

Such professional groupings are not based on kinship or specific aspects of space; rather they are based upon shared interests and values. These people can be said to be related to *non-place communities,* as territorial distance provides few limits to their interaction. Their social propinquity has little to do with their spatial propinquity; because their social interaction is based on common interests, they may travel many miles for even casual social interaction. In a way, such people are multidimensional and supraterritorial, as they function in extensive space, not only in one country but all over the world. They often change their personal residences and, in doing so, extend urbanization. They adapt easily to change and different space or place opportunities, because their knowledge and experience in various conditions enable them to anticipate conditions at different places and times. They look to the future and believe in the possibility of determining their own destiny. Not only their space is extensive but so is their sense of time; they feel primarily concerned about the future.

The Working Class and Space. At the other end of the social continuum Webber and Webber see the *working class;* this group has counterparts in many areas of the world. Whether these people live in the central city areas in deteriorated housing conditions or farther away from the city, they have a close-knit network of social relations composed of individual kinship systems and neighbors. The primary social unit is the extended family, although these family units are not always complete. In childhood, interpersonal relations are primarily with members of the family and neighbors. Older children and adolescents maintain close relationships with local and organized peer groups, men keep close association with co-workers in the daytime and with neighbors in the evening, and women have many social contacts with their neighbors. These relationships build up a network of association, closely related to space and area of residence. Many live within the same block for a generation; family and neighborhood ties keep them close together even through the life span. Because of this social interaction with neighbors, the space of residence includes the street and areas of the block in which much social action takes place. In contrast to that of the intellectual elite, social organization among working-class people is territorially related to their immediate space and departure from this spatial environment is rare.

Just outside the working-class residents' own circle of territory live families with quite similar cultural characteristics and life styles, and yet these other residents are viewed with some suspicion and distrust. This hostility toward similar people outside the immediate life space is exemplified by members of an adolescent gang who will at times fight to the death to keep their street corner or alleyway clear of neighbors who live only a few blocks away. In this way the life space seems to have an individualized and highly personal significance. Physical characteristics of the space, the streets and the buildings, are seen as more than physical structures; they have emotional valences. The perceptual world of the residents, even their perception of themselves, is spatially organized and related. The alleys, streets, and basements are assigned to social groups, as are the rigid rights and obligations associated with them. This delineation of space in a working-class social structure contrasts with the less defined lines of the intellectual elite. The contrast makes it easy to understand the psychosocial consequences of threats to working-class residents' space that come through urban renewal programs and to see how destruction of houses and changes of residence affect the social position in the hierarchies of the social order dependent upon spatial organization and structures.

Territoriality. Certain prerogatives and obligations are associated with these emotional valences of territoriality. Women who work in factories and as domestic servants devote part of their activity to their own households and child care; the only other important interpersonal relationships are with neighbors and family relatives. The men are interested in work only as a livelihood; they do not see it as a means for self-development or social advancement. Their concern is for the immediate time and for the immediate life space. Characteristically, then, the people in this class are oriented to a specific locale or space and to immediate time, the present.

The significance of life styles and emotion about space is especially clear in urban renewal programs. After the land has been cleared and the old neighborhoods have been destroyed, that which had appeared to be a slum amid deterioration is seen to have been in fact a neighborhood with social unity. Although the housing was both unhygienic and unsafe, important advantages in social organization and interpersonal relationships existed. Lacking the support of old patterns of social interaction associated with feelings about the territory, many residents removed to new surroundings developed anxiety and depression.

Urban renewal and housing policies in the United States and Europe have not usually taken into account the social interactions of the people as related to their space. In Britain, the new housing provided for working-class people reflected middle- and upper-class values in the sense of privacy and the use of space; for example, in some of the new towns established after World War II, the people were moved into houses surrounded by considerable space in the front and back. But this imposed a measure of isolation unknown in their former crowded neighborhoods; the frequent daily contact with neighbors and families was now lessened.

Because they missed these contacts, some people tried to move back, while others made frequent trips to the old neighborhoods. Despite the fact that the new housing was much improved in quality, the change had brought little satisfaction. In view of these difficulties, in some new towns in Britain, individual gardens and yards were replaced by spaces designed for community use similar to that to which the people had been accustomed. Here in the United States mistakes also have been made, and building designs and the use of space have not been in keeping with the past orientations of the people. For example, the walls of new housing were built to keep out noise, and privacy was enhanced by hallways accessible only to the families living on them. But the people liked the sounds of neighbors. Women found it difficult to travel to the new shopping centers, and more importantly the new shopping centers lacked the personal quality of the small shops and groceries of old neighborhoods.

Questions have thus arisen about the use of the center of cities as social, economic, political, and residential areas. What does the center of the city offer to residents? One of the compelling reasons to ask such questions is that the centers are increasing in size for some unknown reason. It may be that the centers provide a greater range of specialties that individuals need (Ullman, 1967). Socioeconomic factors significant in change will be discussed in later chapters.

In any event American society's attainments of the future will likely come from the great urban areas. Understanding the many influences on human development in urban society and the consequences of their effect for the society is of much importance (Glass and Singer, 1972).

IN PERSPECTIVE

Man is now seeing himself in a new perspective within the ecosystem of the earth. He has discovered that the world's natural resources are limited, and he has glimpsed the spector of mass destruction resulting from alteration of the earth's envelope of air and its great oceans. This new perspective has brought a realization also that the actions and policies of one group of people affect others half-a-world away. Collaborative effort to use space on earth in such a way that aspects of it are not destroyed is imperative for all.

As a result of technological advances many more people have become aware of their neighbors' activities. Communication with other men on earth is now instantaneous. Such possibilities have brought an increased awareness of the variance in cultures that leads people to regard objects and behavior in differing ways. Acceptance of these cultural differences is part of the "new awareness."

Each person's view of his life space is highly individual. Reality for a person is the way in which it is perceived, and no one else can see the environment in quite the same way. Because of differences in genetic components and learning experiences, each man's view of the environment differs from that of any other man, although it is similar to that of all men.

In the latter part of this century, a new kind of environmental perspective has developed, heretofore only dreamed of, as man's footsteps have been left in strange dust thousands of miles in space. The world is now indeed seen in a new perspective since it can be seen all at once by one man.

REFERENCES

BACON, E. *Design of cities.* New York: Viking, 1967.

BALDWIN, A. L. *Theories of child development.* New York: Wiley, 1967.

BANDURA, A., & WALTERS, R. H. *Social learning and personality development.* New York: Holt, Rinehart, & Winston, 1963.

CALHOUN, J. B. A glance into the garden. In D. Bowers (Ed.), *Three papers on human ecology.* Berkeley, Calif.: Gillick Printing, Inc., 1966. Pp. 19–36.

CARLSON, L. D., & HSIEH, A. C. L. Cold. In O. G. Edholm & A. L. Bacharach (Eds.), *The physiology of human survival.* New York: Academic Press, 1965. Pp. 15–51.

CHERMAYEFF, S., & ALEXANDER, C. *Community and privacy.* New York: Doubleday, 1963.

COLEMAN, R. P., & NEUGARTEN, B. L. *Social status in the city.* San Francisco: Jossey-Bass, 1971.

DODWELL, P. C. Spatial and geometric concepts. In I. E. Sigel and F. H. Hooper (Eds.), *Logical thinking in children.* New York: Holt, Rinehart, & Winston, 1968. Pp. 118–140.

DOLLARD, J., & MILLER, N. E. *Personality and psychotherapy.* New York: McGraw-Hill, 1950.

DOXIADIS, C. A. *Architecture in transition.* New York: Oxford University Press, 1963.

DRIVER, A. F. M. Sensitivity to heat and cold of summer and winter preferrers. *Ergonomics,* 1964, 7, 475–479.

DUBOS, R. *Man adapting.* New Haven: Yale University Press, 1965.

DYCKMAN, J. W. Societal goals and planned societies. In H. W. Eldredge (Ed.), *Taming megalopolis,* Vol. I. Garden City, New York: Doubleday, 1967. Pp. 248–267.

ELDREDGE, H. W. People: Urbanization and city growth. In H. W. Eldredge (Ed.), *Taming megalopolis,* Vol. I. Garden City, New York: Doubleday, 1967. Pp. 4–19.

FORRESTER, J. W. *Urban dynamics.* Cambridge, Mass.: Massachusetts Institute of Technology Press, 1969.

FOX, R. H. Heat. In O. G. Edholm & A. L. Bacharach (Eds.), *The physiology of human survival.* New York: Academic Press, 1965. Pp. 53–79.

FREUD, S. (A. A. Brill, Ed.). *The basic writings of Sigmund Freud.* (Translated and edited, with an introduction by A. A. Brill) New York: Modern Library, 1938.

GLASS, D. C., & SINGER, J. E. *Urban stress.* New York: Academic Press, 1972.

HECKSCHER, A. The city: Work of art and technology. In B. J. L. Berry & J.

Meltzer (Eds.), *Goals for urban America*. Englewood Cliffs, N. J.: Prentice-Hall, 1967. Pp. 10–21.

HELLMER, L. A. The effect of temperature on the behavior of the white rat. *American Journal of Psychology*, 1943, 56, 408–421.

LEBON, J. H. G. *An introduction to human geography*. London: Hutchinson, 1966.

LEWIN, K. *Principles of topological psychology*. New York: McGraw-Hill, 1936.

LOVINGOOD, B. W., BLYTH, C. S., PEACOCK, W. H., & LINDSAY, R. B. Effects of d-amphetamine sulphate, caffeine, and high temperature on human performance. *The Research Quarterly*, 1967, 38, 64–71.

MILLS, C. A. *World power and shifting climates*. Boston: The Christopher Publishing House, 1963.

ODUM, H. T. *Environment, power, and society*. New York: Wiley-Interscience, 1971.

OLGYAY, V. *Design with climate: Bioclimatic approach to architectural regionalism*. Princeton, N. J.: Princeton University Press, 1963.

PIAGET, J., & INHELDER, B. *The child's conception of space*. London: Routledge, 1948.

REINER, J. S., & REINER, T. A. Urban poverty. In H. W. Eldredge (Ed.), *Taming megalopolis*, Vol. II. Garden City, New York: Doubleday, 1967. Pp. 917–929.

SEARS, R. R. A theoretical framework for personality and social behavior. *American Psychologist*, 1951, 6, 476–482.

SHIMKIN, D. B. Adaptive strategies: A basic problem in human ecology. In D. Bowers (Ed.), *Three papers on human ecology*. Berkeley, Calif.: Gillick Printing, Inc., 1966. Pp. 37–52.

SKINNER, B. F. *Beyond freedom and dignity*. New York: Knopf, 1971.

TREICHEL, G. Man, nature, and the landscape. In D. Bowers (Ed.), *Three papers on human ecology*. Berkeley, Calif.: Gillick Printing, Inc., 1966. Pp. 9–18.

ULLMAN, E. L. The nature of cities reconsidered. In H. W. Eldredge (Ed.), *Taming megalopolis*, Vol. I. Garden City, New York: Doubleday, 1967. Pp. 71–93.

VIESSMAN, W. Man and his thermal environment. In B. H. Jennings & J. E. Murphy (Eds.), *Interactions of man and his environment*. New York: Plenum Press, 1966. Pp. 75–85.

WAGNER, P. L. *The human use of the earth*. Glencoe, Ill.: Free Press, 1960.

WEBBER, M. M. The post-city age (the conscience of the city). *Daedalus, Journal of the Academy of Arts and Sciences*, Fall, 1968, 1091–1110.

WEBBER, M. M., & WEBBER, C. C. Culture, territoriality, and the elastic mile. In H. W. Eldredge (Ed.), *Taming megalopolis*, Vol. I. Garden City, New York: Doubleday, 1967. Pp. 35–53.

WHEATON, W. L. C. Form and structure of the metropolitan area. In W. R. Ewald (Ed.), *Environment for man: The next fifty years*. Bloomington, Ind.: Indiana University Press, 1967. Pp. 157–196.

WILLEMS, E. P. An ecological orientation in psychology. In N. S. Endler, L. R. Boulter, & H. Osser (Eds.), *Contemporary issues in developmental psychology*. New York: Holt, Rinehart, & Winston, 1968. Pp. 29–49.

WOLMAN, A. The metabolism of cities: Water and air. In H. W. Eldredge (Ed.), *Taming megalopolis*, Vol. I. Garden City, N. Y.: Doubleday, 1967. Pp. 54–71.

INDIVIDUAL DESTINY IN MODERN SOCIETY

2

Not only has man modified the natural environment in order to create favorable conditions for living, but also he has created certain social structures, organizations, and institutions that affect individual development. Life in this society begins in a social organization, and thereafter throughout his life span the individual interacts with various kinds of organizations and institutions that are significant not only in the enculturation process but in determining his destiny in society.

Although differentiation among the terms *organization, structure,* and *institution* is not clear, social organization usually refers to the ways human behavior is placed in some order. Two concepts in basic social organizations are used: the concept of a structure of social relationships in some group or collection of people and the concept that the shared beliefs of people in a group will determine their behavior (Blau and Scott, 1967). Here the view is that social relationships bring about a structure and that the resulting structure, in turn, provides patterns for social behavior.

THE ORGANIZATION OF SOCIETY

The patterns of culture determining the order of behavior in daily living cover (1) socially approved directions for training children; (2) activities relating to survival, security, and production and distribution of material things; (3) relationships and activities associated with supernatural beliefs; and (4) the control of the behavior of individuals in the group in their relationships with each other. This ordering of behavior predetermines that within each organization a number of roles contribute to the attainment of the goals of a society.

Social structures are essential in a society because they provide patterns for achieving its goals, order, and continuity. The more obvious the pattern of behavior, the more likely it is to survive and to continue from generation to generation. Once a structure institutionalizes behavior, the probability is heightened that the structure will be continued. The continuity of a social structure is also assured when it becomes a part of a system of cultural values, often by ritual.

Generic Social Structures and Individual Behavior

The Family. The family is the most universal of social structures, as it provides the means for care of the young, the possession of wealth, and the transmission and security of material things. Despite its universality, it is probably the most vulnerable of the structures to hostile forces in that it can be easily affected by adverse economic conditions and other threats to the security of the society (Merrill, 1965).

The basis for the family's universality stems in part from man's biological nature. Physiological functions associated with reproduction, fulfillment of biological needs through cooperative endeavor, and the care and training of the young are part of family life; psychological and social activities are inextricably a part of the family's biological functioning. The members of the basic family unit are the father, mother, and offspring, although in many societies other relatives are included in an extended family. In American society the basic family generally lives independently of relatives.

Although the family is an organization for which the culture generally sets functional limits and boundaries, it develops some variation and identity of its own; that is, each family adopts some values different from those of other families surrounding it. Such differences include preferences for food, dress, social relationships, occupational goals, and the like. Despite the fact that individual family differences occur, some support can be found for the contention that much similarity in family structure and role behavior is transcultural. One study found that the interrelationships of family roles were fundamentally similar in four different cultures. The investigators concluded that their data supported the view that role behavior is relatively invariant across cultures (Foa, Triadis, and Katz, 1966).

Increasingly in American and Western society, the family is becoming less centralized, particularly in reference to economic activities (Green, 1968; Nelson, Ramsey, and Verner, 1960). Members are no longer engaged in a unified effort to work together in one household or in one economic activity. In many families, at least one member becomes part of a large, impersonal economic organization. Some functions of the family have been usurped by social organizations: religious training of the children has often been preempted by the church; protection has been assumed by the state through the legal system; welfare for many families has been provided by the state; and family activity in the educational process has lessened as children come under the influence of the state-controlled educational system.

The social status of the family is still closely linked to the occupational role of the father, and his employment usually determines the place of residence. Even if the mother is also employed outside the home, she sees her responsibility to the family as of greater importance than her employment. The family has resisted inroads attempted by the other social structures in society. The other structures have tended to intervene in children's lives, but they have been able to assume only partial responsibility for training or for a program of activities. The family, therefore, remains primarily responsible for fulfilling most of the child's needs.

The Educational System. The educational system, another social structure, also has an important place in modern society. It has come partly under the control of the state through its dependence upon government for support, but because of its function, the structure is considered separate from government. For the individual in this society, education is of paramount importance. Public educational functions have been extended not only to very early age levels, but also even into old age.

The transmission of knowledge and skills by the educational structure in a complex society is beset by many problems. Leadership in social change would not seem to be an appropriate requirement; yet, paradoxically, educational institutions are expected to be originators of social change and distributors of new knowledge. Such activity brings controversy because, on the one hand, they are expected to lead in social change and, on the other, they are expected to represent the culture, a role which tends to limit or even inhibit social change. In addition, social roles are now changing so rapidly that training cannot be linked with certainty to the requirements of roles in the future. Educational preparation, therefore, must be broad and indirect. The complexity of society provides many barriers to the selection of knowledge and skills to be transmitted. Many are critical of the curriculum, particularly students. Today many children and adolescents see little reason to acquire the range of modern knowledge and necessary skills. Institutions of higher learning find it difficult to inspire students to make the intensive effort required to master complex material. In spite of these problems the system has great importance in American society.

Governmental Structures. Governmental institutions making up the government structure have a larger range of activities than they have had in the past and are now responsible for many of the changes that occur in society. Some of the changes result from activities of ideological groups possessing sufficient influence to affect governmental processes. Whatever their source the activities associated with the functioning of the government are the basis for many of the impersonal processes of modern society.

One recent and significant change in society has come with the shifting of some responsibilities of the family to the government. Such functions being changed include protection of the home, education of children, health care, and welfare administration. Control of social behavior on the basis of folkways and mores has declined in favor of control based on laws and governmental regulations. Individual behavior results less from the customs passed on verbally from generation to generation than it did in the past; now formal sanctions and directions from the government prescribe much of an individual's social behavior.

Governmental structures can be divided into three categories: (1) the legislative structures concerned with making rules and laws to provide standards for behavior, (2) the executive and administrative structures concerned with carrying out and enforcing regulations, and (3) the legal and judicial structures that deal with the meaning and application of rules and laws. The legal structure has the power to interfere directly in the lives of people by taking away property from some and giving it to others or by punishing according to the sanctions of the society.

Modern governments are frequently described as bureaucracies because the units for carrying out specific functions tend to grow and proliferate. Bureaucratic governments usually exert considerable effort to define roles and to make rules, because a primary function is to provide a guide for normative behavior. Norms are established by rules and regulations about behavior, and in this way valued characteristics of the culture are preserved. Organizations are also set up to compel people to conform. Because in most societies statements of rules are not always clear and overlapping laws and regulations provide a basis for conflict, part of governmental legal activity is concerned with the interpretation of laws and clarification where conflict occurs.

As societies have moved from agrarian to urban organizations, political structures have extended their areas of activity. Now governments are involved in health, education, agriculture, industry, utilities, and research programs. They have taken over some activities related to economic institutions and deal with prices, credit, labor, regulation of banks and money, utilities, and the like. They have also assumed educational and welfare obligations. Accordingly, modern governments tend to absorb the functions of the other institutions in society.

Further, the functions of all of the types of government are being centralized with the national government despite verbal adherence to the ideal of decentralization. The problems of a complex society are not now easily solved by the skills, abilities, or resources possessed by local governments. The transfer of function has been facilitated by improved transportation and communication which make centralization much easier. Once the government has major control of certain aspects of the functioning of local governments, it seldom transfers control back to the local level.

The Economic Structure. Economic activities associated with the production of goods, their processing, distribution, and related services comprise the economy or economic structure. This structure has undergone rapid change, especially since the Industrial Revolution in the latter part of the eighteenth century. At that time the urbanization of American society began to bring profound changes in the lives of the people in this society. With the development of an urban and industrial society, sweeping technological changes have taken place causing, in turn, significant changes in the family, in education, and in the government.

These changes have had far-reaching psychological effects, as new kinds of economic activities involving new social roles have altered individuals' perceptions of themselves and others. In fact, people have come to identify themselves with their social roles and status levels in economic institutions. Certain perceptual sets and principles of behavior and conduct have evolved. Many within a corporation, for example, see themselves not only as part of their own economic institution, but as part of other economic institutions with which the corporation has interconnections.

In recent years, four important changes have taken place within the economic structure. First, vast corporate organizations are managed by people relatively unknown to the public, whereas a half century ago the corporations were headed by such well-known people as Carnegie, Rockefeller, Mellon, and Ford. A second change in the economic structure is the considerable effort at selling goods and materials. Advertising has become a significant activity and, in fact, its cost and the number of people involved in it has come to rival the production of the goods themselves. The study of the susceptibility of people at all age levels to this form of persuasion now involves scientific research. A third important recent development is the decline of the significance of the trade union. Even though employment has continued to grow, membership in unions has not. This slowing of growth is in contrast to conditions in the early part of the century when unions had a profound effect on American society and the lives of workers. A fourth important change is the newly developed influence of economic institutions on educational institutions. With increasing frequency, curriculum and research programs have been modified by technological advancement in corporations.

An affluent society, according to Galbraith (1967), is dependent upon success in productivity and income as well as the organization of corporations. As a result of affluence, the behavior of people cannot be predicted as well currently as in the past on the basis of economic motivation. Increased discretionary income makes prediction about how this income will be spent less and less feasible. Because of the growth of the large corporations, many of the fundamental activities of society have come to be dependent upon a small number of select corporations: electric power, transportation, manufacturing, and retail trade are carried on by perhaps 500 or 600 firms. The two parts of the economy—the few hundred massive corporations and the thousands of small business proprietors —are very different. Their activities diverge fundamentally; as power has been transferred from individuals to organizations, power and influence in turn have passed to the corporations.

In modern corporations, the owner of capital often is separated from control of the enterprise. In many corporations the stockholders have little influence. As corporations have come to have such an important place in the lives of people and in social processes, their influence on individual development and destiny is indeed great.

The Religious Structure. The religious social structure, consisting of various types of organizations, seems to have three basic functions in a society. First, the structure assists individuals in the determination of a concept of identity, in justification of goals, and in choice of activities. It aids its members in dealing with frustration or suffering and provides explanations for events in the environment that are difficult to understand. Religion also lessens feelings of isolation in the environment, assists in maintaining emotional equilibrium, and provides an integration of individual goals. It also assists in bringing together values and beliefs within a social order; many religious rules add to the cohesion of society, as is shown by the church's emphasis on the protection of life and property.

Like the other social institutions in society, religious organizations are undergoing change. These institutions have a long history, and change has come slowly in the past. Through most of the modern era much controversy has occurred about the response of the religious structure to change. One issue at present is its involvement in social activities, particularly in aid to the poor and to people unable to cope with the problems of living. Some believe that involvement in social problems has removed the structure from religious activities; others believe that it has not become sufficiently involved in modern social problems and that it still adheres to the ritualistic behavior of years gone by.

Social Structures and Power. Although fundamental interconnections and similarities exist among the social structures, an essential basis for differences among them lies in the extent of the power any one of them can exercise. Decisions of a broad nature in the government, for example, especially those involving international affairs, are usually made cooperatively by the governmental, military, and economic structures. Yet the real power of these structures comes from technology provided by corporations within the economic structures. That is, people who direct the giant corporations have worked so closely with both governmental and military units that their influence extends to key decisions made within these units. The flow of government employees to corporation positions, largely because of political changes of party power, serves to strengthen the base of corporate power. Governmental, military, and economic structures have many points where interests and well-being coincide; circumstances which benefit one benefit the others. The countervailing powers of other social structures do not substantially affect the activities of these three powerful structures. The less powerful labor unions and educational and professional organizations generally make decisions of less significance for society. American society to this extent is therefore said to be unbalanced. Whether or not such a view of American social structures is tenable cannot be determined with certainty, nor can certainty be reached about the significance of the influence of such a power complex, as ways of appraising the relative power of social structures are unavailable.

Since the beginning of this century most of the social structures in American society have become large and complex, and their great size and power bring many advantages to the society. One advantage is the success of great projects through the cooperative endeavor of a large number of people. This success is especially evident in the physical sciences and in the technological ventures related to them. Another advantage lies in the fact that in large organizations social power is increased by the pooling of wealth and facilities that, in turn, attract capable people. A further advantage is that large organizations can divert energy and work capability from immediate activity to planning for the future, thereby increasing efficiency in the effort to reach significant goals.

In recent years, social scientists have given some attention to the power of people who are not in an organization. This is sometimes referred to as the power of "unorganized masses." When some new policy is needed, large numbers of voters without organization band together to bring pressure to bear on legislators to pass measures of benefit to them. The measure can also influence the production of items. Some items have been rejected by the public and thus people without organized effort have affected the policy of large companies. (More about the "masses" is covered in Chapter 13.)

The people who control political activity in American society are predominantly socially elite and middle-class individuals. Such control is not surprising, because middle-class parents teach their children the importance of striving for positions of influence and power. Although the power positions in American society are, in the main, held by people who tend to come from the middle class, some positions tend to be occupied by people from the upper class. Those in high diplomatic corps positions, for example, are usually from the upper class, because the social life of the corps usually requires a background of wealth. It is generally conceded that success in the role of diplomat is dependent upon personal financial resources beyond those supplied by the government.

In the first half of the twentieth century, controls were established to limit the activities of various power structures in American society, although the effectiveness of these controls has varied. Early in the century, for example, antitrust laws were passed to prevent large combines of corporations from gaining a monopoly which would allow them to market goods and fix prices solely for their own benefit; and, periodically, concern about control of large corporations causes legislative action. In a complex society, although vigilance is necessary to prevent some social structures from influencing human affairs unduly, arousal of public concern about such problems is increasingly difficult.

Social Stratification

Only a few in modern and urban society are in the most prestigious and rewarding social roles, only a few live in the upper social stratum, and only a few feel little need to strive to better living conditions. Most feel the necessity for dealing with a stratified society stretching above them with rewards unequally distributed. Some, of course, live at the bottom and for generation after generation follow life styles characterized by dissatisfaction and despair.

Generalized concern about people in the lower social strata has increasingly led to a search for means to alter their destiny of poverty and dissatisfaction. The genesis of the increasing overall social concern will not be dealt with here, but attention will be given to the modern and urban society itself—its social strata, its conditions for mobility, its means for social change, and some of its problems of dysfunction that to varying extent affect the destiny of the individual.

The *stratification* of a society is a means of allocating social roles to the members of the society in accordance with individual opportunities and capabilities, the needs of society, and individual motivation. At least in theory, the rewards accompanying the roles of power, prestige, and property are the basis for motivation to participate cooperatively. Opportunities for rewards must be within individuals' capacity to obtain, and once roles are achieved, people in them must be able to carry out the proper functions to contribute to society and fulfill its needs.

A number of approaches to understanding the origin of social stratification have been advanced, but generally it is believed that because society rewards some roles with prestige and power more than others, stratification results from some individuals' seeking and obtaining the more desirable roles (Barber, 1968; Coleman and Neugarten, 1971).

Stratification is found in all societies and so is some degree of dysfunction. Theoretically, a society should not have social inequality, as to some extent stratification represents dysfunction in that the needs of some members are not served. Some positions with much prestige and reward require little effort, although other roles that require great effort and result in considerable contribution to the well-being of society are poorly rewarded. The inequalities of a society have much significance for all individuals growing up within it. Even though they may not be aware of the fact that they are in a stratified system, their behavior is influenced by its constraints and opportunities.

Effects of Stratification. The concept of stratification may be dealt with theoretically by using the concept of social class, although certain drawbacks in this approach are apparent. The concept includes the idea that a certain degree of homogeneity in behavior is prevalent within a class; individuals within a social class have similar educational and occupational pursuits. Consequently, within one class a similarity of life style is found. As a specific type of life style is characteristic of a class, children brought up within one social class tend to have an orientation toward a particular life style.

Close social contacts do not necessarily bring satisfaction in living. People in the lower class, while having closer social relationships and more frequent contacts with other people than the middle class, nevertheless do not consistently gain satisfaction in these relationships. It follows that the more intense the social relationships within a group the more control will occur. That is, close interpersonal relationships necessitate some restraint on individual behavior. Greater numbers of relationships in crowded areas result in more rules and obligations or controls. Such can be the source of stress and frustration.

Once the individual feels some alienation, he may become insensitive to nurturance or favorable emotional responses from others. Apparently one group of first-grade working-class boys was less affected by either nurturance or its withdrawal than either working-class girls or middle-class boys and girls (Sgan, 1967). This investigator sees her results as suggesting that children who had experienced satisfaction in human interaction indicated preferences similar to those of the experimenter, and that the working-class boys who had apparently not had such satisfaction were not as much influenced by the experimenter's responses to them as were the others.

Lower-class children seem to have less tolerance for disapproval and a greater need for approval than middle-class children. Rosenhan (1966), in a study of 72 first-grade boys from the lower and middle classes, hypothesized that children in the lower class would be more responsive to praise after performance in a task than middle-class children. Also, he thought that the performance of lower-class children would be more disrupted by disapproval than that of middle-class children. As an experimental task, he used two switches that activated lights on a board visible only to the experimenter. The experimenter responded with praise or disapproval according to a planned percentage of responses. He found that the performance of lower-class subjects was indeed better under conditions of praise than was that of middle-class children. He also found that under disapproval lower-class boys performed less well than did middle-class boys.

Stratification of a society does not insure that the most rewarding roles are filled with people having the greatest competence. Now, and historically, people in the most prestigious positions and in positions rewarded most by society come from a small segment of the population, and stratification and role functioning have not been fair or democratic. No society has as yet achieved a fair type of functioning, and inequalities and a lack of opportunity for some individuals exist. To some extent, then, stratification implies that a relatively permanent class system is characteristic of a society and that within it status is relatively stable from one generation to the next. Stratification means that individuals have different life chances and different opportunities to achieve satisfying social roles. Thus, one of the problems of any modern and complex society is to find ways to attract people with ability to strive for positions of influence and responsibility and to contribute to the welfare of the society. Generally, societies persuade and condition individuals to seek positions of responsibility. Continuing effort has been made in American society to establish stratification on the basis of ability rather than hereditary factors.

Social Mobility. Success in mobility is related to symbols of status. Symbols such as automobiles, clothing, houses, and membership in certain organizations provide a basis for an appraisal of a person's position. In a relatively stable society, these symbols provide continuing opportunities for assessment. In American society, because of its complexity, individuals sometimes may feel uncertain about their position in the social hierarchy and seek to proclaim their status by the use of symbols.

The stratification of society and its organization into classes in the early days of the United States was a dynamic system in comparison with the stratification system of the seventeenth- and eighteenth-century European societies. Since opportunity for social mobility became greater in the United States, many migrated from Europe to the New World.

Currently, the belief is widespread that opportunity for social mobility is declining and that modern societies as a result are becoming more rigid. However, some believe that the social structure is becoming more open, as technology has brought a wider range of occupational opportunity for mobility. The data in Table 2–1 about social mobility show the

TABLE 2–1
Social Mobility

Level of Occupation and Education	PERCENT		
	Upwardly Mobile	Stable	Downwardly Mobile
Occupational Level:			
Sons' higher than fathers'	69	31	. .
Sons' equal to fathers'	11	86	3
Sons' lower than fathers'	. .	56	44
Educational Level of Sons:			
Above average for class of origin	58	39	3
Average for class of origin	27	56	17
Below average for class of origin	12	54	34

Adapted from R. P. Coleman and B. L. Neugarten, *Social status in the city,* p. 245. Copyright 1971 by Jossey-Bass, Inc. Publishers. By permission.

changes in social status encountered in a study by Coleman and Neugarten (1971). From these data they concluded that sons (86%) usually remained in the same social status as their fathers.

Changes in American society during the last century have probably slowed the rate of mobility for many people and have formalized cultural differences among the social classes at least at the extremes of the hierarchy. Contributing factors have been the closing of the frontier and the transformation of the society from agricultural to urban. As more and more people came to settle the land, those arriving later found less and less opportunity. The ones who had arrived earlier set a high rate of mobility for the country, but as the frontier closed, the rate necessarily slowed. A second major factor in change was the curtailment of immigration in such a way that few people came into the country with low status; the rate of mobility, therefore, slowed merely because of the altered numbers of people seeking to move upward.

Several very recent factors have tended to reduce opportunities for mobility. First, status in American society has been related to the control of wealth, and, with the concentration of wealth among a few families and the rise of the "industrial state," opportunity for individuals with little capital to build and control successful business enterprises has lessened. Control of corporations in this country has come to rest in a comparatively small group, an industrial elite. Second, the necessity for education and skill in occupations is growing. Managerial positions in corporations usually are occupied by individuals who have long and expensive training as well as social connections, both of which are difficult for a person from the working class to acquire. Finally, the development of automation and the use of machines accompanying technological advancement have affected the opportunities for individuals with minimal education and skill.

In the latter half of the twentieth century a new element has been introduced into the complexity of social mobility. As the structure of American society has changed and as the demand for education in occupational activities has been extended, the number of individuals who have a strong drive toward upward social mobility has lessened. If individuals in a society define social status in terms of possessions, little reason remains to cause them to strive further once these possessions are obtained.

Aspiration varies within American society because, in part, it is related to individual assessment of opportunities for social mobility. Social mobility is thus not dependent alone upon motivation and the desire to obtain certain goals within a social order, but also upon social conditions offering opportunities. In the past, individuals in our society have been taught that it is an important social value, indeed a moral duty, for an individual to strive to attain a higher social status than the one into which he was born. This has been a part of American cultural tradition; however, such teaching has lessened as opportunities have lessened. (This topic is further discussed in Chapter 9.)

SOCIAL CHANGE

In understanding the significance of change for individuals in a society, the concept of the life space is again useful, as certain changes may only slowly affect the surroundings of some individuals, while rapidly altering the life space of others. For some individuals the life space may change so slowly that during one lifetime little adaptation is required. But because of urbanization and rapid communication, such a situation is much more unlikely for the future than it was in the past. Individuals in American society will of necessity be required to adapt to rapid social change.

The Dynamics of Social Change

Social change in societies creates difficulties for a number of reasons. First, adaptation to change may be unsuccessful for some people because of their inability to deal with stressful situations resulting from a failure to foresee difficulties, to set realistic goals, to discard patterns of response after they are no longer useful, and to discontinue loyalties to organizations that have become outmoded. A second basis for failure in adaptation is biological. Human beings must obtain from the environment the ingredients necessary for life; thus biological rhythms and processes cannot be in significant conflict with conditions within the life space (Bloch and Prince, 1967; Dubos, 1967). Physical aspects of the environment, therefore, such as heat, cold, and climatic changes cannot require adaptive responses beyond human capacity if people are to thrive.

Emotional support from others can help people to adapt to change with less difficulty. Affiliation of people with others in an urban environment was studied by Babchuk (1965). For the study, a *primary friend* was defined as a person with whom one interacted in a wide range of activities and with whom exchange of positive affect was frequent. Subjects were 117 couples with an age range of 19 to 58 years. A structured interview schedule was used to obtain the data.

This study indicated that people generally did not differ in the number of primary friendships, which were limited to two. It is significant, however, that half of the people in the study indicated that they did not have any primary friends. The study did not indicate whether or not the small number of friends was adequate; however, the subjects thought the number was sufficient. Perhaps two or three primary friends provide adequate emotional support and a basis for integration into the society.

Even though people have the insight and physical capacity to meet social change, still the mere fact of constantly being required to change is in itself a source of difficulty. Under much change, a feeling of futility or instability occurs, as accomplishments worked out with some intricacy and effort must soon be discarded in order that new ways may be developed. (Social change will be discussed in reference to a number of topics in later chapters.)

Impersonal Qualities of Social Change. Forces bringing social change are usually perceived by individuals as impersonal and powerful. Such perceptions develop and persist despite the fact that, upon analysis, the forces are discovered to result merely from the activity of other persons. These impersonal social forces are sometimes beneficent and sometimes inimical to individual or group welfare. Conflicts among values, cultural discontinuities, change in social goals, activity changes in government and industry, technological advances, new scientific discoveries, change in governmental forms, population increase or redistribution, and war— all may be beyond the control of any one individual but may result in fundamental alteration of the society.

Knowledge of trends, obviously, is of consequence to an individual in modern and urban society. Polls in elections, for example, although an area of controversy, represent a way of determining trends on the basis of sampling. With the advent of automatic data processing and the categorization of information from many sources, polls will be increasingly used in the future. This search for trends in social change has already permeated much of society, and even educational systems endeavor to predict population shifts to support long-range planning. Predictions are also being made in various aspects of economic activity, for example, in marketing to predict public demands for commodities.

Any one individual's influence on trends in social change is minimal. Often a particular individual seems to be a leader in change, but usually such a person is more a mirror of the change than an initiating force. It is important to see too that while some individuals seem to control human destiny and to dramatically influence human development in a society, they are in reality only part of fundamental and basic social movements.

In a complex society any social change is uneven in that it affects parts of the society more than others, and frequently the chronology of events associated with social change causes social dislocation and dysfunction. Dramatic discoveries and change in transportation or communication first affect the areas where population density is greatest; it may be years before these changes affect remote areas. The changes may also come to the latter with a different effect because of the difference in time. Social changes in the economic structure or governmental structure of society in turn affect other social structures, and all of the society must change. It is apparent, therefore, that as change comes about in any of the fundamental structures of the society, it eventually affects the other structures.

As social roles, individual self-perceptions, and perceptions of the social order are interdependent, rapid structural change requiring drastic alteration in behavior results in individual anxiety. Consequently, under conditions of rapid change people tend to see new trends as hazardous and try to cling to cultural continuities and refuse to alter their life styles. Because a response style to the environment is internalized, no other way of behaving seems open.

As social change inevitably occurs, the power of various social structures as well as individuals changes. One social structure is in power for a period, and then conditions shift and another structure assumes power. Such shifts affect some individuals adversely while bringing satisfaction and fortune to others.

Change brings frustrating conditions of many kinds; for some individuals the society is in a state of dysfunction all of the time (Allardt, 1966a; Lemert, 1967; Van Doorn, 1966). The number of people so affected varies. In the Great Depression, for example, the economic condition of the country affected the lives of millions of people, and the whole society was in a state of dysfunction for several years.

Social Change and Social Dysfunction. In all societies and within all structures certain culturally approved behavior patterns are established to deal with social dysfunction. These behavior patterns include opportunities for expression of tension and dissatisfaction in regard to the operation and functioning of the structure. In principle, at least, stockholders can cause a change in management; educational organizations can change administration; and governmental units can be altered. But for many individuals the means of changing and altering a social structure or preventing its dysfunctioning are not available. It is then that individuals and groups must find other ways of dealing with the causes of their dissatisfaction. Culturally approved as well as legally approved means of seeking redress to bring about change or to alter the structure must be sought. One way of forcing change is to bring about some disruption in the normal course of events and processes within a structure. The twentieth century has seen the development of many such methods of bringing about change. At the beginning of the century, the rise of the labor union movement and the development of a means of bargaining with corporations effected change in the lives of millions of individuals.

If opportunities to change social status and to deal with some forms of social dislocation such as unemployment are limited, any repression of activity directed toward dealing with the problem is likely to result in aggressive counteraction. While some individuals and some groups eventually accept repression, normal behavior is more likely exemplified by aggressive attempts to overcome barriers. Because of the complexity of human behavior, the manifestation of aggression used to deal with blocking of goals is not easily identified and may not even be apparent to those involved. Aggression is not always realistic; it may be directed toward certain groups of individuals who are available but who are not responsible for the frustration. Hostility may even be turned inward, and some members may select those of their own group as an outlet for aggressive feelings.

In a social organization, the consequence of overt expression of hostility resulting from frustration is likely to be unfavorable to the individual. Most adults, particularly those in the middle class, have learned the consequences of such overt expression and as a result find it necessary to repress feeling; they know that they must personally deal with their own emotions when deprived of a reasonable and direct outlet. The results of such repression in terms of psychosomatic functioning, as well as the effect on covert aspects of interpersonal relationships, make life within modern social organizations quite difficult. An essential requirement of middle-class members of social organizations is that they keep a close control on their emotions and be willing to postpone immediate gratification for long-term goals. But because the uncertainty of attainment of long-term goals is always greater than for short-term goals, general anxiety is increased.

In modern society a tendency to challenge authority and to express feelings of frustration openly and overtly has become generalized even though the means of expression often is irrational. For example, some ghetto residents of big cities have burned and looted the property of their neighbors. (More on this topic is found in Chapter 11.)

Although social change has always been brought about to some extent by revolutionary and aggressive action in social organizations throughout history, it has taken a different form in modern and urban society. Most of the action begins with "demonstrations" and with expressions of "peaceful intent" even though demonstrations eventually involve physical aggression when thwarting of the activity occurs. Often it is the youth who have sought to change characteristics of the social order. As certain techniques are found useful in obtaining change, they are emulated by others.

In a number of societies, the success of the youth's demands has been remarkable—even the course of government has been changed. Some societies are accordingly undertaking various types of reform in government and other social structures. Many young people feel, however, that the complexity of society and the power of certain groups have had a tendency to thwart opportunities for individuals to be influential in change. One of the major tasks of the future will be to provide means within society by which desires for social change can be realized.

Revolution and Social Change

Today, most of the societies of the world are undergoing social change. Changes are taking place in the Eastern and Western nations, in modern and complex societies, as well as in those which still have many characteristics of the nineteenth century or earlier. Perhaps the rapid change has a number of causes, but Sanger (1967) believes that it stems from the fact that man has discovered that he does not have to live on a dirt floor because his father did or because his father's parents did before him.

The Roots of Revolution. The revolutions of today are not characterized, as in the past, by formal war, but they have nevertheless destroyed a tremendous amount of wealth and thousands of people over the world. This violence associated with rapid social change has caused Sanger to label this present period in history as the *Insurgent Era.* Revolution may result from the shifting of power from an aristocracy to a rising middle class, from segments of a middle class to segments of the lower class, from a nation seeking to extend its boundaries, or from a nation seeing revolution and an attack on a neighbor as related to ideology and the spread of its form of government. Revolution usually stems not so much from the seeking of personal power as from a desire for some change in political or economic conditions. In a revolution one of the participants in the conflict is the government. The revolutionary opponent has some degree of organization but is less well organized than the government; sometimes a revolutionary group is very disorganized and is described as engaging in "mob behavior"; and sometimes revolution is caused by the activities of a charismatic person (Timasheff, 1965; Wolfenstein, 1967).

According to Timasheff, the terms *revolution* and *social change* should be distinguished. Rapid social change in the absence of revolution is brought about by change in a social structure, particularly if the structure is the government. Other social phenomena involving force, which should be seen as neither revolution nor war, are riots, violence involving labor, raids, and looting. While violence takes place in these conflicts, they are not considered a revolution that jeopardizes the power or position of the government on a wide scale throughout the society. A revolution is unlikely in a society where it is possible for individuals to satisfy new needs and meet new expectations. It also is improbable that a revolution will occur where people have no expectation that their lot can change. In terms of preventing revolutions, the only alternative to a suppressive force is continuous effort on the part of governments to meet the emerging needs and expectations of the people in the society. Although their outlook has improved, many of those in the lower strata of American society believe that, relative to progress in other forms of social change, they have not made enough progress. On the other hand, their demands to some extent necessitate that progress be slowed in other areas of society despite the fact that people there wish to continue the progress they have made in their life styles. Because progress in one area means a slowing of progress in another, conflict seems inevitable.

Wars and revolutions come and go, but the normative goal for a society is that of peace and social processes based on order. Although frequent periods of conflict can be found throughout man's history, an analysis of the amount of time spent on either peace or conflict indicates that peace and order are more nearly normal than a state of revolution or conflict.

Yet coexistence of stable social conditions and social change is a problem, as the existence of each is to a degree antithetical to the other. The state forms a lasting structure with cultural continuity, but social change means a modification of it. For a state as a social organization to be compatible with social change, individuals within the state must be willing for it to change. Compatibility demands that on the one hand ruling individuals defend the state against disorder and those who seek to modify it for their own benefit and that, on the other hand, they be willing to change it as a reflection of the ideas of people who believe that it should change.

Even in modern social organizations little thought has been given to the provision of avenues for social change. Groups or individuals sponsoring revolution find violence and conflict are their only resource, as paths to influence the structure toward social change do not exist. Some modern governments now are attempting to set up organizational means in order to reflect change sought by individuals and groups.

The Effects of Change. Extremely rapid social change such as that brought by a revolution is very difficult for any society, even for primitive societies. An example of the effect of rapid social change is provided by the people who live in New Guinea. During and since World War II these Stone Age people were suddenly exposed to highly technical social organizations. Now, especially in the Australian territories, a period of modernization is underway, and the tribesmen believe that their artistic wood carvings are no longer of value. These creations, formerly a source of pride, fade into insignificance in comparison with items they see from the modern world. Pride in an intricately carved and decorated canoe paddle of rare hardwood diminishes quickly when the creator is confronted with an outboard motor. As many products of their culture have suddenly lost their value, one entire tribe in a distraught mood deliberately destroyed all their artistic objects. Although for them the old had lost its value, the new had not yet become available. The modern objects belong to someone else. It is not surprising in view of the change that even in this primitive country a number of riots have already occurred in the settled areas where outsiders also live.

A changing society, therefore, means some disharmony; the very fact of social change means discontinuity. New ways of behaving are introduced into an old pattern, often before sufficient examination of the new can be completed. Further, as the parts of a changing society change at unequal rates and further maladjustment results from variance in the speed of change, the change affects the meaning of the culture for the individuals guided by it. Even though a change may be beneficial and lead to the betterment of the lives of some individuals within the culture, it still may have an adverse effect on the whole culture.

Individuals in a changing society seek improvement in their way of life; they seek better ways of fulfilling their needs; they believe that there are better ways if they can only be found. Hence, part of a cultural behavior pattern consists of exploring new ways to accomplish the tasks of everyday life. In a changing society, too, because of the dysfunction related to change, less value is placed on rules and customs and respect for the law is less. Moral codes are less effective than in a stationary or stable society. Sentiment for old institutions declines, and ceremonial behavior associated with them is discontinued, while teachings about religion become minimal. These difficulties seem to be characteristic of all changing societies and cultures (Lipset, 1965; Moore, 1967; Ogburn, 1964).

Any cultural system, however, has consistent elements which provide a solidarity and unity not only within the structure but within a society and culture. These connections within cultural systems are desirable in that they provide for human needs and satisfactions. Specific changes within a social structure need to be in accord with the overall trends within the total society and culture, if they are to be successful and if they are to continue.

Social trends and social change are, of course, bound inextricably to the socialization process. Those forces in society primarily responsible for the socializing experiences of developing individuals need to be understood; as they change, so does the course of human development. As they hold out hope and promise, or confusion and despair, they affect the destiny of the individual in becoming a part of the whole of society.

IN PERSPECTIVE

A significant part of man's environment lies beyond the natural features of mountains, valleys, rivers, cities, and towns. It consists of the *social organizations* of society. Because of their influence and continuity these organizations play an important part in the socialization of all human beings. The two most important are the family and the educational system. Increasingly, however, governmental agencies are taking over larger portions of their functions as work roles change and as women spend more time in activities away from the home.

The relationships of individuals to social organizations differ according to social status. Most people in modern societies are in a vast middle group with a medium amount of goods and income. Only small parts of the population are at the very top and at the very bottom. Factors significantly affecting social mobility from one group to another are difficult to assess, but it seems that movement out of the group into which one is born is quite difficult.

In most complex societies, social change is a particularly important influence on human development. These societies are changing at a rate that affects, often adversely, all of the values and cultural guides of the social structures. Children taught a way of behaving often find in a short while that the way no longer serves and in fact may be a hindrance in coping with the daily problems of living. Thus, a new and heavy burden in modern times has been placed on socializing agencies in their effort to prepare the young for adult roles.

Impetus for modern social change has come from the demands of people for a better opportunity to fulfill their needs and desires. These extensive demands have caused some to call this "The Insurgent Era." Although social change means progress and better opportunity for some people, it also destroys values that have been useful in dealing with the world and social relationships. Consequently, important distinctions must be made by the family and the educational system between values that need to be maintained and those which can be discarded.

REFERENCES

ADAMS, B. N. *Kinship in an urban setting.* Chicago: Markham, 1968.

ALLARDT, E. A theory on solidarity and legitimacy conflicts. In W. J. Goode (Ed.), *The dynamics of modern society.* New York: Atherton, 1966a. Pp. 167–178.

ALLARDT, E. Reactions to social and political change in a developing society. *International Journal of Comparative Sociology,* 1966b, 7, 1–10.

AMATORA, SISTER MARY. Home interests in early adolescence. *Genetic Psychology Monographs,* 1962, 65, 137–174.

ANDREWS, J. D. W. The achievement motive and advancement in two types of organizations. *Journal of Personality and Social Psychology,* 1967, 6, 163–168.

ARENSBERG, C. M., & NIEHOFF, A. H. *Introducing social change.* Chicago: Aldine, 1964.

BABCHUK, N. Primary friends and kin: A study of the associations of middle class couples. *Social Forces,* 1965, 43, 483–493.

BARBER, B. Social stratification structure and trends of social mobility in Western society. In T. Parsons (Ed)., *American sociology: Perspectives, problems, methods.* New York: Basic Books, 1968. Pp. 184–195.

BERKOWITZ, L., & FRIEDMAN, P. Some social class differences in helping behavior. *Journal of Personality and Social Psychology,* 1967, 5, 217–235.

BERTRAND, A. L. *Basic sociology: An introduction to theory and method.* New York: Appleton-Century-Crofts, 1967.

BLAU, P. M., & SCOTT, W. R. The concept of formal organization. In G. D. Bell (Ed.), *Organizations and human behavior.* Englewood Cliffs, N. J.: Prentice-Hall, 1967. Pp. 77–81.

BLAU, Z. S. Class structure, mobility, and change in child rearing. *Sociometry,* 1965, 28, 210–219.

BLOCH, H. A., & PRINCE, M. *Social crisis and deviance.* New York: Random House, 1967.

BROTZ, H. Social stratification and the political order. In A. M. Rose (Ed.), *Human behavior and social processes.* Boston: Houghton Mifflin, 1962. Pp. 307–320.

COLEMAN, J. S. *Resources for social change.* New York: Wiley-Interscience, 1971.

COLEMAN, R. P., & NEUGARTEN, B. L. *Social status in the city.* San Francisco: Jossey-Bass, 1971.

COSER, L. The functions of conflict. In N. J. Demerath & R. A. Peterson (Eds.), *System, change, and conflict.* New York: Free Press, 1967. Pp. 307–311.

DAVIES, J. C. Toward a theory of revolution. *American Sociological Review,* 1962, 27, 5–19.

DELGADO, J. M. R. The changing brain in a changing society. In C. C. Walton (Ed.), *Today's changing society—A challenge to individual identity.* New York: Institute of Life Insurance, 1967. Pp. 37–49.

DEUTSCH, K. W. Toward a theory of power and political structure. In H. W. Peter (Ed.), *Comparative theories of social change.* Ann Arbor, Mich.: Foundation for Research on Human Behavior, 1966. Pp. 60–74.

DRUCKER, P. F. The revolution in higher education. In T. R. Ford (Ed.), *The revolutionary theme in contemporary America.* Lexington, Ky.: University of Kentucky Press, 1965. Pp. 86–99.

DUBOS, R. J. Science and the human person. In C. C. Walton (Ed.), *Today's changing society—A challenge to individual identity.* New York: Institute of Life Insurance, 1967. Pp. 27–36.

EISENSTADT, S. N. Social change, differentiation and evolution. In N. J. Demerath & R. A. Peterson (Eds.), *System, change, and conflict.* New York: Free Press, 1967. Pp. 213–229.

ETZIONI, A. *A comparative analysis of complex organizations.* New York: Free Press, 1961.

FELDMAN, A. S., & HURN, C. The experience of modernization. *Sociometry,* 1966, 29, 378–395.

FESTINGER, L. *A theory of cognitive dissonance.* Evanston, Ill.: Row, Peterson, 1957.

FLETCHER, R. *Human needs and social order.* New York: Schocken Books, 1966.

FOA, U. G., TRIADIS, H. C., & KATZ, E. W. Cross-cultural invariance in the differentiation and organization of family roles. *Journal of Personality and Social Psychology,* 1966, 4, 316–327.

GALBRAITH, J. K. *The new industrial state.* Boston: Houghton Mifflin, 1967.

GARTNER, D., & IVERSON, M. A. Some effects of upward mobile status in established and ad hoc groups. *Journal of Personality and Social Psychology,* 1967, 5, 390–397.

GESCHWENDER, J. A. Explorations in the theory of social movements and revolutions. *Social Forces,* 1968, 47, 127–135.

GHISELLI, E. E. Psychological properties of groups and group learning. *Psychological Reports,* 1966, 19, 17–18.

GLOCK, C. Y., & STARK, R. *Religion and society in tension.* Chicago: Rand McNally, 1965.

GOODE, E. Social class and church participation. *American Journal of Sociology,* 1967, 72, 102–111.

GOODE, W. J. *World revolution and family patterns.* New York: Free Press, 1963.

GOODWIN, R. N. The person and his political environment. In C. C. Walton (Ed.), *Today's changing society—A challenge to individual identity.* New York: Institute of Life Insurance, 1967. Pp. 87–110.

GREEN, A. W. *Sociology: An analysis of life in modern society.* New York: McGraw-Hill, 1968.

GREER, S. A. *Social organizations.* New York: Random House, 1955.

HAGEN, E. E. *On the theory of social change.* Homewood, Ill.: Dorsey Press, 1962.

HAWLEY, A. H. Ecology and human ecology. In G. A. Theodorson (Ed.), *Studies in human ecology.* New York: Harper & Row, 1961. Pp. 144–154.

HEIST, P. Higher education and human potentialities. In H. A. Otto (Ed.), *Explorations in human potentialities.* Springfield, Ill.: Charles C Thomas, 1966. Pp. 261–274.

HIELD, W. The study of change in social science. In N. J. Demerath & R. A. Peterson (Eds.), *System, change, and conflict.* New York: Free Press, 1967. Pp. 251–263.

HIMES, J. S. *The study of sociology.* Glenview, Ill.: Scott, Foresman & Co., 1968.

HOFFMAN, L. R., & MAIER, N. R. F. Social factors influencing problem solving in women. *Journal of Personality and Social Psychology,* 1966, 4, 382–390.

HOLLINGSHEAD, A. B. Stratification in American society: Culture and the family. In M. Hillson, F. Cordasco, & F. P. Purcell (Eds.), *Education and the urban community.* New York: American Book, 1969. Pp. 54–65.

JANOS, A. C. *The seizure of power: A study of force and popular consent.* Research Monographs, Princeton University Center of International Studies, 1964, No. 16.

JOHNSON, C. A. *Revolution and the social system.* The Hoover Institution, Stanford University Press, 1964.

KIRKPATRICK, C. *The family as process and institution.* New York: Ronald, 1963.

KORNHAUSER, W. Power elite or veto groups. In W. J. Goode (Ed.), *The dynamics of modern society.* New York: Atherton, 1966. Pp. 376–383.

KUHN, A. *The study of society: A unified approach.* Homewood, Ill.: Dorsey Press, 1963.

LAUMANN, E. O. *Prestige and association in an urban community.* Indianapolis: Bobbs-Merrill, 1966.

LAWRIE, J. W. Motivation and organization. *Personnel Journal,* 1967, 46, 42–49.

LEMERT, E. M. *Human deviance, social problems, and social control.* Englewood Cliffs, N. J.: Prentice-Hall, 1967.

LERNER, M. Six revolutions in American life. In T. R. Ford (Ed.), *The revolutionary theme in contemporary America.* Lexington, Ky.: University of Kentucky Press, 1965. Pp. 1–20.

LINDSAY, J. *The city.* New York: W. W. Norton, 1970.

LIPSET, S. M. Revolution and counter-revolution—the United States and Canada. In T. R. Ford (Ed.), *The revolutionary theme in contemporary America.* Lexington, Ky.: University of Kentucky Press, 1965. Pp. 21–64.

MARCH, J. G., & SIMON, H. A. Dysfunctions in organizations. In G. D. Bell (Ed.), *Organizations and human behavior.* Englewood Cliffs, N. J.: Prentice-Hall, 1967. Pp. 91–96.

MARCH, R. M. *Comparative sociology.* New York: Harcourt, Brace & World, 1967.

MARTINDALE, D. *Institutions, organizations, and mass society.* Boston: Houghton Mifflin, 1966.

MAYER, K. B., & BUCKLEY, W. *Class and society.* New York: Random House, 1970.

MEAD, M. Culture and personality development: Human capacities. In H. A. Otto (Ed.), *Exploration in human potentialities.* Springfield, Ill.: Charles C Thomas, 1966. Pp. 137–153.

MEAD, M., & METRAUX, R. *A way of seeing.* New York: McCall Publishing, 1970.

MERRILL, F. E. *Society and culture.* Englewood Cliffs, N. J.: Prentice-Hall, 1965.

MERTON, R. K. *Social theory and social structure.* New York: Free Press, 1968.

MILLER, N., & BUTLER, D. C. Social power and communication in small groups. *Behavioral Science,* 1969, 14, 11–18.

MILLS, C. W. The structure of power in American society. In W. J. Goode (Ed.), *The dynamics of modern society.* New York: Atherton, 1966. Pp. 366–375.

MOORE, W. E. *Order and change: Essays in comparative sociology.* New York: Wiley, 1967.

MORRIS, R., & BINSTOCK, R. H. *Feasible planning for social change.* New York: Columbia University Press, 1966.

MURRAY, H. A. *Thematic apperception test.* Cambridge, Mass.: Harvard University Press, 1943.

NELSON, L., RAMSEY, C. E., & VERNER, C. *Community structure and change.* New York: Macmillan, 1960.

ODEGARD, P. H. *Political power and social change.* New Brunswick, N. J.: Rutgers University Press, 1966.

OGBURN, W. F. *On culture and social change.* Chicago: University of Chicago Press, 1964.

PRITCHETT, C. H. The judicial revolution and American democracy. In T. R. Ford (Ed.), *The revolutionary theme in contemporary America.* Lexington, Ky.: University of Kentucky Press, 1965. Pp. 65–85.

ROACH, J. L., GROSS, L., & GURSSLIN, O. R. Stratification theory. In J. L. Roach, L. Gross, & O. R. Gursslin (Eds.), *Social stratification in the United States.* Englewood Cliffs, N. J.: Prentice-Hall, 1969. Pp. 11–16.

ROACH, J. L., GROSS, L., & GURSSLIN, O. R. Social class: Concepts and research methods. In J. L. Roach, L. Gross, & O. R. Gursslin (Eds.), *Social stratification in the United States.* Englewood Cliffs, N. J.: Prentice-Hall, 1969. Pp. 74–83.

ROSENHAN, D. L. Effects of social class and race on responsiveness to approval and disapproval. *Journal of Personality and Social Psychology,* 1966, 4, 253–259.

SANDERS, I. T. *The community: An introduction to a social system.* New York: Ronald, 1966.

SANGER, R. H. *Insurgent era.* Washington, D. C.: Potomac Books, 1967.

SCHERMERHORN, R. A. *Society and power.* New York: Random House, 1961.

SGAN, M. L. Social reinforcement, socioeconomic status, and susceptibility to experimenter influences. *Journal of Personality and Social Psychology,* 1967, 5, 202–210.

SHIBUTANI, T., & KWAN, K. M. *Ethnic stratification.* New York: Macmillan, 1965.

SPADY, W. G. Educational mobility and access: Growth and paradoxes. *American Journal of Sociology,* 1967, 73, 273–286.

SPICER, E. H. Developmental change and cultural integration. In A. Gallagher (Ed.), *Perspectives in developmental change.* Lexington, Ky.: University of Kentucky Press, 1968. Pp. 172–200.

SUTTLES, G. D. *The social order of the slum: Ethnicity and territory in the inner city.* Chicago: The University of Chicago Press, 1968.

TALMON-GARBER, Y. Social change and family structure. In B. Farber (Ed.), *Kinship and family organization.* New York: Wiley, 1966. Pp. 88–101.

THOMAS, W. I. *On social organization and social personality.* Chicago: University of Chicago Press, 1966.

TIMASHEFF, N. S. *War and revolution.* New York: Sheed & Ward, 1965.

VAN DOORN, J. A. A. Conflict in formal organizations. In A. de Reuck & J. Knight (Eds.), *Conflict in society.* Boston: Little, Brown, 1966. Pp. 111–132.

WERTS, C. E. Career changes in college. *Sociology of Education,* 1967, 40, 90–95.

WOLFENSTEIN, E. V. *The revolutionary personality.* Princeton, N. J.: Princeton University Press, 1967.

SOCIALIZATION

Generally, the approach to the study of *socialization* has been concerned with the development of individual characteristics of social behavior. Here, however, the concept is not limited to social skills or to the process of acquiring acceptable and approved behavior. The term refers both to the process of learning behavior that fits the individual for life within his society and to environmental influences, that is, the effect of the environmental context. The term *context* includes the physical environment, social organizations, and the expectations of the society and culture. Such a broad approach to the meaning of socialization is perhaps better described as a perspective than as a definition. This meaning, however, is in keeping with a new trend toward convergence of theoretical approaches and viewpoints. Heretofore, viewpoints tended to deal separately with the process of learning and with the settings in which the learning takes place.

A number of issues relevant to developmental theory and research are dealt with in this section: (1) the significance of early childhood experience for later response styles (of particular relevance to programs such as Head Start and day care); (2) the importance of motivation during the developmental years and in adult role behavior (to be discussed at greater length in a later section); (3) the origins of difficulty for children growing up in environmental contexts different from the mainstream of American culture (children in the city's ghettos, for example); (4) the place and function of agents of society in the socialization of children; and (5) the relation of work and leisure in modern society. These topics lay a foundation for an understanding of behavioral control, autonomy, social conflict, and power to be covered later, particularly in Part V.

Part II also deals with variations in behavior patterns among social classes and cultures. Cultures vary as to content and as to the manner in which the content is passed to the next generation. A significant aspect of cultural content is that of *normative behavior.* In theory, norms consist of the culturally defined behavior usually transmitted to the next generation. For complex societies, the transmission of normative behavior in some sort of discrete entity is virtually impossible, primarily because of rapid social change.

Cultural conditions and transmission methods cause frustration. This frustration in turn affects individual motivation to develop approved or normative behavior. Definition of the problem areas in the content and in the transmission process and the amelioration of their effects are important goals for modern society.

THE
DEVELOPMENT
OF URBAN
LIFE STYLES

3

The life styles found today in urban society reflect the complexity and changing aspects of American culture. For youth this means that models of living patterns currently visible cannot be perceived as appropriate for adoption during their adult years. For those in the early years of adulthood, it means that they must look forward to a change in their life styles and living patterns, sometimes drastic and immediate. Even if they do not encounter sudden change, they can expect to alter their life styles and occupations substantially during their lifetime. This is a new condition in man's living. For most of the time in the world's history, man has been able to follow the model of his father, or even that of his earlier ancestors, as life styles in most societies have changed only gradually; but now with such rapid social change, youth cannot envision satisfactory life styles. Socialization, accordingly, is a much more difficult process now for the adults endeavoring to carry on the process with the young and for the young who must look forward to life in an unpredictable society.

SOCIALIZATION IN URBAN SOCIETY

One significant cause for change in life styles in American society is the great migration to the cities. Small towns and even some states are experiencing substantial losses in population as the greatest movement of people in history is taking place. The way of life in the small town isolated from the urban centers no longer serves. The causes of migration are complex and will be dealt with in more detail in later chapters, but, in part, the migration has to do with human motivation and desire. Relatively simple life styles in rural America were followed a few years ago because products of technology were accessible to only a few people in relation to the whole of society. But as technological products have become increasingly available, the old living patterns are no longer satisfying or even tenable. The man on the farm can no longer use a team of horses to plow but needs an expensive late-model tractor. His wife cannot wash clothes in tubs on the back porch, but needs an electric washer and dryer. His children clamor for color television. The state demands that he discard his old car as a hazard on the highways and as a source of pollution. Further, even the limited market for his produce is disappearing as conglomerates buy the neighboring farms and set up their own complex communication system with urban markets. As his children complete high school and can find no opportunities for work, they decide even before they graduate to migrate to the cities.

Obviously, much of the socialization process has not been relevant for these youth. They are ill-prepared for life in the cities. Consequently, as socialization is discussed here, attention is given to the "traditional" theoretical positions and research strategies, but at the same time attention is directed to the need for new concepts in keeping with the urban age.

It is not surprising that in many parts of American society both adults and youth have doubts about the offerings and goals of the socialization process. It is highly probable that youth's turning away from the patterns their parents have shown them is, in part, because of the parents' realization that their own styles are no longer appropriate. Perhaps, too, their dissatisfaction with their education results from the fact that educators have failed to perceive the need to change their training and goals in order to be relevant to a new age.

Concern about the process of fitting a child for life in modern society is heightened as the process is viewed in a small and dying town in rural America. How are the youth being prepared for their migration? How can the people who remain make sweeping changes in their lives as the new technology of the urban age reaches out to engulf them? Concern is heightened by the plight of many youth already living in the great urban centers who also find their education irrelevant.

The concept of socialization assumes that an individual must meet to some extent the requirements demanded of him by society. Each individual's role requires that some behavior must be in accord with patterns already established. This role behavior is necessary for the functioning of groups forming the larger system of society. Such role requirements are laid down by society in order that certain results and goals will be obtained. The individual's successful performance of his role is necessary for the satisfaction of others who are a part of an interrelated social order. The development of appropriate role behavior is not the entire meaning of socialization, however, as ultimately the satisfaction of the individual in society is paramount. Concern for the individual's socialization experience leads to concern for his chances of satisfaction in society.

Theoretical Foundations

No one theory suffices to explain socialization, but *social learning theory* seeks to explain the process of socialization and the ways the child moves from earlier forms of behavior into those forms desired by society. It holds that although at the beginning of life much of the infant's behavior is undirected and that he is uninformed about cultural expectations, it is incorrect to see infancy as a period in which behavior is unrestrained. Even in infancy the effect of models, conditioning, and reinforcement molds response patterns. The child changes his behavior during development, at least in part, because new kinds of behavior and accomplishments bring increasing satisfaction and pleasure. Thus, in the socialization process, simple and pleasurable kinds of behavior are relinquished for behavior that is more complex. Sometimes the new behavior requires denial of earlier forms of satisfaction.

Cross-cultural studies attribute many similarities among children to common elements in their environment and in their learning process. Certain physical laws, such as gravity and the danger of fire, cause children in one culture to behave similarly to children in other cultures, and expectations as to time for walking, talking, and the control of excretory processes are common to most if not all cultures. Societies over the world, however, have different ways of teaching children about these and other developmental accomplishments.

Social learning theory is currently in the process of modification and change. Its primary contribution is its effort to make principles explicit so that empirical investigation can be carried out. As social learning theory is based in part on psychoanalytic and stimulus-response theories, the difficulties inherent in those theories have been carried over to social learning theory. Thus, the difficulty in empirically substantiating such a psychoanalytic theory, for example, as the "latency stage of middle childhood" makes that part of social learning theory resting on psychoanalytic theory difficult, if not impossible, to verify. Stimulus-response theory also has certain deficiencies. Although at one time the sequence of stimulus-response was thought to be objective and easy to define or conceptualize, the meaning of *stimulus* or *response* has not been made explicit. Connections in the brain have been shown to be much more complex than as first described by the theory. An important contribution, however, of the aggregate of social learning theory is the emphasis on objectivity and on testing hypotheses through research.

Means of Socialization

Environmental conditions in the life space vary in effect on the individual not only because of their direct influence, but also because their effect depends on variance in individual capacity for response. Variation of environmental effect also results from previous experience and the ability to provide meaning for current stimuli, to arrange those newly perceived in patterns, to interpret them, and to derive appropriate responses. Variation also comes from differences in motivations, stimuli, and developmental maturity.

An individual responds to environmental opportunities not only because of his own needs and motives but also because his behavior elicits responses from others which in turn contribute to fulfillment of his needs. Responses to the child by individuals about him are significant in his learning because they reinforce behavior desired by the society and culture. This social reinforcement becomes the foundation for response patterns in social interaction.

Affectional factors condition the infant's and young child's responses to others. The range of emotional interchange is gradually extended as the individual grows, and his own characteristics become apparent to the mother as she responds on the basis of these characteristics; as a result, he is treated as a person different from others. Those who consistently interact with the child eventually develop a response pattern to the child that becomes predictable. Thus elements of the environment become familiar and continuous.

The socialization experiences of childhood not only contribute to such accomplishments as acquisition of language but also contribute to the increase of cognitive capacities and the development of a successful cognitive style that enables the child to move efficiently from one kind of learning experience to another. He learns to establish satisfying and appropriate social relationships with people of various ages, to make appropriate responses to both impersonal and personal aspects of the environment, and to initiate effective approaches in problem-solving behavior. Thus, in the socialization experience a child learns to make responses in accord with the external controls provided by the social order and culture; he develops a capacity to delay need fulfillment and to establish culturally approved controls of emotional response.

Goals and Developmental Accomplishments. Some specific goals of the socialization experience are: (1) acquisition of language, (2) cognitive development in reference to problem-solving, (3) acquisition of roles in social relationships, (4) orientation toward reality and a capacity to deal with fantasy, (5) motivation and willingness to explore novel situations, (6) learning appropriate behavior for gratification of needs, and (7) motivation to engage in goal-directed activities (Yarrow, 1968). Other important goals of socialization that have been suggested are proper nourishment and health, environmental consistency and repetition, opportunity for stimulation with playthings and objects, kinesthetic stimulation in physical handling, and opportunity for exploration of the environment through play in a variety of situations (Provence, 1968).

As the child begins to explore his life space, he needs little training in locomotion, but his environment should provide such things as climbing apparatus and wheel toys with handles in easy reach. He should also be allowed to explore materials varying in texture, shape, and weight and to manipulate objects in association with other objects—spoons with cups or container, geometrical forms that fit into holes, pegs on which rings can be placed, blocks or large pegs that can be pounded in a pegboard, and simple figures for puzzles. Most young children enjoy playing in water and sand. Freedom in exploring these things can lead the child to continue to seek new modes of learning and new experiences.

Young children between twelve and eighteen months begin to vocalize extensively. With the beginning of language, learning about the environment is greatly accelerated. Because language is so much a part of the learning process, it will be discussed in more detail in Chapter 6.

Socialization Models. Although it is difficult to determine how much of the socialization process depends on observation of others and imitation of their behavior, much of what the young child learns about the culture comes through the observation of other people. Some of the observed models provide emotional exchange, while others merely show ways of meeting problems and solving them. The actions of other people illustrate behavioral organization and predictability, as the behavior of most models takes place in a context of the culture's expectations. The behavior of models helps the child learn appropriate problem-solving methods. Other people define reality in the child's world and through reinforcement and sometimes punishment assist in channeling his behavior into culturally approved actions. If the child's behavior is in keeping with the expectation of models, he often receives affection or some kind of reward. And conversely, if his behavior is not in accord with expectations, he may be ignored, rejected, reprimanded, or punished.

Models, in addition to exemplary behavior, give direct instruction through explanation of techniques or by demonstrating appropriate actions. They reflect normative behavior about morality or specific kinds of social interchange. They also provide cultural values associated with objects, kinds of work, and emotional responses to others. The child learns these values and uses them as guides for his own actions. The influence of exposure to models ranges on a broad continuum from the provision of examples of simple behavior to strong emotional alliances that have significant or permanent effects on the young person's psychological and behavioral characteristics. Models whom children imitate can be quite real and close, they may be half real and half shrouded in fantasy, or they may exist wholly in fantasy. The first models are usually parents, but as children approach school age, others exert influence over their behavior.

Frequency of association with a model is an important factor in influence, especially when opportunity for emotional interchange exists. If a child is fearful about engaging in some type of behavior, an emotional relationship with another person helps him overcome his inhibitions or anxiety about the behavior. Responses that bring satisfaction tend to become established while those responses that cause dissatisfaction tend to diminish and disappear. Previous satisfaction is thus important in determination of a *set* or readiness to follow a model's behavior.

Children have been found to prefer models who have power to reward, and they consider such adults as more attractive than those without power (Bandura, Ross, and Ross, 1963). These investigators concluded that the children in their study tended to identify with a source of *power* rather than with a person with a subordinate role. These same research workers found that children in a nursery school who were allowed to observe models engaged in physical and verbal aggression against a doll reproduced this behavior when they had the opportunity. Those subjects who observed nonaggressive models showed little or no aggressive behavior when given the opportunity (Bandura, Ross, and Ross, 1961).

On the evidence of available studies, a child exposed to a successful model, a model who has social power and who reinforces emulated behavior, will carry the initiated behavior over into other similar situations. And, in addition, if a strong emotional alliance with a model exists, emulation of the model's behavior will likely become a part of the individual's life style and continue throughout his adult years.

Children from the lower socioeconomic class are often left at an early age with peers and thus have more sex-role models than is usually the case with middle-class children. This availability of peer models occurs in part because a large number of children from this class, especially those in the deteriorated areas of cities, come from one-parent families in which older children care for younger ones and adults seldom if ever provide care. Peer models alone, however, cannot fulfill the children's needs.

The school causes some conflicts in regard to models for the lower-class child in that the middle-class teacher may disapprove of the child's emulation of models in his life space. Further, the lower-class child is left on his own in groups that have little or no adult influence. Children in these groups turn to other group members to find "significant others" who can only partially serve as cultural agents. Middle-class young children placed in a nursery school interact both with peers and adults and thus have better opportunities for identification and imitation of a satisfying nature. Such experience usually leads to continuing and stable behavior patterns.

As children grow older, peers become of more significance as models, and by adolescence peers are valued as models more than are adults. Some parents and teachers are dismayed at the significance of adolescent models, but it should be remembered that much previous teaching about the importance of models has taken place and therefore the importance of models to adolescents is not surprising.

Those adolescents who continue their education in a university usually continue to emulate peers as they did earlier; at the same time, they find adult models who sometimes approve their behavior and sometimes bring them into conflict with earlier behavioral patterns. Some adolescents create ideal persons with whom to identify. This personification of ideals sometimes begins in middle childhood with the development of imaginary companions who are often fanciful persons of daring. In adolescence, the ideal imaginary person usually has some foundation in reality. The ideal may be a teacher who in imagination is endowed with desirable characteristics. Sometimes such a person is referred to as an *ego ideal,* meaning that the adolescent sees the person as having qualities that he desires. This personification of ideals may involve sex-role behavior, as the admired person may be of the opposite sex and one with whom the adolescent would like to have an emotional relationship. Because of the prevalence of intense feelings during adolescence, such fantasy can result in a traumatic experience if the adolescent is rejected or discovers behavior which is incongruent with the fantasy. Personification and fantasy occur in many if not most individuals and often form a powerful basis for motivation and inspiration toward culturally approved behavior.

DETERMINANTS OF URBAN LIFE STYLES

The structures of society are essential to the socialization process. Each of the structures has both a broad and a specific concern in the process, and taken together they constitute the social order. Each structure must for its own preservation and continuity function so that its values are inculcated in the young. The trends in their change and their influence are of paramount concern in understanding the development of an individual in modern society. Toward the end of the early childhood period, social structures outside the family become of increasing significance in socialization.

The Influence of Urban Social Structures on Human Development

The School as an Agent of Society. The child's first experience in school brings a significant change in his pattern of interaction with the environment. At school he is surrounded by people who differ from his family, people who have taken over responsibility for his safety and for the experiences to which he is exposed. Most children begin school with favorable anticipation, but some find it a time of stress and begin to develop behavior problems. An urban setting, especially the area of the central city, makes early demands on children for flexibility, for new ways to deal with the environment, and for personal adaptation to change despite their limited ability for cooperative social endeavor or for organized play. Although children need to develop a capacity to cope with frustration and to deal with complex social relationships, they usually have insufficient help in dealing with these complexities. Those living in deprived areas usually have more difficulty than do middle-class children in dealing with various aspects of the new environment, because they have deficiencies in sensory, motor, cognitive, linguistic, and affective experience.

In the middle years the child completes his training in elementary school and gains a great deal of information and new skills. Because knowledge has expanded so greatly in the twentieth century, the child learns much more than his parents did at his age.

In middle childhood the social significance of one's own physique, health, skin color, and social status is discovered. Individuals find, too, that social status is related to ability on the playground and skills in physical activities. Boys develop skills in gross motor activities such as basketball, football, and the like; girls develop skills in the use of small muscles for activities of writing or sewing. And, during this period sex differences in social behavior become established, and boys and girls move rapidly toward development of sex roles. This period is considered the latency period in psychoanalytic theory; however, interest in the opposite sex develops at an accelerated rate during the middle years. At the beginning of middle childhood, most children have learned something about cleanliness and the care of their bodies; in fact, so much has already been learned that the educational system usually needs only to reinforce the parents' training. Some children from deteriorated areas and from lower socioeconomic circumstances, however, have difficulty if they go to a school in a middle-class neighborhood. They may encounter disapproval of their language and of a lack of cleanliness or social and verbal skills. If they go to a school in their own deteriorated area and to teachers who represent the same general socioeconomic status, they may easily adapt to the school's requirements but their performance on achievement tests and intelligence tests will continue to be lower than the average of children who attend middle-class schools.

The influence of peers in school becomes increasingly important as the child spends more time away from the family, and the values and behavioral expectations of agemates become an important factor in behavior. Sometimes the child's continued adherence to a parental value system brings him into conflict with his peers. Because of such frequent conflict in values during the middle years, ability to make moral judgments independently must be learned.

In middle childhood, when the child is first introduced to the rules of the school, he has difficulty in understanding many of them. Children from the ghetto of the city have difficulty making distinctions between behavior that requires permission and behavior that does not. Some research findings indicate that the ability to make judgments about moral behavior is dependent upon intellectual ability (Whiteman and

Kosier, 1964). Available information about children's development of moral behavior is not definitive, however. One study of children in middle childhood found, for example, that moral judgment was related to age level, but was not significantly related to socioeconomic class or to sex differences (Boehm and Nass, 1962). Defining moral behavior for research studies is a difficult task. Nevertheless some research workers believe that study of the ways moral values are learned and of the methods of teaching them will prove productive; but moral values or rules about behavior may require learning conditions no different from those needed for other behavior.

Acquiring skills and meeting the demands of the school are abilities related to the child's perception of the appropriateness of sex roles. Some investigators believe that children are more willing to master school tasks and learn the skills required by the school when these seem to be appropriate to their own sex. In a study of children in the early grades in school, Kagan (1964) found that many objects which the child had to deal with were associated with femininity because the woman teacher used them. He concluded that girls were more likely to be interested in school tasks than boys. If this kind of information can be expanded and substantiated, it means that some consideration should be given not only to the curriculum but to the constituency of the child's life space in school. Many parents of children in center city, particularly those who are black, believe that the school's offering does not meet the needs of their children.

Concern about the crises in urban educational systems has been linked to concern about other crises in society. The linking of concerns has resulted not only from riots and alarming increases in crime, but also from the realization that as pressing as some of the immediate social problems are, long-term solutions are required. Most gang members for years were unsuccessful in meeting educational standards before they dropped out of school (Ahlstrom and Havighurst, 1971). Educational experiences to meet the needs of such children before adolescence is seen as one approach to the problems of these youth. Improvement of educational opportunities for children in the inner city has become more difficult in recent years because of the changing tax base associated with the changing living patterns of city inhabitants as well as the movement of commercial enterprises to the periphery of the city. Demands for services and welfare programs of the cities have risen, but the sources of tax revenue have not. Added to the difficulties of increased costs has been the great migration of the poor to the cities. Thus, a major cause of difficulty in education results from the problems of large numbers of people living in poverty in the cities. While the crisis in the educational system may be the most important of the social crises, education of the black child from the city ghetto, for example, cannot be separated from the socioeconomic problems of his family and the other problems in his life space. Neither can it be separated from the outlook of his destiny in society. The urban crisis in education is consequently inextricable from the socialization of the child in center city, his cognitive characteristics, emotions, and motivation.

The crisis in urban education is also linked to the poverty of many children in the central part of the city. The term is not relative merely to our own society; more and more it will be relative to the cultures and societies of the world. One definition of poverty is that a fraction—one fifth or less—of a society can be perceived as poor. If this definition is used, no solution to poverty exists, as there will always be a lowest fraction of income. Some believe, however, it would be better to use a definition that depends on an income figure below which everyone would be designated as poor.

Poverty can also be defined in terms of the characteristics of those with very low incomes. Some people with very low incomes are found among those who try to farm land of marginal productivity. The majority of this group are whites living in the South. The aged are another group; perhaps one fourth of the very low incomes are in this category. Families without a father and families with both parents but in which the father is employed in unskilled and low-paying jobs, make up another group. Many in this group are black. The largest group of poor, however, are white families living in urban areas. Reasons given for their poverty are low intelligence and physical disabilities, but the basic reasons for the poverty of this group are not clear (Miller and Woock, 1970). Many have emphasized the importance of the fact that black people are overly represented among the poor, and this information is a basis for insistence on fundamental change in American society.

Education as a means in the eradication of poverty must be perceived as part of a complex of variables. The children in Head Start, for example, who made the most progress on psychological tests were those who lived with both parents and whose parents had the most education and the highest incomes. Even though the educational experience was equal for all, those from families with a higher income and a higher socioeconomic level progressed further; thus the educational variable was less significant than the variables of family characteristics (Alexander, 1969). The problems of the poverty during the developmental years need to be approached in conjunction with efforts to bring about other changes in the urban setting.

The Role of Government. The influence of governmental organizations in the lives of children is likely to be greater in urban areas than in small towns. As children in the latter part of middle childhood and in adolescence move away from the family, significant influences on their behavior tend to come from peers, school, and governmental institutions. A number of governmental organizations have been established to take an active role in dealing with child behavior on the basis of legal authority. They may be set up as organizations to replace parents or they may function in a way similar to foster parents. Courts and social agencies make decisions about the placement of children and the kind of training or care they are to have. Courts have the power to remove children from their own parents if the children are judged to be neglected, because most people believe that children are entitled to care according to certain standards. Juvenile courts deal with the deviant behavior of children, as well as with violations of the law. They endeavor to solve the problems of children who have been abandoned or neglected by their parents. Thus, some governmental institutions have been established for children who need only protection. Others are concerned primarily with punishment, but even these provide educational programs. Still other institutions for children with physical and mental defects—blindness, deafness, and mental deficiency—have rehabilitation as the goal.

The institutional system has drawn increasing criticism. All too often children are placed in institutions on the basis of expediency. In other instances, the families of mentally deficient children have to wait years for them to be admitted. The purpose of institutions is to provide specialized care and education, but frequently the advantages of institutional care are offset by the long delays in admission. Further, many institutions operate with limited staff and equipment. Because of overcrowding, children are sometimes released with inadequate preparation to find a place in society. Institutions established to deal with specific difficulties of some children usually find that these children have overlapping problems.

Children placed in institutions because of aberrant social behavior still must adapt to a restrictive environment, though on a reduced scale. If they find even more difficulty in establishing satisfying emotional relationships with others in an institution, they are unlikely, once they are released, to meet the social requirements of the society any better than when they entered.

Economics and Socialization. Many people see television as a significant influence on children, not only in the urban setting but throughout the society. Both "commercials" and programs are believed to be influential. Widespread violence in programs has been of concern. Although most children spend many hours viewing programs, the extent of influence of such experience is still in controversy. One study seeking to determine the effect of television used a model's behavior on videotape as a means of influence. The results showed that the model's advocacy of rule-breaking affected the behavior of the children in reference to following rules (Stein and Bryan, 1972). Another study of elementary school children indicated that subjects who were shown a videotape of aggressive activity (fist fighting, shooting, and knifing) tended in the latter part of the experimental procedure to be more likely to "hurt" another child than were subjects in the control group who had watched a "neutral" program. Thus, in general, children who had been shown the fighting program were more willing to engage in aggression themselves than were those who had not seen the aggressive tape (Liebert and Baron, 1972). Still, the results could be interpreted as only temporary "modeling behavior" and of no lasting significance. Permanent and long-term effects of aggression or violence have not yet been established. It does seem reasonable, however, to believe that repeated exposure to "violence" is an inappropriate experience for anyone.

Industry has influenced children's lives through their families, not only in the production of goods, but in the control of their fathers' lives and occupations. Families in America have been increasingly mobile; transfers from one city to another are far from infrequent. This changing of the family environment affects children's lives in diverse ways, especially by establishing patterns of mobility which they are likely to continue when they become adults.

Religious Influence. The influence of religious organizations on developmental experience, like that of other social institutions, varies from society to society. In some societies the church is powerful and has considerable influence on functions of the other social organizations, particularly on the education and training of the young. In other societies the church's function is primarily spiritual and has little influence on other organizations. In American society the church varies considerably in its function, from the many rituals of the Catholic Church to the very simple ones of some denominations.

In Western society religion has had considerable influence on normative behavior, as the Ten Commandments have prescribed restrictions and forms of behavior for most of recorded history. With such beliefs, religion provides a cultural pattern of behavior that assists the individual in role behavior and in developmental changes throughout his life. The functioning and influence of religion in complex cultures is less important than in primitive ones, according to Merrill (1965), because religious beliefs lose power if many in the society do not believe, religious rules are more easily evaded without notice in complex societies than in primitive ones, and some religious practices may be a disadvantage in urban life styles. In American society religious influence on the training of children seems to be lessening. In part this change is associated with the great technological advances in society and the increasing emphasis on independence of thought and activity as opposed to any extra-individual control or dictation.

Middle-class religious organizations are divided ideologically over their roles in civil-rights activities. Some religious leaders have seen their role as a militant one and have advocated open disobedience of laws that restrict demonstrations and assemblies devoted to the accomplishment of social change. Religious leaders from all of the major religious organizations have at times been active in confrontations with police and the legal system. Sentences of fines and imprisonment have been given to those leaders who have sponsored causes of desegregation, rights of workers, freedom to assemble, and black demands for economic opportunity.

Some black civil-rights workers have demanded reparations from urban religious organizations of all faiths. They demand money as reparation for the church's silence and participation in a society that deprived black people of their legal and social opportunities. Some religious organizations respond favorably to these demands not so much because of the concept of reparations but through sympathy for the struggle of black people for economic independence. The cause of civil rights has been perceived as a moral cause, and thus it has always been closely linked to both middle- and lower-class religious beliefs.

The social phenomenon of the second half of the twentieth century is that the church has come into conflict with the state over social causes rather than over religious issues as has occurred throughout so much of history. An example of the involvement of state and church in pursuit of the same goal is the presence of Head Start (preschool) classes for black children in religious buildings. This agreement came about in part because of the unavailability of adequate space and also because of the commitment of the religious organizations to social change. Although these programs receive support primarily from the Federal government, they are carried out on property belonging to religious groups.

Not all members of religious organizations believe that so much of their resources and effort should be directed to social goals. Some believe that religious groups are becoming social agencies and that religious beliefs and purposes are being neglected. Religious organizations therefore are involved in new sources of controversy and they, like society as a whole, are undergoing change. The change is uneven, as it is in society. Strong areas of resistance exist throughout the organizations, and resistance also has come from other social structures that contend that religious organizations are infringing upon their traditional roles and activities. Nevertheless the role of governmental and religious organizations has changed; there is cooperation not only in social programs but in the reduction of the separate effort in educational programs.

Urban Life Styles

Social change does not bring change in life styles easily because patterns established in earlier years are difficult to alter. In a rapidly changing society, incongruity in adult patterns of living is apparent. Incongruities in parental behavior are to be expected, as life styles cannot be quickly altered to conform with all aspects of cultural change. Perception of parental incongruities sometimes causes the young to reject adult life styles entirely even though some characteristics are appropriate.

The area of urban space that in the future will see the greatest change in life styles is the periphery of large cities. Although much of this area today is still suffering from "urban sprawl," its proximity to center city and the relatively low population density make it the most attractive living area of the future. Some of this area still has the advantages of wooded areas, accessible creeks and rivers, and other natural characteristics. The older established areas and developing peripheries will be a new ecological unit of the post-industrial society. This kind of space has been designated the *Urban Field* (Friedmann and Miller, 1968). As an enlargement of the space of the center city, it can enhance social and cultural life.

Income, Work, and Leisure. Income in America is expected to rise, and time spent at work is expected to lessen. As the demarcation between leisure and work lessens, a merging of both types of activity will characterize urban life styles. This bringing together of activity will accompany changes of economic and psychosocial characteristics so that the living areas can no longer be distinguished as urban and rural. The center core of the cities will still influence the periphery by retaining the great museums, musical and art centers, universities, and economic and business units, but the influences of these will also be scattered into the periphery by various branches, communications, and rapid public transportation.

Personal life styles will include much more time spent in leisure, and the adult models available to children will tend to change from the absolutely work-oriented parents to those enjoying leisure and extended activities not necessarily directly related to their vocations. Increased flexibility of women's roles will allow more choices of activity in both industry and in the community. The life space and activities within it will reflect the dispersion of activities formerly found only in certain parts of the urban area. In the future, education, government, and commercial organizations will be more responsive to people's needs and life styles.

While new transportation forms and technical advances make mobility more feasible, a countertrend in technical advances will likely lessen the need for personal mobility. Dispersion of working places is possible by communication developments, and thus reasons for the location of business firms close to each other are being reduced. Now the convenience and desires of the working force can be taken into account, and living environments of the future will have more variety. Multiple living space will be increased for more and more people, as space will be maintained in populous and active areas as well as in areas where leisure and recreational activities are possible. The present concept of second homes will be altered so that living patterns easily flow through space and *separateness* will not be part of the concept. Because income, availability of diverse activities, and mobility will increase, individuals will participate in a wide range of organizations. The use of urban space will have to insure the conservation of scenic values and historical sites. Industrial pollution will have to be controlled. Newly constructed living areas will have to be appropriate to the life styles of the people who will live in them. Such a vision of an improved quality of life depends upon the development of programs related to the varying needs of diverse styles of living as well as insight into the effect on both the physical surroundings and people.

Work and the American Dream. As changes are envisaged in life styles, it is well to remember that the American Dream is one of an open-class society. The Dream implies that being born in poverty or in a disadvantaged area should not determine an individual's destiny beyond his own control. Although the child born in poverty should have the same opportunity for education and achievement as does the child born into the middle or upper class, the opposite realities of current society are becoming increasingly clear. The present structures and their programs have not as yet been able to offset the disadvantages of a poor family background. Parents who are successful in modern and urban society in fulfilling their needs and establishing a successful life style provide better models and better socialization experiences for their children than do those parents living in poverty. The teaching of the successful parent about the culture, role behavior, and social skills remains a significant factor in the prediction of the child's future life style in society. For the American Dream to approach reality, the vast areas of the cities where thousands of people live in poverty and frustration will have to be changed, not only by adequate housing and living space but by education which must provide opportunities so that individuals living in these areas can find their way into the mainstream.

IN PERSPECTIVE

Life styles in urban society reflect the conflicts over social change as well as the changing character of social roles. Some adults have found that a life style formerly approved or desired must be altered. Age differences in life styles are especially marked, as many of the young have developed their own at extensive variance from adult models.

In the early part of the century, the development of technology and principles of mass production brought many changes in work. Unions did much to improve safety, wages, and pensions. But as the latter decades of the century are reached, traditional concepts of work are undergoing change. In recent years work has not brought the satisfaction found earlier. As the attitudes of workers in many "service" occupations have altered, their concern for accomplishment of a high level of performance has lessened. Work on assembly lines has never held much satisfaction; recently, mass "slow-downs" have occurred to protest the current stultifying conditions. Even those in the professions have become dissatisfied. Work provided by society is not now generally considered as a means of fulfillment; rather, satisfaction is sought in leisure. Work weeks are being shortened, and much more time is available for leisure than was true earlier in the century.

Predictions have been made that the "post-industrial age" will not provide enough meaningful work opportunities in the future and that large segments of the population will not be able to find work for which they have been trained. Thus, proposals have been made for a "guaranteed income" to provide a realistic form of social security.

Perhaps the greatest problem in socialization today, however, is the rejection by youth of life styles long advocated by society. This rejection, although signifying need for change in the learning experiences provided for youth, has not brought creative and empathic reactions from society's agents. It should be noted that the rejection of society by many youth is a new development in the social history of man, and it is not surprising that society's dependence on cultural continuities has not as yet allowed substantial change in training experience, objectives, or content.

REFERENCES

AHLSTROM, W. M., & HAVIGHURST, R. J. *400 Losers*. San Francisco: Jossey-Bass, 1971.

ALEXANDER, T. Emotional characteristics of disadvantaged children of Appalachia. In T. Alexander (Ed.), *Annual Report: Child Development Research Center*. Philadelphia: Temple University, 1969. Pp. 97–108.

ANDRY, R. G. *Delinquency and parental pathology*. Springfield, Ill.: Charles C Thomas, 1960.

BALDWIN, A. L. *Theories of child development*. New York: Wiley, 1967.

BANDURA, A., & HUSTON, A. Identification as a process of incidental learning. *Journal of Abnormal and Social Psychology*, 1961, 63, 311–318.

BANDURA, A., ROSS, D., & ROSS, S. A. Transmission of aggression through imitation of aggressive models. *Journal of Abnormal and Social Psychology*, 1961, 63, 575–582.

BANDURA, A., ROSS, D., & ROSS, S. A. A comparative test of the status envy, social power, and secondary reinforcement theories of identification learning. *Journal of Abnormal and Social Psychology*, 1963, 67, 529–538.

BANDURA, A., & WHALEN, C. K. The influence of antecedent reinforcement and divergent modeling cues on patterns of self-reward. *Journal of Personality and Social Psychology*, 1966, 3, 373–382.

BENNETT, I. *Delinquent and neurotic children*. New York: Basic Books, 1960.

BOEHM, L., & NASS, M. L. Social class differences in conscience development. *Child Development*, 1962, 33, 565–574.

BRIM, O. G., & WHEELER, S. *Socialization after childhood*. New York: Wiley, 1966.

CALDWELL, B. M. What is the optimal learning environment for the young child? *American Journal of Orthopsychiatry*, 1967, 37, 8–21.

DeLUCIA, L. A. The toy preference test: A measure of sex-role identification. *Child Development*, 1963, 34, 107–117.

ELKIN, F. *The child and society*. New York: Random House, 1960.

EMMERICH, W. Continuity and stability in early social development. *Child Development*, 1964, 35, 311–332.

FRIEDMANN, J., & MILLER, J. The urban field. In J. A. Winter, J. Rabow, &

M. Chesler (Eds.), *Vital problems for American society.* New York: Random House, 1968. Pp. 479–499.

GRINDER, R. E. Relations between behavioral and cognitive dimensions of conscience in middle childhood. *Child Development,* 1964, 35, 881–891.

GUMP, P. V., & KOUNIN, J. S. Milieu influences in children's concepts of misconduct. *Child Development,* 1961, 32, 711–720.

HARTUP, W. W. Peers as agents of social reinforcement. In W. W. Hartup & N. L. Smothergill (Eds.), *The young child: Reviews of research.* Washington, D.C.: National Association for the Education of Young Children, 1967. Pp. 214–228.

HARTUP, W. W., & ZOOK, E. A. Sex-role preferences in three- and four-year-old children. *Journal of Consulting Psychology,* 1960, 24, 420–426.

HETHERINGTON, E. M., & FRANKIE, G. Effects of parental dominance, warmth and conflict on imitation in children. *Journal of Personality and Social Psychology,* 1967, 6, 119–125.

KAGAN, J. The child's sex-role classification of school objects. *Child Development,* 1964, 35, 1051–1056.

KIRKPATRICK, C. *The family as process and institution.* New York: Ronald, 1963.

KUHN, A. *The study of society.* Homewood, Ill.: Dorsey, 1963.

LIEBERT, R. M., & BARON, R. A. Some immediate effects of televised violence on children's behavior. *Developmental Psychology,* 1972, 6, 469–475.

LYNN, D. B. A note on sex differences in the development of masculine and feminine identification. *Psychological Review,* 1959, 66, 126–135.

MERRILL, F. E. *Society and culture.* (3rd ed.) Englewood Cliffs, N. J.: Prentice-Hall, 1965.

MILLER, H. L., & WOOCK, R. R. *Social foundations of urban education.* Hinsdale, Ill.: Dryden Press, 1970.

MONAHAN, T. P. Broken homes by age of delinquent children. *Journal of Social Psychology,* 1960, 51, 387–397.

MONAHAN, T. P. Family status and delinquency. In M. E. Wolfgang, L. Savitz, & N. Johnson (Eds.), *The sociology of crime and delinquency.* New York: Wiley, 1962. Pp. 321–330.

MORRIS, R. R. Female delinquency and relational problems. *Social Forces,* 1964, 43, 82–89.

MUSSEN, P. H., & PARKER, A. L. Mother nurturance and girls' incidental imitative learning. *Journal of Personality and Social Psychology,* 1968, 2, 94–97.

MUSSEN, P., & RUTHERFORD, E. Parent-child relations and parental personality in relation to young children's sex-role preferences. *Child Development,* 1963, 34, 589–607.

PROVENCE, S. The first year of life. In C. A. Chandler, R. S. Lourie, & A. D. Peters, *Early child care.* New York: Atherton, 1968. Pp. 27–39.

PROVENCE, S., & LIPTON, R. C. *Infants in institutions.* New York: International Universities Press, 1962.

RHEINGOLD, H. L. The modification of social responsiveness in institutional babies. *Monographs of the Society for Research in Child Development,* 1956, 21 (2).

ROSENHAN, D., & WHITE, G. M. Observation and rehearsal as determinants of prosocial behavior. *Journal of Personality and Social Psychology,* 1967, 5, 424–431.

SANDERS, I. T. *The community.* New York: Ronald, 1966.

STEIN, G. M., & BRYAN, J .H. The effect of a television model upon rule adoption behavior of children. *Child Development,* 1972, 43, 268–273.

SYKES, G. M., & MATZA, D. Techniques of neutralization: A theory of delinquency. In M. E. Wolfgang, L. Savitz, & N. Johnson (Eds.), *The sociology of crime and delinquency.* New York: Wiley, 1962. Pp. 249–254.

TYLER, B. B., TYLER, F. B., & RAFFERTY, J. E. The development of behavior patterns in children. *Genetic Psychology Monographs,* 1966, 74, 165–213.

WHITEMAN, P. H., & KOSIER, K. P. Development of children's moralistic judgments: Age, sex, I.Q., and certain personal-experiential variables. *Child Development,* 1964, 35, 843–850.

WHITING, J. W. M., & CHILD, I. L. *Child training and personality: A cross-cultural study.* New Haven, Conn.: Yale University Press, 1953.

YARROW, L. J. Conceptualizing the early environment. In C. A. Chandler, R. S. Lourie, & A. D. Peters, *Early child care.* New York: Atherton, 1968. Pp. 15–26.

SOCIOCULTURAL
VARIANCE
IN
RESPONSE STYLES

4

The geographic location of birth, the extent of family involvement in community life, the parents' place in the strata of society, and their success in attaining normative standards of behavior determine to large degree an individual's place in society. The position of the family in an economic structure, for example, determines the adequacy of prenatal care as well as the characteristics of the space immediately surrounding the child. The life space, as the child's immediate context in the total culture from the very beginning, is the essential factor that impels him inexorably toward his destiny in the social order.

SOCIOCULTURAL PATTERNS

The family's social class defines the nature of the family members' problems as well as the methods to be used in solving them. The child sees in family life an enactment of that part of the culture in which his family lives. Because his training is in accord with the part of the culture in which he spends his early years, it is to be expected that his aspirations, his feelings about himself, and his family relationships will induce certain behavioral patterns that vary from those of children growing up in another class and in another place (Baumrind, 1972; Marjoribanks, 1972). Still, some common threads are found, and in American society a lessening of class differences in child training has been observed. Prominent in this reduction of differences are the increasing numbers of people who come under the prolonged influence of the educational system.

Social-Class Variance

At one time it was believed that several important differences existed in child-rearing practices of lower and middle socioeconomic classes. A study by Davis and Havighurst (1946) suggested that middle-class parents used more strict measures for control in child training than did lower-class parents. Some years later a study by Maccoby and Gibbs (1954) obtained different results; at this time middle-class parents were found to be more tolerant of the child's behavior than lower-class parents were, particularly in reference to aggression, sex play, and toilet training. Still a few years later, Miller and Swanson (1958) concluded that social-class differences in child rearing were indeed becoming less observable. A subsequent review showed that child-rearing disparities between the lower and middle socioeconomic classes have gradually decreased over the years (Waters and Crandall, 1964). The extremes of behavior in American society seem to have been progressively reduced, in that there are fewer extremely poor people and fewer extremely rich people. A greater amount of the material of the culture is now available to those in the lower socioeconomic class than formerly, and although many people still live in poverty in deteriorated areas of large cities, many families have also been able to move out of such areas. An increasing number of people from the lower socioeconomic class now stay in the educational system for longer periods of time, more opportunities are available in industry for on-the-job training, and modern communication media have extended knowledge of the culture. All of these developments have affected child training. Consequently, training customs such as emphasis on the delay of gratification, the importance of planning, and the learning of techniques to successfully cope with the problems of the culture have become generally observable. As a result of these changes and of the increasing complexity of American society, it is difficult to characterize a large group of people as middle class or lower class, because heterogeneous characteristics of the life space of each class limit the effectiveness of such generalizations. It does not seem possible, either, to compare social classes on the rather abstract qualities of "permissiveness" or "strictness" in child training. Such concepts are abstract and difficult to evaluate in practical terms.

Despite the reduction of social-class differences and the difficulty in making generalizations about variations in child rearing, the fact remains that many parents cannot provide for their children's fundamental needs in nutrition, health care, or psychological nurturance (Caldwell, 1967; Goldstein, 1967; Yarrow, 1968). These parents living under adverse conditions do not provide planned activities to benefit their children or specific experiences to contribute to the development of effective ways to deal with the environment. The parents' life styles tend to be related only to the present, in part because of the recurring crises with which they must try to cope.

Such parents also have problems in teaching cognitive development. The effect of cultural deprivation on children growing up in deteriorated sections of large cities is exacerbated by limitations on verbal communication between mother and child (Hess and Shipman, 1965). The cognitive environment of these children is controlled by status roles rather than by attention to the characteristics of a situation. That is, the lower socioeconomic class environment causes the child to be concerned about authority rather than reasoning; he may conform to demands, but he does not consider the appropriateness of the demands, and he is taught to view the consequences of his behavior in terms of immediate reward or punishment rather than long-range goals. Mothers and children tend to respond without sufficient time for planning, for dealing with causation, and for reflection about the possible results of their decisions. The behavior of both tends to be insufficiently related to the situational context.

If assistance to children in the lower socioeconomic class is to help them achieve the normative behavior of the whole society, the environment must provide patterns of experiences that emphasize the proper behavioral systems (Gewirtz, 1968). A desirable system of behavior may also be enhanced by changing the conditions of the immediate space surrounding the child and by providing the optimal number of peers and adults (as empirically determined). In early childhood, socialization by imitation is more likely if a number of somewhat older children in the environment provide examples of desired behavior rather than if young children are allowed to come in contact only with age peers.

Cultural Variants in Enculturation

Cross-cultural studies of child-rearing practices have been undertaken to determine the general types of influences they have on adult role behavior. Barry, Child, and Bacon (1965) see child rearing as an effect of culture. They ask questions like these: Why do certain child-rearing practices occur in certain cultures? Is it because this particular kind of training produces behavior in adult life appropriate to the society or culture? Is it because the type of economy in a culture requires certain adult roles, and individuals must be fitted for these roles by certain child-training practices?

Behavioral Differences in Relation to Food. One variable these investigators believe important is the extent to which food is acquired and cared for. For example, some primitive societies depend on animal husbandry for food; in others in which agriculture is important, certain kinds of behavior are encouraged in order to insure the growing of food.

The production of food in both ways requires care in performing certain roles, and appropriate behavior patterns are established for children to follow. These investigators argued that if economic roles tend to be generalized to other behavioral patterns within the culture, it might be possible to predict typical social behavior.

These investigators hypothesized that in societies where it is difficult to accumulate food, adult behavior should be individualistic and assertive. In societies where a considerable amount of food is accumulated, adults should be conscientious and conservative. One hundred four societies were rated on the following aspects of child training: (1) obedience, (2) responsibility, (3) nurturance, (4) achievement, (5) self-reliance, and (6) general independence. The study indicated that societies with very high accumulation of food showed more pressure toward obedience and responsibility and less pressure toward achievement, self-reliance, and independence than was shown by those societies with a low accumulation of food. Nurturance was the only child-training variable which was similar in rank in both types of societies. The study suggested that in socialization of the young child, the family undertakes to provide the child with specific problems appropriate to the culture and to teach him when he is confronted with other problems to select culturally desired solutions. In general, the problems provided are increasingly complex, because, as a child grows older, he is expected to behave in more complex ways.

The Role of Competition. Cultural differences in behavior patterns have been studied in other ways. Differences between Cubans and Americans, for example, were studied by Shaw (1967). Cuban culture more often rewards "good" behavior and encourages dependence than does American culture, whereas American culture more often punishes "bad" behavior and encourages independence than does Cuban culture. The subjects were children 11 to 13 years of age and adolescents 16 to 19 years of age equally divided as to sex. Part of the information obtained was by reading short stories to the groups. The subjects made choices of positive or negative outcomes for the stories. Among other differences encountered, Cuban subjects, especially younger ones, more often preferred positive outcomes for the stories than did the American subjects.

Cultural variance occurs not only in teaching methods but also in what is to be taught. Some cultures emphasize time, but others have little interest in it and may in fact have no language to describe past or future events; some cultures emphasize various forms of measurement in addition to time, but others have no methods of measurement; and some societies maintain a history carefully delineated according to chronology, but history in others has no reference to the chronology of events. Some societies teach children to compete at a very early age, and competition is often used as motivation by encouraging children to perform at a level superior to that of their peers. But some societies do not teach competition; in fact, they may disapprove of it. In our society, the mother has primary responsibility for the care and training of the child, but in some societies this is not the case. In the Trobriand Islands, for example, and in some other islands of the Pacific the mother's brother has been described as having primary responsibility for the training of the child (Malinowsky, 1935). Parental control of children also varies considerably from society to society and even within cultures; it also varies according to social class and geographical areas. American society differs from some European societies, for example, in its concern about the social behavior of very young children (Gardner, 1964; Stevenson, 1967).

Other evidence indicates a number of cultural differences in child-training methods, but within a similar framework of overall social control. One study of child-rearing practices gathered information in six societies: a town in New England, a community in Eastern Kenya, a community in Northern India, a village in Okinawa, a tribe of Indians in Southwestern Mexico, and a group in the Northern Philippines (Whiting, 1966). Observations showed that social control was relatively uniform in most respects: leaders in the societies held positions on the basis of merit, and group sanctions were used to induce desired behavior and usually consisted of avoidance or expulsion. Enforcement of desirable behavior in Okinawa, India, and the Philippines was related to identification with the group. In the Mexican society, the group sanctions were related to the fear of being ostracized. In Kenya, leadership served as social control, as the leader had considerable power and prestige.

Social Role Relationships. A study of several hundred middle-class five-year-old children in Japan sought information about their ideas of kinship categories, sex and age roles, and adult occupations (Goodman, 1967). The investigator found that in their concepts of the social order, identification, especially in regard to age and sex, was one of the most common and systematic principles described by her subjects. The Japanese girls, for example, had been taught that as women they should be gentle and kind. In general the children tended to identify with older siblings or with grandparents, uncles, and aunts. Goodman noted that in the interviews the children referred to themselves only rarely and referred to others in traditional Japanese nonindividualistic terms, by the status labels of "teacher," "doctor," or "learned person."

An individual in any society lives within complex interpersonal relationships that always involve some degree of communication and dependence; some of these relationships are important and some are fragmentary and transient. Children must learn how to deal with these various kinds of opportunities for social relationships. One of the essential tasks for the child is to learn what to expect in various social relationships; part of the socialization and child-rearing process must help children to make these distinctions. Knowledge about social relationships is also fundamental to making decisions about what goals to pursue and the appropriate behavior for achieving them. This knowledge is gained primarily through contact with those in the life space.

Some patterns of social relationships are common among all societies, as all societies have status differentials in age and sex (Nash, 1965; Cole,

Gay, Glick, and Sharp, 1971). For example, very young children cannot perform in adult roles. Because of the biological bases for child bearing and care, sex roles are also universally differentiated. Men usually perform tasks which require time away from the family, because women must stay close to the home in order to take care of children, and many tasks surrounding the living space fall to women because they are close by.

Specialist roles in a society tend to affect personal relationships by increasing formality and separation. Urbanization may adversely affect the satisfaction obtained in personal relationships, as is suggested by comparison with primitive societies. Observations of the Hopi Indians, for example, indicate that a child growing up in a village feels a part of it. Even if starvation threatens the whole village, the threat is not for the individual alone, in that he can be assured of a share as long as there is any food. The Hopi child also grows up with an assured place in the society; he does not have to try to find some unknown occupational role, nor does he have to face a complex society where he can see no place for himself. Rather, he sees an attainable social role and always feels a part of the social order (Dennis, 1965). An urban and highly complex society such as the American, has, by contrast, some disadvantages for the individual. Personal relationships are few in number and often difficult to retain. Mobility and shifts toward formal relationships often result only in relationships that are nonreciprocating. Parts of the urban environment, however, offer exceptions to such conditions; kinship and neighborhood organizations in the ghettos of large cities give the individual some measure of support; and in other parts of the society, among people in the upper classes, for example, there is a sense of community and of reciprocation, once an individual is included.

Behavioral Norms

Normative behavior is established by feelings, or affect, associated with a behavioral pattern or response in such a way that either positive or negative value is attached to the behavior. As *norms* are really concepts of behavior believed to be appropriate for the society and culture, they can be dealt with symbolically and transmitted from generation to generation as part of the cultural heritage. Norms are of two types: "performance norms" and "ideal norms" (Ullman, 1965). People may maintain that as one form of behavior is ideal, everyone should strive for it; yet their everyday living performance may actually follow a different pattern from the ideal. Adherence to norms depends on motivation as well as on practicality.

The Meaning of Normative Behavior. Although it is quite important to develop a satisfactory definition of normative behavior, definitions now are ambiguous (Gibbs, 1965); more than a decade ago, different meanings were given to the word norm, especially in terms of quantity and quality (Newcomb, 1958). The origin of norms depends on group expectations; if a group of people interact over a period of time, they come to expect certain behavior in the relationships within the group. A society delineates expected behavior so that the members can predict the behavior of others and can respond accordingly. The expectation of this behavior effects conformity to group demands and determines the individual's response pattern. The individual comes to have expectations for others as well as for himself. Life in a group thus requires an individual to live within a network of social expectations (Merrill, 1965). Apparently expectation establishes the norm, rather than the degree of social conformity. Even those who believe that neither the statement of the norm nor the degree of conformity wholly establishes it do agree that expectation is consequential (Homans, 1961). The definition of normative behavior may include the concept of conscience, or at least, the idea that the norm makes an individual feel that he ought to conform to it (Johnson, 1960). Definitions of normative behavior should be determined by specific groups within a society, not only those groups that provide a frame of reference or a basis for comparison of individual behavior but also by those groups that provide rewards or reinforcement for conformity to stated norms. Three types of reference groups may be described by their functional characteristics: (1) a normative group that delineates role behavior for the individual, (2) a group that provides role models for examples of performance, and (3) an audience or group that provides an opportunity for reward for successful performance in a role (Kemper, 1968). Group behavior is not completely uniform, and in most societies an individual has a range of acceptable behavior in which he can operate. This range of operation may be narrowed, however, by some concept of moral or ethical behavior.

Benefits and Conflicts of Normative Behavior. Benefits accrue to an individual if he conforms to cultural norms; he receives the approval of other members of the group and experiences satisfaction himself in knowing that he has met their expectations or that his behavior is considered appropriate. Acceptance of the individual and his admission to the group depend on his internalization of norms appropriate for his status or social role. In this way the individual develops a response style in accord with the group. This response style is related to his capacity and ability, his perception of the environment, and his own perception of normative behavior. In part, he has positive feelings about himself to the extent to which he feels he meets the expectations of the group. The family is the most important origin of the child's knowledge of social norms, but his understanding is also affected by the play groups of his peers or by the gangs and loose social organizations of adolescence.

Sometimes individuals feel that the norms are for the benefit of society and not for their own benefit. Given the opportunity, these individuals do not behave according to the social norms of the group. As deviation occurs in primitive societies, as well as in modern and urban societies, some deviation should probably be considered normal. Usually some accepted patterns of behavior can be followed to circumvent required norms. In complex and urban society, individuals avoid to some extent a number of norms related to sex behavior, advertising, governmental procedures, academic activities, and functions in professional roles (Merrill, 1965). Failure to abide by norms may result from the belief that normative behavior is unimportant or not required. From any point of view, judgments about norms should take into account *cultural relativism,* which means that individual human behavior is to be approved or disapproved on the basis of the culture in which the individual lives. But as communication will more and more affect every society on earth, cultures will have greater similarities than in the past.

Comparisons among cultures and societies have discovered normative behavior common to them. Some universality occurs in norms related to language, marriage and family systems, age and sex differentiation, government functions, religion, systems of knowledge, economic systems, recreational activities, and art forms (Bertrand, 1967). The conception of the cultural appropriateness of human behavior varies between two extremes; at one end of the continuum the individual is autonomous, but at the other his behavior is a reflection of society's expectations. Most behavior within American society lies between these extremes.

In modern, complex, and urban societies, variations in normative behavior provide some conflict. Normative behavior may, for example, differ geographically within a society. Such variation sometimes stems from a discrepancy between the standards of the basic social structures—church, family, and educational system—and the broad standards of behavior characteristic of the whole culture. The function of social organizations is important in the establishment of normative behavior, as norms provide in them a basis for power in the control of individual members. Individuals within an organization must accept its norms and believe them legitimate. A number of ways have been devised to encourage acceptance and belief, such as the awarding of honors, titles, grades, or citations for prescribed behavior (Etzioni, 1961).

Through socialization an individual learns to recognize the cues that allow him to discriminate among the variety of stimuli in his *life space* and to respond in a way that will lead to approved behavior. Through socialization an individual also develops feeling about aspects of the social environment and his personal ability to cope with them. He learns to deal with the demands of social agents—the family, the government, the educational system, and others. Through knowledge about norms he can develop a social response style that will eliminate the necessity to experiment in every situation in order to find expected or approved behavior. Conformity to norms makes it possible for an individual to benefit from the experience of many others in the society before him.

THE PATTERNING OF BEHAVIOR

The socialization process channels behavior and accordingly results in a denial or postponement of need fulfillment. Inevitably some frustration accompanies child training. In certain instances an individual's goals are merely modified, but in other cases he finds that they can be reached only through specified behavior. Denial, postponement, modification, and channeling all place strain on the individual and thus affect motivation, self-perception, response to novel experience, and behavioral effectiveness.

Contradictions of the society and culture should also be taken into account in understanding the origin of an individual's response style. Contradictions can result in a public and private differentiation in role behavior. A prominent person may establish an *image,* so constructed that certain goals can be achieved in a profession or in political office. Normative standards in regard to dress, interpersonal relations, financial activity, sexual behavior, and political views may be of one kind for public view and of quite another for a private life. Such role division is relatively common in modern and urban society. This division comes about in part because values remaining "on the book" in certain social institutions have been replaced by custom yet not by fiat. Political and economic expediency may account for some of the reluctance to recognize a general change in normative standards.

Personal idiosyncrasy and individuality also may account for role differentiation. Certain roles, often in the professions, make demands on the personal lives of people which prevent need fulfillment within the prescribed roles. A private life is then sought in which a different set of standards is followed. As urban society becomes more diverse and as complexity in roles increases, differentiation between private and public roles will probably lessen.

Reaction to Frustration

The first significant training experiences are in reference to the infant's biological processes. He is soon put on a schedule in which he is fed and required to sleep at certain times. Many parents begin the teaching of excretory control before their child is a year old. Within these areas of control, the degree of interference with the child's desires and behavior varies. When he is first given solid food, for example, he may wish to explore it with his hands or drop it on the floor, but usually these impulses are denied. He may also wish to continue nursing and to avoid changing to solid foods or drinking from a cup.

This early blocking process is seen by a number of investigators as a *critical experience* (Mussen, Conger, and Kagan, 1969). The child's adaptation to these early forms of blocking may set patterns that become part of a general response style lasting into adulthood. The blocking process may influence the child's problem-solving behavior by lessening his interest in exploring novel situations. Moreover, blocking may reduce general motivation to work toward goals by leading the child to see himself as a person who cannot expect to reach his goals.

Because various types of interference with the child's behavior can influence the development of behavior patterns, *frustration* is an important problem in socialization, even though it is not easily defined. In fact, investigators have used the term with various meanings for many years. Frustration has sometimes been used to refer to the whole process involved in action toward a goal—both the blocking agent and the goal itself; it has also been used to refer to the emotional state or condition of the organism—the result of blocks between the individual and the goal. The latter interpretation, that is, the condition of the organism, was emphasized in the early work of Brown and Farber (1951).

A number of investigators believe that the effects of frustration can be cumulative and that prolonged frustration may cause the child's behavior to become socially unacceptable. Interference with his actions and disruption of his feeling of well-being may in some instances result in asocial behavior. Definite cause-and-effect relationships are difficult to establish, however, and as Yarrow, Campbell, and Burton (1968) suggest, investigations have not sampled types of frustrating experiences very well nor has a concept of frustration been well enough defined to prevent conflict in research findings.

Frustration and Aggression. Frustration is believed to result in aggressive behavior in some instances. This point of view is emphasized by Sears and his collaborators (1953; 1961; 1965). Generally, investigations indicate that punishment (any ill or penalty) is positively associated with a child's aggressive behavior, but research results are inconclusive. A follow-up study, six years later, of children originally studied at five years of age gathered information about 160 of the original 379 children (Sears, 1961). Attitude scales which were used to study five aspects of aggression consisted of sentences to which the subjects were to respond on a five-point scale ranging from "agree" to "disagree." The data obtained in the follow-up study suggested that "antisocial aggression" was positively related to "high permissiveness and low punishment." "Antisocial aggression" was defined as aggression ". . . normally unacceptable socially in the formal pattern of our culture."

Other investigations suggest that the specific effects of punishment in the development of aggression in the socialization process are unclear (Yarrow, Campbell, and Burton, 1968; Boe, 1966; Boe and Church, 1966). Empirical investigation of the effect of punishment may well be hampered by the fact that the same punishment may have quite different effects on children who have different relationships with socializing agents; further, laboratory studies and experimental controls in situations involving punishment and its effects on the child's tendencies to aggression are very difficult to design or carry out. Even though the effect of punishment on the child's aggressive tendencies may be equivocal in present-day research findings, investigators generally hypothesize that punishment is likely to increase aggression.

The Problem of Motivation and Efficiency. Frustration, defined as an emotional state of the organism, can impel the organism to further effort; thus it is possible for frustration to be a motivating factor. Frustration, under such circumstances, might turn one type of behavior directed to an undesirable goal toward some socially acceptable goal. Or frustration can cause feelings of hostility and aggression not toward a goal at all, but toward some other person or object (displaced aggression); it may cause physiological concomitants related to the agitated state of the organism which would persist too long for normal physiological tolerance; it may have psychological effects that would prevent realistic perception or effective problem-solving activity; and it may result in a state of anxiety that would have a generally undesirable effect on cognitive processes.

Another type of frustration, that caused by parental disapproval, may adversely affect general learning, as is suggested by a study of the effect of social disapproval on children's motor responses (Patterson, 1965). Subjects in the second, third, and fourth grades were asked to drop marbles into a box. Boys who were particularly responsive to disapproval of their performance in dropping the marbles were those described by teachers as "inefficient" in the classroom and were those who came from homes that were punitive and restrictive.

Perhaps ways can be found to help a child benefit from frustration; the socialization process could include training in ways to deal with frustration—to develop a special capacity to overcome obstacles and to fulfill needs in socially acceptable ways. If this could be achieved, then the socialization process could be defined as the development of socially acceptable ways to fulfill needs despite the problems inherent in the process.

Sociocultural Contradictions

Much of individual behavior and family functioning reflect the society and culture. Not all the problems of individuals in society result from ineffectiveness in the family system, as some problems undoubtedly stem from the family's conformity to contradictory or unfavorable requirements of the society and culture (Alexander, 1969).

Cultural Lag. In a rapidly changing urban society cultural lag is a possibility. *Cultural lag* occurs when a culture prescribes certain behavioral patterns for individuals, even though such behavior no longer serves in a highly technical society (Ogburn, 1964). Cultural lag may be implemented by family child-rearing practices that teach the child behavior no longer appropriate in a changing society. But it could be that the technological changes in the society are not suited to important functions of the family and that the changes which have taken place in the society, rather than the behavior patterns, are undesirable. The belief is widespread that individuals in this society need to develop behavior in accord with its highly technical developments. This may be an oversimplification, as Bloch and Prince (1967) suggest, because, as adaptation is a two-way process, it might be better to emphasize bringing technological developments into line with satisfaction for individuals living within the society and culture. In the long run, theoretically at least, technological goals are set in order to bring satisfaction to those within the society.

The Effects of Contradictions. Contradictions exist in any social order, in that the culture and society demand one kind of behavior and also demand behavior which conflicts with it. Social roles may involve contradictions. Some individuals, for example, required to exercise rigid authority in their occupational roles are also expected to be flexible within their families. Such contradictions can cause emotional disturbances which threaten stability and health. Contradictions in the society and culture tend to produce dissatisfaction and emotional disturbance within individuals, because of the conflict between behavior deemed appropriate for the overall good of society and that which is for the good of an individual. In some instances, one must behave in contrast to established social norms in order to find personal satisfaction (Rosow, 1965). In other instances, social status cannot be attained without behaving in conflict with a personal social value taught by the culture. It is possible that *sociopathic* behavior, behavior deemed pathological in terms of social goals, may be passed on from generation to generation for reasons of realistic expedience.

Families range in functioning from those who are successful in fulfilling individual needs and meeting cultural requirements to those who fail to reach either goal. Social factors external to the family affect its functional level, and if social conditions adversely affect the family, the children are likely in turn to affect society adversely later in their lives. Child-rearing practices and response styles developed in the family can thus be expected to influence social patterning and cultural characteristics. Ideally a family system should be thoroughly integrated within the social order and the social order should have a minimum of contradictions for the family. The goal of the family should be to bring satisfaction to individuals within it and at the same time to meet the prescribed behavior required by the social order.

Research investigations have only in recent years studied the effects of certain kinds of child-rearing practices and parent behavior on children and the later result of these influences in the lives of the children. Concern about such practices as early weaning, bottle feeding instead of breast feeding, permissiveness in teaching the child control of excretory processes, and the like is also rather recent. Even now beliefs are often contradictory, and generally acceptable principles have not yet been derived.

Contradictions and Social Mobility. Another problem in modern society that is associated with contradictions is the social mobility of parents. Behavior necessary for mobility may cause tension and conflict. The family that moves upward in the social strata is likely to change its life pattern, but some family members may prefer to maintain their former behavior and to continue to associate with people from whom they obtained emotional support in the former stratum. Yet these old associations and old response styles are inappropriate for the new social position. Feelings of insecurity may also be generated by doubts about former behavior associated with religious and educational goals, by changes in values related to work, or by feelings about the acquisition of possessions. Mobility may also cause difficulty by emphasizing the importance of further achievement beyond the capacity of the individual. Or mobility may change the family's values so much that behavioral controls once associated with a value system no longer operate. Children growing up in such families may attach little importance to meeting the requirements of society. Middle-class youth at the present time have thus adopted some behavior of the lower class. Those who find satisfaction in the present use of force, in compliance with fads, in adoption of certain language characteristics, and in the enjoyment of certain types of music reflect the acquisition of lower-class values (Pine, 1967).

Social Class and Cultural Discontinuity. Some children grow up with few opportunities that fit them for life in modern or urban societies, for two basic reasons: (1) *socioeconomic and cultural deprivation* of their entire family in relation to the majority of people in the society and culture and (2) *institutional deprivation* of children not in families who, even though they may have adequate physical care, are still deprived of psychosocial experiences needed for development.

Empirical evidence as well as observation suggests that parents in the lower socioeconomic or working class usually provide an inadequate psychosocial environment for their children and that they engage in unfavorable child-rearing practices, particularly in teaching their children (Hess and Shipman, 1965; Chilman, 1966). An analysis of available information suggests that the child-rearing practices of the poor provide inconsistent and harsh punishment and that the parents are fatalistic in their attitudes, unconcerned with the future, authoritarian, and rigid about sex roles (Chilman, 1968). To some degree, the parents themselves are models of alienation from the society, and at the same time they limit their children's experience outside the immediate environment. They engage in little verbal communication in child training and place little emphasis on abstract concepts. They have low self-esteem, distrust the opposite sex, and are inconsistent in nurturance. The effects of such inadequate training are apparent in the children's performance of certain standardized tasks. Results of studies of children within the extensive research sample of the Head Start program indicate that those from deprived areas perform less well on many kinds of tests than do average children. Their vocabulary has also been found to be less extensive (Alexander, Stoyle, and Kirk, 1968; Alexander and Stoyle, 1972). (See Figure 4–1.)

The general environmental deprivation and the lack of learning opportunities reduce the children's capabilities to meet school requirements or to perform successfully on varied tasks. While the Head Start program seeks to compensate for the lack of favorable experiences of the children enrolled in its classes by providing opportunities for social interaction and for learning tasks similar to those in school, the children usually continue to live in deteriorated physical conditions of the city

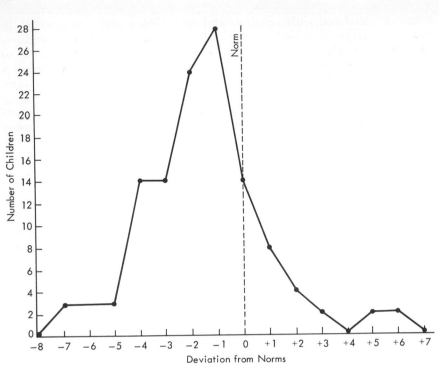

FIGURE 4–1
Picture vocabulary scores compared to Stanford-Binet norm for black
three- and four-year-old children showing that their scores were
significantly below the test norm.
(Adapted from T. Alexander, J. Stoyle, and C. Kirk, The language
of children in the "inner city." *The Journal of Psychology,* 1968,
68, 215–221. Copyright 1968 by the Journal Press, and used by permission.)

and in unfavorable psychosocial conditions. Although evidence indicates
some progress by these children as a result of the enriching Head Start
experience, unless special experiences are continued and an effort is
made to deal with the problems within their living space and unless the
children later attend schools where the favorable Head Start experiences
can be built upon and enlarged, the benefit of the program is likely to
be less significant as time passes.

The unfavorable effects of discontinuity in psychosocial relationships
in even very young children are apparent from studies of infants who
have been separated from their mothers and placed in institutions (Flint,
1966). Information indicates that continuing care by one person is needed.
Children, whether in institutions or in families that provide little emotional support, seem to require opportunity for continuing individual

relationships. They need specific help in problem-solving approaches, in seeking varied types of materials and implements, in developing interest in varied kinds of activities, and in learning to rely on themselves to solve problems. Children from deprived environments need special experience to learn the variations in meaning of language forms used outside their life space. The learning of language should also be associated with experiences in affect in which the teacher as a model can show sympathy and empathy. Often deprived children—unlike children of middle-class families—have not had opportunities or models that can provide these experiences.

Affective and Cognitive Patterns

An appraisal of the theory and research concerned with the process of socialization or enculturation reveals that progress is not uniform, that some theoretical conceptions are more advanced than others, and that some areas of both theory and data are incomplete. It is possible, however, to bring together some principles.

Affective Exchange. Two basic areas are important in the process of fitting a child for life in a social order. First, relationships should be established for affective exchange. Without this kind of exchange with others, the individual cannot find satisfaction in any life style, nor is he likely to fit into a society or social order. There is a fundamental need for close and continuing affectional relationships with a few people. It is particularly important that the behavior of individuals associated with the child be consistent, so that he can predict the kind of experiences he will have with people who are significant for him. These affective relationships are a foundation for the motivation to become socialized and to participate actively in a social order. The effect of the lack of such experience is not only seen in infants reared in institutions, but also evident in adolescents engaging in delinquent behavior, those with emotional disorders, and those with various forms of psychopathology. Common in all of these abnormal conditions is the inability to establish lasting close affectional relationships with others.

A number of essential needs are fulfilled in affective exchange with others. First, the individual establishes an *identity.* One of the most devastating of experiences for a human being is to be lost in large numbers of people in which individual characteristics go unrecognized. The feeling of individual identity is necessary because the individual must feel capable of solving the problems of everyday living and meeting the expectations of society. A person should feel that his biological and psychological characteristics have fused in a resulting uniqueness, that he differs to some degree from others, that these differences are of value, and that as a result of his composite of similarities and differences he has a personal identity. As urbanization has increased and large numbers of people have come to live and work in concentration, an individual sense of identity has been threatened. Many young people today see this lack of identity as one of the outstanding faults of modern society. The second benefit gained in affective exchange is that a child will internalize values of significance to people with whom he has a close emotional alliance. Because of his concern about the welfare of the person with whom he has an affectionate exchange, he will not destroy or treat with disdain the values held by such a person. The child thereby comes to have an investment in the welfare of society because of his emotional relationship with a significant person who values the society's success. Some young people reject the society and those responsible for it because they feel emotionally rejected themselves. The third benefit from emotional exchange is in self-perception. In order to develop a response style in which values of the social order are internalized, the individual must be aware of these values. He must learn to perceive them and to respond to stimuli from others if he is to be concerned about their welfare. As part of this concern the individual learns to perceive himself as a person of value.

Stimulus Availability. The second basic area of concern in the process of socialization and enculturation involves the development of capacities to deal with physical aspects of the life space. A variety of stimuli should be available to the child so that he can progress in all the necessary developmental accomplishments. In fact, throughout the life span opportunity should be available to perceive novel stimuli and to pursue variations in one's own life style. Children growing up in deprived areas of cities often have limited experiences with novel stimuli and consequently are impaired further in meeting the challenge of complex urban environments. Dealing with the characteristics of the life span is dependent upon the development of language and symbolic behavior. (This topic will be discussed more in detail later.) Through language the child learns to give meaning to stimuli in his environment and to deal with them symbolically. In the childhood years, with the development of a capacity for abstract thinking and symbolic behavior, the child should come to see the relevance of past experience in dealing with the environment.

In learning to deal with the environment, however, a number of difficulties can occur. For example, some children adequately perceive elements in a current situation, but have difficulty in relating them to past experience—they cannot profitably use the analogous or relevant situations previously encountered. Others are incapable of examining, through imagination, the results and consequences of a response. Some cannot see the value of a projected response in a search for alternatives or new types of reactions.

It is apparent that the urban environment, with its values often in conflict and with the meaning of essential elements often unclear, requires considerable capacity in abstract thinking and in testing solutions symbolically. It is also apparent that the demands of urban living are becoming an even greater challenge in this era of accelerating social change.

IN PERSPECTIVE

Modern societies are difficult to characterize in regard to child-rearing patterns even when an effort is made to be specific about variants growing out of socioeconomic or cultural differences. A general description of patterns in American society seems feasible, as over the years research investigations indicate a generalizing tendency in child-training methods. Substantive differences exist, however, between most of the population and the segment living in the city ghettos. Children from these areas have less stimulation in their training, particularly in complex language and abstract activities. As society seeks to ameliorate and offset cultural deprivation, it is essential that programs involve opportunities for *affectionate interchange* in children's relationships with teachers and models. This is necessary as evidence is at hand to indicate that the essential motivating force in a child's socialization according to norms is an affectionate relationship with cultural agents and models.

A number of significant variations are still found to exist among different societies and cultures. Competition, a principle of goal-directed behavior and social interaction, is especially emphasized in American culture, but in a number of other cultures it is disapproved. On the other hand, several forms of child-rearing principles are found to be cross-cultural. For example, in all cultures similar tasks fall to women because they are necessarily close to food preparation when children are present. In urban society this is a less general finding than it is among the undeveloped societies. To a certain extent, urban society allows some freedom from role requirements because of the anonymity of the individual in vast numbers of people.

There are both benefits and conflicts for the individual in society's provision of role expectations or norms. Among the benefits: conformity brings group approval and thereby satisfaction; decisions about behavior are easily made in a society where social roles are clearly delineated; and self-perception in terms of group requirements and normative rules is favorable and thus doubt about goals or accomplishments is lessened. Conflict, however, may arise under conditions of strict role prescriptions because individual spontaneity and creative endeavor are circumscribed. Some members will feel that the norms prescribed by the state are not to their benefit. If prescriptions for roles lie in the hands of the few in an elite group, considerable power over the lives of many inevitably results. And normative behavior prescribed by society often contains contradictions and conflicting rules. As a result of such contradictions people find it difficult or impossible to make satisfactory decisions; frustration then becomes a significant social problem.

REFERENCES

ALEXANDER, T. *Children and adolescents: A biocultural approach to psychological development.* New York: Aldine-Atherton, 1969.

ALEXANDER, T., & STOYLE, J. Culture, cognition, and social change: The effect of the Head Start experience on cognitive patterns. (Unpublished manuscript, 1972).

ALEXANDER, T., STOYLE, J., & KIRK, C. The language of children in the "inner city." *The Journal of Psychology,* 1968, 215–221.

BARRY, H., CHILD, I. L., & BACON, M. K. Relation of child training to subsistence economy. In A. D. Ullman (Ed.), *Sociocultural foundations of personality.* Boston: Houghton Mifflin, 1965. Pp. 291–306.

BAUMRIND, D. An exploratory study of socialization effects on black children: Some black-white comparisons. *Child Development,* 1972, 43, 261–267.

BERTRAND, A. L. *Basic sociology: An introduction to theory and method.* New York: Appleton-Century-Crofts, 1967.

BIERSTEDT, R. *The social order.* (2nd ed.). New York: McGraw-Hill, 1963.

BLOCH, H. A., & PRINCE, M. *Social crisis and deviance.* New York: Random House, 1967.

BOE, E. E. The effect of punishment duration and intensity on the extinction of an instrumental response. *Journal of Experimental Psychology,* 1966, 72, 125–131.

BOE, E. E., & CHURCH, R. M. The permanent effect of punishment during extinction. Paper presented at the meeting of the Eastern Psychological Association, New York, April, 1966.

BROWN, J. S., & FARBER, I. E. Emotions conceptualized as intervening variables—with suggestions toward a theory of frustration. *Psychological Bulletin,* 1951, 48, 465–504.

CALDWELL, B. M. What is the optimal learning environment for the young child? *American Journal of Orthopsychiatry,* 1967, 37, 8–21.

CHILMAN, C. S. Poor families and their pattern of child care: Some implications for service programs. In C. A. Chandler, R. S. Lourie, & A. D. Peters (Eds.), *Early child care.* New York: Atherton, 1968.

CHILMAN, C. S. *Growing up poor.* Washington, D. C.: U. S. Department of Health, Education, and Welfare, Welfare Administration, 1966.

COLE, M., GAY, J., GLICK, J. A., & SHARP, D. W. *The cultural context of learning and thinking.* New York: Basic Books, 1971.

COOPER, J. B., & McGAUGH, J. L. *Integrating principles of social psychology.* Cambridge, Mass.: Schenkman, 1963.

DAVIS, A., & HAVIGHURST, R. J. Social class and color difference in child rearing. *American Sociological Review,* 1946, 11, 698–710.

DENNIS, W. *The Hopi child.* New York: Wiley, 1965.

DOLLARD, J., DOOB, L. W., MILLER, N. E., MOWRER, O. H., & SEARS, R. R. *Frustration and aggression.* New Haven: Yale University Press, 1939.

ETZIONI, A. *A comparative analysis of complex organizations.* New York: Free Press, 1961.

FLINT, B. M. *The child and the institution.* Toronto: The University of Toronto Press, 1966.

GARDNER, D. B. *Development in early childhood.* New York: Harper & Row, 1964.

GEWIRTZ, J. L. The role of stimulation in models for child development. In C. A. Chandler, R. S. Lourie, & A. D. Peters (Eds.), *Early child care.* New York: Atherton, 1968. Pp. 139–168.

GIBBS, J. P. Norms: The problem of definition and classification. *The American Journal of Sociology,* 1965, 70, 586–594.

GOLDSTEIN, B. *Low income youth in urban areas.* New York: Holt, Rinehart and Winston, 1967.

GOODMAN, M. E. *The individual and culture.* Homewood, Ill.: Dorsey Press, 1967.

HESS, R. D., & SHIPMAN, V. C. Early experience and the socialization of cognitive modes in children. *Child Development,* 1965, 36, 869–886.

HOMANS, G. C. *Social behavior: Its elementary forms.* New York: Harcourt, Brace, Jovanovich, 1961.

JOHNSON, H. M. *Sociology.* New York: Harcourt Brace Jovanovich, 1960.

JOHNSON, R. C., & MEDINNUS, G. R. *Child psychology: Behavior and development.* New York: Wiley, 1965.

KEMPER, T. D. Reference groups, socialization and achievement. *American Sociological Review,* 1968, 33, 31–45.

MACCOBY, E. E., & GIBBS, P. K. Methods of child rearing in two social classes. In W. E. Martin & C. B. Stendler (Eds.), *Readings in child development.* New York: Harcourt Brace Jovanovich, 1954. Pp. 272–287.

MALINOWSKY, B. *Coral gardens and their magic.* 2 vols. New York: American Book, 1935.

MARJORIBANKS, K. Environment, social class, and mental abilities. *The Journal of Educational Psychology,* 1972, 63, 103–109.

MERRILL, F. E. *Society and culture.* (3rd ed.). Englewood Cliffs, N. J.: Prentice-Hall, 1965.

MILLER, D. R., & SWANSON, G. E. *The changing American parent.* New York: Wiley, 1958.

MUSSEN, P. H., CONGER, J. J., & KAGAN, J. *Child development and personality* (3rd ed.). New York: Harper & Row, 1969.

NASH, M. *The golden road to modernity.* New York: Wiley, 1965.

NEWCOMB, T. M. *Social psychology.* New York: Holt, 1958.

OGBURN, W. F. Cultural lag as theory. In W. F. Ogburn, *On culture and social change.* Chicago: University of Chicago Press, 1964. Pp. 86–95.

PATTERSON, G. R. Parents as dispensers of aversive stimuli. *Journal of Personality and Social Psychology,* 1965, 2, 844–851.

PAVENSTEDT, E. A comparison of the child rearing environment of upper-lower and very low lower-class families. *American Journal of Orthopsychiatry,* 1965, 35, 89–98.

PINE, G. J. The affluent delinquent. In H. W. Bernard & W. C. Huckins (Eds.), *Readings in Human Development.* Boston: Allyn & Bacon, 1967. Pp. 303–312.

Rosow, I. Forms and functions of adult socialization. *Social Forces,* 1965, 44 (1), 35–45.

Sears, R. R. The relation of early socialization experiences to aggression in middle childhood. *Journal of Abnormal and Social Psychology,* 1961, 63, 466–492.

Sears, R. R., Rau, L., & Alpert, R. *Identification and child rearing.* Stanford, Calif.: Stanford University Press, 1965.

Sears, R. R., Whiting, J. W. M., Nowlis, V., & Sears, P. S. Some child rearing antecedents of aggression and dependency in young children. *Genetic Psychology Monographs,* 1953, 47, 135–236.

Shaw, M. E. Some cultural differences in sanctioning behavior. *Psychonomic Science,* 1967, 3, 45–46.

Stevenson, H. W. Studies of racial awareness in young children. In W. W. Hartup & N. L. Smothergill (Eds.), *The young child.* Washington, D.C.: National Association for the Education of Young Children, 1967. Pp. 206–213.

Ullman, A. D. *Sociocultural foundations of personality.* Boston: Houghton Mifflin, 1965.

Waters, E., & Crandall, V. J. Social class and observed maternal behavior from 1940 to 1960. *Child Development,* 1964, 35, 1021–1032.

Whiting, B. B. (Ed.). *Six cultures.* New York: Wiley, 1966.

Yarrow, L. J. The crucial nature of early experience. In D. C. Glass (Ed.), *Environmental influences.* New York: Rockefeller University Press, 1968. Pp. 101–113.

Yarrow, M. R., Campbell, J. D., & Burton, R. V. *Child rearing.* San Francisco: Jossey-Bass, 1968.

INTELLIGENCE, LANGUAGE, AND CREATIVITY

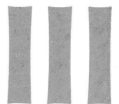

Satisfaction in the process of interaction for both the individual and society depends to a considerable extent on the capacity of the individual to respond with effective and creative behavior. Capacity develops from innate neurological foundations and from information, models, and complex learning opportunities in the environmental context or life space. The discussion here, in contrast to earlier chapters, emphasizes individual capacity and the processes of learning; less emphasis is placed on the environmental context, although integration is attempted.

The cognitive processes of perception, comprehension, memory, symbolism, and concept formation, in their totality, comprise an individualistic cognitive style. This style is characteristic of the person in interaction with the environment. A person must achieve, to some degree, a changing style, as both individual and environment are continuously being altered.

A significant capacity or foundation for response is language, which greatly facilitates environmental interaction and cognitive development. Verbal ability is an important factor in intelligence, as any inadequacy in language is considered to be both a result and a cause of mental deficit.

Language is of particular interest to those concerned with cultural deprivation of children in the deteriorated sections of the large cities. Young children from the ghetto, entering school with a lack of verbal ability, experience difficulty in most areas of the school curriculum. Language facility is perceived as a basic requirement for these children if they are to become socially mobile.

Creative or original behavior associated with superior mental ability is believed to be particularly valuable in finding satisfaction in living in modern society. Some believe that creativity and intelligence are separate abilities. But it has been observed that many people with superior intelligence are creative and that those individuals with low intellectual capacity usually exhibit little behavior that can be termed creative.

The search for a certain "quality of life," a goal for many in modern society, seems to depend upon a creative and highly individual approach to a life style. For people to achieve a creative life style, it is important during their development that they have an openness to experience and an opportunity to explore the environment with minimal control by others. The ordinary school experience today, a number of theorists believe, is greatly lacking in such conditions.

Part III, in a broad sense, deals with the foundations of the individual's total capacity to adjust to and cope with the environment. Its three chapters contain a summary of theoretical and research findings about the development of an overall capacity to respond. Intelligence, language, and creativity are each discussed in a separate chapter because of their significance in the individual's interaction with the environment. A satisfying life style in modern society seems to depend substantially on an ability to find new solutions to many types of problems.

THE
FOUNDATIONS
OF
RESPONSE

5

As this society and the life styles in it have become more complex, the young have encountered a socialization experience much more demanding than that of their fathers. This complexity of society, so greatly heightened in the twentieth century by advances in technology, has made attainment of satisfaction in society much more difficult to achieve. Not only is there more complexity in occupational roles, but much more complexity characterizes private life styles. With the changeover from an agrarian society to a highly industrialized one, increasing emphasis was placed on the ability to solve intricate problems and make decisions involving extensive information. In association with these demands for the individual to "reason" and to "know," a considerable preoccupation with intelligence testing and with techniques to enhance cognitive development occurred early in the century.

In the preceding century when family and occupational roles in American society did not require complex behavior, little attention was given to the nature of individual capacity to learn. But as the twentieth century advanced, much more interest in the "capacity" to learn arose. Much more emphasis was placed on the importance of educational experience. Many came to believe that achievement of prestige and power roles required a capacity for a wide range of responses enhanced by many years of training in the educational system.

It also became apparent that even in a democratic and open society those born into families in the mainstream of society still were the ones who achieved in the educational system and who later attained the most desired roles in the society. As a result of this observation, the controversy over the relative significance of heredity and environment in human intelligence is periodically renewed. The roots of this controversy reach far back into history. Some groups thousands of years ago perceived themselves as chosen and superior. Even some tribes of primitive people today describe themselves as the Real People and see themselves as cast in a better mold than their neighbors. This belief in bloodlines has, of course, been the basis for social prestige of the nobility and royal kinship systems that have dominated much of the history of civilization.

Concomitant with the "rise of the common man" and the endeavor to apply the ideals of democracy, the principle of inherited superiority came to be questioned and even rejected by many. But over the years, even with the discovery of many of the principles of genetic inheritance, complete rejection has been far from general. With the advent of the twentieth century and the increase in the application of scientific discoveries to everyday life, interest in determination of individual differences in capacity for complex responses was extended. Widespread use of intelligence tests produced results that indicated that those of "better birth" who enjoyed prestigious social roles made higher scores and therefore demonstrated greater intelligence than those in the lower socioeconomic strata of society. Thus, blood did seem to tell after all. In spite of these findings some still argued that where opportunities for education and attainment of prestigious roles were possible, those from the lower socioeconomic levels of society achieved as much or more than some of those from elite families.

This controversy continues (Jensen, 1969; Coleman, 1968, 1971; Kagan, 1969). Because black children generally make lower scores than white children make on intelligence tests, the earlier argument that "blood will tell" is seen as applying to them, too. However, the question of social opportunity and access to education must be taken into account in the low scores because black people have not had sufficient opportunity for education or prestigious positions. Coleman thinks that the school cannot offset the family influence and social conditions that may adversely affect a child. The controversy is perpetuated because it provides a basis for the demands of the disadvantaged for more opportunities as well as a justification by the elite for positions of power already held.

An understanding of this controversy requires (1) basic information about biological foundations for response, (2) a perspective of history, and (3) knowledge of the changing nature of human development in the urban age. A new direction of concern is now emerging. Although they view the problem of the significance of heredity and environment differently, Jensen and Kagan are concerned about academic achievement in the *traditional tasks* of the school. The new perspective, associated with the development of the "open classroom," holds that a concern about mastery of skills and specific information by certain grade levels is inappropriate. Those taking this view maintain that *development of individual initiative* in the acquisition of knowledge is of greater importance. Thus, it may be that the basic controversy, in time, will be irrelevant.

DEVELOPMENTAL CHANGES IN THE
CAPACITY TO RESPOND

The foundations for response are laid down at conception. Within the germ cells, in the nuclei, chromosomes determine hereditary characteristics through the influence of their genes. While the methods of genetic influence are complicated and the processes incompletely understood, some basic information about the determinants of individual capacities is available. Within the nuclei of the cells the substance DNA (deoxyribonucleic acid) directs cell development to form the complex parts of the new individual. The process of growth extends from one cell to billions. By the beginning of the third month of pregnancy, the weight of the fetus is six billion times the weight at conception. Resemblance to human form now is apparent, and muscular development has progressed to the point that movement of the limbs is possible. In the next few months, the body systems move toward functioning; and by seven months independent life becomes possible, though precarious.

A brief time immediately following birth is called the *perinatal* period; it lasts for about thirty minutes. During this time the infant begins to breathe and maintain its own temperature level, although with some variation. During the *neonatal* period, lasting for about two weeks, the infant sleeps a great deal, and its response is general. The mouth can move and the hands can grasp, but body movement is minimal. The infant cannot raise its head or turn over. Nevertheless substantial progress is made toward an efficient and independent existence by progress in blood oxygenation, temperature constancy, ingestion and digestion of nutrients, and functioning of the excretory systems. During much of the first few months subsequent to birth, the infant sleeps between 15 and 20 hours of the day. After about six months, sleep lasts through the night, and daily waking periods are extended.

Sensory and Perceptual Capacities—
Infancy through Adolescence

Environmental awareness is at first quite limited for the very young infant. The principal means of awareness are the visual and auditory sense organs, but visual perception is particularly limited as the anatomical structures on which vision is dependent are poorly organized. In recent years, studies of visual perception have added to the understanding of infant capacities for response. For example, investigations of infants' interest in stimuli in the first few months of life have determined the length of time of visual fixation and the changes in heart rate resulting from introduction of stimuli into the visual field. In a study of visual discrimination it was found that infants as young as four months respond more frequently with smiles to a "regular face" than to a "scrambled face" (Kagan, Henker, Hen-Tov, Levine, and Lewis, 1966), and in another study a sex difference in the length of time of visual fixation was found (Lewis, Kagan, and Kalafat, 1966). Perceptual constancy, that is, stability in perception of objects under varying conditions, has also been studied in infants. An object that is close stimulates a larger area of the retina than it does at a greater distance; a bird flying away causes a change in the stimulated area of the retina, but the bird seems to remain the same size. Even in infancy a child can distinguish between nearer and farther objects.

The auditory sense is fairly well developed at birth. Even in the first few days of life the infant's response to auditory stimuli can be shown by the measurement of changes in heart rate. Cardiac response is apparently affected by changes in the intensity of auditory stimuli; intense stimuli are more likely to elicit responses than are low-pitched and less intense stimuli.

Some information about other sense modalities is available, but other modalities are difficult to study in infants. During the neonatal period, taste is apparently not highly developed; but the neonate seems to distinguish between sweet and sour, if facial expressions are any indication. There is also some evidence that infants respond to olfactory stimulation (Engen, Lipsitt, and Kaye, 1963).

The child's interpretation of the environment improves as he becomes capable of discrimination and response to varying qualities of the environment; discrimination is thus linked to thought processes. Learning and the association of stimulus with response brings *arousal;* in states of high arousal, the child develops *perceptual curiosity,* that is, he becomes curious in response to stimuli that are novel, complex, or surprising. As a child becomes aware of more characteristics of the stimulus, the state of arousal is reduced. As he learns more about his environment, his perception becomes less centered on himself; and he begins to respond in a much more realistic manner (Berlyne and Fromme, 1966; Berlyne, 1960; Berlyne, 1964).

As maturity increases, children become more interested in novel experience. But responses to novel experience are affected by past experience, and effectiveness in dealing with new stimuli is limited by the opportunity to utilize past response patterns in the new experience. For example, adolescents in one study were asked to view figures through a stereoscope. Some of the figures were in the form of letters such as an "E" and some were only geometric designs. Those that could be identified verbally (perceived as a letter of the alphabet) were less likely to "fragment" or to have parts disappear during viewing than were the unidentifiable geometric designs. Such results demonstrate the importance of *identification* of stimuli in perception and environmental awareness (McKinney, 1966).

Perceptual Learning in Early and Middle Childhood

As has been indicated, the influence of environmental properties in an individual's life space is determined by the *configuration* or pattern of his capacities and acquired abilities. Each person, because of his biological individuality (heredity) and variations in experience in his culture, has a unique learning experience within the environment (Odom, McIntyre, and Neale, 1971). He responds accordingly to the real world, consisting of physical characteristics involving distance, orientation (for example, up and down), color, texture, and temperature, on the basis of perceptual individuality. He is influenced not only by these individual realities, but also by cultural realities that cause whole groups of individuals to perceive the environment in ways that may or may not be in accord with actual physical properties.

The infant begins to give the environment his personal meaning as some responses bring satisfaction; he gives meaning, for example, to stimuli associated with feeding and sources of physical comfort. In addition to the development of individuality in modes and styles of response to the environment, the child also acquires expectations or *sets* for satisfaction or dissatisfaction associated with objects.

Characteristics of Perceptual Learning. Several classes of variables or determinants have been suggested as necessary to the perception of objects in space. One suggestion is that there are four classes of such determinants. The first of these includes *ocular capabilities* and the capacity to determine distance and objects visually; this class includes the physical characteristics of visual anatomy and function. The second class consists of *retinal projections,* capabilities determined in part by anatomical structures as well as psychophysical characteristics. These latter are basic, as they enable most individuals to make judgments with minimal information. The third type of determinants are those directly attributable to *learning.* And a fourth class of determinants consists of *aptitudes* of visual and perceptual performance (Smith and Smith, 1966).

Perceptual Development. Piaget's view of cognitive development in stages from sensorimotor through perceptual to abstract response was discussed earlier; however, other approaches to cognitive growth similar to his have been advanced. Bruner (1964), for example, suggested three modes in sequential order: the *enactive,* or motor response; the *iconic,* or images of the perceptual field; and the *symbolic,* or representation involving remoteness. Whatever the approach, the development of perceptual processes is considerably influenced by skills achieved because of demands made on the individual by the culture.

In an investigation of early perceptual learning the play activities of three- and four-year-old children were studied. The variables were *perceived depth, visual direction,* and *perceived distance.* The meaning of *perceived depth* was indicated, for example, by the length of a play block; the meaning of *visual direction* was defined as locomotion toward an object, following a path, pouring liquids, painting, and reaching. Evidence of the *perception of distance* was obtained from the subjects by observing their behavior on steps or in stepping over something. "Errors of size perception" were determined by observing the child's effort to reach for objects that were too high. The investigator (Smith, 1965) concluded that perception of *direction* and *depth* accounted for most of the space perceptions the children used in play activities. Evidence of response based on the *perception of distance* was limited. It was also concluded that the transition from depth to distance perceptions increased with age. In a similar study of children in middle childhood in grades one through six, much the same conclusion was reached as chronological age and accurate perceptions of distance were found to be significantly correlated (Towler and Nelson, 1967).

Perceptual Complexity. Studies dealing with complexity and patterns in the environment have shown that children are increasingly able to deal with ambiguous stimuli as they get older (Elkind and Scott, 1962). These findings provide some support for Piaget's theoretical contention that perception is "centered" in childhood and gradually "decentered" with age. Evidence of perceptual change with age comes from a study of children from four to nine years of age. Using drawings as stimuli, the investigation demonstrated that the ability to perceive both parts and wholes increased with age (Elkind, Koegler, and Go, 1964). By the time most children reach nine years of age they are able to integrate parts into wholes. The "decentering" theoretical concept that older children are able to organize parts and wholes into configurations by using logical principles seems to be substantiated by such studies (Elkind, Anagnostopoulou, and Malone, 1970).

An important aspect of awareness of the environment is discrimination among forms of objects by using various types of cues. That is, an aspect of the object (size, shape, or the like) is used as an aid in identifying it. Developmental changes in *form discrimination cues* used by nursery school children were observed in a study of thirty boys and girls aged three to six. The children were shown stimuli consisting of five irregular pentagons made of black paper and placed in a circle on a field of grey cardboard. The task was to match a pentagon in the middle of the field to one of the surrounding figures. The investigators concluded that younger children tended to use the bottom lines of the pentagonal stimuli as cues to discriminate among them, but at successive ages the subjects increasingly used a top-to-bottom scanning approach (Kerpelman and Pollack, 1964).

Spatial Perceptions. Sex differences in spatial perceptions are not usually apparent until after the age of six years, as the research findings of several studies suggest (Maccoby, 1966), but girls seem to have difficulty performing spatial tasks (Anastasi, 1958; Tyler, 1965). Girls are more field dependent in certain tasks than boys, particularly on such a test as the Embedded Figures Test (a test in which a figure is so surrounded by other stimuli that it is difficult to perceive the figure). A study of the performance of subjects on a wide variety of geometrical tasks led to the conclusion that girls were less skilled than boys, especially in visualization of spatial factors (Werdelin, 1961). Information available about differences in spatial perception suggests that the deficit of girls need not necessarily be due to basic or innate differences in perceptual capacity, because boys are given different kinds of experiences that are likely to add to their spatial perception ability. Boys are encouraged, for example, to work with construction of models, building blocks, and other materials that contribute to their spatial skills more than do the kinds of experiences provided for girls (Sherman, 1967).

Social Perception and Experience in Middle Childhood and Adolescence

Social Schemata. In the perception of persons, unit-forming principles termed *social schemata* or *response sets* assist in dealing with ambiguous social situations (Kuethe, 1962; Estes and Rush, 1971). Just as the placement of two objects together depends on the use of a schema, the placement of people (or symbols for them) together depends on a social schema. The use of similar schemata by a number of individuals indicates similarity in perceptual learning, and similarity in use is evidence of normative behavior within a culture. Information about social schemata used symbolically by young male adults was obtained by using figures cut from cloth (felt), which were placed on a large field of the same material by the subjects in the study. The figures consisted of a man, a woman, a child, and rectangles of different dimensions. The subjects were asked to arrange these figures in "sets" as they placed them on the "field." A majority of the subjects placed the human figures close together as shown in Figure 5–1. The findings indicated that different schemata were used for people and objects.

There is evidence that children learn to apply social schemata to parents. Verbal labels assigned to parents are particularly significant in the child's social interaction with his parents and in his understanding of sex roles. Children in middle childhood (six to eight years) were studied for the concepts of father, mother, and self. One part of the study investigated the children's response to 66 pairs of picture stimuli by asking them questions along such dimensions as "strong-weak, big-little, nurturant-nonnurturant." A questioner would say, for example, "Here's a strong rabbit and here is a weak rabbit. Which one reminds you of your father (mother, or self)?" The subjects perceived the father as "stronger" and "larger" than the mother, among other differences.

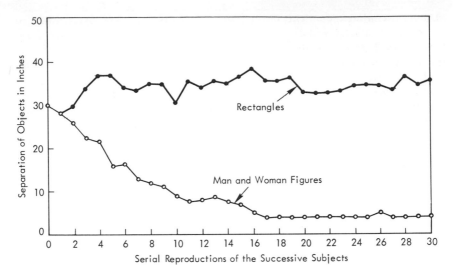

FIGURE 5–1

Illustration of the difference between the social schemata for objects and for people. The graph shows how each subject, after viewing the preceding subject's placement, placed the rectangles and the figures.

(Adapted from J. L. Kuethe, Social schemas. *Journal of Abnormal and Social Psychology,* 64, 1962, 31–38. Copyright 1962 by the American Psychological Association, and reproduced by permission.)

These investigators (Kagan, Hosken, and Watson, 1961) suggest that children's interaction with the environment, especially through communication media, determine their perceptions of masculinity; males are associated with size and strength and the like.

Social Perceptions and Social Class. Social-class differences seem evident in social perceptions. A questionnaire study of several hundreds of boys, ages nine through eleven, from middle and lower socioeconomic classes, reported that the middle-class boys tended to see their parents as more interested in their performance than did the lower-class boys (Rosen, 1964). Differences between the groups were greater in the perception of the father than of the mother. Middle-class boys were much more likely than were lower-class boys to perceive the father as interested in their performance in school and as attentive to their interests.

Perceptual Deprivation. Some research psychologists assert that it is essential that the infant or young child should have specific experiences during early developmental years that contribute to his capacity to differentiate, discriminate, and form into patterns and concepts his experiences with the environment. As perception normally occurs before any action, the child's capacity to interact with the environment may be considerably impaired if his perceptual experience is limited (Gewirtz, 1968; Taylor, 1962). Assuming that there is some order in the process of development and that the child moves from one period to another by using his past experience to interact with the environment, then early deprivation means inadequate development. Perhaps doubts about the child's eventually overcoming such deprivation are justified. Theoretically at least, the deprived child must greatly accelerate his developmental accomplishments at a later time if he is to overcome deprivation in early life. To keep up with a child. who has progressed in the normal experiences for his culture, he will need not only to match the other child's growth resulting from expanding experiences, but also to make up for the experiences he formerly missed. This accelerated development is much to expect for any child.

Although a child formerly deprived must continually operate at an expanded and accelerated rate in interaction with the environment, he can be expected to have difficulty in dealing with his present experience. Overcoming deprivation is therefore quite a complex process. If expanding experience and learning affect the development of morphological characteristics, severe deprivation thus may alter physical capacity to the extent that the child becomes incapable of benefiting from subsequent experiences designed to offset his earlier deprivation.

It is possible that a minimum amount of stimulation is necessary for the development of a child's abilities and that increasing complexity in the structure of the environment is necessary for the acquisition of adequate response capabilities. This view suggests that the child should have experience with objects, events, and opportunities for emotional exchange in the context of the main part of the culture. It may well be that beyond a certain maximum level the stimuli can be too many or too complex for the young child's benefit. Perhaps beyond this maximum of experience the child's development may actually be inhibited. Accordingly, this view implies that an optimal range of stimulation in early life exists; the individual may be harmed if stimulation is below or above the normal range. Such a range probably is culturally relative.

In other aspects of development, it is generally believed that affective experience depends upon the child's perceptual sensitivity to emotional responses from the individuals about him in his life space. Not only are the young child's responses determined by his interaction with adults or other individuals around him who are models, but his behavior is channeled by reinforcement, identification, and imitation associated with affective interaction.

COGNITIVE CAPACITIES

Cognition, the process of knowing, depends (in addition to perceptual experience) upon the processes of comprehension, association, and memory, the projection and carrying out of solutions, and the development of a cognitive style. Ultimately each individual develops a life style, usually in such a way that behavior is relatively congruent with cultural rules as well as with other characteristics of the life space.

In practical terms, cognition includes in its meaning the manner of perceiving, comprehending, remembering, and reasoning about possible ways of solving problems. Solutions to problems may be carried out in overt response with some evaluation and feedback. Some theorists and investigators believe that it is important to distinguish the cognitive from the affective aspects of behavior; although such a distinction may be useful in some theoretical considerations and perhaps in some investigative procedures, it is difficult, if not impossible, to make in practice. Basically cognition depends on physiological and biochemical processes of great complexity, involving many actions and events about which knowledge is only slowly being gained.

The Foundations of Cognition

The processes of life and interaction with the environment depend primarily on one body system, the Central Nervous System (CNS). The functioning of this system is essential for other body systems and is the foundation for the organism's interaction with the environment. The development of CNS capacity is complex; it is interdependent with other body systems and with experience in receiving external stimulation. Activity of the CNS also depends on the activity of receptors and sense organs to extend response patterns as the individual matures. An essential activity of the CNS is to integrate current stimulation with that experienced in the past. As the past stimulation has been labeled, interpreted, and associated with some sort of response, in some instances an effective response has already been stored in memory and thus is easily available. A pattern of these ready responses can be termed a *response style*.

A living organism is constantly in some state of interchange with the environment. The processes taking place within a cell and the functioning of body systems depend on an interchange of substances. This necessity for interchange is closely related to instinct, drive, and motivation, in that the organism must engage in certain behavior to survive; for example, hunger will compel behavior of some kind. (These concepts will be discussed further in a later chapter in connection with motivation and drive.)

The relation of physiological processes and functioning to response style or cognitive style in a culture is difficult to describe. Increased understanding of biochemical processes and genetic bases of behavior may provide a foundation for integrating biological and cultural information into theoretical and practical explanations of essential cognitive processes.

The basic units of the CNS are the neurons (billions of them), with the larger neurons linked by many connections called synapses. *Receptors* and *effectors* function in such a way that stimulation of a receptor will in turn influence an effector, which then influences another receptor. These interconnections and networks of the CNS are the foundations of behavior.

In the process of evolution, the brain and spinal cord have come to be well protected by membranes and bone. Further, the cerebrospinal fluid in the canal, running the length of the spinal cord, lessens the effects of shocks or blows that might have an adverse effect on the brain. Through the cord run *afferent* and *efferent* fibers; the former conduct nerve impulses to the brain, and the latter carry them away and downward in the cord and from there to parts of the body. The primary mass of the brain itself, consisting of the cortex and the cerebellum, is probably a later evolutionary development than the brain stem. Only in recent years has some detailed information been available about the functioning of these various parts of the brain. Experimentation to discover changes in electrical potentials has been carried out since the discovery that stimulation of the brain brings about changes in neural routes and that these changes can be observed in their effect on various types of response. Muscular movements, for example, have been found to be controlled by the part of the *frontal lobes* of the brain designated as the *motor areas.* The *sensory area* lies behind the motor areas in the front part of the *parietal lobes;* its function is associated with tactile or kinesthetic stimulations as well as stimulations of temperature. Neural paths from the eyes lead to the *occipital lobes* at the back of the brain. Taste and smell involve the lower part of the brain, the *temporal lobes.* Since most of the cerebral cortex does not have specific functions, much of the frontal, parietal, occipital, and temporal lobes are designated as *association areas.* These association areas have to do with complex behavior and the cognitive processes. The integrative functioning of the CNS depends primarily on the association areas.

Through learning and experience, responses can become automatic and reflexive, and environmental exchange is thereafter made with less energy; once complex skills are achieved, energy can then be used for acquisition of other complex responses. The brain, of course, can instigate behavior, that is, it can function without sources of outside stimulation. It can also seek new information related to responses, in order to make them more effective than previous ones.

The brain stem has three sections: the hindbrain, related to respiration and cardiovascular function, the midbrain, which functions in hearing and vision reflexes; and the forebrain, in which the thalamus has an important role in sensory impulses traveling from the receptors to the cortex. (See Figure 5–2.) Just below the thalamus is the hypothalamus; its function is related to body temperature, chemical balances, metabolism, blood pressure, sleep, and emotional responses.

Nutrition and oxygen are essential to the brain. The brain is particularly sensitive to the deprivation of oxygen—depletion of oxygen for only a few seconds drastically affects its capacity, and depletion of only a few minutes is lethal. Energy for mental processes comes primarily from carbohydrates, but the brain cannot store these to any extent, and deficiency of even moderate amounts can adversely affect behavior. Not only can the brain be impaired by deprivation of nutrients, but its func-

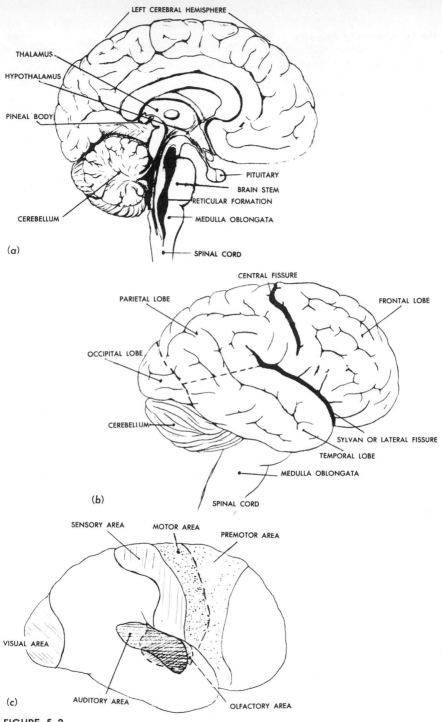

FIGURE 5–2
(a) Left cerebral hemisphere viewed from the right. (b) Brain, right view. (c) Localization of function of the cerebral cortex.
(Reproduced from T. Alexander, *Children and Adolescents: A biocultural approach to psychological development,* pp. 53–55. Copyright 1969 by Aldine-Atherton. By permission.

tioning may be improved by administration of some substances. Considerable experimentation in recent years has been under way with psychoactive drugs. Some of these substances are used to stimulate and others to calm. In the future, biochemical reactions and the general functioning of the nervous system may well be enhanced, controlled, or made more effective by conditions or stimuli induced from the environment. Understanding the effects of such stimuli will probably require not only knowledge of genetic and embryological factors, but also of internally and externally based biochemical influences. Philosophical and ethical issues will be more in evidence as time passes, since it seems that youth is increasingly seeking to alter experience through the use of a wide range of drugs.

Although knowledge about cognitive processes requires basic concern with the structure and function of the CNS, it should be kept in mind that other systems are so closely related in their functioning that the functioning of the nervous system and the cognitive processes ultimately depends upon the functioning of the whole organism.

Cognitive Processes

Perception and Comprehension. In the beginning processes of cognition, in perception and comprehension, the individual becomes aware of the stimulus-pattern, labels it, and interprets it. The selection of stimuli to attend to is sometimes determined by a relatively fixed channel of behavior; that is, as a result of conditioning and experience only certain stimuli are attended to and interpreted. Although situations change and maturation occurs, still the individual tends to use the same bases for selection and interpretation. Because of this tendency toward a fixation of responses, development is to some extent an uncomfortable process; responses learned through effort must in time be discarded, and new effort must be devoted to learning even more complex tasks.

Effective perception and comprehension are influenced by age, by individual differences in capacity, and by experience. Some individuals, for example, can attend to stimuli in spite of distraction by extraneous stimuli, while others find it difficult to devote sufficient attention to the problem to become aware of its essential aspects. Inability to attend sufficiently for adequate appraisal and interpretation can be a cause of inadequate response and ineffective learning.

Some information about the effect of any intervening educational experience on cognitive processes in very young children is provided by a study of three -and four-year-old children who lived in the deteriorated part of a large city (Alexander and Stoyle, 1972). They were given the Stanford-Binet Intelligence Scale at the beginning of the school year and again at the end of the year. The items comprising the Binet were grouped into the following categories: Comprehension, Visual Perception, Memory, Verbal Ability, Performance, and Drawing. During the school year the children improved in the tasks grouped under Comprehension, answering such questions as "Why do we have houses?" and carrying out instructions: "Here's a pencil. I want you to put it on the chair. . . ." Another category in which the children improved was Visual Perception. The tasks consisted of such questions as "Which ball is bigger?" and "See all of these animals? Find me another one just like this up here." (The wording of the Binet is quoted.) Virtually no change was apparent in the other categories of Memory, Performance, Drawing, or Verbal Ability. (See Figure 5–3.) The results of the study suggest that although some capacities involved in cognitive processes can be effectively altered, a general experience will not necessarily bring general improvement. (For Binet items, see Terman and Merrill, 1960).

Memory. Upon perception of an event, that is, when labeling or interpretation takes place, a *trace* is thought to be left in the cerebral cortex that becomes the basis for memory and association, two other essential cognitive processes. Memory has for some time been assumed to be a physiological modification of the brain, perhaps an alteration within the brain cells. Such a view seems reasonable, as some alteration in structure or function seems to be necessary for the event of memory to take place, but the idea of a trace is theoretical. Some prefer to use a concept of *interconnections* similar to the storage or memory bank of computers (Oldfield, 1964). The trace view of memory lends itself well to explanations of forgetting, as the trace can be seen as fading. But memory is also seen as an active process, in which changes over a time period result in

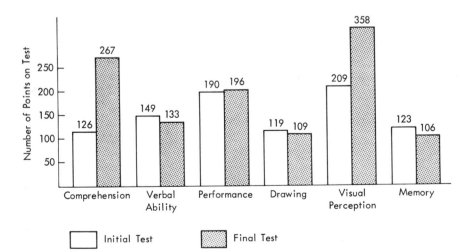

FIGURE 5–3
Change in scores on Binet items in the mental ability categories over the school year of children in Head Start classes.
(Adapted from T. Alexander and J. Stoyle. Culture, cognition, and social change: The effect of the Head Start experience on cognitive patterns. Unpublished.)

more effective and useful organization than the original form of the remembered event (Chaplin and Krawiec, 1968; Guilford, 1971). That is, explanations and new knowledge can make the original remembered event more meaningful or useful. Such an active memory process results in stronger or more viable images than those in the first perceptual experience. Memory in this way is a part of perceptual learning. Subsequent experience and association accordingly become part of learning and ultimately contribute to a response or cognitive style (Cole, Frankel, and Sharp, 1971). Memory is thus interrelated with other cognitive processes.

Set is important in memory and is related to selectivity. Attendance to a specific pattern of stimuli will enhance memory, even in very young children (Blank and Frank, 1971). When the expected stimuli appear, energy is then devoted to the pattern and is not dissipated in relation to other stimuli. But set can also be a handicap. One study illustrating differences among children (five, eight, and eleven years) in their "attribute fixation" or set involved the task of sorting geometrical figures of varying shape, size, and color. The stimuli were paper cut-outs mounted in the center of a white card about three inches square. The investigators (Kofsky and Osler, 1967) concluded that the subjects at each age level could sort the stimuli into logical groups, that the youngest children had more difficulty in the sorting task than the older children, and that all of the subjects had attribute preferences. Adherence to these preferences provided more of a handicap for the younger children than the older. In some aspects of the task, the younger group tended to depend on color while the older subjects depended on form. All three groups showed least preference for sorting on the basis of size. The youngest group had the most difficulty in shifting from one criterion for sorting to another. Apparently, their previous set interfered with changing to a different basis for sorting, but shifting of set did improve with age.

Another factor in memory is *motivation*. It is easier to remember things which have either fulfilled a need or posed a threat (Cuvo and Witryol, 1971). And persistence in perceiving and comprehending a situation is required if the pattern of stimuli, events, or the totality of events is to be remembered. Fleeting attention may not suffice. Both quantity and quality of memory are functions of persistence in attention to events to be remembered.

Memory seems to improve with maturation and experience, as children begin to improve in memory on entering first grade, and continue to do so throughout middle childhood. Even infants have some ability to respond to a remembered stimulus or lack of it. At five years of age, a child usually can repeat four numbers that have been read to him; by the time a child is ten, he can usually repeat six digits. Other accomplishments of memory can be illustrated by naming objects from memory. In testing a child with the Stanford-Binet Intelligence Scale, for example, three toys—automobile, dog, and shoe—are placed in front of the child.

The child is asked to close his eyes while the experimenter covers the toy dog with a cardboard box. The child then is asked to look and decide which object is missing (Terman and Merrill, 1960). A number of investigators today are interested in such tasks and study the capacity for short-term memory (Calfee, 1970; Belmont, 1972).

Imagery and imagination are also part of memory. Almost as soon as cognition became a subject for investigation, *eidetic imagery* was studied as a part of investigations of memory. This phenomenon can be discovered by showing a child a picture with many details and then removing it. Some children can describe the details of the picture as if the stimulus were still present and visible; the image may last for several minutes or more (Doob, 1970). Eidetic imagery seems to be very rare. In a study of 150 eminent men and women of whom a large proportion had superior memories, only about 25 had "photographic memory" (Cutts and Moseley, 1969). More than a thousand adults were tested but no eidetic imagery was found, although some individuals with superior memory were found. One way of testing memory consisted of showing the subjects a poster-size picture for 30 seconds and then asking the subjects to answer questions about it. Another test requested the subjects to repeat a hundred-word passage after one reading. The investigators found a close relation between excellent memory and achievement in school, college, and careers. Students in the upper quartile on the memory tests were also in the upper quartile in scholastic standing. Memory should be considered to be multioperational, Cutts and Moseley believe, and to include learning, storage, recall, and recognition. Ability to hold information in mind provides an individual with a reservoir of information with which to develop solutions to problems.

In spite of the availability and widespread use of such test items, investigations of memory development are difficult to carry out, in part because of the subjective quality of the data and in part because of the difficulty in showing differences in quality or quantity. As the gathering of data depends on the verbal reports of children, variables such as differences in linguistic ability are likely to interfere with results of the study.

A number of factors probably determine differences in memory ability. Children from the lower socioeconomic class seem to have more difficulty with tasks of memory than do middle-class children. And educational programs with very young children in the lower socioeconomic class have not been notably successful in improving their ability on memory tasks as was indicated earlier.

Symbolic Processes and Solutions. In environmental interaction and in complex situations, *solving a problem symbolically* is essential. Symbolic solutions conserve organismic energy and effort, but more importantly they make it possible to avoid the consequence of an inadequate or catastrophic response. In one sense symbolic solutions are a way of testing proposed or hypothetical responses against reality. Perhaps this is one of the meanings of psychoanalytic and theoretical postulates about the functioning of the ego. The individual seeks a response in accord with his conception of reality.

Symbolic solutions and projection of possible responses can also be a way of predicting others' responses. "Internal conversations" can take place: a response can be symbolically tried, then the results can be projected for possible evaluation. Perhaps a change in the symbolic response can be made and the results can be tried again. Such a process provides internal feedback. The advantage of such symbolic testing of a hypothesis is obvious. It has even been extended by present-day computers. Through simulation (or creation of hypothetical solutions) with a computer, considerable time can be saved. Computers thus extend the symbolic functioning of the brain.

One study of human ability to project solutions was based on the assumption that once stimuli are given meaning, an individual must engage in complex behavior to associate the meaning with past experience or learning (Alexander, Kugel, Cushna, and Snider, 1964). That is, on being confronted with a new stimulus, it is necessary to search in one's "memory bank" for a way to determine the significance and meaning of it. This search usually involves an effort to explain the occurrence or existence of the stimulus. An understanding of the cause of its existence then contributes to judgment about the response to be made and the likelihood of its success.

The investigation involved 435 children in middle childhood (aged 7 to 12). Thirty of the children had been diagnosed as having some type of behavior disorder and 32 as having some central nervous system disorder; the remainder were normal. The stimuli ranged from the very simple tasks of completing a formboard to telling a story about pictures of children and adults. In this latter task, the responses were scored on the basis of the kind of response a subject made to the stimuli (pictures). Categorization of the level of complexity of subjects' responses consisted of: (1) a *listing* of the content of the picture, (2) a *description* of characteristics of the people, (3) *causation*, an explanation of antecedent events, (4) an *incomplete prediction* of future conditions or relationships, and (5) a *complete prediction* of future conditions in keeping with the description of the stimuli and the antecedent conditions. The responses of some subjects consisted of only listing the characteristics of each picture shown to them. For example, the type of response placed in this first category (Listing) would be: "This is a boy." Another subject might give a more complex response and say "This is a boy who has on a striped shirt." Such a response indicates some awareness of characteristics of parts of the stimulus-pattern represented by the picture—this response would be placed in the second category (Description). Still another subject might show an ability to reason about antecedent events or causation and would say: "This boy has just put on a striped shirt that has been given to him as a birthday present." This response would be placed in the third category of antecedent conditions (Causation). Another subject might respond by saying: "This is a boy who has just put on a striped shirt given to him as a birthday present by his mother. He is now going out in the yard." This response is an *incomplete prediction* since it does not definitely indicate what will happen next. A *complete prediction* would be: "He is going out to be with his friends who have been invited to his birthday party. The party will be in a new tent where there is already waiting lots of good things to eat including his favorite dessert—chocolate cake." Thus, the steps of a continuum are indicated ranging from a simple listing of stimuli to a specific prediction of future conditions.

In Figure 5–4, it can be seen that children with CNS disorder perceived or were aware of the stimuli but had difficulty associating them with past experience or reaching some idea of causation. Generally the subjects were unable to predict future conditions. The test scores of children with behavior disorders were similar to the scores of normal children.

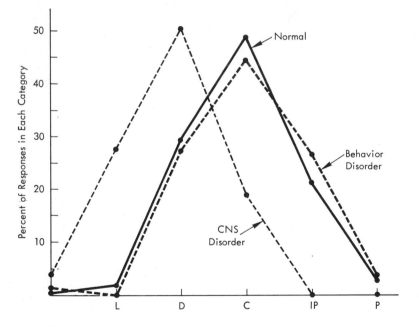

FIGURE 5–4
Percent of subjects attaining each category of a continuum of a complexity of response. (1) L = *listing* the content of the picture; (2) D = a *description* of characteristics of the people; (3) C = *causation,* an explanation of antecedent events; (4) IP = an *incomplete prediction* of future conditions or relationships, and (5) P = complete *prediction* of future conditions in keeping with the description of the stimuli and the antecedent conditions.
(Adapted from T. Alexander, R. B. Kugel, B. Cushna, and B. Snider. Studies of complex behavior. I. The processes of perception, association, and prediction of response. *The Journal of Psychology,* 1964, 58, 23–32. Copyright 1964 by the Journal Press, and used by permission.)

Children with behavior disorders and normal children were able to describe the stimuli in terms of present conditions and causative events. However, only a few were able to describe *future* possibilities. Prediction of effects of a stimulus or the responses required by it is essential to appropriate or goal-obtaining behavior, yet only a few individuals were capable of it. Behavior in complex and urban society increasingly requires that an individual be able to try out results of his behavior in his thought processes before making a response or taking a course of action. But this study suggests that normal children in middle childhood have developed little capacity to engage in such behavior.

Concept Formation. Another factor in the projection of solutions is *concept formation*, which is defined as the perception of patterns of relationships among stimuli and responses (Goss, 1964). The simplest concept-formation tasks can be described under the term "stimulus generalization," that is, the tendency of similar stimuli to evoke similar responses. A concept exists when two or more objects are grouped separately from other objects on the basis of a common feature, property, or characteristic (Bourne, 1966; Nelson, 1972). A careful definition is necessary for experimentation, since the word *concept* has many meanings. Grouping according to a common feature can be exemplified by the word "bird"; not all birds are similar, but even an unfamiliar or strange bird can be classified as a "bird" on the basis of characteristics already learned by the perceiver. Such categorizing of things and events is necessary for coping with the diversity and complexity of stimuli in the surrounding life space. The individual uses concepts to encode stimuli into manageable groupings; to this extent he makes his complex environment more manageable than when he perceives it in unrelated units. Objects can be classified according to a great number of characteristics. The simplest categorization is probably made on the basis of physical identity. The category of *black birds* involves "blackness" and "birds" as characteristics for grouping. The grouping of objects into concepts insures some similarity of response to these objects by people within the culture. Part of the response will very likely be verbal, because objects will be called something; they will be given some type of label (Hollenberg, 1970).

Characteristics and meaning of stimuli are essential in the use of concepts. Stimuli have many dimensions like size or color; but as not all of them are used in conceptual behavior, some characteristics can be considered irrelevant to the concept. Those characteristics of the stimuli relevant to the concept do influence response. If the relevant characteristics of the whole category of stimuli included in the concept consistently or quite frequently evoke the same response, this response becomes associated with the concept. Such a response to a concept—or to the category of things it represents—is called a *categorical response*.

Environmental objects can be categorized according to simple concepts similar to the principles developed by Kagan, Moss, and Sigel (1963). First, objects can be organized on the basis of *part-whole relationships*. That is, "parts" of a number of "wholes" can be grouped on the basis of the similarity of the specified part; for example, all birds that have webbed feet can be grouped together. Another type of organization can be on the basis of *spatial relationships*. An example would be the classification of birds that build their nests in dark, enclosed places. A third basis for a concept is that of *functional relationships*. Objects would be grouped in this concept on the basis of use—for example, the group of objects which transport passengers. A fourth organizational basis involves *classificatory relationships*. Objects grouped on this basis would have similarities of appearance that would put them all in one class; for example, a tent and a wigwam would be classified as shelter.

Very young children can form concepts in tasks of visual perception, as was demonstrated by a study involving two-year-old children (Heiser, 1969). The task consisted of finding a raisin under the larger of two measuring cups. The children attained the concept of selecting the larger cup in approximately three trials. In another part of the study using geometric figures, the concept of larger was somewhat more difficult, as the figures were in only two dimensions. But the children in the study did attain the concept of larger with a variety of geometric figures.

Maturation and experience enable older children to use more concepts, and more complex concepts, than can younger children. Classificatory concepts are probably more complex than concepts of function or use. The larger vocabulary and more complex response patterns of older children clearly facilitate the development of conceptual response patterns. The formation of concepts is increasingly important in the projection and exploration of possible solutions as children grow older.

Cognitive Style. The final cognitive process to be discussed here, the development of a *cognitive style*, can be called the action phase of problem-solving. (Davis, 1971; Garrettson, 1971). In it the individual selects a response and carries it through. The results of the response may be immediately apparent or they may take some time for evaluation. If the response is effective or successful, and if it fulfills the individual's needs, it may then be reinforced. The satisfaction attained constitutes a reward and allows feedback on the response, which may cause it to be extended or improved. Successful responses lead to a patterning of cognitive processes into a cognitive style. Perceptual selectivity, memory, projected solution, and the action phase are all affected by the results of earlier responses and by the degree of success or failure. Evaluation of patterns of success becomes a part of the individual's repertoire of behavior or cognitive style. But if the response is ineffective and unsuccessful, perceptual selectivity may be altered and the labeling or perceptual learning may be "forgotten." The failing responses will be avoided in projecting future possible solutions; that particular action phase is unlikely to be repeated. By evaluation of the results of the response, the individual develops rules of behavior that influence his cognitive style. These rules may consciously or unconsciously determine his future reasoning and cognitive processes.

Social interaction within the family and the life space in the child's very early years affects the development of response styles and patterns, as is illustrated in a study by Pedersen and Wender (1968). Their subjects were 30 boys studied at two years of age and then again at six. Information obtained from observations, teachers' ratings, and parent interviews was used to rate behavior in the categories of "physical contact, attention seeking, orality, and sustained directed activity." The subjects were asked to perform three cognitive tasks: (1) the Wechsler Intelligence Scale for Children, (2) a "Categorization-style Test" (this test used the Sigel Sorting Task, made of twelve arrays with four pictures each—a stimulus picture and three response pictures; from the latter three the subjects were to choose the one most like the stimulus picture and give reasons for their choice), and (3) a field dependence-independence task consisting of an embedded figures test. The findings indicated that maternal behavior that encouraged independence and interaction with the physical environment was associated with high nonverbal ability. Subjects who were autonomous in their play with manipulative objects also tended to have a higher performance IQ on follow-up four years later. The authors concluded that encouragement of independence at an early age facilitated the development of capacities to perform tasks involving spatial relations, color and form choices, and manipulative dexterity.

Quantitative Systems and the Study of Cognition

As studies of human performance have multiplied, the use of quantitative techniques in investigations has also increased. Problems in understanding cognitive development have also multiplied, as research in neurophysiology has revealed the complexity of the central nervous system. Theoretical models of wide diversity have now developed. And, the use of computers, particularly in simulation of neural functioning, has extended greatly the conceptual possibilities for investigation.

Quantitative Methods. A review of quantitative methods in the study of behavior reveals a number of significant developments in the first half of the twentieth century. Interest in such methods has steadily increased since the early days of the laboratory studies of Francis Galton. Galton, however, made a particularly important contribution to quantitative methods by his use of the *median,* the *standard score*, and *correlation* in the statistical treatment of data. This work, coupled with that of Karl Pearson (for example, his *product-moment coefficient of correlation*), provided the essential basis for modern descriptive statistics. James McKeen Cattell influenced development of investigations by using tests to study mental processes. He and his associates at Columbia University began the first large-scale testing of mental ability to study the range of individual differences.

As is well known, mental testing began with the work of Binet and Simon in 1905 in France (Peterson, 1969). Their scale was based on a concept of intelligence that included a direction for mental processes, ability to reach solutions to problems, and ability to make judgments. The scale was constructed of many heterogeneous items related to information, vocabulary, performance tasks, and reasoning. Binet and Simon gave the group of tests to a large number of subjects and arranged the items according to age by selecting and placing the items so that a person of any given age could successfully complete from 50% to 75% of the test for his age group. The scale was thus based on the premise that intelligence developed according to chronological age and that an individual child's development could be measured against the scale's items for a child of that age. That is, a five-year-old child should be able to pass the items at the five-year-old level, and by comparing the child's performance to a standardization group, his intellectual ability could be determined. The concept of *mental age* grew out of the idea that if a child passed all the items at the five-year-level, his mental age was five no matter what his chronological age was.

Critical questions about the scale have been raised over the years. Does the heterogeneous group of items of the scale represent mental ability? And is it justifiable for a single test score, based on a successful completion of a group of unrelated items, to represent intelligence? Two approaches have been developed to answer these questions. One approach consists of an assessment of intelligence on the basis of reasoning and observed behavior, and the other approach consists of an analysis of test items to determine what they measure. Both approaches are still subject to controversy after a half century of research effort.

Other uses of quantitative methods in the study of cognition are exemplified by the development of cybernetics, the application of information theory, and computer research. These approaches seek to create models of learning which will predict behavior and problem-solving responses.

Cybernetics is a new science formed to relate behavior in the nervous system and in machines to the principles of the social sciences. The systems of thought developed by the cyberneticists depend upon analogies between the human nervous system and electronic circuits. The function of the basic units in the nervous system, the neurons, is suggested to be analogous to the function of computers. The computer is composed of many relays which operate on an "on or off" basis, as does a neuron. The computer can store items or remember them, as does the brain. Both the computer and the brain operate with feedback mechanisms, which allow conditions external to the unit to alter the functioning of the unit. *Feedback* can be illustrated by modern room temperature controls. When the temperature of the room changes, a thermostat will turn an airconditioning unit on or off. Physical and physiological processes in the body function in a similar way. Circulation in the body, for example, changes in relation to outside temperature, moving blood toward or away from the skin in order to keep the body's internal temperature constant. Many other analogies are possible. Research on these mechanisms has led to wide diversity in studies.

Information Theory. The application of information theory has attracted the attention of many investigators of human behavior in recent years. *Information theory* holds that cognitive processes can be studied and understood as if they were similar to those of electronic communication systems. An individual receives, processes, and responds to messages as does an electronic unit that receives signals, stores them, and makes them available on demand. If given a problem, a modern machine can store information and go through complex procedures with it in order to arrive at a solution. When it uses units of information (bits), it applies stochastic or probability methods to the problem to be solved. *Input* and *output,* important concepts in the operation of machine models, can also be applied to cognitive processes. The signals that come into the system (input) are similar to sensory data entering an organism, and the output of the machine is similar to the reactions or responses of the organism.

In the view of Schroder, Driver, and Streufert (1967), human information processing, or thinking, has more alternatives than that of lower animals. Human thinking can assign more meanings to objects and therefore is less stimulus bound. Human thought and its related action as a result contains more uncertainty and ambiguity than that of animals. Through the use of computers, these investigators believe, complex sets of instructions and rules can be applied to data in an almost limitless way. But despite their great capacity, computers are very simple in comparison with human thought; as creative or adaptive mechanisms, they are quite limited. The significant use of computers is to store a large amount of information and to process the data according to rules devised by human experimenters.

Schroder and his colleagues believe that information processing involves two independent properties: (1) the dimensions and (2) the integrating rules. They see *dimensions* as "units of conceptual functioning"—judgments about a range of stimuli. Judgments about variation in light, for example, can be made on at least three dimensions: brightness, saturation, and hue. The more dimensions involved, the greater is the likelihood of the development of complexity in *integrating rules.* They suggest a "low integration index" and "high integration index" to describe a variation in "level of conceptual structure," the way an individual processes information. "Needs, concepts, beliefs," and the like, are "structures" for processing information. Interaction between persons and environmental variables is thus dependent on the structures that determine the complexity of information processing. If intelligence is measured by the amount of information that can be brought about by new combinations of rules, the more complex and higher levels of information-processing structures would be considered characteristic of more intelligent activity.

Social Change and Cognitive Development

Just as the advent of the industrial age at the beginning of the century brought great interest in the human capacity to respond to an increasingly complex environment, so have new developments in urban society brought altered views in conceptualizing human intelligence.

Certain recent trends have appeared which seem to lead to far-reaching changes in all basic concepts and principles of human development. In spite of revival in some circles of the controversy about the relative importance of heredity and environment as bases for intelligence, there is an overwhelming trend toward belief in experience and education as significant determinants in the capacity to find satisfaction in a life style in modern society. Illustrations can be found in the vast governmental program of Head Start where thousands of children below norms in ability on intelligence tests are being provided experience to help them perform at a higher level in the school system and thereby ultimately have a better prospect for a satisfying role in society than would ordinarily be expected. Similarly, thousands of students are being admitted even to the most prestigious institutions of higher education who only a few years ago would have been considered "incapable of profiting from college training" by reason of their low scores on intelligence or aptitude tests.

Perhaps an even more significant and shattering trend is the widespread demand for change in the content of the entire educational system. Youth now demand that relevance be shown; content "to train the mind" is irrelevant and is quickly rejected. In addition, they show a tendency to reject striving behavior and the long hours required to master difficult cognitive tasks or skills, the use of which is not easily seen. These are but a few of the trends that are altering old concepts and principles. There are others.

Although much emphasis is still placed on the importance of learning to read, many children go through the educational system without being proficient. Reading, of course, is dependent upon complex psychoneurological processes as well as cultural experience. It has been suggested that in urban society reading proficiency is less valued because of new forms of communication. Youth finds much of their interaction in modern society is not dependent upon reading; for example, no reading is necessary in the hours spent every day in their early years with television. Yet other forms of social change affect cognitive behavior. These forms relate to the concepts of work and occupational roles: (1) the effect of the three- or four-day week, when at least half of a person's life will be in activities unrelated to achievement in an occupation; (2) the changing character of occupations, particularly in relation to machines and automation; and (3) the revolutionary ideas of dissociating income from work. These significant trends in modern society will be discussed subsequently. Mention is made of them here to indicate that social change is altering principles and concepts of human development as derived in the first part of the century. Principles, it is apparent, can be affected by social change, in part because principles are dependent upon concepts of normative behavior. The usefulness and relevance of earlier principles are therefore being altered by the accelerating social change now taking place in the last half of this century.

IN PERSPECTIVE

Attainment of satisfaction in modern society has become an increasingly difficult task in recent years because of the advance of scientific technology and the complexity of social role requirements. To obtain a rewarding and prestigious role, much training and individual effort in the educational system are required. Many educators assert that if an individual is to be successful in a training program, he must have the basic capacity to learn a myriad of complex tasks and many intricate bits of information. Such a learning capacity is believed to depend upon a number of biological traits and a varied environmental experience. This means that the central nervous system, primarily the brain, must function sufficiently well to meet the demands of the culture. Also, experience during the developmental years must be of such a nature that the input of appropriate stimulation and information is in accordance with the cultural mainstream.

Because of the importance of education in this society, controversy over the relative importance of heredity and environment in the development of the capacity to engage in complex behavior has continued to occupy the attention of behavioral scientists for most of this century. It is possible, however, that asking about the relative importance of heredity and environment is not a question that can be answered, as it implies that structure and function are separable in application.

It ought to be expected that an individual will develop adequately and find a satisfying social role if his learning experiences are appropriate. Consequently, the view seems to be emerging in modern society that concerns about qualities of motivation and emotional stability transcend concerns about innate biological differences.

REFERENCES

ALEXANDER, T., KUGEL, R. B., CUSHNA, B., & SNIDER, B. Studies of complex behavior: The processes of perception, association, and prediction of response. *The Journal of Psychology,* 1964, 58, 23–32.

ALEXANDER, T., & STOYLE, J. Culture, cognition, and social change: The effect of the Head Start experience on cognitive patterns, 1972 (unpublished).

ANASTASI, A. *Differential psychology; individual and group differences in behavior.* (3rd ed.). New York: Macmillan, 1958.

BELMONT, J. M. Relations of age and intelligence to short-term color memory. *Child Development,* 1972, 43, 19–29.

BERLYNE, D. E. *Conflict, arousal, and curiosity.* New York: McGraw-Hill, 1960.

BERLYNE, D. E. The influence of complexity and novelty in visual figures on orienting responses. In J. C. Harper (Ed.), *The cognitive processes.* Englewood Cliffs, N. J.: Prentice-Hall, 1964. Pp. 120–129.

BERLYNE, D. E., & FROMME, F. D. Some determinants of children's questions. *Child Development,* 1966, 37, 176–189.

BLANK, M., & FRANK, S. M. Story recall in kindergarten children: Effect of method of presentation on psycholinguistic performance. *Child Development,* 1971, 42, 299–312.

BOURNE, L. E. *Human conceptual behavior.* Boston: Allyn & Bacon, 1966.

BRUNER, J. S. The course of cognitive growth. *American Psychologist,* 1964, 19, 1–15.

CALFEE, R. C. Short-term recognition memory in children. *Child Development,* 1970, 41, 145–161.

CHAPLIN, J. P., & KRAWIEC, T. S. *Systems and theories of psychology.* (2nd ed.). New York: Holt, Rinehart & Winston, 1968.

COLE, M., FRANKEL, F., & SHARP, D. Development of free recall learning in children. *Developmental Psychology,* 1971, 4, 109–123.

COLEMAN, J. S. Academic achievement and the structure of competition. In *Reprint Series No. 1, Socialization and schools.* Cambridge, Mass.: Harvard Educational Review, 1968. Pp. 1–22.

COLEMAN, J. S. *Resources for social change: Race in the United States.* New York: Wiley, 1971.

CUTTS, N. E., & MOSELEY, N. Notes on photographic memory. *The Journal of Psychology,* 1969, 71, 3–15.

CUVO, A. J., & WITRYOL, S. L. The influence of incentives on memory stages in children. *The Journal of Genetic Psychology,* 1971, 119, 289–300.

DAVIS, A. J. Cognitive style: Methodological and developmental considerations. *Child Development,* 1971, 42, 1447–1459.

DOOB, L. W. Correlates of eidetic imagery in Africa. *The Journal of Psychology,* 1970, 76, 223–230.

DUBIN, R., & DUBIN, E. R. Children's social perceptions: A review of research. *Child Development,* 1965, 36, 809–838.

ELKIND, D., ANAGNOSTOPOULOU, R., & MALONE, S. Determinants of part-whole perception in children. *Child Development,* 1970, 41, 391–397.

ELKIND, D., KOEGLER, R. R., & GO, E. Studies in perceptual development: II. Part-whole perception. *Child Development,* 1964, 35, 81–90.

ELKIND, D., & SCOTT, L. Studies in perceptual development: I. The decentering of perception. *Child Development,* 1962, 33, 619–630.

ENGEN, T., LIPSITT, L. P., & KAYE, H. Olfactory responses and adaptation in the human neonate. *Journal of Comparative and Physiological Psychology,* 1963, 56, 73–77.

ESTES, B., & RUSH, D. Social schemas: A developmental study. *The Journal of Psychology,* 1971, 78, 119–123.

FISHER, G. H. Developmental features of behaviour and perception: I. Visual and tactile-kinaesthetic shape perception. *British Journal of Educational Psychology,* 1965, 35, 69–78.

GARRETTSON, J. Cognitive style and classification. *The Journal of Genetic Psychology,* 1971, 119, 79–87.

GEORGE, F. H. *Cognition.* London: Methuen, 1962.

GETZELS, J. W., & ELKINS, K. Perceptual and cognitive development. *Review of Educational Research,* 1964, 34, 559–573.

GEWIRTZ, J. L. The role of stimulation in models for child development. In

L. L. Dittmann (Ed.), *Early child care.* New York: Atherton, 1968. Pp. 139–168.

GLINER, C. R., PICK, A. D., PICK, H. L., JR., & HALES, J. J. A developmental investigation of visual and haptic preferences for shape and texture. *Monographs of the Society for Research in Child Development,* 1969, 34 (6, Whole No. 130).

GOSS, A. E. Verbal mediating response and concept formation. In R. J. C. Harper, C. C. Anderson, C. M. Christensen, & S. M. Hunka (Eds.), *The cognitive processes.* Englewood Cliffs, N. J.: Prentice-Hall, 1964. Pp. 133–161.

GOTTHEIL, E., COREY, J., & PAREDES, A. Psychological and physical dimensions of personal space. *The Journal of Psychology,* 1968, 69, 7–9.

GUILFORD, J. P. Varieties of memory and their implications. *The Journal of General Psychology,* 1971, 85, 207–228.

HEBB, D. O. Drives and the C. N. S. (Conceptual Nervous System). In C. R. Evans & A. D. J. Robertson (Eds.), *Brain physiology and psychology.* Los Angeles: University of California Press, 1966. Pp. 67–83.

HEISER, R. B. Some notes on concept formation in young children. *The Journal of Genetic Psychology,* 1969, 114, 219–227.

HOLLENBERG, C. K. Functions of visual imagery in the learning and concept formation of children. *Child Development,* 1970, 41, 1003–1015.

JENSEN, A. R. How much can we boost I.Q. and scholastic achievement? In *Reprint Series No. 2, Environment, heredity, and intelligence.* Cambridge, Mass.: Harvard Educational Review, 1969. Pp. 1–123.

KAGAN, J. Inadequate evidence and illogical conclusions. In *Reprint Series No. 2, Environment, heredity, and intelligence.* Cambridge, Mass.: Harvard Educational Review, 1969. Pp. 126–129.

KAGAN, J., HENKER, B. A., HEN-TOV, A., LEVINE, J., & LEWIS, M. Infants' differential reactions to familiar and distorted faces. *Child Development,* 1966, 37, 519–532.

KAGAN, J., HOSKEN, B., & WATSON, S. Child's symbolic conceptualization of parents. *Child Development,* 1961, 32, 625–636.

KAGAN, J., MOSS, H. A., & SIGEL, I. E. Psychological significance of styles of conceptualization. In J. C. Wright and J. Kagan (Eds.), Basic cognitive processes in children. *Monographs of the Society for Research in Child Development,* 1963, 28 (2, Whole No. 86). Pp. 73–112.

KERPELMAN, L. C., & POLLACK, R. H. Developmental changes in the location of form discrimination cues. *Perceptual and Motor Skills,* 1964, 19, 375–382.

KESSEN, W. Questions for a theory of cognitive development. In H. W. Stevenson (Ed.), Concept of development. *Monographs of the Society for Research in Child Development,* 1966, 31 (5, Whole No. 107). Pp. 55–70.

KIDD, A. H., & RIVOIRE, J. L. The culture-fair aspects of the development of spatial perception. *The Journal of Genetic Psychology,* 1965, 106, 101–111.

KOFSKY, E., & OSLER, S. F. Free classification in children. *Child Development,* 1967, 38, 927–937.

KUETHE, J. L. Social schemas. *Journal of Abnormal and Social Psychology,* 1962, 64, 31–38.

LEIBOWITZ, H. W. *Visual perception.* New York: Macmillan, 1965.

LEWIS, M., KAGAN, J., & KALAFAT, J. Patterns of fixation in the young infant. *Child Development,* 1966, 37, 331–341.

LOWENFELD, V. *Creative and mental growth*. (3rd ed.). New York: Macmillan, 1957.

MACCOBY, E. E. Sex differences in intellectual functioning. In E. E. Maccoby (Ed.), *The development of sex differences*. Palo Alto, Calif.: Stanford University Press, 1966. Pp. 25–55.

MCKINNEY, J. P. Verbal meaning and perceptual stability. *Canadian Journal of Psychology/Revue Canadienne de Psychologie*, 1966, 20, 237–242.

NELSON, K. The relation of form recognition to concept development. *Child Development*, 1972, 43, 67–74.

ODOM, R. D., McINTYRE, C. W., & NEALE, G. S. The influence of cognitive style on perceptual learning. *Child Development*, 1971, 42, 883–891.

OLDFIELD, R. C. Memory mechanisms and the theory of schemata. In J. C. Harper (Ed.), *The cognitive processes*. Englewood Cliffs, N. J.: Prentice-Hall, 1964. Pp. 356–366.

PEDERSEN, F. A., & WENDER, P. H. Early social correlates of cognitive functioning in six-year-old boys. *Child Development*, 1968, 39, 185–193.

PETERSON, J. *Early conceptions and tests of intelligence*. Westport, Conn.: Greenwood, 1969. (Originally published in 1926.)

QUINTON, A. The problem of perception. In G. J. Warnock (Ed.), *The philosophy of perception*. London: Oxford University Press, 1967. Pp. 61–84.

RABINOWITZ, F. M., & ROBE, C. V. Children's choice behavior as a function of stimulus change, complexity, relative novelty, surprise, and uncertainty. *Journal of Experimental Psychology*, 1968, 78, 625–633.

ROSEN, B. C. Social class and the child's perception of the parent. *Child Development*, 1964, 35, 1147–1153.

SANDERS, A. F. Short term memory for spatial positions. *Nederlands Tijdschrift voor de Psychologie en haar Grensgedieden*, 1968, 23, 1–15.

SCHRODER, H. M., DRIVER, M. J., & STREUFERT, S. *Human information processing*. New York: Holt, Rinehart & Winston, 1967.

SHERMAN, J. A. Problem of sex differences in space perception and aspects of intellectual functioning. *Psychological Review*, 1967, 74, 290–299.

SMITH, O. W. Spatial perceptions and play activities of nursery school children. *Perceptual and Motor Skills*, 1965, 21, 260.

SMITH, O. W., & SMITH, P. C. Developmental studies of spatial judgments by children and adults. *Perceptual and Motor Skills*, 1966, 22 (Monograph Supplement 1).

TAYLOR, J. G. *The behavioral basis of perception*. New Haven, Conn.: Yale University Press, 1962.

TERMAN, L. M., & MERRILL, M. A. *Stanford-Binet Intelligence Scale*. Boston: Houghton Mifflin, 1960.

TOWLER, J. O., & NELSON, L. D. Spatial concepts of elementary school children. *Alberta Journal of Educational Research*, 1967, 13, 43–50.

TYLER, L. E. *The psychology of human differences*. New York: Appleton-Century-Crofts, 1965.

WERDELIN, I. *Geometrical ability and the space factors in boys and girls*. Lund, Sweden: University of Lund, 1961.

SYMBOLIC SYSTEMS AND ENVIRONMENTAL INTERACTION

6

The individual can deal with environmental complexity much more efficiently through the use of symbols than directly; in some instances he can deal with his environment only through symbols (Furth, 1967). The use of symbols enables man to manipulate the qualities of his life space, to store them in memory, and to put them through complex processes, thereby increasing the effectiveness of his interaction with the environment. The entire environment, in fact, can exist in his memory in the form of symbolic systems.

Language itself is a system of symbols that can recreate the environment in a form capable of many types of manipulation and exploration. Each symbol stands for an object or event in the environment, in reality. Because emotions and bodily states may also be associated with the symbol for an object, idea, or event, symbols can affect behavior even in the absence of the corresponding objects and conditions. Indeed, some symbols evoke the same response patterns as the actual objects or events. Passages from a book or scenes from a play may elicit intense emotional reactions, although they are only symbolic forms of objects or events. Symbols, therefore, in one sense become the environment; they evoke responses just as "reality" would. Symbols may be connected to the real world by *similarity:* that is, a symbol may appear to have characteristics similar to the object which it represents. Or symbols may be *associated* with an object; in such a way lines with cross-bars on maps indicate railroads. Or the symbolic relationship may be based on intersensory connections, as when a sound suggests a color; this type of relationship is called *synesthesia*.

Primitive man used concrete and simple symbols, often natural objects, but modern man usually uses artificial objects such as drawings, writings, and sounds. In modern language and in modern societies, the words or symbols associated with objects usually have little connection with them and seem to be arbitrarily chosen. The systems of symbols used in modern societies have become exceedingly complex. A further complication occurs when symbols stand for symbols; when HMS is used for *Her Majesty's Ship,* the letters stand for words that are symbols in themselves. Such symbols are sometimes difficult to decode, particularly when they are mathematical.

SYMBOLS AND IDEAS

Ideas and social information affect the application of symbols to perceptual experience. According to Keasey, Walsh, and Moran (1969), *informational influence* occurs when the judgment of others serves as an "anchor" for an individual's perceptual experience and response patterns. This effect is as influential as the actual physical properties of the stimulus. Keasey and his associates believe that informational influence is of most significance in perceptions that involve some uncertainty. To substantiate this argument, they investigated the effect of social influence and labeling on subjects' perceptions of and responses to color stimuli.

The color blue-green was selected for the study because of its ambiguity. Eight other colors ranging from green to blue were used, with the test stimulus blue-green at the midpoint on the continuum. The subjects for the study were young adults of both sexes, of whom half had identified an ambiguous blue-green stimulus as blue and half as green in an initial phase of the experiment. The subjects were shown the stimuli through a hole approximately one inch in diameter in a 22-inch by 28-inch black panel. The colors were mounted on circular discs in random order. Each subject was shown the blue-green for 30 seconds and instructed to keep it in mind. They were all given different information about the color. They were told that the color had been designated as blue, or as green, by a group of male, or female, artists, or history teachers, in a previous experiment. Each subject was told that other colors would appear and that he would be asked to decide whether or not one was the *same* as the color stimulus (blue-green). The subject was then shown five colored discs from the continuum ranging from green to blue in random orders.

The results indicated that a subject whose tendency was to label the test stimulus *green* in the early part of the experiment responded differently from the subject who labeled the test stimulus *blue,* apparently because his perceptions of other colors shown were anchored by his earlier perception of the test stimulus. Subjects who were informed that the information source agreed with them in their designation of the test stimulus responded differently from subjects who were informed that the information source disagreed with them. For example, of two subjects who responded to the test stimulus as green, the subject who was told that the information source saw it as green was more influenced toward green in other responses than was the subject who was told that the information source saw the test stimulus as blue. The subjects were more influenced by information sources of their own sex than by those of the opposite sex, and the qualifications of the information source (whether he was an artist or a history teacher) did not significantly influence decisions.

The subjects' original ideas, such as perceiving the ambiguous color of blue-green as either blue or green, seemed to persist and to affect subsequent decisions. Perhaps this is the way response styles begin. Corroboration by others was also significant, even though their qualifications or the bases for their judgments were not particularly important. This finding indicates that support from others encouraged the subjects to continue the response in later decisions, whether or not the corroborating judgment was justified.

Sounds as Symbols

The elementary unit of speech is the *phoneme,* a particular speech sound. There are more phonemes than letters in the alphabet, because letters can be pronounced in different ways. The term phoneme is an abstraction; each individual pronounces a phoneme in a different way from other individuals. The individual's pronunciation of a phoneme is called a *phone.* A phoneme is actually a category of similar phones. Grouped into words, phonemes have meaning and psychological significance; words or parts of words with meaning are called *morphemes.* The morpheme is the smallest unit of meaning.

Phonemes. New recording devices make it possible to analyze speech by isolating or combining speech sounds. Through the study of auditory recognition with such devices it has been found that the consonant heard depends not only on the physical stimulus of the consonant, but also on the vowel that follows it. The perception of "p" and "k," for example, depends on the vowel following. This view, according to Brain (1968), illustrates that the perception of a word is more than a sum of perceptions of its phoneme parts. In fact, phonemes can be recognized much better if they are presented in words than if they are included in nonsense syllables.

Learning principles help describe the infant's experience with environmental sounds. For example, his recognition of familiar persons, as shown by his anticipatory movements at their appearance, is *reinforced* by soothing speech sounds in conjunction with other nurturant behavior. He develops *perceptual selectivity* as he comes to associate specific sounds with specific objects, events, and situations. Many sounds come to have meaning. The child learns to label sound stimuli, and he learns the patterns of sounds making up the grammatical structure of language (Mueller, 1972; Friedlander, Jacobs, Davis, and Wetstone, 1972).

   Morphemes. After mastering the sounds of the language—the *phonology*—the child must face the task of producing morphemes and grouping them into sentences. The child's first ventures into the production of morphemes, or words, usually contain errors such as "wound" for "round." But even these errors consist of sounds common to his language. He is not likely to use combinations of consonants from other languages, although until about nine months of age children in different cultures with different languages produce similar sounds.

   A study by Menyuk (1968) of sound combinations provides information about the effect of a child's previous production of language sounds on learning nonsense syllables, as well as the effect of age or maturation on learning phonological sequences. Her subjects were preschool, kindergarten, and first- and second-grade children (aged four to eight years). The stimuli, initial-consonant clusters with a following vowel and consonant, were designated grammatical or nongrammatical on the basis of their occurrence in ordinary speech. Examples of the grammatical clusters are "trut" and "drin," and examples of the nongrammatical clusters are "tsut" and "dlin." Three tasks were devised for the subjects. One task involved five colored circles on a white board, which were given phonological groupings or names; for example, one circle was called "drin." The children were first told the name of each circle and then asked to point to the correct circle as the experimenter pronounced its name. The second task required that the subject repeat the names of each set after they were spoken by the experimenter. The third task asked the subjects to repeat a set of five words after they were spoken by the experimenter. In the analysis of the results (see Figure 6–1), each grade level was compared with another on the basis of the percentage of children who had learned and reproduced grammatical versus nongrammatical sets, and the percentage of correct responses to each type of sequence.

   Among the findings of the study was evidence that all the subjects at the preschool level learned and responded correctly to some grammatical and nongrammatical material. The percentage of correct responses in selecting the named circle was significantly higher for grammatical than for nongrammatical items at every age level. The percentage of children who successfully repeated a set of actual words, such as "truth" or "drive," was also significantly greater than the percentage of subjects repeating the meaningless sequences.

   Menyuk concluded from the study that the older the subjects were, the more successfully they could learn either grammatical or nongrammatical tasks. The older subjects did not, however, reproduce or repeat the names of the nongrammatical sequences any better than did the

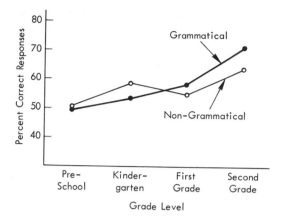

FIGURE 6–1

Percentage of correct responses in learning grammatical and non-grammatical sets of nonsense syllables.

(Adapted from P. Menyuk. Children's learning and reproduction of grammatical and nongrammatical phonological sequences. *Child Development,* copyright 1968 by the Society for Research in Child Development, Inc. 39, 849–859. By permission.)

younger subjects. The experimenter concluded that age does not prevent comprehension of a second language and that difficulties in learning language are primarily in reproducing sound sequences.

Language—Species-specific Behavior. In the normal course of development, much of an infant's early experience (that which is significant to him) is associated with the people around him. From the very beginning he hears language, a portion of which is devoted to him exclusively. Soon objects become familiar to him—his bed, his bottle, his rattle, certain people—and he associates sounds (such as a door opening) with them as well as names. Long before he can produce language he has much experience with it. In addition to associating sounds with objects, he learns a great number of principles about speech sounds (Snow, 1972).

The use of language involves a storage of information. As the names of objects are learned, they become available on instant demand. The information consists not only of single words but of the principles for use of words (Scribner and Cole, 1972). The principles of social interaction connected with the words, too, are learned (Love and Parker-Robinson, 1972). Thus, the learning of language is part of the process of learning to interact with the environment.

Some investigators believe that language is a *species-specific* attribute —that is, that language is a form of behavior peculiar to man (Lenneberg, 1968). Several conditions in man and in his use of language suggest this view.

First, certain characteristics of human anatomy and physiology related to speech—morphological structures of the oral cavity and brain function, lateral dominance (for example, preference for the right or left hand due to the dominance of one side of the brain), the functioning of neurological and respiratory systems, the capacities of auditory receptors, and the mechanisms for integration of systemic response—indicate complex specializations of structure and function that seem to be present to the greatest extent in man, of all species.

Second, the use of language occurs at a specific point in man's developmental sequence. Nearly all children begin to use language at about the same age. Even children of different cultures and languages learn to speak at about the same time in their development.

Third, the accomplishment of language is general. Individuals learn language despite morphological and physical difficulties of many kinds, even with defects in the anatomical structures on which language depends. They also acquire at least some language even when their opportunities to learn are inadequate.

Fourth, certain language characteristics are universal. Languages in diverse cultures and even in isolated areas of the earth have much similarity in grammatical principles and other characteristics. Languages throughout the world, for example, have words for objects, words to describe qualities of things, and words to describe relationships among them. Syntax among all languages shows some similarity in formal characteristics. Any language in existence can be learned by people from even the most diverse cultures.

The Learning of Language. The communication system of language depends upon pronunciation, writing, vocabulary, and grammar; it is a ". . . formalized and traditionalized set of spoken, written, or gesticulated symbols and signs which serve to express and communicate feelings and thoughts" (Alexander, 1967). The child learns this system in five stages: (1) some response to spoken sounds of others, with an attempt at imitation; (2) experimentation with sounds and less effort toward imitation; (3) direct effort toward imitation and the repetition of speech sounds; (4) application of sounds to objects by providing labels for them (at this stage, sounds are used as a tool and a means of communication); and (5) the transition from one-word statements to combinations of words in sentences (Alexander, 1967).

These stages of learning involve much effort and many errors. Some errors come from the application of concepts and generalizations to cases that are exceptions. All large animals with four legs may be called "horses," even those which are cattle. Other errors result from treating all verbs as regular; "finded" may be used instead of "found."

Part of the difficulty in learning language is related to the irregularities in the language, usually remnants of the past. In a rapidly changing society and culture, the language changes. As new objects, experiences, and life styles emerge, so do new words and language patterns, yet older remnants remain and in some parts of the society tend to continue in prominent usage.

Modification of language, according to Alexander (1967), often is determined by the ease with which words can be transformed. He explains that in the history of English there have been two ways of changing adjectives into nouns—by adding *th* and by adding *ness*. The *th* has proved to be less viable, although the method still is used, for example, in transforming *warm* into *warmth*. The other method is used in changing *wary* into *wariness*.

In addition to learning the grammatical structure of a language, the child must perform other related tasks: (1) speaking with appropriate word fluency—an ability dependent in part on a large store of words and concepts and (2) writing in a grammatical and acceptable literary style. To achieve such goals, the child must learn relationships in addition to words. A simple word may have several meanings, and the intended meaning in a given context is revealed by the word's relationship with other words around it. The word *brook,* for example, can mean a stream of water or it can mean "endure," as in "he will brook no opposition." Sentences or groups of words are necessary to indicate meaning in complex language (Kramer, Koff, and Luria, 1972).

The child must learn further that some sentences are actional and some are attributive (Alexander, 1967). In the *actional* sentence, the verb describes the action and the nouns name the doers and objects. An example would be: "The conductor starts the train." In this sentence, the subject "conductor" is the doer, the verb "starts" describes the action, the object "train" is acted upon. In an *attributive* sentence some condition is attributed to the subject; for example, "John is the guide." In this sentence the subject is given a classification which covers a kind of activity. As Alexander points out, the types of English sentences are many, but their basic forms are centered around nouns and verbs. For the meaning of a sentence to be clear, its subject and predicate must be clear. He also describes basic word functions in four primary categories: (1) nouns or noun substitutes, (2) verbs, (3) adjectives, articles, and adverbs, and (4) prepositions and conjunctions. Thinking processes and logical analyses depend upon the relationships of these fundamental parts of language.

It is generally agreed that certain grammatical structures are common in all languages and that the child uses them when he begins to use language. The responses infants make before they learn to talk also suggest that they understand nonverbal cues, such as facial expressions, prior to speech (Fraser, Bellugi, and Brown, 1968). Children may also understand grammatical rules before they actually use them. If the child, for example, holds up his shoe and his foot and says "shoe," he understands the verb and action to be "put on my shoe."

Because variations in sentence structure are limited in the child's early speech, much of his language consists of naming objects. Probably this tendency in young children also derives in part from parental teaching. The child sees certain objects frequently—his shoe, for example—at the same time that he hears the sound of "how it is called." The parents often use only the name of the object to refer the child to it. As the child eventually masters words and the sounds of speech, however, he discovers the usefulness of extended language, as well as the satisfaction of the people around him with his achievements. The parents' expansion and transformation of words the child uses account for about one third of his language (McNeill, 1968). If the child says, "Car go," for example, a parent may respond, "Yes, the car is going." In this way the child learns to deal linguistically with objects and at the same time to use his own language as a base. The child's learning of language also includes constructing a dictionary and rules for its use, learning the phonetic principles (speech sounds), and learning the principles for using linguistic knowledge in speech and listening (McNeill, 1968).

Studies of children's language development have indicated that they have a particular or "private" language that is differentiated from universal or "public" language. Such a distinction further illustrates the complexity of the individual's development of language. Private or egocentric speech is common in early childhood in the age between four and six years; in the ensuing years it is largely absent in children engaging in logical thought processes (Kohlberg, Yaeger, and Hjertholm, 1968). In general, these investigators concluded from their findings that the child's private speech results not only from his inability to pursue logical processes without verbalizing them, but also from his inability to differentiate between talking to himself and talking to others. (See Figure 6–2.)

Children also seem to learn some word groupings better than others, particularly words in a noun-verb-noun sequence. Such a sequence is learned more easily than a sequence, for example, with the words in a noun-conjunction-noun sequence. One possible reason is that the former is a complete sentence, while the latter is a sentence fragment. Suzuki and Rohwer (1969) hypothesized that the *deep structure,* the structural meaning of the noun-verb-noun sequence, is the basis for the facilitated learning and that it assists in the storage of units of information in memory. In order to test this hypothesis, Suzuki and Rohwer placed 24 pairs of nouns in declarative sentences in the form: article-noun-verb-article-noun; for example, "The *ROCK* hit the *BOTTLE.*" A different verb was used for each sentence. A noun-conjunction-noun experimental sequence was devised by substituting *and* and *or* for the verbs, for example, "The *ROCK* or the *BOTTLE.*" The subjects were fifth-grade children and college students. They were required to memorize pairs of nouns so that when one noun was given, they could respond with the other. They were told that the nouns would be presented in a sentence, underscored and capitalized. The investigators reported that the children learned the nouns more rapidly when the noun pairs were connected by verbs than by conjunctions. The interpretation of the results indicated that the subjects were using the underlying structure of the sentences. As there were no differences in adult learning of the two sequences, the investigators suggested that possibly the adults memorized the sentences as units.

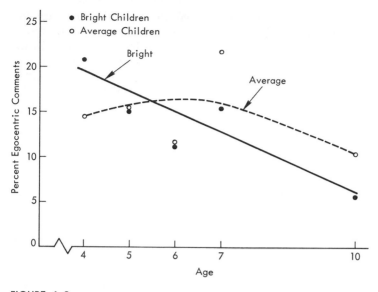

FIGURE 6–2
Trends In egocentric speech for bright and average children. Marked
decrease does not occur before age seven.
(Adapted from L. Kohlberg, J. Yaeger, and E. Hjertholm. Private
speech: Four studies and a review of theories. *Child Development,*
copyright 1968 by the Society for Research in Child Development,
Inc. 39, 691–736. By permission.)

Generalization in Environmental Interaction

A *generalization* is a statement of the main, overall fact or condition
resulting from inference applied generally to things grouped together to
form a class. Generalization grows out of sensory experience with visual,
auditory, olfactory, kinesthetic, and tactile stimuli. These stimuli must
be organized, given abstractions, and dealt with in some way; then the
experience in its totality is given a verbal label. Subsequent experiences
of a similar nature tend to elicit associations with the original experience
that invite the application of the verbal label to them as well; in this
way the generalization is extended to cover a larger category. This activity is similar to the development of a concept, since both involve the
recognition and grouping together of similar qualities.

Complexity of Response. Generalization is obviously useful in dealing
with the complexities of the environment. It increases efficiency in recog-
nizing stimuli similar to those associated with responses already stored
in memory. Old responses can be called upon and new complexities of
response developed with a reduced expenditure of energy. Some examples
of analogous functions may be found in stored programs for computers.

The machines' stored responses can be used to avoid the necessity for working out new programs, which would require much repetitive effort.

The Use of Abstractions. Involved in the complexity of generalizing is the use of abstractions. Abstractions are used to compare new stimuli with those stored in memory from past experience. The developmental sequence in the use of abstractions was studied by Al-Issa (1969). His subjects were boys ranging in age from five to ten; they were asked to define 30 words, such as *soldier, dog, orange.* The children's definitions were placed in three categories: concrete (descriptive), functional (in terms of use or function), and abstract (categorical, such as "an apple is a fruit"). The proportion of both concrete and functional responses decreased with age, while the proportion of abstract definitions increased with age. The information indicates a gradual change from concrete and functional methods of conceptualization to a higher level, that of the abstract. If, as the author suggests, the results are interpreted in Piaget's terms, it can be said that as children progress in cognitive development and reach a level of formal operations, their thinking and language processes begin to operate in a different way, they begin to use abstractions to a greater extent than they did earlier. The findings of this study thus suggest further evidence that the linguistic and cognitive processes develop concomitantly.

Response Class. Another important concept related to generalization is *response class* (Salzinger, 1967). A class of responses may have variations within it. Lever pressing is a response class, for example, but a laboratory rat may depress the experimental lever with either his left or his right paw, thus varying the response within the class. The rat depresses the lever in response to some stimulus and generalizes that either paw will suffice. Often in such experimentation, generalization from the reinforced response to other responses related to the reinforced one may indeed lead to a new response pattern or a new response class. Even the learning of language itself—which is a great help in such generalization, as verbal labels can assist in establishing connections and relationships—consists of developing classes of responses, with new reponse patterns growing out of older ones. As a result of generalization, Salzinger concludes, a person can develop responses that he has never tried before, which have thus not been reinforced, simply because they are similar to responses that were reinforced. In a way, then, responses are never entirely new, but are related to previously developed ones.

Behavioral Control. The development of generalization in the very early years was explored by Moore and Olson (1969) in their study of the effect of explicit instructions on a *behavioral prohibition.* The subjects were middle-class children of both sexes in a preschool. They were given a group of building blocks and told they could use some of the blocks, but not others. One half of the subjects were given *explicit information* about the characteristics of the forbidden blocks; they were told, for example, that in the group of blocks they would be given, the characteristics of the forbidden blocks were that they were red, with a dot on each surface. The experimenter specifically called the child's attention to the *dot* for the explicit instructions. The children were told to put these aside. The other half of the children were given *inexplicit information;* they were merely *shown* the red dotted blocks and told not to play with any such blocks. In the first group of blocks given to both groups, all of the blocks with dots were red. After the children had sorted and played with the selected blocks, all of them were given a second group of blocks; some of these had dots, but none of them were red. Because none of the second group were the same as the ones that had at first been forbidden, the children had to infer which were forbidden and thus to generalize to the new situation.

The children with the inexplicit information did not question the adequacy of their earlier judgment of the first group of blocks and sorted the second group of blocks—as they apparently had sorted the first group—on the basis of the color, red. But of the 15 children in the explicit information group, 13 eliminated the dotted blocks from the group they were to play with. The experimenters concluded ". . . that clarifying information facilitated the appropriate generalization of a prohibition in a situation in which a fine discrimination must be made between a permitted and a prohibited behavior" (Moore and Olson, 1969).

Rote Learning. Generalization may occur even in tasks that seem un-related to other cognitive tasks, for example, in the rote learning of nonsense syllables. Such tasks, however, are not entirely different from other cognitive processes. Ordinarily in a rote learning task a subject is required to memorize a list of nonsense syllables or unrelated words. Some type of previous experience nevertheless is likely to be associated with the task—not only associated meanings and similarities, but even the methods of categorizing and organizing, as well as decisions as to which types of problem-solving approach to use. Varying degrees of stim-ulus selection also occur. Perhaps similar syllables can be grouped to-gether, or chance associations may be possible. Individual variation in response patterns in such a task as rote learning may result not only from types of past experience, but also in part from available associations stored in memory.

Mediation and Motivation. Jung (1968) suggests that the term *medi-ation* be used to describe the process of using past associations to establish new associations. Association of current stimuli with stimuli in memory is basic to the mediation activity. Associations, by mediating between stimuli perceived in the confronting problem and the stored responses to similar stimuli in the past, can help develop effective responses.

Although many hold the concept of motivation to be essential in learn-ing (as motivation in learning tasks is frequently thought to be main-tained by reinforcement of successful performance), Jung asserts that the concepts of motivation and reinforcement have little interest for investi-gators of verbal learning. He seems to suggest, though, that the state of the organism and conditions relative to need fulfillment are essential for verbal behavior to occur. Jung does acknowledge some organismic conditions, particularly arousal levels, as significant in verbal learning.

The *transfer of training* also is associated with generalization. The close association of the two processes comes from the idea that the performance of one task can subsequently affect the learning of a similar task. A similar function can be ascribed to response style—one response style may be of value in new situations different from but similar to familiar ones.

Generalization is a broad concept and a fundamental one in cognitive functioning. Most broadly conceived, it can be thought of as the utilization of past experience.

ENVIRONMENTAL CHARACTERISTICS AND INTERACTIONAL PROCESSES

In order to interact effectively with his environment, the individual must know its characteristics and the principles that allow him to deal with its many systems. He must learn to make distinctions and generalizations, if he is to benefit from the experience he gains. Part of this development involves learning to use language and the various patterns of language that are related to cognitive processes. As cultural influences and social class affect linguistic and cognitive response styles, individuals of different cultural background or social class tend to use somewhat different systems of language and so to interact with their environments in dissimilar ways.

Language as a Determinant of Response Style

The difficulties of using language in interaction with the environment are illustrated, according to Luria (1968), by the "inhibitory" function of speech. A child of three years of age, asked to press a rubber bulb each time a red light appears but not to press it when a blue light is shown, is unable to carry out the task; the selection of responses is too complex for him. Even though he understands the directions and executes them at first, his sense of selectivity fades and he presses the bulb at the appearance of either light. Even though the child understands the semantic meaning of the inhibitory directive "don't press," his responses become diffuse and impulsive. Verbal directives will be effective, however, if the child is told each time a red light appears, "press," and each time a blue light appears, "don't press." Directions given with the appearance of the light are effective in producing the correct response.

That the accomplishment of self-instruction develops over the early childhood years seems apparent. If a child of three is given instructions to use his own commands of "press" for the red light and "don't press" for the blue light, his own inhibitory speech will still not keep him from pressing the button at the appearance of the blue light. Another year must pass before his own verbal directive of "don't press" produces a successful inhibitory response. In the intervening year the child develops more complex behavior in connection with his acquisition of language.

The "oral language style" of children in middle childhood was studied by Lerea and Sinclair (1968). They sought to determine whether similarity or contiguity was used more frequently by children who had difficulty articulating phonemes than by normal children. The *similarity* category was defined as those responses that consist of "naming" or "delineating," and the *contiguity* category was defined as "descriptive" and "functional" expressions. Both categories are generally used, but the study hypothesized that preferences for one type of response over the other are characteristic in verbal behavior. These investigators wished to determine whether the responses of children with functional articulation defects would depend predominantly upon similarity or contiguity.

The subjects of the study were 48 children between the ages of six and twelve assigned to three groups: (1) those with normal speech, (2) those with a functional articulation defect characterized by difficulty with one or two phonemes, and (3) those with an articulation defect consisting of three or more phoneme errors. The subjects were given the Columbia Mental Maturity Scale, a test consisting of a series of cards with various types of drawings and pictures (Burgemeister, Blum, and Lorge, 1972). Each subject was instructed to point to the picture that did not belong in the series and explain his decision. The explanations given by the subjects were categorized as based on either similarity or contiguity, according to the principles of the definitions just given. The results of the study indicated that in response to the less difficult items (cards 1 to 50) all subjects preferred explanations based on similarity. Explanations for the more difficult items (51 to 80) were more often based on contiguity than similarity. The children with articulation problems tended to give more responses in the contiguity category than did the normal group, but variance was large and the differences were not statistically significant.

Such investigations of verbal behavior, even when statistically inconclusive, contribute information about the development of response styles. Response styles developed in interaction with the environment may hinder or contribute to successful problem-solving and need fulfillment. In this study, as is sometimes found generally, a slight defect may lead an individual to a determination to meet successfully the demands of the culture; in such a case, the defect may motivate the individual to develop a more complex response style, which is an asset to his interaction with the environment. But some individuals with such a defect may be so acutely aware of it as an obstacle to effective action—or the defect may be so severe—that they become incapable of problem-solving behavior. A factor other than the defect itself may thus determine whether an individual with articulation problems develops a response style that will lead to success in environmental interaction or one that will lead to failure (Shouksmith, 1970).

By adolescence, individuals should be quite adept at the language of their culture, but the rapid changes of this period might be expected to affect linguistic development. Comparison of word usage of those at the beginning of adolescence and those nearing the end of that period was undertaken by Beier, Starkweather, and Miller (1967). These investigators sought to determine whether or not a significant and positive relationship exists among frequent occurrence of words, a small amount of variety, and shortness in length. They studied twelve- and sixteen-year-old boys to determine whether they used a larger number of different words as the frequency of occurrence became smaller and whether the magnitude or length of the words they used was inversely related to the number of occurrences of a given word. The subjects were asked to speak extemporaneously and to operate a recorder while they were speaking. About 5000 words were obtained from each subject; 2700 words were selected and placed on data-processing cards. The data were analyzed according to certain categories: *positive* words (yes, okay), *negative* words (no, never), *self-reference* words (I, me, we), and *type-token ratio* (the number of different words over the total number of words).

In an analysis of the information gathered, Beier and his fellow investigators compared the words of the subjects with "American newspaper English" and found considerable similarity. They also found that the number of different words increased as the frequency of occurrence decreased. There were, however, some differences between their data and those from "newspaper English." The spoken language of the subjects included about half as many different words as the sample of newspaper English. As words decreased in length, they also increased in frequency. Age also seemed to influence the length of words used. Among other age differences, the older subjects spoke faster, used more positive and negative words, more self-reference words, more references to others, and more question words than the younger subjects. The type-token ratio showed no differences according to age.

One of the findings of this study suggests that adolescents avoid word complexity in their speech. If verbal variety and complexity are related to complex thought processes, it would seem that, as some investigators have suggested, adolescents do not generally use their full mental potential for complex behavior.

Environmental Context and Language

The learning of language is related in part to environmental context: the child perceives objects in certain relationships that he comes to expect and ultimately deems to be appropriate. When objects appear in inappropriate or unusual settings, his response to them is either slowed or inaccurate. This slowness of response can also affect his verbalization of the experience.

Language, too, seems to be learned in an expected context. Studies have shown differences, for example, in the time individuals take to respond to color-words in unusual and in expected relationships. The word "red" printed in green requires a longer period between appearance and naming than if it were printed in red.

Context and Cognition. To study interference of unusual context with response patterns, Sichel and Chandler (1969) used color blots, congruently and incongruently colored color-words, paired combinations of color blots, and paired combinations of congruently and incongruently colored color-words. The subjects for the study were young female adults. Stimuli projected from slides onto a screen consisted of colored rectangles (red, blue, and green), congruently colored color-words (for example, the word "red" printed in red), incongruently colored color-words ("red" printed in blue or green), pairs of colored rectangles (red with blue, blue with red, and so on), pairs of congruently colored color-words ("red" printed in red and "blue" in blue), and pairs of incongruently colored color-words ("red" in green with "green" in red; "blue" in red with "green" in blue).

The time the subjects required to respond, the latency period, differed according to color for both the colored rectangles and the colored color-words. Time was shortest for response to red, next shortest for blue, and still longer for green. When color-words were shown in colors incongruent with their meaning, the time for verbal response was longer than for words congruently colored. When interference by pairing was introduced, latency time was also increased. Incongruence, the appearance of unexpected relationships, generally interfered with the verbal response. Such information suggests that language is learned in relation to objects and that its fluency and effectiveness probably depend on cultural associations in the life space.

Behavior Anomalies and Language. Context is important in certain cognitive processes, especially in making comparisons of objects and in making generalizations. The place of context and language in certain cognitive functions—in the processes of memory, discrimination, and generalization—was studied by Hagen, Winsberg, and Wolff (1968). These investigators emphasize, as has Piaget (1952), the importance of memory, particularly memory of recent experience, and, with Werner (1961), the importance of simultaneous perception of action and result, which involves the correlation of current perceptual experience with past perceptual experience stored in memory. These investigators recognized the importance to cognition of *discriminative functioning,* which enables the organism to respond to variations in environmental stimuli. They also maintained that language is necessary to memory and discrimination, in that language helps to establish memory by rehearsing the material and by transferring experience into symbols. They noted that a change in the characteristics of stimulus cues can be dealt with more efficiently if it is verbalized and that generalization is facilitated by the use of verbal symbols. Tasks of transposition—for example, choosing the larger of two objects—seemed to them to depend to a great extent on the use of language.

The study by Hagen and his associates compared children with a mental disorder with normal children on a number of language-related cognitive abilities: short-term memory, discrimination, generalization, transposition, and discrimination reversal. One group of subjects consisted of ten children with a mental disorder (psychosis) between the ages of five and eleven. The subjects in this group were ranked according to their language proficiency. Thirty normal children were used as a comparison group. Equipment for the study of transposition, discrimination, and generalization consisted of four wooden cylinders almost 3 inches in diameter and ranging in height from about an inch to about 4 inches, and a series of "three sticks" of varying length. A hole in the bottom of each item could hold candy to be found as a reward. The subjects were trained to develop the concept of *largest* by having them search for candy in the base of the *largest* cylinder or stick. The memory task used 12 different series of cards containing colored pictures of such objects as a truck, a doll, a clown, and a sailboat. The subjects were first shown the cards, which were then turned face down. The subjects next were shown a *cue* card and asked to find in the series they had seen a card similar to it. In the second session of testing, the investigators used a reversal shift in the rewarded stick; the reward was to be found in the smallest item. In the short-term memory test the cards were used as before; but as each card was shown, the experimenter pronounced the name that the subject had given for that card.

The performance of the children with mental disorder was significantly lower than that of the normal children. Language functioning and cognitive performance seemed to be related, as the investigators found that performance in the mental disorder group was related to language ability. While a number of possible reasons can be given for this relationship, the most tenable one seems to be that as the intervening factors causing overall behavioral and cognitive dysfunction varied, they also impaired the capacity for language. This does not mean that language is only a symptom, but rather—as was mentioned earlier—that it is an essential part of cognitive functioning. As individual capacities vary because of organismic deficit, so does the ability to use language. As intervening causes are ameliorated, language should improve.

Studies of this type are difficult to carry out, and often only a small number of subjects are available for them, which makes statistical analysis of dubious value. Further, to treat as a homogeneous group children who have mental disorders severe enough to be termed psychoses has apparent disadvantages, as the causes of their organismic defects can vary so much. But the study described here at least indicates that language dysfunction occurs concomitantly with cognitive malfunctioning and that the children with mental disorder were clearly differentiated in their performances of the varied tasks.

Cultural Deprivation and Language. As ameliorative programs have been established for children from poverty areas to improve their performance in the educational system, many investigators have seen the language characteristics of such children as a particularly important concern (Minuchin and Biber, 1968; Quay, 1969; Quay 1972). Because language is related to cognition, differences in linguistic characteristics might well be expected to affect children's learning of other required cultural skills and information.

Some fundamental questions need to be considered in reference to the so-called culturally deprived children, according to Baratz (1969). For example, what is the language system of children of low-income blacks? Are these children generally linguistically deficient or simply different? The answers to these questions should determine the characteristics of ameliorative programs, Baratz believes. She points out that investigations of the problem have customarily studied middle-class tasks; standard English (the language of the middle-class child) has been used as a criterion of measurement. Baratz asserts that linguistic research supports the view that the language of the low-income black child results not from failure to learn the rules of a linguistic system, but rather from the fact that he has learned different rules of language behavior. A task given to both middle-class white and low-income black children in the language of middle-class children, is not, according to Baratz, the same task for both. She planned a study based on the assumption that lower-class children learn "a well-ordered but different system" of language. She set up a study that required white children to use the black children's language as well as they did or be classified as deficient.

The subjects in the study were black children in the third and fifth grades from a center-city school and white children from a middle-class suburban school. The task consisted of a sentence repetition test containing 30 sentences, of which 15 were in standard English and 15 were in nonstandard English. Each subject was asked to repeat a sentence after hearing it twice. After the repetitions, each subject was asked to listen to other speech stimuli and select from a group of pictures of black, white, and Oriental men, women, boys, and girls a picture he believed to be that of the speaker.

The results of the study indicated that white middle-class children were significantly better than black children in the repetition of standard English sentences, whereas black children were much better than white children in the repetition of the nonstandard sentences. It was found that the black children used systematic nonstandard speech patterns when they repeated the standard sentences. The investigator concluded that the language of low-income blacks does not represent a language deficit but a difficulty in "code switching" and that the code (standard English) is not as well known to them as the nonstandard English.

The study supports the view that language is related to response style and thus to cultural norms. Each group tended to use its own interpretation of the stimuli. The results of the study reveal an example of the way behavior (in this case language) is conditioned to form a response style (the use of standard or nonstandard English), and the tendency to construct reality according to these styles (translation of nonstandard English into standard English when repeating a sentence). Whether one group or the other should be considered deficient is not crucial; the main consideration is that learned responses need to agree with group norms and the requirements of cultural roles. Such agreement is necessary if individuals are to be successful in the cultural mainstream. In reality, individuals find the role requirements easier to meet if their own response styles are in accord with cultural expectations. Although the details are not included here, Baratz also demonstrated a number of specific differences in the language of the two groups and thus provided information for ameliorative programs.

Another study of black and white children, eight to ten years of age, from low and middle socioeconomic classes, required the children to listen to uneducated and educated white women and educated and uneducated black women as they read lists of monosyllables (Eisenberg, Berlin, Dill, and Frank, 1968). The black children generally listened less attentively than the white children. Not surprisingly, the investigators found a significant relationship between the listening scores of the subjects and their ability to rearticulate the lists.

Another approach to the influence of social class on developmental and linguistic behavior was made in a study of the ability to integrate information from one sensory modality with information from another modality (Connors, Schuette, and Goldman, 1967). This study investigated the problem of cross-modal transfers, in this case from haptic (touch) to visual, and the influence of social class on such transfers. These investigators hypothesized that the performance of lower-class children would be less successful than that of middle-class children on tasks requiring intersensory communication. They felt that the poorer performance would confirm the significance of language in relating information from different sense modalities. They used an information-theory model, which described a geometric form as having a number of *stimulus dimensions* such as size, shape, and angle of orientation. They assumed that: "The amount of information for any dimension depends on the number of variations that can occur for that dimension in the total set from which the stimuli are drawn."

The subjects for the study were 80 children in kindergarten, first, third, and sixth grades; that is, twenty children at each age of five, six, nine, and twelve. One school was a lower-class school in an impoverished area of a city, and the other was an upper-middle-class school in the suburbs. Ten children were included from each of the four chosen grades in the two schools. Both sexes were equally represented. The stimuli for the study were 27 different geometric forms of varying size, shape, and angle. The shapes were arranged on an 18-inch by 24-inch panel. The subject sat facing the panel and reached into a box beneath it to feel a geometric form hidden from view. He then pointed to the similar form on the display panel. Each of the 27 forms was presented to a subject 3 times for a total of 81 trials for each subject.

The investigators found that in the transfer of information from the haptic to visual modalities, social class and age caused significant differences between the lower-class and middle-class children. Differences between social classes substantially lessened, however, by the age of six. The information from the study does not explain the reason for the disappearance of the difference between the social classes, but the experience the lower-class children gained by entering school in the first grade may be a factor.

Language Deficit and Reasoning Ability

Another investigation concerned with social class and the development of very young children under adverse conditions of poverty in an urban environment endeavored to determine the characteristics of such children's language deficit, as well as the basis for their deficiency in reasoning ability (Blank and Solomon, 1968). These investigators asserted that current ameliorative programs were not sufficiently specific and usually introduced a wide range of stimuli without concern for the causes of such deficiencies. They believed that supposedly enriching stimuli provided in a general way will not overcome individual difficulties and that children need to be involved in activity consisting of an "internal manipulation of experience." Such experience should include the "ability to organize thoughts, to reflect upon situations, to comprehend the meaning of events, and to structure behavior so as to be able to choose among alternatives." Blank and Solomon took the position that "an internal symbolic system" can best be developed through the use of language, including its complex use. They asserted that experience in merely providing labels, for example, was insufficient —children should learn to use terms and language referring to abstractions, concepts, and categories. Relative judgments about quantity and quality, as well as an ability to use complex structure in language, seemed to these investigators to be essential. Ordinarily, especially in middle-class homes, such experience is gained in interaction with adults, but children from deprived environments lack such opportunities.

On the basis of these views they developed four guidelines for their study: (1) Adequate development of language can come only with consistent guidance on an individual basis. (2) Because the child learns with some "resistance," he ". . . should not be permitted to leave a task unfinished." Further, the child should be made to meet the demands of the teacher. (3) Because frequent reinforcement is needed, each child should have tutoring for 15 to 20 minutes per day. (4) Improvement in language will enable the child to cope effectively with the disadvantages of his environment.

Certain techniques based on these assumptions were developed. The first technique was designated as *selective attention:* assistance was to be given the child to "recognize essential elements," by requiring him to attend to stimuli and objects which the teacher deemed consequential. Second, the investigators emphasized *categories of exclusion,* that is, they felt it was important that the child make decisions "within the confines set by the teacher" and that he work within a specific "frame of reference." A third technique consisted of encouragement of *imagery of future events.* It was suggested, as an example, that if a child finds a doll on a table, he should be asked: "Where would the doll be if it fell from the table?" Other similar techniques were used. The purpose of the techniques was to help the children go beyond "labeling" to the complex use of language, in order to enhance their cognitive development and increase their opportunities for success in interaction with the environment.

The subjects for the study were 22 three- and four-year-old children divided into four groups. Two of the groups were tutored individually and two were not. The children were taught individually for 15 to 50 minutes, five times a week for one group and three times a week for the other. Children in one of the untutored groups had individual sessions with the teacher but were not "specifically taught." The teacher was described as being "responsive" to the child but did not "initiate any cognitive interchange." The other untutored group was part of the regular school program.

It was reported that changes in the four groups on the Stanford-Binet Intelligence Scale were significantly different and that the gain in the tutored groups was significantly greater than in the untutored groups. No significant difference was found between the group receiving attention—that is, the group whose teacher was only "responsive" —and the group without attention. Interaction with the children on an individual basis in the teaching situation seemed to benefit them, at least in the improvement of their ability to perform the tasks of the Binet test. Interpretation of the results should be cautious, as the groups were so small that the results are statistically questionable. Even the statistical significance of the gain in IQ of the most-tutored group would be questioned by some investigators. The study does nevertheless point to an important issue and concern, the relationship of individual interaction with very young children to their learning and socialization.

Blank and Solomon take the view that the interaction must be of a "tutorial" quality in that "attention" as given one of the control groups was not sufficient to produce measurable changes. At the same time they emphasize that they encountered changes in the behavior of some of the children, particularly those who were "withdrawn" at the beginning of the study. They assert: "The most striking gains in the program were the apparent joy in learning and the feeling of mastery which the children displayed as the tutoring progressed."

While such an interpretation fits the hypotheses of the investigators, those who have worked in clinical settings with children who have had inadequate opportunities for emotional exchange with adults would hypothesize that any adult satisfaction with a child's behavior establishes an interactional cycle which would bring the same results and that the "tutoring" could be of any nature and achieve the same ends. Merely being "responsive," as in the attention or control group, could be expected to be of little consequence to a child in need of emotional exchange with an adult. Such a view would suggest that the tutoring provided a vehicle and the enthusiasm for learning resulted from the satisfaction gained in interaction with the adult.

These issues are important in understanding the socialization processes of all children, as well as in the particular goal of benefiting children from an inadequate environment in a large city (Tizard, Cooperman, Joseph, and Tizard, 1972). Such investigations as that pursued by Blank and Solomon, in conjunction with other studies of the fundamental bases for interaction between young children and adults as it occurs in clinical processes, are needed. This is not to suggest that young children cannot benefit from preschool experiences designed to help them learn abstract information and acquire skills or that such specific experiences are not also needed. But the child's fundamental needs for emotional exchange with adults cannot be discounted or masked by concern only for his development of a successful linguistic style. The child may indeed benefit much more from such specific experiences as those provided in this study, if his basic emotional needs are recognized and dealt with. A basic hypothesis of socialization seems to be at issue: A child can be socialized, tutored, or trained to develop in many directions, once a significant interactional system is established. He will learn or master what is demanded, if in the process his needs can be fulfilled.

One further hypothetical premise of the Blank and Solomon study should be discussed; that is, their view that the child should learn to make decisions within the "confines set by the teacher." In the society of the future such a view of child training may well be less valued. As the individual is allowed increasing amounts of free time away from work, and as values change and arise from more personal origins, the individual will have to make decisions *without* the confines of others. Socialization in the early years which emphasizes decision-making within a dictated framework seems to be antithetical to successful individual behavior in a complex, changing culture. In fact, many young people today are asserting their intention to make their decisions without "the confines of the teacher." If this is the trend, it would seem important to provide experiences in the early years that would be consonant with later experience.

Many young people are concerned about the current emphasis on learning and educational processes rather than on emotional needs and personal interests. They maintain that educational procedures and the direction of educational experience should grow out of personally derived goals. This concern may be in part the result of a lack of opportunities for emotional exchange in their earlier years. It may be in part the result of an insight gained from experience in the complex and impersonal educational institutions of modern society. But Blank and Solomon, although they direct attention to the importance of individual interaction for their young subjects, seem to see the interaction as derived from the goals of the teacher.

An important question today is: How can the young individual be educated or enculturated and at the same time find satisfying interactional relationships that will not lead to alienation from society in years to come?

IN PERSPECTIVE

Learning is greatly facilitated by the use of symbols, particularly linguistic symbols. Through language, a form of symbolic behavior, interaction with the environment can take place on a complex level. Information from the past, for example, can be used to deal with future projections; neither past nor future has meaning without symbolization or some form of language. Language itself can cause responses similar to those made when real objects are present or when real events occur.

Overemphasis on the importance of language in life styles in modern societies is hardly possible because complex cognitive processes are dependent to such a great extent on linguistic skills. Emotions and motivation are also dependent upon language, and these significant experiences in human behavior are inextricably involved in symbolic processes.

One of the most important ideas about language is the implications for all learning to be found in its development. Most investigators easily agree that language is of paramount importance in complex behavior, but they do not always agree about the nature of the process of learning language. A child accomplishes the singularly difficult task with little direct instruction. Language is learned with the aid of models and by individual experimentation. "Programmed learning" and "reinforcement" are not the most prominent features of the experience. It is important to note that the child learns language through his own effort and program design.

The process of this learning, the settings in which it takes place, and the use of models ought to be given consideration in relation to other learning experiences. Study is warranted because this most complicated of learning tasks in all of human behavior is learned largely without direct teaching. Observations of the process and conditions of learning can therefore be instructive to those concerned with other forms of learning.

Another important idea about language is related to social-role behavior. It has long been observed that language is of much significance in meeting role requirements. An excellent example is found in Shaw's *Pygmalion*. The idea is advanced in the story that "As a woman speaks, so is she." An essential point about the importance of appropriate role behavior is made. Even minute linguistic characteristics are of significance.

Language behavior is so much a part of a person's fixed response system that change is difficult. Speech patterns persist even though the individual makes great effort to alter them. Clues about behavior and environmental experience are easily revealed, and even though the person can engage in role behavior appropriate to a new status, if language remains inappropriate, success is unlikely.

REFERENCES

ALEXANDER, H. G. *Language and thinking*. Princeton, N. J.: D. Van Nostrand, 1967.

AL-ISSA, I. The development of word definition in children. *Journal of Genetic Psychology*, 1969, 114, 25–28.

BARATZ, J. C. A bi-dialectal task for determining language proficiency in economically disadvantaged Negro children. *Child Development*, 1969, 40, 889–901.

BEIER, E. G., STARKWEATHER, J. A., & MILLER, D. E. Analysis of word frequencies in spoken language of children. *Language and Speech*, 1967, 10, 217–227.

BLANK, M., & SOLOMON, F. A tutorial language program to develop abstract thinking in socially disadvantaged preschool children. *Child Development*, 1968, 39, 379–389.

BRAIN, R. The neurology of language. In R. C. Oldfield & J. C. Marshall (Eds.), *Language*. Baltimore, Md.: Penguin Books, 1968. Pp. 309–332.

BURGEMEISTER, B. B., BLUM, L. H., & LORGE, I. *Columbia mental maturity scale*. New York: Harcourt Brace Jovanovich, 1972.

CONNERS, C. K., SCHUETTE, C., & GOLDMAN, A. Informational analysis of intersensory communication in children of different social class. *Child Development*, 1967, 38, 251–266.

EISENBERG, L., BERLIN, C. I., DILL, A., & FRANK, S. Class and race effects on the intelligibility of monosyllables. *Child Development*, 1968, 39, 1076–1089.

FRASER, C., BELLUGI, U., & BROWN, R. Control of grammar in imitation, comprehension and production. In R. C. Oldfield & J. C. Marshall (Eds.), *Language*. Baltimore, Md.: Penguin Books, 1968. Pp. 48–69.

FRIEDLANDER, B. Z., JACOBS, A. C., DAVIS, B. B., & WETSTONE, H. E. Time-sampling analysis of infants' natural language environments in the home. *Child Development*, 1972, 43, 730–740.

FURTH, H. G. Concerning Piaget's view on thinking and symbol formation. *Child Development*, 1967, 38, 819–826.

HAGEN, J. W., WINSBERG, B. G., & WOLFF, P. Cognitive and linguistic deficits in psychotic children. *Child Development*, 1968, 39, 1103–1117.

JUNG, J. *Verbal learning.* New York: Holt, Rinehart & Winston, 1968.

KEASEY, C. B., WALSH, J. A., & MORAN, G. P. The effect of labeling as an informational social influence upon color perception. *Journal of Social Psychology,* 1969, 79, 195–202.

KOHLBERG, L., YAEGER, J., & HJERTHOLM, E. Private speech: Four studies and a review of theories. *Child Development,* 1968, 39, 691–736.

KRAMER, P. E., KOFF, E., & LURIA, Z. The development of competence in an exceptional language structure in older children and young adults. *Child Development,* 1972, 43, 121–130.

LENNEBERG, E. H. A biological perspective of language. In R. C. Oldfield & J. C. Marshall (Eds.), *Language.* Baltimore, Md.: Penguin Books, 1968. Pp. 32–47.

LEREA, L., & SINCLAIR, J. K. A preliminary study of verbal style among normal and speech defective children. *The Psychological Record,* 1968, 18, 75–80.

LOVE, J. M., & PARKER-ROBINSON, C. Children's imitation of grammatical and ungrammatical sentences. *Child Development,* 1972, 43, 309–319.

LURIA, A. R. The directive function of speech in development and dissolution, part I. In R. C. Oldfield & J. C. Marshall (Eds.), *Language.* Baltimore, Md.: Penguin Books, 1968. Pp. 70–81.

McNEILL, D. The creation of language. In R. C. Oldfield & J. C. Marshall (Eds.), *Language.* Baltimore, Md.: Penguin Books, 1968. Pp. 21–31.

MENYUK, P. Children's learning and reproduction of grammatical and nongrammatical phonological sequences. *Child Development,* 1968, 39, 849–859.

MINUCHIN, P., & BIBER, B. A child development approach to language in the preschool disadvantaged child. In M. A. Brottman (Ed.), Language remediation for the disadvantaged preschool child. *Monographs of the Society for Research in Child Development,* 1968, 33 (8, Whole No. 124). Pp. 10–18.

MOORE, S. G., & OLSON, F. The effects of explicitness of instructions on the generalization of a prohibition in young children. *Child Development,* 1969, 40, 945–949.

MUELLER, E. The maintenance of verbal exchanges between young children. *Child Development,* 1972, 43, 930–938.

PIAGET, J. *Origins of intelligence in children.* New York: International Universities Press, 1952.

QUAY, L. C. A comparison of disadvantaged Negro children on the Stanford Binet administered in standard English and the Negro dialect under two conditions of reinforcement. In T. Alexander (Ed.), *Annual report: Child Development Research Center.* Philadelphia: Temple University, 1969. Pp. 73–96.

QUAY, L. C. Negro dialect and Binet performance in severely disadvantaged black four-year-olds. *Child Development,* 1972, 43, 245–250.

SALZINGER, K. The problem of response class in verbal behavior. In K. Salzinger & S. Salzinger (Eds.), *Research in verbal behavior and some neurophysiological implications.* New York: Academic Press, 1967. Pp. 35–54.

SCRIBNER, S., & COLE, M. Effects of constrained recall training on children's performance in a verbal memory task. *Child Development,* 1972, 43, 845–857.

SHOUKSMITH, G. *Intelligence, creativity, and cognitive style.* New York: Wiley-Interscience, 1970.

SICHEL, J. L., & CHANDLER, K. A. The color-word interference test: The effects of varied color-word combinations upon verbal response latency. *The Journal of Psychology,* 1969, 72, 219–231.

SNOW, C. Mothers' speech to children learning language. *Child Development,* 1972, 43, 549–565.

SUZUKI, N., & ROHWER, W. D. Deep structure in the noun-pair learning of children and adults. *Child Development,* 1969, 40, 911–919.

TIZARD, B., COOPERMAN, O., JOSEPH, A., & TIZARD, J. Environmental effects on language development: A study of young children in long-stay residential nurseries. *Child Development,* 1972, 43, 337–358.

WERNER, H. *The comparative psychology of mental development.* New York: Science Editions, 1961.

CREATIVE
BEHAVIOR

7

Originative behavior is behavior that produces things, events, situations, or experiences that are novel, different, unique, or original. While interest in artistic or novel creations is very old, study of the process of creation either by critical examination or by scientific method is comparatively recent. Original creations, especially new products that appeal to consumers, are indeed valued by modern society. A new sports-car design may bring huge profits to an industry; a new drug may not only bring profits to man, it may even change the mores of a society; and a new scientific exploration may set the imagination of the whole world aflame. In most areas of activity in modern society there is, accordingly, a preoccupation with new ways to sell a product, to attract students to a course or institution, to entice patrons to a theater, and to persuade readers to buy or subscribe to a literary production. There are, of course, countertrends; there is resistance to change, both to individual change and to changes in society and its order.

An aspect of originality is the *uniqueness* of a product, the quality that insures that counterparts of the product are few or nonexistent. Another aspect of originality is *relativity:* if a product has qualities never "known" before, it may be impossible to perceive, because perception of a new thing is possible only in terms of past experience with known objects. If the product is unusual it may be unnoticed or deemed of little value (Anderson, 1965). As definitions of reality are culturally derived, culture determines what is to be judged creative or original.

Originality is generally viewed as an essential element of creative behavior, but some see it in broader terms. There is evidence that those who engage in creative behavior are able to tolerate ambiguity and to explore in areas of endeavor where order, relationships, and meanings are not immediately clear (Chambers, 1972). Creative individuals have a tendency to gain satisfaction in such exploration; great confidence is often displayed as people impulsively try different types of solutions, even though the solutions are not immediately successful. Further, investigators of this topic place importance on fluency in thought and action and on flexibility.

When new responses are devised, new situations are created, and further new responses or life styles may then follow. Creative behavior is far-reaching in its effects. It may not only alter the life space but (and perhaps more importantly) also transform the creator as well as his life style. Consequently, there is in creative behavior the emergence of a product accompanied by alterations in the life space; ultimately a change in the individual's life style and changes in the culture may spread from one to the other.

CHARACTERISTICS OF CREATIVITY

Because originality is felt to be rare, creative persons are considered of great value to a social organization or to society at large. However, a degree of creative behavior is encountered in most individuals; it therefore seems that true originative behavior should be considered in terms of quantity as well as quality. Creativity is a characteristic of all people, to a degree, and only certain conditions need be fulfilled for a person to be termed creative: his product, or idea, must become public and it must be considered novel and valuable (Eisner, 1967). Some believe that an essential element in the concept of creativity is that the trait be measurable, that is, that tests of it can be constructed that allow a quantitative approach to it (Anastasi and Schaefer, 1971; Cropley, 1972). Similarly it has been asserted that creativity is a dimension, a trait that can be ranked on a scale of degrees of creativity (Guilford, 1965). Although measurement and valuation of original products may sometimes be considered inappropriate to a definition of creative behavior, some judgments are nevertheless made. Even the judgment that the product is original represents an evaluation, a discrimination, and perhaps an insight.

The developmental sequence of originative behavior is significant in relation to socialization and education, as it seems reasonable to expect that as children mature, they will engage in more originative behavior (Anderson, White, and Stevens, 1969). The course of such development is not smooth, as apparently an increase in creativity takes place in the first and second grades, followed then by a decrease. The curve rises again, and decreases at the beginning of adolescence, or about the seventh grade. From the eighth grade through the tenth, the rise in creativity is slow (Torrance, 1962).

An essential characteristic of originative behavior is that it seeks new problems to solve and does not merely deal with methodology. Thus originative behavior also consists of the formulation of new hypotheses not previously tested (Bloomberg, 1971). Even though machines are now being extensively used in problem-solving, the ideas necessary to direct research effort and data processing still come from creative individuals (Reese and Parnes, 1970). It is also now recognized that general problems involving several disciplines ought to be studied together in order to discover relationships among known facts. The design for such investigations must be made by individuals capable of original thinking, people who go beyond the ordinary ways of environmental interaction (Mackworth, 1965).

Individual Abilities in Originative Behavior

Novelty and uniqueness are characteristics of life. With the exception of identical twins, no two individuals are exactly alike in their genetic determinants. Even on a cellular level, characteristics are unique on the basis of both constituency and process. In one sense, the birth of each individual is a biological original. To a degree, therefore, the life that extends before a person would be guaranteed some amount of originality even if it were possible to see development as only biologically based. When influences from the environment are taken into account, with all of their variability in the interactive process, individuality is indeed greatly enhanced.

Theoretically there are two trends in the developing individual: a trend to continue the early functional and behavioral uniqueness resulting from inheritance and developmental functioning and a conditioning of the life processes toward achieving similarity in behavior that will serve societal and cultural goals. The latter trend means that individual identity and uniqueness will be lost in conformity to social and cultural patterns. The conflict between these trends of course becomes internalized. The individual feels a need to be unique, to be valued for his own differences, his own contribution to human relationships and organizations; at the same time, he feels comforted by being one of a group, approved and accepted by his fellows through the merging of personal identity with group identity.

Socialization processes have an inherent conflict. On the one hand, there is the goal of various agents to socialize behavior to bring it into accord with cultural norms; and on the other hand, there is the concomitant desire of the person for independence and an opportunity for divergent behavior in a unique response style. The only way such conflicting trends can coexist is to mark out "spheres of influence" and areas in which individual innovative and originative behavior are acceptable. Such spheres differ for the various social roles, with some allowing much more divergence than others. There are, it is easy to observe, changes in developmental levels of tolerance of divergent behavior. Behavior acceptable at earlier stages or at younger ages may no longer be tolerated at later periods. Or, behavior not required at earlier ages may be demanded in later years. Accordingly, originative behavior is allowed within a framework of cultural demands, but at times is proscribed by written and unwritten cultural codes.

Developmentally, originative behavior is to some extent *emergent behavior* that comes into being as a result of growth and maturational processes. Although certain developmental accomplishments (such as walking) are similar among people, they are for each individual, at one point, original accomplishments. Original accomplishments, however, can be grouped under conceptual categories. For example, musical compositions or paintings in oil or watercolor can be grouped, but they may vary greatly within such categories. And, currently, there is a fluid boundary between what is considered an artistic product and what is not. *Art* seems indeed to be a broad term.

One characteristic of originative behavior is that it must be spontaneous, that is, it must emerge from the capacity or will of an individual. If it could be produced on demand, it would not be original, because it would then have to exist within the conception of the demanding authority. Then, too, as even the individual cannot know what the creative behavior will be, he must explore either in his mental processes or with some media the development of the product. This exploration is dependent on freedom of action. The young child is encouraged to explore his environment with some degree of freedom; usually he is allowed more spontaneity in the development of response patterns than when he is older. Cultural imprint is therefore less demanding on the very young child (although the demands increase rapidly). Perhaps this early freedom accounts in part for the young child's often spontaneous and divergent behavior. Because his perceptions are not so likely to be stereotyped or previously conditioned as are those of adults, his products are more likely to be novel or original.

The socialization process and cultural conditioning may proceed so strongly, however, that the child's individuality and spontaneity come to be limited. Motivation to diverge in behavior is so circumscribed that he tends to search for the correct way, the expected way, in order to continue the customary reinforcement. Novel ways are often unrewarded; they may even be punished. In this respect, socialization during the developmental years is often inimical to originative behavior.

Originality and Cognitive Processes

The creation of a new product is dependent upon certain cognitive processes. For example, an artist determines that his work will be on canvas; this decision of itself excludes work in marble, wood, or iron and even determines the dimensions of his product in several ways. Such a decision results from memory, stored information, perceptual selectivity, reinforcement, feedback, and insight. In this way, originative behavior is much like any other behavior, but perhaps it requires more complex cognitive processes, more motivation, and more of certain types of past experiences than does conventional behavior.

Intelligence and Originality. Although some believe (Getzels and Jackson, 1962) that intelligence and creativity are disparate concepts, others believe that there is a close relationship between originative behavior and intelligence. Guilford (1967a; 1967b) includes creative thinking in the concept of intelligence, but only under a broad definition. He sees the concept of intelligence as including many of the concepts discussed in Chapter 5 in reference to cognition, and he maintains that creative abilities are part of intelligence.

Guilford has created a complex model of intelligence and explains that creative outcomes are derived from the interaction of the individual with the environment. His model, he believes, provides an operational definition of the attainment of originality—behavior that is characterized by the production of unusual responses and the perception of remote connections.

Not all the model's components, mainly derived from factor analysis of test scores, can easily be defined in practical terms. The parts do provide labels for groupings of relationships among test scores. While it may be that the groupings are too constricting, the model places originative behavior within the conceptual framework of cognitive processes.

Information Processing. Those interested in information-processing techniques have also formulated some theoretical postulates. They advocate that creativity be studied by discovering the different ways in which information is sought. The extent of variety in methods used in seeking information is indicative of the degree of originality. To investigate such a conceptual approach, Karlins (1967) evaluated the effectiveness of the explanation of creativity based on information-processing concepts provided by Mednick (1962) and Schroder, Driver, and Streufert (1967). The latter's approach, as discussed in Chapter 5, stressed cognitive structure and integrative complexity. High *integrative complexity*, in contrast to low, refers to the capacity to use large numbers of perceptual categories in acquiring information about the environment. A similar approach to the study of creativity, the *associative theory* advocated by Mednick, depends upon the idea that associative or perceived elements are combined in new ways. The more remote the elements are from each other, the more creative the process of thinking. Variations from one individual to another in creative activity may result from the number of "associative elements" available. Karlins used a technique that allowed subjects a limited amount of time to solve a complex problem. They were required to learn enough about an island culture to find the "best possible way" to secure the inhabitants' approval and co-operation in building a hospital. Information was provided in the form of words or phrases on cards from which the subjects in their information search were required to obtain facts about the problem; they were then required to develop assumptions and solutions. The subjects (young male adults) were divided into four groups; two groups had high and low scores on a technique devised by Schroder and associates to indicate integrative complexity, and two had high and low scores on a technique devised by Mednick to indicate the use of associative elements. The study indicated that according to the theory of Schroder and associates, "integratively complex" subjects showed greater breadth of information search and used more categories than did "integratively simple" subjects. The "complex" subjects asked more questions and indicated more willingness to explore their environment directly, and they were less interested in information about how others dealt with the problem. No significant differences were found between the high and low subjects (differentiated by Mednick's associative creativity technique) in their behavior on the experimental task (the building of the hospital). The investigator did not conclude that the associative creative theory was untenable, but rather that there was a difference between it and Schroder's approach. He did conclude that the wide environmental exploration found in Schroder's "integratively complex" group should be related to creative interaction with the environment.

A conceptual approach that places originality in information searching about aspects of the environment should be of consequence. Increasingly, in modern and urban society, individuals must obtain a wide variety of information for solving the problems of complex existence. Originality in finding ways to gain essential or particularly appropriate information, as well as originality in relating the various kinds of information units (associative behavior), may mean the difference between satisfaction and dissatisfaction in an urban environment.

Life styles developed in less urbanized environments may necessitate considerable adaptation when the individuals are transposed to more urbanized environments. Perhaps additional attention should be given to information-search techniques both in the home and in the educational system. Experience in seeking information units necessary for complex behavior in modern society seems particularly appropriate for children from deprived sections of the city (Lake and Tedford, 1970). Such children lack ability to deal with the complex demands of the school, partly on the basis of inadequate experience; but they also are likely to lack techniques of information search.

Divergence and Convergence. In making discriminations about originative behavior, a dichotomy has been proposed that uses the terms *divergent* and *convergent* behavior (Guilford, 1967a; 1967b). Others have modified these terms and extended their definitions. Now divergent behavior is seen as growing out of thinking that is speculative and that goes beyond prosaic solutions to problems; it leads away from conformity and established patterns of thought and behavior to create different products or ideas. Convergent behavior is characterized by the use of available information and methods in solving problems; it is behavior that conforms to current thinking and response styles. Convergent behavior specifically refers to responses that lead to the accomplishment of tasks for which there is considered to be only one right answer.

A number of research workers have divided subjects into convergent and divergent groups on the basis of certain tests (Clark, Veldman, and Thorpe, 1965; Hudson, 1966). Clark and his co-workers defined divergent thinking by a composite score based on three tests developed by Guilford; they defined convergent thinking by performance on an intelligence test. Correlation between these two indicators of convergent and divergent ability showed them to be virtually independent. (The subjects were divided in both groups at the median, in order to obtain "high" and "low" groups on each ability.) Among the techniques used to study creativity was the Holtzman Inkblot Technique. The inkblots were shown to the subjects individually, and only one response to each card was required. Another technique was a word fluency test in which the subjects were asked to write as many words as possible, using certain letters such as *S* or *J*. The subjects scoring high on the divergent-thinking tests were much more fluent verbally than were those with low scores. Further, it was found that those subjects scoring high on divergent thinking tended to use larger blot areas in their responses to the inkblot test than did those low on the divergent-thinking measure. The latter predominantly used small details of the blots.

Clark and his associates concluded that they found no relationship between convergent and divergent thinking; consequently, they believed they had evidence that divergent thinking was a separate dimension of cognitive activity. They also concluded that subjects with divergent-thinking ability were more likely to use imaginative responses of a wider range when given the opportunity than were the convergent subjects. The divergent subjects could go beyond the limits set by the stimulus and still remain within the appropriateness demanded by the form of the stimulus. The investigators saw the divergent subjects as having their ideational and perceptual processes controlled but not conventional, and the fantasy of such subjects seemed to them to be "free and active."

The finding that the divergent subjects tended to use larger parts of the blot implies certain characteristic responses in interaction with the environment. Perhaps this characteristic relates to Schroder's concept of integrative complexity in that the subjects tended to relate characteristics of the stimulus and to operate within a conceptual system. This holistic tendency represents a more complex type of response than one primarily devoted to details of the stimulus. Such overall environmental interaction is likely to be at a more complex and effective level (Phillips and Torrance, 1971). More effective solutions can be reached and more difficult problems can be solved than is possible when there is a preoccupation with details. This combining capability seems to be an important principle or concept for creative activity, based as it is on the idea of perceiving relationships and creating new products out of varying stimuli and experiences. Such approaches to environmental stimuli seem to be particularly appropriate for life in complex environments.

THE RELATION OF SPACE AND TIME
TO ORIGINATIVE BEHAVIOR

An individual in his interaction with the environment molds it and is molded by it. Consequently, environmental conditions affect the extent to which he will seek novel experiences or will experiment with response styles differing from the norms of the culture. Conditions within the life space of the very young child begin to affect his exploration and experimentation, his types of learning, and his formation of percepts. Reinforced responses set a course veering toward cultural divergence or convergence. In urban and modern society, factors of wide diversity determine his ultimate response style.

Further, two conceptual approaches exist in relating *time* to originative behavior. One stems from the fact that creativity can be recognized only in retrospect—the action occurs and then is judged as to originality. Sometimes, indeed, many years elapse before recognition takes place. Second, there seems to be a sequence of behavioral units characterizing a creative production. Whether or not such a sequence really exists needs to be determined. Some research has been directed to this end.

Life Space Characteristics and Originative Behavior

Not only do new productions and differentiated response styles characterize individual change, but they also effect environmental change by altering conditions in the life space. In turn, the life space provides response to the creator or innovator, primarily in social interaction, but certainly in other diverse ways. The influencing factors of the life space are so intermeshed that differentiation between personal and environmental factors is usually veiled. Nevertheless some characteristics of the life space itself must be examined and isolated, if only in theory, in order to discover those characteristics which stimulate originative behavior.

The significance of environmental conditions is unclear, as man is biologically relatively adaptable to environmental variation, although adaptation is accomplished by his behavior rather than by any evolutionary proclivities. Man's ingenuity enables him to mediate between his needs and the environmental conditions; if it is too cold he can wear animal skins or build a shelter in order to achieve a biological adaptation. Of course, his behavior to accomplish adaptation is significantly related to possibilities for social cooperation to bring about group adaptation.

Cultural channeling of human behavior does, however, allow some individualization. Most societies provide the possibility of fulfilling individual potential in such a way that creative products can bring satisfaction and social rewards, although within limits. Each individual, to a degree, constructs significant elements of the social milieu in which he lives and, at the same time, he is affected by its totality. Through language and tools a person molds the characteristics of his surroundings and, to a varying extent, determines the effects of the life space on himself. It can be said that he can alter natural laws and the events of nature. Through the powerful accomplishment of language he can extend his experience, learn from others and, at the same time, influence them to fulfill his desires. Through language he transcends his space and time limitations to learn from another place and age.

Some characteristics of the life space provide more favorable kinds of experience for the development of originative behavior than do others. The significance of such variations can be seen in the past. About 500 B.C. outstanding achievements occurred in China, India, Palestine, and Greece. During this time unique social conditions allowed widespread opportunities for individual expression. Then there came decline. But several centuries later another great resurgence of creative endeavor occurred during the Renaissance, bringing with it the threshold of the modern age of scientific development, exploration, and the spread of knowledge (Martindale, 1966). Periods of time when creativity flourished in the past seem to have contained certain qualities such as collective or governmental efforts to encourage freedom of choice of activities. In such a context, it is of value to explore, at least in theory, some conditions in which originative behavior seems to be enhanced.

The Importance of the "Openness" of Experience. There appears to be a need for an open social order. Although "openness" varies over the age span in most cultures, more freedom seems to exist in the years of early childhood, as the young child is allowed freedom in individual pursuits to a greater extent than during later years. But empirical evidence to support or refute such judgments is lacking. From a contrasting point of view, it can be maintained that in these early years, through the impact of the culture, the child is forced into conformity by demands for control of body processes, for protection of objects, for respect for social rules in interaction, and the like. Further, it is during these years that he must accomplish the exceedingly difficult task of learning language, as well as the many tasks associated with motor skills. The reality of freedom in these early years is relative to the freedom possible in the ensuing years. Some investigators (Anderson and Anderson, 1965) see much effort by the agents of socialization to stifle originative behavior in the middle childhood and adolescent years and ask: "What is the meaning of compulsory attendance, of required courses, of core curricula, of specific assignments, of examinations, of rewards, trophies, prizes, 'honor societies,' failures, flunks and the varieties of punishment except as expressions of control?" Such control seems to be based on fear and a lack of confidence in the person over whom the control is exerted. This lack of confidence causes anxiety and a lack of motivation, leaving revolt or submission as the only alternatives for the child.

Cultural limitations arise from social interaction, personal forces, and cultural rules or mandates. But in addition there are impersonal forces, for example, the inexorable passage of time with concomitant biological manifestations in bodily change and the results of these changes on behavior. Associated with time is the irreversibility of many decisions and actions. The behavioral patterns cannot be relived, and their effects often cannot be altered; only future behavior can be altered, but the change takes place in quite different circumstances.

It is obviously possible to view child-rearing experiences in retrospect and to perceive desirable alterations in adult behavior. Anderson and Anderson maintain that parents spend the first decade of the child's life trying to restrict the child's eagerness to be free and the next decade in trying to undo the results. The Andersons also indict the educational system for providing little opportunity for the developing individual to progress beyond cultural dictates. They are opposed to intelligence testing as well as other forms of testing. They see testing as a closed system in which the individual must conform to prescribed standards if he is to be successful; only a narrow range is allowed for response variations.

The problem of determination of the range of freedom for the individual to engage in divergent behavior is complex in that cultural and social norms must be established if a social order is to exist. Social roles with limitations on these roles must be delineated: the artist must not act as a surgeon. And, social norms must provide predictability and security. Social orders could, of course, provide opportunities for a life style in which freedom for divergence could have some assurance of acceptance. Part of the problem is learning to use personal freedom in relation to freedom for society and others. Can the individual use freedom so that his behavior is not solely egocentric? At what point in development should the individual be expected to attain complex social insights and percepts? What is to be done with those who will not or cannot acquire socialized behavioral patterns? These questions represent some of the dilemmas of man in modern society.

Risk Behavior. In divergent behavior of almost any type, several risks are involved. First, as novel responses have not been tried or evaluated, success cannot be assured. Second, in addition to whatever consequences of failure are manifest, there is the possibility of social disapproval, punishment, or ridicule. Society accordingly provides a number of methods in which sanctions for exploration of a life style can be maintained. Very early, children become aware of the sanctions of the culture, and to varying extents they learn to deal with them in relation to originative behavior.

Implicit in the meaning of originative behavior is motivation to undertake unfamiliar tasks; such behavior has been termed *risk behavior*. For some individuals satisfaction is derived in undertaking tasks that

contain some risk. Associated with the desire for risk is the desire to
undertake particularly difficult tasks, tasks that involve the possibility of
dire consequences associated with failure and tasks in which failure can
be perceived by others. Some individuals commit themselves to tasks requiring persistent effort over long periods of time, as well as alteration
of response patterns or life styles.

Social conditions seem to affect the extent to which risks will be
taken, and such conditions may be a determining factor in the production
of creative objects. An investigation of social influences on risk-taking of
five-year-old children is illustrative (Torrance, 1969). Equipment consisted of bean bags and a marker indicating five distances. The experiment was preceded by a training program that included a discussion
about "difficult" and "easy" tasks. The subjects were informed that they
could make the task of throwing the bags into a wastebasket easy or
difficult by deciding about the distance they would stand from the
basket. Three conditions under which they could throw were set up: in
pairs, alone, or before the entire class. The results of the study showed
that the easiest positions were chosen when the subjects were to throw
before the *group* and *alone,* and the greatest risks were taken when the
subjects performed in pairs. When in front of the group none of the
children tried to throw to the target from the greatest distance. The
study suggests that very young children have already been conditioned
to take fewer risks when taking action before a group. Socialization influences for these children were already evident in the development of a
response style, as they were concerned about social reactions in making
choices about the difficulty of the task. If creative behavior includes risk-
ing adverse reactions from peers, these very young children had already
developed a concern that interfered with originative behavior.

As a result of social reactions, self-perceptions are formed that affect
not only risk-taking but motivation to undertake difficult tasks or to
persist in ambiguous ones. Descriptions of self-perceptions by individuals
who create original products provide information (even though of a subjective nature) on characteristics that may be significant in determining
their life style. Even though such information is self-descriptive and
therefore may reflect influences or desires rather than actual characteristics, such perceptions are likely to affect their behavior, especially in the
determination of a response style. For example, if an individual sees
himself as "confident," it would seem that this expectation for himself
would influence behavior when he perceived a situation necessitating
confidence.

Self-perception and Impulse Control. Support for the belief that views
about oneself are of consequence in originative behavior is found in a
study of creative adolescents by Schaefer (1969). The following characteristics of the adolescents were noted: a *preference for complexity* and
a bringing together of remote factors; a high degree of probability to
engage in *impulsive behavior,* combined with an interest in the novel
aspects of the environment; and a preference for *autonomous behavior*
and self-assertiveness. Creative adolescents were found to have a tendency

to engage in socially undesirable behavior and also to recognize behavioral traits or tendencies in their own life styles that apparently conflict. Nevertheless they sought to resolve these conflicts and to achieve some success in reconciliation. These traits or tendencies apparently are related to the capacity to engage in impulsive behavior, at times, to engage in behavior without weighing the consequences.

The tendency toward a lack of deliberation is seen by some investigators as related to an interest in novel experience (Maw and Maw, 1970). Such experience calls for responses that often must be derived at the moment, and in this way such behavior is related to impulse behavior. Control of impulses and reasoning about consequences are not self-imposed, but the satisfaction of the immediate experience at hand is viewed as paramount. Accordingly, new relationships may be taken into account, especially those which are social in nature. Closely allied with these tendencies are ones toward autonomy and the desire to be free of external control. Further, tendencies indicating aggressive motivation to overcome obstacles or take independent courses of action are frequently observed. Often this behavior is emulated by peers, although such emulation is not of particular importance to the idiosyncratic and creative individual. This description of behavioral patterns and perceptions is supported by the information obtained by Schaefer as the result of his study of the kinds of adjectives (through the use of the Gough Adjective Check List) that adolescents apply to themselves. In his study he divided a large number of subjects according to scores on a test of creativity (Guilford's Alternate Uses and Consequences Test); the students low on the test and teachers' judgments as to creative behavior were used as a comparison group. The creative adolescents saw themselves as creative, independent, iconoclastic, complicated, and asocial. The control subjects on the other hand saw themselves as dependable, cooperative, contented, conventional, quiet, and silent.

The study of creativity as a behavioral process or a pattern requires among other things a definition that allows objective experimentation. Further, natural conditions must be simulated. That is, the tasks in which subjects are to be creative must provide opportunities for originative behavior and the conditions must be similar to conditions under which other creative individuals can produce novel products. In considering these assumptions, a number of difficulties are at once apparent: Can tests be devised which provide a simulated creative opportunity? Do such conditions as time limits, authoritative directions, and group associations separate the test or laboratory situation from the more natural conditions? How much are motivational and emotional factors a problem in research or laboratory experimentation?

Research Methods. A test situation by definition implies a structured situation with directions and imposed limits. These implications and impositions have been seen as opposed to creative behavior by some experimenters. Based on such concerns, one study sought to differentiate between test situations and game-like situations (Kogan and Morgan, 1969). The latter were considered to be more like natural conditions than tests. The game-like context for the experimental tasks, however, did not enhance creative behavior, at least as it was defined in the study. The test context was found to enhance fluency and uniqueness. The reasoning of the investigators in undertaking the study was that the game-like context would provide relaxed and informal conditions that would foster creativity. Games, however, are like many psychological tests, in that success is relative. Consequently, one of the problems in the study was that there may not have been enough difference between the tasks of the experiment and tests. The investigators considered the possibility, too, that some individuals might be more creative on tests because of previous experience. This study illustrates some of the problems of investigating originative behavior and providing experimental conditions in artificial settings that will allow the study of creative behavior.

A different approach to the problem of studying the process of creativity was taken by the Andersons (1965). They viewed creativity in philosophical and ethical terms by asserting that creativity involved "living truthfully." The perception of truth was seen as idiosyncratic for the creative person: If truth is perceived as anyone else sees it, the perception is a conforming one and therefore is not creative. They advocated an internal criterion that emphasized that a person is what he purports to be. They also described as concomitants of such perceptions the ability to live harmoniously without concern for threats or feelings of defensiveness. The Andersons further asserted that the environment must facilitate creativity by social acceptance of the characteristics of the person and by stimulation through interaction that allows for individual differences.

The general hypotheses were that a restricting environment affecting creativity would be encountered in countries that were traditionally authoritarian and that more originative behavior would be found in democratic cultures. Additional hypotheses were that children developing in authoritarian cultures would be different in interpersonal interaction from those reared in democratic cultures; that the former would be anxious, conforming, aggressive, intolerant, and the like. The children in the democratic countries, it was hypothesized, would be spontaneous, integrative, and harmonious in their behavior.

With such a theoretical orientation, they undertook to study creativity through the use of a projective technique. One part of the technique consisted of a series of six short incomplete stories involving a social conflict, for example, a conflict between a teacher and a child. A second series included five incomplete stories, three of which indicated that an adult had made a mistake.

An example of one of the stories used in the projective technique follows:

The teacher suddenly discovers that fifty cents has disappeared from her desk. She looks up and sees that all the class are working on their arithmetic. She wonders what happened to the money and what she should do. What does the teacher do? *Finish* this story with a few sentences. Tell what happened to the money and exactly how the teacher feels and what she does.

The children from cultures considered to be authoritarian tended to see the money as stolen, while those in the democratic countries saw the money as lost. The implication of these findings is that environmental conditions and learned social percepts affect response style and in fact may epitomize personal relationships in cultural patterns. The choice of money for intercultural comparisons may have affected the results, not only from a standpoint of monetary exchange but because various teachings about the importance of money in different cultures may have affected the students' interpretations.

The Chronology of Creativity

It is seldom possible for an observer to obtain information about the creative process or to be present during the creation. Available information about the process is therefore subjective by nature; perhaps even the originator himself cannot adequately describe it. Associative thinking in the process stretches back into the creative individual's past; it is intertwined with various perceptions, connections, symbols, and feelings stored in memory, perhaps for years. The energy, perceptual reorganization, the trial-and-error responses, the insights, the failures, the discouragement, the pleasure, or the exhilaration thus are primarily known from subjective descriptions.

On the basis of such descriptions a number of stages have been advanced as characteristic of the process of problem-solving or creation. These stages are given different terms but generally consist of preparation, incubation, and evaluation. Such conceptual descriptions have not been empirically substantiated and are unlikely to be (Guilford, 1965).

A sequence of four stages has been described as the following: *preparation,* the organization of material and the desire to solve problems; *incubation,* a waiting period often characterized by frustration; *insight,* an idea accompanied by emotions related to the solving of the problem, as well as by anxiety about reaching the solution; and *verification,* the part of the process in which proof is sought and satisfaction associated with success is achieved (Haefele, 1962). It may be that such a description applies to small or limited solutions, or it may be entirely misleading. The actual production, solution, or final idea seems to be omitted from the sequence. The origin of the production may lie much earlier in experience and the description of the process and thus can better be described in terms of cognitive processes and psychoneurological functions than with Haefele's sequence. Description in terms of new associations with perceptions stored in memory, new combinations of response patterns, and similar concepts would seem to be more useful than a sequential description. While solutions may apparently come suddenly, the process actually may be of long duration, perhaps of years. Processes may vary greatly with the kind of activity as well as with individuals.

Characterization of the environmental conditions, too, has been recognized as important, so that the creative individual's relationship with his life space can be taken into account. Accordingly, all the factors already recognized as influential in the determination of behavior seem to be important in problem-solving. The utilization of environmental information within the life space is probably best categorized as the utilization of "additional experience." Additional experience may be used through memory, by which past associations with former solutions can contribute to a new solution. The formations of new connections and the alteration of ineffective perceptual sets are likely to require a period of time. The sequences of working on the problem and then putting it aside for a time make possible the establishment of new associations as well as a redirection of energy into new perceptual and conceptual systems.

An example of the operation of a sequence of stages is provided by Dreistadt's (1969) study of creative problem-solving in young adults. The subjects were divided into four groups: those who were given the problem with no aid; those who were provided with picture analogies; those who were given an incubation period; and those who were provided both pictorial analogies and an incubation period. One of the problems used in the study is shown in Figure 7–1. The subjects who had an incubation period of eight minutes were required to guess the identity of playing cards during their incubation period. Following this period they were given seven more minutes to work toward a solution of the problem. Those having the benefit of the analogy pictures and the incubation period made the best scores. The next highest scores were obtained by the subjects who were provided the analogies without the incubation period. The lowest scores were made by those subjects without the aid of either an incubation period or analogies. It seems that incubation alone did not have a significant effect on the performance of the subjects. It may be that experimental conditions did not simulate natural conditions in the way that creative people use such periods. Then, too, the same amount of time for an exploration of the problem is not likely to be equally beneficial for all subjects. The guessing of cards during the incubation period may have been a distraction, as many artists and creative persons see the incubation period as one of relaxation, idleness, and often solitude.

Common and Uncommon Behavior

One characteristic of the creative person is that he gives unusual responses in a problem situation in addition to many of the common ones. It has been suggested that an individual who lacks creative ability

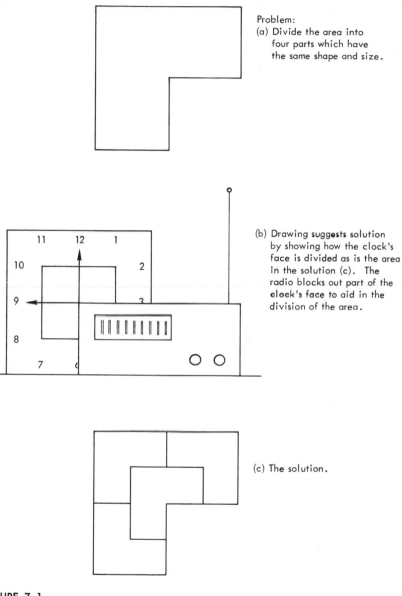

Problem:
(a) Divide the area into four parts which have the same shape and size.

(b) Drawing suggests solution by showing how the clock's face is divided as is the area in the solution (c). The radio blocks out part of the clock's face to aid in the division of the area.

(c) The solution.

FIGURE 7–1

The drawing in (b) illustrates how an analogy can aid in obtaining an insight into the problem (a) and in arriving at a solution (c).

(Adapted from R. Dreistadt. The use of analogies and incubation in obtaining insights in creative problem solving. *The Journal of Psychology,* 1969, 71, 159–175. Copyright 1969 by the Journal Press, and used by permission.)

will be likely to produce stereotyped responses and will offer few alternative responses. It is probable that the number of possible solutions
proposed to a problem decrease over time for everyone; that, at first,
there will be largely common responses with unusual ones more likely
to occur subsequently. Ward (1969) suggests that a creative individual
will differ primarily from one lacking in creativity in the following ways:
the *probability* of uncommon responses will be higher in the creative
person's productions in problem situations; the *rate* of the production
of uncommon responses will be greater; and, the *continuance* of the
production of unique responses will extend beyond the general responses
of others. These ideas come from an investigation of the differences between creative children (seven and eight years of age) and those of low
creative ability on tests modified from those developed by Wallach and
Kogan (1965). The subjects were required to provide as many ideas as
possible that would apply to a problem. The subjects' responses were
scored for "fluency" (number of ideas) and "uniqueness." The scores on
the various tests were combined to form a single index of creativity in
order to compare the *rate* and *uniqueness* curves of children designated
creative and those lacking in creativity ability. The subjects in the creative group did not produce a generally higher proportion of unique
responses, nor did they increase their proportion of unique responses in
successive opportunities. Ward suggested that it is possible that "personality" and "motivational" variables outweighed the significance of any
difference in number and richness of responses between the creative
groups and those low in creativity.

Perhaps originative behavior is a response style and should be conceptualized as a cognitive process. That is, there is the possibility that
the concepts of intelligence and creativity are insufficiently differentiated.
Then, too, the concept of motivation might well be included within the
concept of cognition and that, as was discussed in Chapter 5, cognitive
processes ultimately should be considered as a part of the holistic behavior
of the individual. The study also is illustrative of problems inherent in
the definition of originative behavior. Ward used an operational definition of *fluency* as the total number of acceptable solutions. Implicit in
such a definition is the emphasis on quantity as a characteristic of
creativity. Although such a view is tenable, it means that originative
behavior comes to be original by sheer numbers and that qualitative
characteristics are unnecessary. On the other hand, qualitative characteristics in some fields of endeavor are the basis for originative behavior.
On such a basis, objects considered to be esthetic have intrigued man
over the centuries. *Uniqueness* was operationally defined for the study
on the basis of *rarity* of the response. That is, if the response was acceptable for a possible solution and, at the same time, only one or a few
persons produced it, then it was seen as particularly creative. Of course,
one characteristic of a creative product is that it is rare; but, again in
this study esthetic qualities are not a facet of the definition and rarity is

related to quantity. It is apparent that cultural values should be included in any concept of creativity. Dependence on quantitative concepts and the absence of esthetic qualities are two aspects of the definition of creativity that are likely to vary in emphasis with variation in cultural values.

The place of originative behavior in urban society is yet to be made explicit. New ways of fulfilling needs for individuals or a society are needed to improve the quality of life and to open new doors to achievement and satisfaction. As life becomes increasingly difficult in urban environments, new life styles must emerge. Theoretical and empirical studies need to be undertaken to place originative behavior in some favorable perspective during the developmental years.

IN PERSPECTIVE

Each person has original and unique characteristics, some biological, some learned. From one point of view, then, every person is capable of original behavior, that is, original behavior is not unusual. The rather puzzling aspect of the concept of originality is that a creation must lie within a certain predetermined range if it is to be recognized or accepted. A product, for example, must be more unusual than others in existence, yet if it is too different, it will either remain unrecognized or be rejected. Creative products consequently must exist within a range of cultural tolerance.

Aside from cultural limitations other constraints exist. If examples of creative products are examined, it is usually discovered that they are related to human needs or longing. The products may be a musical score that creates a mood, a painting that causes an emotional response, or a new building design that brings a pleasant visual sensation. Emotion is an important factor in the acceptance or acknowledgment of an original product.

Originality to some extent is antithetical to conformity to rules or acceptance of standard conditions. Research workers have given attention to conditions that foster creativity. Society, its social institutions, and its agents are, however, in a dilemma in trying to encourage creativity: Individuals must be trained to conform to cultural rules, but original or different approaches must be encouraged. Hence, some conflict is involved for both the culture and the individual as he pursues paths not recommended or at least not previously approved as worthwhile. Autonomy is necessary if an individual is to create something new, yet society and its agents expend much effort to insure that the child is "shaped" by his environment in culturally approved ways. Perhaps some compromise is possible; if a wide range of choices for behavior are provided by society, an individual can pursue creative activity and thus still fulfill needs to be original within a culturally approved range.

REFERENCES

ANASTASI, A., & SCHAEFER, C. E. The Franck drawing completion test as a measure of creativity. *The Journal of Genetic Psychology,* 1971, 119, 3–12.

ANDERSON, H. E., WHITE, W. F., & STEVENS, J. C. Student creativity, intelligence, achievement, and teacher classroom behavior. *The Journal of Social Psychology,* 1969, 78, 99–107.

ANDERSON, H. H. On the meaning of creativity. In H. H. Anderson (Ed.), *Creativity in childhood and adolescence.* Palo Alto, Calif.: Science and Behavior Books, 1965. Pp. 46–61.

ANDERSON, H. H., & ANDERSON, G. L. A cross-national study of children: A study in creativity and mental health. In I. J. Gordon (Ed.), *Human development.* Chicago: Scott, Foresman, 1965. Pp. 307–315.

BLOOMBERG, M. Creativity as related to field independence and mobility. *The Journal of Genetic Psychology,* 1971, 118, 3–12.

CHAMBERS, J. A. *College teachers: Their effect on creativity of students* (Project No. 9-D-046, Grant No. OEG-4-9-190046-0057-057). Washington, D.C.: Office of Education, U. S. Department of Health, Education, and Welfare, 1972.

CLARK, C. M., VELDMAN, D. J., & THORPE, J. S. Convergent and divergent thinking abilities of talented adolescents. *Journal of Educational Psychology,* 1965, 56, 157–163.

CROPLEY, A. J. A five-year longitudinal study of the validity of creativity tests. *Developmental Psychology,* 1972, 6, 119–124.

DREISTADT, R. The use of analogies and incubation in obtaining insights in creative problem solving. *The Journal of Psychology,* 1969, 71, 159–175.

EISNER, E. W. Research in creativity: Some findings and conceptions. In H. W. Bernard & W. C. Huckins (Eds.), *Readings in human development.* Boston: Allyn & Bacon, 1967. Pp. 429–435.

GETZELS, J. W., & JACKSON, P. W. *Creativity and intelligence.* New York: Wiley, 1962.

GUILFORD, J. P. A psychometric approach to creativity. In H. H. Anderson (Ed.), *Creativity in childhood and adolescence.* Palo Alto, Calif.: Science and Behavior Books, 1965. Pp. 1–19.

GUILFORD, J. P. *The nature of human intelligence.* New York: McGraw-Hill, 1967a.

GUILFORD, J. P. Some theoretical views of creativity. In H. Helson & W. Bevan (Eds.), *Contemporary approaches to psychology.* Princeton, N.J.: Van Nostrand, 1967b. Pp. 419–459.

HAEFELE, J. W. *Creativity and innovation.* New York: Reinhold, 1962.

HUDSON, L. *Contrary imaginations.* New York: Schocken, 1966.

KARLINS, M. Conceptual complexity and remote-associative proficiency as creativity variables in a complex problem-solving task. *Journal of Personality and Social Psychology,* 1967, 6, 264–278.

KLINGER, E. *Structure and function of fantasy.* New York: Wiley, 1971.

KOGAN, N., & MORGAN, F. T. Task and motivational influences on the assessment of creative and intellective ability in children. *Genetic Psychology Monographs,* 1969, 80, 91–127.

Kogan, N., & Pankove, E. Creative ability over a five-year span. *Child Development,* 1972, 43, 427–442.

Lake, A. E., III, & Tedford, W. H., Jr. Influence of creativity on formation of subjective units. *The Journal of General Psychology,* 1970, 83, 227–237.

Macworth, N. H. Originality. *American Psychologist,* 1965, 20, 51–66.

Martindale, D. The sociology of man's creative potential. In H. A. Otto (Ed.), *Explorations in human potentialities.* Springfield, Ill.: Charles C Thomas, 1966. Pp. 36–45.

Maw, W. H., & Maw, E. W. Nature of creativity in high- and low-curiosity boys. *Developmental Psychology,* 1970, 2, 325–329.

Mednick, S. A. The associative basis of the creative process. *Psychological Review,* 1962, 69, 220–232.

Phillips, V. K., & Torrance, E. P. Divergent thinking, remote associations, and concept attainment strategies. *The Journal of Psychology,* 1971, 77, 223–228.

Reese, H. W., & Parnes, S. J. Programming creative behavior. *Child Development,* 1970, 41, 413–423.

Schaefer, C. E. The self-concept of creative adolescents. *The Journal of Psychology,* 1969, 72, 233–242.

Schroder, H. M., Driver, M. J., & Streufert, S. *Human information processing.* New York: Holt, Rinehart & Winston, 1967.

Torrance, E. P. Peer influences on preschool children's willingness to try difficult tasks. *The Journal of Psychology,* 1969, 72, 189–194.

Torrance, E. P. *Guiding creative talent.* Englewood Cliffs, N.J.: Prentice-Hall, 1962.

Wallach, M. A., & Kogan, N. *Modes of thinking in young children: A study of the creativity-intelligence distinction.* New York: Holt, Rinehart & Winston, 1965.

Ward, W. C. Rate and uniqueness in children's creative responding. *Child Development,* 1969, 40, 869–878.

Ward, W. C., Kogan, N., & Pankove, E. Incentive effects in children's creativity. *Child Development,* 1972, 43, 669–676.

EMOTIONS, MOTIVATION, AND LEARNING

IV

The concepts of emotion and motivation are abstractions that refer to essential occurrences and factors in human experience. Important characteristics of these conditions are learned; that Is, perceptual experience, set, reinforcement, memory, and other factors involved in the learning process are part of emotion and motivation.

Definitions of the terms *emotion* and *motivation* are not easily obtained, and conflicting theories and research findings indicate that present-day knowledge is inadequate for their definition. Much is known, but even more is unknown. Emotions can be described in terms of physiological changes due to them, but little meaning results from such a theoretical position. A quickened heartbeat occurs during the onset of an emotion, for example, but a similar event also occurs during exercise. Subjective qualities of emotions are still essential for a complete definition. The same reasoning applies to motivation. Hunger, a condition that leads to behavior to obtain food, involves a biochemical condition. But in human beings, the manifestation of hunger is more complex than just a biochemical state.

In the two chapters in this section, theory and research are emphasized. Some of the discussion is complex, but these are complex topics that require a background of knowledge based on theory and experimental results.

HUMAN
EMOTIONS $\qquad$ 8

Although emotional experience is an important part of everyone's life, complete understanding of the cognitive and organic processes of the experience remains beyond reach. Nor are the values associated with emotional behavior clearly established, as some people believe emotionality worthy of encouragement while others hold that emotions should be repressed. Those who value emotions maintain that emotional experience gives life meaning and variety; those who do not value them believe that socialization should insure the avoidance of emotions, which interfere, they believe, with reasonable social exchange and with problem-solving.

Many believe that emotions have a significant influence on the developing individual and that positive emotions are important motivating forces in acquiring new skills and knowledge (Plutchik, 1970). Feelings of satisfaction in accomplishment seem to be necessary for the reinforcement of socialized behavior and for the establishment of effective responses in environmental interaction. Negative feelings (depression, anger, fear, and the like) also have a function in the socialization process. Anxiety, usually a persistent negative emotion, affects social behavior by influencing the individual to conform to cultural rules. Anxiety can prove a definite disadvantage, however. With other negative emotions, it sometimes disrupts reasoning processes and problem-solving behavior and can even have a deleterious effect on body function (Lazarus, Averill, and Opton, 1970; Millon, 1969). Negative emotions are especially harmful when they cause perceptual distortion of the meaning of the behavior of others or of environmental characteristics (Bakwin and Bakwin, 1972; Rosen, Fox, and Gregory, 1972). And negative emotions often arouse antagonistic responses in other people, thus interfering with attainment of group goals and social change.

THE DEVELOPMENT OF EMOTIONAL BEHAVIOR: THEORIES AND SYSTEMS OF THOUGHT

A fundamental difficulty in understanding the emotions lies in the problem of defining them. Disagreement about definition stems from uncertainty about the respective roles of the visceral organ systems and the central nervous system. Concern about the relative importance of one over the other was evident several thousand years ago in the writings of Plato and Aristotle, who emphasized visceral activity and paid little attention to the place of the brain in the emotions. Today's questions revolve around the relative significance of the activity of the visceral organs and the brain.

Some theorists hold that *emotion* is a behavior pattern dependent on the activity of visceral organs innervated by the autonomic nervous system, that any manifestation of the experience in the brain is secondary or of little significance, and that the individual's musculature or brain may be active but is not necessarily so. In contrast, other theorists have declared that emotional experience depends primarily on the activity of the brain, with simultaneous or resulting changes in the visceral organs (Wenger, Jones, and Jones, 1962; Mirsky, 1971).

A quite different view of emotions advocated several decades ago, but still considered relevant by some theorists, is one in which the very term *emotion* is seen as useless and meaningless (Duffy, 1941). This view holds that treating emotional behavior as if it were set apart from any other response of the organism is unwarranted and that an emotion is not distinguishable from any other body condition. Those subscribing to this view believe it impossible to determine the point at which a condition of an organ system can no longer be characterized as an emotional state. Some basis for this argument exists: Although a quickened heartbeat can be considered a sign of emotion, all quickening of the heart should obviously not be viewed as a result of emotion. Emotions, such theorists as Duffy maintain, should be viewed as responses to situations perceived as having potentially favorable or unfavorable effect—responses which depend upon an individual's goals, his perceptual learning, and his response patterns acquired earlier in development. Conditions of emotion should be treated as high or low degrees of motivation, involving high or low degrees of energy expenditure. If emotional responses cannot be placed in differentiated categories and a specific condition cannot be designated an emotion, the responses are no different from the pleasantness or unpleasantness of all experience. In brief, what is usually described as an emotion is only an extreme characteristic of a response, one that is part of the individual's response pattern at any given time.

Some consideration of various theoretical points of view concerning emotion is valuable in interpreting the results of modern research studies as well as the current ideas about the place of emotions in human development. Characteristics of emotionality become especially important when large numbers of people work and live in close proximity.

The Search for the Origin of the Emotions

The James-Lange Theory. Is happiness the result of laughter, or is sadness the result of crying? Happiness *is* laughter, William James asserted. He believed that emotion followed organic condition; he maintained that visceral changes occur right after the perception of the stimulus, that awareness of the body change is, indeed, the emotion. James took the position that, if one doubted his theory, one should try to describe emotions without dealing with body sensations. If that is done, he said, a neutral and intellectual description of perception is all that is left; no "emotion" exists.

William James was a professor at Harvard who with the Danish psychologist, Lange, developed the James-Lange theory of emotions, which describes all organic changes as reflexive events resulting from a stimulus situation. Because he perceived emotions as reflex acts and because so many different types of body manifestations are apparent in the emotional state, James asserted that the categorizing of different kinds of emotions is impossible. Because the emotions of different people vary indefinitely, no typical expression of anger or fear can occur. Judgments about the usefulness of James' theoretical approach should be reserved until other theoretical viewpoints and research studies are taken into account (Chaplin and Krawiec, 1968).

Behavioristic Theory. According to behavioristic theory, origins of emotional experience are based on three innate emotions (Watson, 1929). Watson believed that emotions can be ranked on a pleasantness—unpleasantness continuum. He maintained that emotions are primarily dependent on the activity of the muscles and endocrine glands and that the origin of emotions is primarily in the sex glands (Bergmann, 1962). The three innate emotions of fear, rage, and love were thought to comprise total infant emotional experience. Watson saw several specific sources of stimuli that cause emotions in infants: for *fear,* a loud noise or the loss of support; for *rage,* the prevention of movement on being tightly held; and for *love,* the stimulation of the erogenous zones. Watson's view of emotions was soon questioned, as experimentation indicated that only when observers were aware of the kind of stimuli being applied to an infant could his categorization be correctly employed. Investigators concluded that observers projected their own perceptions into interpretation of infant behavior; that is, the observers tended to "let the response fit the stimulus."

Despite difficulties with Watson's explanations, his theory stimulated research and had significant influence on twentieth-century psychology. His views were included in other theoretical orientations, and research growing out of Watson's ideas led to the *Cannon-Bard theory of emotions* (Chaplin and Krawiec, 1968).

The Cannon-Bard Theory. The emergency theory of emotions developed by Cannon and Bard sees extreme states as readying the organism for supraordinary responses; it holds that the autonomic nervous system is responsible for emotions. According to this theory, a number of events take place upon perception of a certain stimulus complex: blood circulation changes so that blood volume is reduced around visceral organs; heart rate increases; and changes take place in hormonal activity. Epinephrine (adrenalin) poured by the adrenal glands into the bloodstream enhances the conditions brought about by the action of the autonomic nervous system. Other complicated effects of epinephrine, such as an increase in the rate of blood clotting and changes in the musculature, ensure that the body can maintain action for increased periods of time.

The central point of the Cannon-Bard theory of emotions is the emphasis on the role of the *hypothalamus,* a small area below the thalamus in the lower region of the brain. Evidence that the hypothalamus influences emotions came from the discovery that the removal of this region of an animal's brain affects its capability for emotional response and that electrical stimulation of the hypothalamus causes emotional reactions. This early work of Cannon and Bard was carried on by Delgado, Rosvold, and Looney (1956), who showed that stimulation of a portion of the hypothalamus brought about avoidance behavior in animals, and by Gelhorn (1957), who indicated that electrical stimulation of a part of the hypothalamus in cats would create a display of aggressive behavior.

Further support for the theory was obtained by removing the cortex, the outer part of an animal's brain, and finding that emotional response still occurred, although the emotion was limited or occurred without association to the stimulus. The removal of the cortex prevented perception of external stimuli and attachment of meaning to them. In essence, this thalamic theory of emotions holds that neural impulses entering the hypothalamus cause impulses to travel to the cortex and also along efferent pathways to the viscera. Meaning is given to the emotional state by the cortex, and body changes are brought about by impulses affecting the various body systems.

The essential difference between the James-Lange theory and the Cannon-Bard theory is this: the James-Lange theory holds that the emotions are dependent upon afferent impulses from the viscera to the brain, these impulses causing consciousness of the emotion; the Cannon-Bard theory views cortical and visceral action as occurring simultaneously from action of the hypothalamus in response to impulse from the receptors.

Both of these theories make contributions to an understanding of the emotions. Emphasis by James on the awareness of body conditions must be taken into account because the conditions of a rapidly beating heart, trembling limbs, and shortness of breath do come to awareness and are likely to be influential in response patterns. An essential contribution of Cannon and Bard is their assertion that emotions include *both* cognitive and visceral functions. Duffy's contention that emotional conditions are no different from any other organismic response still cannot be discounted, because subsequent research has not as yet disproved her ideas.

The work of Cannon and Bard leading to the idea of a seat of the emotions in the hypothalamus caused investigators to search for other areas of the brain as possible alternate sites of the emotions. As a result of research with improved techniques for electrical stimulation of the brain, it was found that visceral organ systems were affected by a part of the brain's cortex, the limbic portion of the forebrain. The relationship (stimulation of one area affects the other area) established between the limbic area and visceral organ functioning suggested to some investigators (originators of the Papez-MacLean theory) that this cortical area is the origin of emotional experience (Morgan, 1965). This view of emotions differed from the Cannon-Bard theory primarily in respect to the area of the brain in which emotional activity originated, as Papez and Mac-Lean saw the limbic forebrain rather than the thalamus as the emotional center. Other parts of the brain have been found to influence organic activity in the viscera, however, and a complete dependence on a limbic center for emotional experience has been questioned (Cofer and Appley, 1964; Jacobson, 1972).

Hedonistic and Activation Theories. Some theorists see the explanation of emotional experience as falling into two broad categories, the hedonistic theories and the activation theories (Cofer and Appley, 1964). Hedonistic theories suggest that human behavior is determined by pleasantness and unpleasantness or feelings usually less intense than emotions. One proponent of a hedonistic theory, Paul Thomas Young (1961), extensively studied affective processes by investigating the food preferences of rats. His studies led him to conclude that habit and palatability (characteristics of the food) are important in food selection. He saw food as capable of causing *affective arousal,* which means that responses to food occur in terms of liking or disliking in varying degrees of intensity. Evidence indicated that needed foods are generally the foods enjoyed. If affective processes are significant in food preferences, the existence of "specific hungers" as opposed to a "general hunger drive" seems to be indicated. Additional to the selection of food to fulfill nutritional requirements is relief from the stress of hunger. Such relief is accompanied by the enjoyment of food. These states of relief and enjoyment can be considered response patterns that leave some neural trace in the organism. Other explanations of these events are possible, however, as it is not necessary to see affect as associated with food preferences, because "reinforcement or a reward mechanism could explain food preferences" (Cofer and Appley, 1964).

When a person experiences a pleasant emotion, stimuli from the environment are associated with it. If at some other time these same stimuli occur, they stir up the emotion again, or at least part of it. This explanation means that indicators of activity associated with the functioning of the autonomic nervous system (for example, cardiovascular and respiratory changes) register the existence of affect but not its pleasantness or unpleasantness. This theoretical approach advanced by McClelland (1955) further holds that unlearned affect stems from situations where unexpected events occur. Expected events arouse little affect. Whether or not the affect is positive or negative depends on the size of the discrepancy between what is expected and what occurs. Small discrepancies are positive, large ones negative. Some difficulty is immediately apparent in such an idea, however. If one unexpectedly gains a fortune, this event (according to the explanation) should arouse an unpleasant emotion. The theory is based on experimentation with mild affective reactions and does not deal with turbulent emotions or drives (Cofer and Appley, 1964).

Activation theories are based on principles derived from experimental data that the efficiency of a sequence of behavior varies in accordance with the energy mobilized and the muscular response accompanying it and that functioning of the cortex is related to *arousal potential* in the brain stem (Cofer and Appley, 1964). Representatives of the activation theory are Schlosberg, Malmo, and Lindsley. A major point of emphasis in the Schlosberg (1954) view is that activation ranges on a continuum from sleep, a state of low activation, to high activity as in running or in complex problem-solving. Since emotion is a degree of activation level, research should be directed to measuring the various levels and relating them to other characteristics of behavior. Malmo (1958) emphasized the concept of an emotion as an arousal of the organism. Such arousal is related to a generalized drive. The term *generalized drive* means that although the organism is in a state of activity, the activity is not directed toward a specific goal. Hebb (1955), another activation theorist, believed that there is only one general drive or arousal condition. He believed that the condition could be brought about by the mechanisms of hunger, pain, and the like. Lindsley (1951) based his approach to a large extent on data obtained from the electroencephalogram (EEG). He found that tracings of the brain's electrical activity when an emotion was experienced showed an *activation pattern*.

Theoretical approaches such as those described in this chapter have increasingly depended on laboratory experimentation, much of it with animals. These representative theoretical systems provide a background for current research findings and indicate the significance of emotions in all of human experience.

The Freudian Explanation of Emotions

According to Freud, much behavior is determined by the *pleasure principle*. This principle, related to the life instincts, indicates that the person seeks to increase *affective* pleasure and to reduce tension or pain. Freud (1938) believed that a fundamental drive in human behavior stems from the sexual instinct and that pleasure is obtained by the reduction of tension in the sex organs. Control of the sexual instinct is based in the *ego,* interpreted to mean the "I" or the "self." The ego has as its main purpose the bringing of satisfaction (primarily sexual) within limits determined by the environment and culture.[1] Additionally, the person functions according to the *reality principle.* This principle means that the needs of the organism can be fulfilled only in terms of the reality of the environment. During the developmental years, an individual's behavior is predominantly guided by the pleasure principle, but in adult life the reality principle becomes uppermost. The trend away from an egocentric concern with pleasure to a recognition of the demands of reality brings about social behavior and the structure of social orders.

The Freudian view of emotions places anxiety into three categories. One fundamental type of anxiety is *reality anxiety* caused by threats from the life space. Associated with this basic type of anxiety are two others, neurotic anxiety and moral anxiety. *Neurotic anxiety* arises from the fear that basic instincts will overcome the control of the ego and cause behavior disapproved by the culture or the society. Such anxiety stems from fear of punishment accompanying the fulfillment of instinctual desires. It begins during the developmental years from punishment by parents and by others with power over the child.

Moral anxiety comes from the influence of the *superego* (conscience). If the superego is strong, the child will be concerned about transgressions of the moral code and will experience guilt if he even considers such transgression. Moral anxiety is part of social learning by which the child is taught that if he does something wrong, punishment will follow.

Although anxiety is not considered a pleasant state, it can serve some purpose in the individual's interaction with the environment by providing a warning of possible punishment or disaster. The warning creates a state of tension that includes some disruption of ordinary body processes. Anxiety differs from the tension of hunger in that hunger results from an internal biochemical condition, whereas anxiety is related to environmental conditions, to learning from the past, or to events that may take place in the future.

The psychoanalytic view of emotions seeks to provide a foundation

---

[1] Freud agreed that, in addition to the sexual drive, there were other drives such as the hunger drive. He grouped them all under the term *ego instincts.* These instincts have as their main goal self-preservation (Baldwin, 1967). Freud did not develop a systematic theoretical approach for an explanation of emotional experience, and he did not believe that his theory should be applied to all behavior (Bolles, 1967).

for the relationship between emotional experience and organic well-being. The relationship is illustrated by the description of the psychosomatic disorders. The origin of these disorders, as explained by neo-Freudian psychoanalysts, is in hostile impulses arising from conflict caused by the incompatibility of motives. The person with a neurosis may want to receive affection and to enjoy favorable contacts with people but may be hostile in social interaction to the point that he prevents opportunity for fulfilling his need for affection. As a result of failure, anxiety develops, and a cyclic effect is set in motion that may worsen the neurosis.

Another explanation having wide acceptance is that anxiety begins in childhood with a lack of parental affection. Usually the reason that children do not receive sufficient affection lies in the parents' incapacity to provide it because of their own difficulties. Parental rejection of their children is often hidden by behavior that masks real feelings, but children become aware of the parents' feelings despite protestations of affection and demonstrations of devotion.

The causation of psychosomatic disorders or certain types of body dysfunction is believed to be associated with prolonged anxiety. The continuing stirred-up state usually affects a specific body system. For example, if the gastrointestinal tract is affected, excess acidity results, contributing to ulceration in the stomach or duodenum. Severe conditions may even cause death. The psychoanalytic view holds that such psychosomatic disease processes of the colon as those occurring in ulcerative colitis are associated with negative emotions about the self and the environment. Children with this disease differ from normal children in the extent of their negative emotions. Such children perceive the feelings of others as negative, hostile, or depressed. When they are shown a series of ambiguous pictures of children and adults, they assign negative emotions to these neutral stimuli more often than normal children do (Alexander, 1965).

Other body systems can be affected by anxiety, especially the respiratory and cardiovascular systems. Even the function of the skin can be affected. Although some people have organic upset apparently associated with emotions, others can be emotionally disturbed and yet not have an organic system malfunction. The existence of little or no organic malfunction in some cases of emotional disturbance has suggested the possibility that in certain individuals organic propensities allow emotional states to result in organic impairment.

It may be that some causative relationship exists between certain emotional states and certain body systems. It is thought that duodenal ulcers are likely to occur in aggressive executives who strive for success in large corporations. Perhaps anxiety and fatigue combine to affect a particular organ system. Hypotheses about causative effects of anxiety and body function have not been completely established, although increasing evidence supports the contention that an important relationship between psychological or cognitive processes and abnormal body conditions does indeed exist.

The Idea of Affectional Systems

The Information from Animal Studies. The place of affection in the understanding of emotional behavior has attracted attention in recent years, as shown by a series of studies of the behavior of young monkeys (Harlow and Harlow, 1966). Substitute monkey "mothers" made of wire mesh or of wooden frames covered with rubber and terry cloth were used in the experiments. In this well-known work half of the baby monkeys were fed through the wire mothers and half through the cloth mothers, but all the monkeys preferred to spend their non-nursing time with the cloth mothers, even those fed from the wire figures. When the young monkeys were experimentally frightened, they would flee to the cloth mothers rather than to the wire mothers. As the monkeys grew older, both groups of animals developed unusual behavior and abnormal social responses, although those reared with the cloth figures had fewer abnormal responses than the other group. Abnormal behavior was reduced in the animals if they were allowed to associate with their peers. Later experimentation with different heads on the figures as well as different covers for the frames did not reveal significant differences in preference. Experimentation with different materials to cover the frames showed that the young monkeys definitely preferred cloth coverings. Variation of the temperatures of the figures showed preference for warm over cold "mothers," and movement of the figures showed preference for "rocking mothers" over stationary ones (Harlow and Suomi, 1970).

Information from these studies has been interpreted as indicating the existence of an infant-mother *affectional system* that is less variable than the system among peers or the sexual system between adults. The infant-mother affectional system is characterized by four stages: a reflex stage, a comfort and attachment stage, a security stage, and a separation stage. The reflex stage lasts for the first few weeks of life and is a time in which behavior consists of nursing and grasping. The comfort stage is essentially one of seeking fulfillment of body needs for warmth, contact, and nursing. In the security stage, the young go to the mother when they anticipate danger. In the separation stage, the young engage in interaction with others without depending on the mother.

In appraising the information gained from these studies, attributing human qualities to the relationships between the animals is a possible disadvantage. The figures were designated "mothers" by the investigators; however, such a designation may cause others to perceive the behavior of the animals on the basis of their experience with their own mothers. The information from the studies does indicate sensory differentiation and preference in these animals. If the sensory experience with the terry-cloth figure was generally more satisfying than the experience with the wire figure, it is not surprising that, when frightened, the monkeys would seek the more comforting experience. If one proceeds on a stress-reduction theoretical approach, then preference for the soft stimuli should be expected. While the studies indicate that the terry-cloth figure had significance beyond that of being a source of food, preference for it does not necessarily preclude the possibility that other drives are significant in the development of an infant-mother affectional system. If the ethological concept of *imprinting* is applied here, the infant monkeys' behavior can be said to depend on a complex sensory mechanism or instinct. Imprinting was at first defined as an emotional bond between the young and the parent, which in birds is dependent on the first moving object seen after hatching. Experiments have shown that "parent" can be a mechanical object or even human (Hess, 1968). In drawing conclusions from the studies, caution should be exercised, as affection may be a singularly human capacity.

The significance of emotions in development is supported by other animal studies. In several experiments, rats were exposed to novel three-dimensional visual, social, and tactual stimuli. They were then tested in a number of exploratory situations. In these studies, significant relationships were found between handling in infancy and the amount of exploratory behavior occurring when the animals were older. Apparently handling and other stimuli increased exploratory behavior and reduced emotional reactivity (Denenberg, 1967).

Children in Institutions. Certain studies with human subjects have some similarity to the animal experiments. In one study, a control group of infants in an institution received the ordinary amount of handling and attention, while the experimental group received 20 additional minutes each day of handling and tactual stimulation for a month after birth. The subjects were so chosen that no differences were found on the basis of a developmental test (Gesell Schedules), rate of weight gain, or general health. At 111 days of age, both groups were given a number of tests; it was found that the experimental or "handled" group engaged in significantly more visual exploration of the environment than did the group treated in the ordinary way in the institution (White and Castle, 1964).

In another study of institutional infants, tactual stimulation was used as an independent variable. The subjects were matched on Gesell scores, age, length of time in the institution, and age at time of admission. At the beginning of the study, the mean age of the infants was about 22 weeks. The experimental group received about 20 minutes of extra stimulation each day (for a 5-day week) over a 10-week period. At the end of the period, the infants were again tested with Gesell Schedules. Although the developmental quotients for the infants declined over the 10-week period, those in the nonstimulated group declined to a significantly greater extent than did those in the experimental group. This line of investigation with both animals and infants should be extended and the amount of stimulation should be varied to obtain more information concerning subsequent performance and development, especially with reference to emotional and social behavior (Casler, 1965).

Psychophysiological Approaches

The *neurophysiological theory of emotions* is based on the concept that emotional experience interrupts an ordinarily "stable configuration of neural systems" (Pribram, 1967). The theory holds that two organismic mechanisms are to be found: a mechanism that works toward stability by mobilizing subsystems in the organism to exclude disturbing stimuli and a mechanism that changes behavior in some way to deal with disturbing inputs. *Preparatory* and *participatory* processes are emphasized to bring about control over the disturbing character of emotional experience by an internal control that excludes the input or by working input into a system where it can be controlled. In such a way an internal and external system of control is achieved.

This theory differs from other approaches in several ways: it relies on the functioning of memory mechanisms instead of drives originating in the viscera. Some essential criticism has been made of this approach. The theory maintains that emotion interferes with goal-seeking and planning behavior, but it seems that emotion can also assist in goal-directed behavior. If a cat chases a rat, the cat has a plan; and the rat behaves as if he also thinks the cat has a plan (Flynn, 1967).

The functioning of the endocrine-gland system in reference to emotions has been of interest to a number of investigators. Although change in hormonal levels in emotional experience was recognized almost a half-century ago with the experiments of Cannon, capability and techniques for chemical analysis necessary for measurement of such changes have been available only in recent years (Brady, 1967).

The task of relating events in the endocrine system to subjective and cognitive experience is not easily accomplished. The significance of various levels of hormonal substances in the blood is difficult to interpret, because some amounts disappear rapidly from the blood by way of metabolism and by excretion through the kidneys (Kety, 1967). In emotional states, as was indicated earlier, substances secreted by the adrenal glands are associated with stressful situations. One product of those glands, hydrocortisone, normally circulating in the blood, has been found to be elevated in the blood of disturbed or anxious patients in hospitals. In fact, normal persons under stress have shown an increase in the secretion of hydrocortisone (Lykken, 1968).

The influence of the hormone serotonin on cognitive processes has created interest in recent years. Serotonin, secreted by the brain itself, functions in direct relationship between cognitive activity and emotional states (Woolley, 1967). Support of this view comes from experimentation that indicates that normal individuals behave similarly to people with schizophrenia when they take chemical analogs of serotonin. Other analogs sufficiently similar in chemical structure to take the place of serotonin cause excitement and agitation. Some analogs are antagonistic to serotonin and cause depression. Two synthetic analogs, psilocybin and lysergic acid diethylamide (LSD), which resemble serotonin, cause a number of specific changes in behavior. LSD induces hallucination and frequently causes extensive changes in behavior. Psilocybin, long used by natives in Yucatan, improves sight and sometimes creates a trance-like state (Woolley, 1967).

Some tranquilizing drugs cause deficiency of serotonin in the brain and the body tissues. The drug reserpine is an analog of serotonin, and its reduction of serotonin in the brain is believed to be the source of its tranquilizing effect. Chlorpromazine, another tranquilizer, combines with serotonin to prevent the use of serotonin by tissues. An increase in the serotonin can be brought about by certain drugs, and such an increase causes elation and euphoria.

A possible explanation of schizophrenia is that a serotonin synergist that is present in elevated amounts in the tissues of certain persons apparently makes tissues especially sensitive to serotonin. This responsiveness is thought to bring on mental disorder by causing a normal amount of serotonin to act with the power of an abnormally large amount. These findings need further support by extended research but do promise a valuable line of inquiry into the physiological bases of emotional experience and behavior.

EMOTIONS AND URBAN LIVING

Emotional experience has particular importance in urban living. Whether satisfaction is obtained or the stress of conditions becomes too great depends upon individual adaptive activity, the extent of social control of environmental factors, and the collective effects of the living patterns of large numbers of people occupying a relatively small amount of space. Research methodologies have been developed (with varying degrees of success) to measure individual differences in capacities to avoid or to cope with stressful stimuli and to study the effects of environmental conditions on emotional behavior. These research strategies provide essential information for educational programs and social institutions seeking to improve environmental conditions.

Emotions and the Urban Life Space

The proximity of an individual to others is to some extent related to *affect* and emotional experience. An individual tends to perceive spatial relationships in reference to others on the basis of emotional feelings. Significance of the areas of the life space is related to the individual's emotions about the people within his space. Developmental experience determines his emotions about distances as well as corresponding response styles associated with the distances. As developmental experience generally is dependent on the values and teachings of the culture, both should be significant in determining emotional experience in reference to social interaction. A basic hypothesis growing out of such concepts is that distance from others, when under control of the individual at the center, is likely to be determined by the *feeling* of the person for the others. Even the degree of acquaintance or "information input" about the "perceived others" is significant in determining the distances in interpersonal interaction. Physical closeness thus tends to coexist with closeness of affectional relationships.

Spatial Preference. A study about preferences within the life space was done by Guardo (1969) by dividing space surrounding a person into zones or "spatial spheres." Influenced by the work of Hall (1963), Guardo described the spheres as *intimate* (0–18 inches), *casual-personal* (18–48 inches), *social-consultative* (48–144 inches), and *public domain* (beyond 144 inches). His eleven- and twelve-year-old subjects from middle-class and working-class families were first required to assign the labels of "friends," "acquaintances," or "strangers" to pairs of figures (silhouettes) about 4 inches high. The children were then shown seven more silhouettes, placed at successive distances according to the intimate and casual-personal zones. Next they were required to place a silhouette representing themselves in some proximity to silhouettes labeled by the examiner. The examiner would say: "This is your best friend. Where would you be standing?" Correlations between distance and degree of liking were statistically significant. A sex difference was encountered in the findings: girls placed themselves closer to "liked" figures than the boys did and placed "feared" figures at greater distances from themselves than boys did. The findings of this study are significant in relation to other factors in interpersonal interaction: If positive affect is related to physical closeness and dislike is related to greater distance, then emotional stress should be expected when disliked people are put in close proximity. Such a hypothesis has relevance for grouping in various "spaces" of the urban environment, as individuals are likely to develop varied reaction mechanisms when they are forced into close proximity with disliked or feared persons. Because it is expected that emotions about proximity will start in infancy, the search for understanding such mechanisms should begin with studies of early life.

A fundamental assumption is that feelings about proximity stem from an *ethological-evolutionary* base; that is, they have some innate emotion. In one study in this area, emotion was defined as an "affectional tie" by one person for another which persists over time. The principal characteristic of this emotional relationship is the effort to maintain physical nearness and opportunities for social interaction and communication across distance. A very young infant indicates desire for physical closeness and contact, usually through some motor behavior or vocalization such as sucking, smiling, or crying. This behavior is developmental and evolutionary in that it changes and becomes more pronounced as the individual matures and as influences from the environment increase. Since such behavior begins very early in infancy, it can be assumed to be genetically based, a *genetic bias* that is activated or terminated by environmental events. It can be assumed, therefore, that many developmental factors modify and influence the association of affect and physical proximity.

The Significance of Early Experience. The long period of dependency in infancy makes it necessary for the infant and mother to be physically close in order that the infant can survive. To some extent, the behavior accompanying this long period is species-specific; evolution and the genetic code for the human species are of such a nature that infant care will be insured. Further, the prolonged period of dependency is linked to the behavioral complexity of the species. Because the human potential for complex learning is so great, it is apparent that prolonged existence in a learning environment ultimately contributes to the complex behavior of adulthood. As part of the genetic foundation, some sort of drive in the organism to explore the environment and to take advantage of learning opportunities also exists, and innate exploratory behavior can be expected. Even in early infancy the child seeks to extend his range of stimuli and to attain increasingly complex response patterns in ever-widening areas of the environment. Consequently, while an "attachment" of the infant to the mother occurs, an innate propensity to move away from this attachment to environmental interaction and to other relationships is also present (Ainsworth, 1969). Studies of infant activity may reveal basic principles of the biological bases for behavior and at the same time demonstrate the effect of various types of cognitive environments that facilitate or inhibit complex interaction and learning. The study of infants 49 to 51 weeks of age by Ainsworth and Bell (1970) is illustrative. Observations were made of the behavior of the infants in relation to the mother, to toys, and to the presence of an observer. Laboratory conditions were varied by the presence or absence of the mother and of the observer, whom the investigators designated as a "stranger." Observations were used as a frequency measure of exploratory activity—locomotor, manipulatory, and visual. In 3-minute episodes, intervals of 15 seconds were timed and a score of "1" given for each interval in which one of the types of behavior occurred. Crying of the infant was also scored. A second measure consisted of coding the infant's behavior in relationship to the mother's or the stranger's behavior. Four classes of behavior were rated on a 7-point scale: *proximity- and contact-seeking behavior* (approaching, reaching, and vocal signals given in reference to a specific direction); *contact-maintaining behavior* (clinging, embracing, clutching, and vocally protesting release); *proximity- and interaction-avoiding behavior* (greeting and watching at a distance; avoidance of looking at an adult, turning away, or moving away); and *contact- and interaction-resisting behavior* (attempts to push away or to strike an adult who seeks to make contact, including screaming or throwing oneself on the floor).

The laboratory room had a clear area of floor space marked in squares, a child's chair filled with toys, and chairs for the adults at opposite sides of the room. The infant was placed on the floor at the base of a triangle formed by the three chairs. In one episode the "stranger" entered, sat for a minute while talking with the mother, and then approached the infant and showed him a toy. At the end of the third minute the mother left the room and the stranger remained with the infant. In the next episode, if the infant was engaged in play, the stranger did not participate; if the child was inactive, the stranger tried to interact with him; if he was distressed, she tried to comfort him; but if she could not comfort him, the episode was terminated.

Other activity designated as *search-behavior* was scored for three of the eight episodes in the experiment. *Search-behavior* consisted of following the mother to the door, seeking to open the door, and watching the door or the mother's empty chair.

The results shown in Figure 8–1 indicate the decline of activity with the variance of the presence of the adults in the experimental episodes.

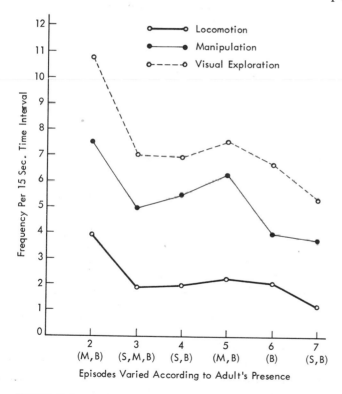

FIGURE 8–1

Incidence of exploratory behavior of one-year-old children (M = mother; B = baby; and S = stranger).

(Adapted from M. D. S. Ainsworth and S. M. Bell. Attachment, exploration, and separation: Illustrated by the behavior of one-year-olds in a strange situation. *Child Development,* copyright 1970 by the Society for Research in Child Development, Inc. 41, 49–67. By permission.)

It is clear that the presence of the mother contributed to exploratory behavior and her absence caused a reduction of exploratory behavior. Other research findings have been similar (Cox and Campbell, 1968; Rheingold, 1969). The behavior observed in the human infants when the mother was absent seems to be similar to behavior reported by investigators of separations of young monkeys from their mothers (Kaufman and Rosenblum, 1967).

From information gained in this study, Ainsworth and Bell suggest five propositions: (1) behavior is heightened or diminished by both environmental and intraorganismic conditions; (2) threatening conditions heighten attachment behavior; (3) strong attachment behavior hinders exploratory behavior, but having an opportunity for attachment and having the person present facilitates exploratory behavior; (4) attachment behavior may disappear in prolonged absence of the mother, but the attachment is not necessarily diminished; and (5) attachments vary in qualitative characteristics according to individual relationships.

Evidence seems to support the general proposition that infants prefer proximity to a specific person and that the presence of the mother contributes to or even makes possible exploratory behavior. Although the term *attachment* does not contribute to the understanding of the behavior, the existence of a generalized response pattern to a stimulus complex consisting of visual, auditory, and tactual stimuli seems to be well enough established. Perhaps the label of "attachment" masks some of the essential characteristics of the behavioral complex that have to do with biological needs, conditioned responses associated with such needs, perceptual sets growing out of experience, emotional patterns including physiological conditions in the viscera and brain, and the persistence of the sets and response patterns continuing through the developmental years. Although the response patterns are linked to the mother and to a specific life space in the early years, a transfer is gradually made to peers, and in adulthood specific attachment behavior occurs in interaction with the individual's own infant.

Affect, as described in this study in relation to the life space, may be applied to social patterns of behavior in the urban environment. It seems reasonable to expect that resistance to strangers at an early age may be continued through the developmental years and that this early conditioning may not be within personal awareness. Adult behavior in urban crowds, for example, can be compared to that of the infants in the study when the infants avoided contact with the stranger by averting their eyes or ignoring the stranger's vocal attempt for exchange.

Emotions and Cognitive Functioning

Anxiety. Some theoretical viewpoints hold that emotion, especially anxiety and fear, can have an adverse effect on problem-solving behavior and on performance in complex tasks. Although the specific processes involved in emotional interference with intellectual functioning have not been made clear, the evidence available indicates that a high level of anxiety and an inadequate performance on certain tasks occur together. Information from several studies suggests that reasoning in complex verbal tasks is more susceptible to interference by anxiety than the reasoning necessary for simpler tasks. One study of the effect of anxiety on five performance tasks carried out by children nine and eleven years of age provides an example of the studies on which current thinking is based. The performance tasks ranged from those requiring "simple association processes" to tasks requiring "complex deductive processes" (the basis of concept formation). Data about levels of anxiety were obtained from the Test Anxiety Scale for children developed by Sarason and his associates (1960). This scale depends on the subject's admission of characteristics associated with anxiety in taking tests and consists of such questions as whether the child is afraid that the teacher will ask questions about what he has learned. The results of the study showed significant negative correlations; that is, subjects scoring high on the anxiety test tended to score low on the paired associates test (a test that required matching certain words with nonsense syllables) or to score low on the anagrams test (a test in which the subjects were required to make from the one word provided as many words as possible within a given time period). These findings were supported by the results of comparison of scores obtained from school achievement tests with those of the anxiety test. The information from the study provides some practical evidence that anxiety has an adverse effect on certain types of tasks, particularly on parts of tests requiring complex verbal behavior (Stevenson and Odom, 1965).

Uncertainty in Perceptual Experience. Uncertainty, a less intense emotional state than anxiety, was the subject of another study of children in middle childhood and early adolescence (six to fifteen years old). The aim of the study was to obtain information about the capacity for dealing with complex stimuli and the capacity to respond to *uncertainty* in perceptual experience. Some individuals prefer novelty and perceptual variability, and the investigators proposed to use the preference for variability as indications of attraction to uncertainty. Because this preference was to be investigated in reference to age, the question was asked: Would younger children prefer shapes with less variability than would older children? The shapes used as stimuli, black figures on white backgrounds, were constructed so that they varied in the number of "turns" from three to forty; or, from a triangle (three turns) to a complex figure with forty turns. They were projected in pairs onto the front wall of the room in which the subjects were seated, and the subjects indicated their preference for one of the figures by marking a test booklet. Subjects of all ages preferred shapes of about ten turns. A significant finding was that younger children preferred more variability than older children. One explanation offered by the investigators (Munsinger, Kessen, and Kessen, 1968) was that the children beyond a certain level of variability did not change their responses. The subjects showed interest in "uncertainty" only up to a certain point. This and other studies suggest that preference for variability depends on the individual's capacity for response, the amount of interesting stimuli in the environment, and the cultural rules that surround the stimuli.

Although a certain amount of uncertainty, or variation in stimuli, is interesting, some kinds of "novelty" occurring in early life can apparently produce persistent anxiety; some infants have been observed to be more fearful than others. Ordinarily, fear of "visual novelty" is first observed in infants at about 6 months of age (Bronson, 1968). Such observations lead to the question: Does fear behavior observed in infancy continue into childhood and beyond? Some information in answer to this question comes from the Berkeley Growth Study at the University of California (a study of the physical and mental development of about 30 boys and 30 girls). Very young children were routinely tested for mental, motor, and physical growth and were observed as to whether the strangeness of the testing had caused them to cry. After 10 months of age, a 7-point rating scale to indicate fear was used to record "wariness" or "reserve" in the testing situation. A third measure was used to indicate the infants' level of sensitivity to "disturbing" stimuli. The amount of time an infant cried during the examination was also noted.

These children showed that individual differences in fear responses persisted over time and that the fear of novelty began between 5 and 10 months of age. Levels of fearfulness in the boys tended to remain constant from the first year through early childhood. A prediction was made that boys who developed a fear of "strangeness" earlier than others would carry fearfulness from infancy into the early childhood years. As several of the subjects were diagnosed in adulthood as having evidence of schizophrenia, their high ratings of fearfulness in infancy suggest that such extreme behavior in infancy is indicative of a potential for later pathology. Information about the girls showed that correlations of fearfulness at 10 and 15 months with ratings at older ages were low and not statistically significant. The investigator (Bronson, 1970) suggested that for males the early onset of fear indicated a predisposition toward such behavior and that it became a basis for the level of fear occurring in subsequent years; for females the first appearance of fear is determined by the infant's sensitivity to distressing stimulation and thus such behavior was more related to external influences than to an internal and persistent condition.

These suggestions are tentative, since some social-learning theorists believe that more demands of a competitive nature are made on boys and that from infancy they are treated differently from girls. Girls are given more protective care during the early years, but "risk behavior" is encouraged for boys. At the present time, corroboration is needed for such sex differences as well as for the varying effects of anxiety on cognitive development.

Research here seems relevant to urban living in that undue anxiety and stress seems to interfere with the cognitive processes and complex behavior required in urban environments. Uncertainty and complexity while of definite interest within limits can become so anxiety-producing that avoidance behavior ensues. A hypothesis might then be that the "stimulating experience" of life in the city is of value only to a limited extent. A further hypothesis might be made that some anxiety about urban living may be brought about in early childhood and persist on into the adult years. With the increasing stress of the urban environment, early anxiety may be translated into adult psychopathology.

The Expression of Emotions and Social Interaction

Although neurological and visceral processes seem to be responsible for much emotional experience, certain kinds of emotional expressiveness are *learned* in human interaction in the very earliest days of life. Emotions related to external or environmental events obviously depend upon a learned discriminative ability to distinguish between those stimuli which mean threat and those indicating comfort. Because most emotional experience takes place in association with other people, one would expect this social experience to be influenced by those responsible for the infant's care. In most instances, the young child's earliest emotional experience is associated with his mother. Through the mother's provision of food and other physical comfort, the infant is conditioned in the first months of life to respond to her presence or absence with anticipation or disappointment. As the mother is the source of certain kinds of stimuli and other people are not, the infant's discrimination and emotions that influence her behavior are steps toward influencing his own environment.

Social Discrimination. It is reasonable to assume that a basic capacity for discrimination is necessary for social interaction. Information about the beginnings of discrimination of social stimuli is important if the earliest kind of emotional behavior is to be investigated or related to the socialization process. An emotional response such as differentiation by the infant between the mother and others should be a clue to the development of this ability.

A fundamental question is apparent: At what age will the infant show an emotional reaction when the mother is no longer within his visual field? In order to obtain such information about this early discrimination of maternal presence or absence, 64 infants from 3 to 19 months were studied in a laboratory setting (Fleener and Cairns, 1970).[2] The placement of the infant, the mother, and the laboratory assistant is shown in Figure 8–2. The procedure required that the mother

---

[2] This experiment is similar to that of Ainsworth and Bell (1970) previously described. In that study the *exploratory behavior* of the infants was investigated as influenced by the presence or absence of the mother. This study is an investigation of *emotional behavior* as influenced by the presence or absence of the mother.

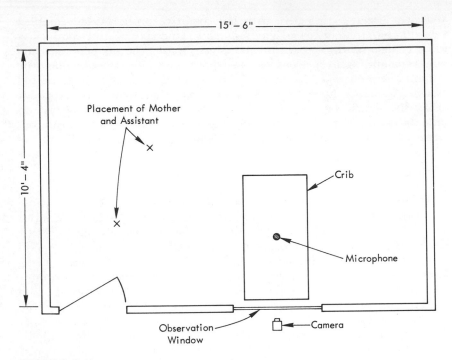

FIGURE 8–2
Dimensions of the experimental room and location of apparatus in a
study of infants' reaction to absence of mother.
(Adapted from D. E. Fleener and R. B. Cairns. Attachment behaviors in human infants: Discriminative vocalization on maternal
separation. *Developmental Psychology*, 2, 1970, 215–223. Copyright
1970 by the American Psychological Association, and reproduced by
permission.)

and the assistant remain in the room for several minutes, with the
infant in a crib. Then the mother would stand, pass by the crib, speak
to the child, and leave the room. The assistant would remain alone with
the infant for about two minutes. Following this period, the mother
would return to the room and say "hello" before seating herself. Then
the assistant would leave and return to the room in a similar way. The
sequence ended with both seated in the room. It was repeated with the
assistant as the first to leave. Data about this procedure were obtained
by means of a one-way mirror, motion picture segments, and sound
recordings. An event recorder was used to make a record of the periods
when the infant cried. The records were divided into five-second segments; if the infant cried during one segment, he was given a score of 1
and if he did not, the score was 0. The infants cried more during the
maternal absence than they did during the absence of the assistant.
Other findings indicated that the onset of crying occurred during periods

when the mother was out of the room and that a sex difference in the amounts of crying from one situation to another did not exist. The investigators concluded that children who were at least one year old showed a significant tendency to become upset when separated from the mother. Although the investigators believe that infant crying is but one aspect of a response pattern in social interaction, they did not consider the question of the normal amount of crying at an early age as part of the socialization process; for example, should an infant be allowed to "cry it out?" Neither was the question raised specifically as to whether or not some of the infants had been conditioned to tolerate separation better than others. If such conditioning had taken place, then the lack of an emotional reaction was not the result of a lack of development of a discriminative capacity.

Judgments about the desirability of early conditioning to adjust to separation will vary. Some would advocate training an infant to adjust quickly to strangers, particularly in view of the trend toward placing infants in day-care centers. Although the infant might successfully be conditioned to tolerate separation, the long-range effect could be detrimental to learning to become emotionally committed to one or a few persons. The results of the study, however, provide some information about the capacity of the infant to be aware of his social surroundings and to respond with emotion to them. Research in the area of early experiences in the socialization process is important, but it should be noted that experimentation such as this must be examined in its effect on infants. Leaving an infant in an anxious state for even the short periods maintained in this experiment could begin unfavorable conditioning. In fact the experimenters remarked about a tendency toward "persistent crying" in some instances, even when the mother returned.

The Persistence of Emotional Behavior. Do the behavioral patterns of emotional expression established in childhood persist through the developmental years? Does a child who has difficulty in social interaction, as shown by withdrawn behavior, continue to react in such a way in social situations in adolescence or adulthood? And, does the active and socially responsive child continue to behave in this way through adolescence and into adulthood? In an effort to answer these questions, data from 64 subjects in the Berkeley Guidance Study were analyzed. Ratings on dimensions of emotion ranging from *expressive—outgoing* to *reserved—withdrawn* obtained from subjects five to sixteen years of age were related to later ratings (at age thirty) ranging from *placid—controlled* to *reactive—explosive*. In both sexes "emotional expressiveness" tended to be associated with "sociability." The "expressive—outgoing" boy, for example, continued to be generally more successful in social interaction than a "reserved—withdrawn" peer. In relating the information about early development to adult behavior on the second dimension (placid—controlled versus reactive—explosive) a sex difference was found. In males, the degree of *control* of emotions tended to persist, and in females the level of emotional *reactivity* persisted. Prediction of adult behavior from early data was difficult and Bronson (1967) concluded that information used to predict adult behavior should be obtained at certain periods during the developmental years. This idea is related to a concept that emphasizes *critical periods* of development. Predictions are apparently enhanced when subjects are studied at certain periods during development and when such periods are related to the behavior to be predicted.

Although the effects of variation on the development of fear and social responsiveness have been observed in infants (Caldwell, Hersher, Lipton, Richmond, Stern, Eddy, Drachman, and Rothman, 1963; Provence and Lipton, 1962; Rheingold, 1961), deliberate alteration of infant experience to demonstrate the effects of deprivation of certain stimuli is not possible. Such experimentation with animals, however, can lead to new hypotheses and perhaps to insightful observations. An example of a study with such intentions was undertaken with young kittens (Collard, 1967). For the study, 30 kittens (five weeks old) were divided into groups of ten (six males and four females). One group was handled by different persons; a second group was handled by only one person, the experimenter; and the third group was not handled but was allowed to explore the test room for two minutes each day. The number of fear responses was determined by the number of attempts to escape when held by strangers (also by the experimenter in the case of the "one person" group). Social responses were determined by the amount of affectionate and playful behavior under three conditions: when held, when called, and when allowed to explore the experimental room. Exploratory responses were measured by the amount of play with a string.

Information from the study showed that varied experience with a number of persons tended to reduce the kittens' fear of strangers. The kittens handled by one person, however, showed more playful and social behavior than the kittens handled by several persons, and they tended to engage in more exploratory behavior than those in the other groups. The reduced level of play of the "multiple-person" group as compared with the "one-person" group suggests that play was influenced by differences in handling experiences. Apparently the "one-person" kittens became accustomed to one person and thus showed more play and social behavior than those of the other groups. The findings indicate, at least for cats, that a one-to-one relationship with a person affects emotional expressiveness, and to this extent the findings are similar to those obtained in the studies of infants in institutions.

Expectancy Sets. Evidence available from both animal and infant studies indicates that infants who have satisfying interpersonal relationships develop a perceptual set of expectancy for future satisfaction, but those who have had frustration and deprivation of opportunity for fulfilling needs tend to see many of the new stimuli in environmental interaction as holding possible dissatisfaction. As the culture is characterized by the perceptions of individuals in it, cultural norms for emotional experience grow out of individual perceptions. Hence, during the developmental years, depending upon the character of the socialization experience, some children learn to expect that new stimuli will turn out to be threatening, hostile, or depressing in some way, while other children learn to expect new stimuli to be satisfying or pleasurable. In a complex society, with all its difficulties, the question can justifiably be asked: Will children develop with a favorable or unfavorable expectation about events occurring within their life space?

One way to investigate such developmental experience is to provide ambiguous stimuli that can be interpreted by the subject either favorably or unfavorably. The individual's response to such ambiguous stimuli thus reflects emotional tendencies growing out of environmental experience. In one study of such tendencies, subjects were shown five cards, one after another, containing human figures depicted in such a way that facial expressions and body positions could be interpreted as showing either positive or negative emotional experiences. Boys and girls, five to twelve years of age, were asked to tell a story about each picture and to include what they thought the people were doing and how they felt. The responses were recorded and placed on data cards. A computer program determined the number of words used by each subject, as well as the number of key words, positive and negative (from a lexicon formulated in a previous study). The words in the lexicon were: (positive) friend, good, happy, playing, and well; (negative) fight, mad, sad, scold, and sorry.

The children's total verbal response increased with age, that is, older subjects tended to use more words in response to the cards. (See Figure 8-3.) The finding that more positive than negative words were used indicated that children increasingly perceive their environment in positive terms in spite of difficulties in the socialization process. Negative emotional responses increased very little from the early years. Some decline in total verbal response took place at nine and ten years of age and a decline in positive emotional response was found at eleven. The meaning of this variation is not immediately apparent, however. The findings suggest that for middle-class children the socialization process does not cause a tendency to see the environment as more negative than positive (Alexander, Stoyle, Roberge, and Leaverton, 1971).

The effects of various stimuli in the life space on emotional experience or expression may not always be within awareness. An experiment with subliminal perception of pleasant and unpleasant words suggests this possibility. In this study, a list of both types of words was projected by a tachistoscope onto a screen at such speed that the subjects, young adults, could not verbally identify the words. When the shutter was opened to display the words on the screen, it also started a timer which was stopped when the subject reacted by depressing a key, indicating his response as either positive or negative. The data indicated that people respond more rapidly to pleasant words than to unpleasant words, even when the words are projected so rapidly that they are below recog-

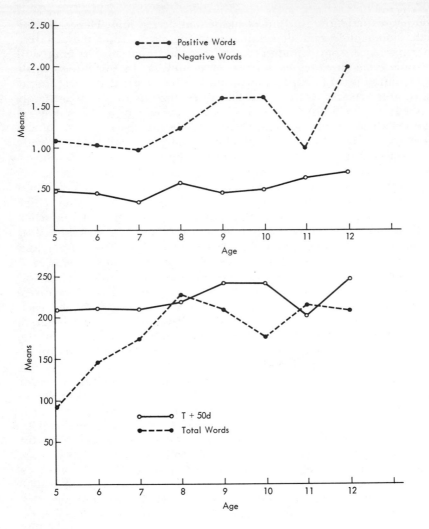

FIGURE 8–3

Adjusted means for each group for the use of positive and negative words in response to the stimuli, the adjusted means for each age group according to the formula T + 50d,* and the means for the total number of words used in response to the five pictures shown to each subject.

* (T = total number of words used in the stories of each subject; d = the algebraic difference between the positive and negative words; and 50 is a weighting factor.)

(Adapted from T. Alexander, J. Stoyle, J. Roberge, and P. Leaverton, Developmental characteristics of emotional experience. *The Journal of Genetic Psychology*, 1971, 119, 109–117. Copyright 1971 by the Journal Press, and used by permission.)

nition level (Watson, 1970). More delay in reaction time for the unpleasant than for the pleasant words showed that motor responses were influenced by perceptual experience with its meaning beyond awareness (or, when the individual's perception was subliminal). Identification or determination of the origin of emotional experience thus is not always within an individual's capacity. These findings seem to be evidence that social interaction and emotional experience are influenced by events of which the individual is not necessarily conscious and that subtle factors with emotional valences in the life space can be expected to affect judgments and responses to others as well as to events.

Expressiveness. In considering emotional expressiveness, it is important to understand that the individual is required to relate his needs to cultural demands and norms. To do this, he must make compromises between attainment of personal goals and cultural requirements. Some balance must be achieved—neglect of personal needs and satisfactions leads to a feeling of futility, and neglect of cultural expectations leads to frustration, conflict, and a lack of social approval. Emotional expressiveness can lead to fulfillment of personal needs, but it must be related to cultural norms. Normative behavior is not always clearly defined and, although youth can follow models, identification with models does not necessarily insure success or satisfaction. Socialization experience for some individuals does not help them learn to engage in the complex reasoning processes necessary for making the required compromises. Because, in a rapidly changing society, the socialization process is not always modified in relation to the changes in society, the individual at times has difficulty in making decisions about his behavior. An appropriate behavioral code in some instances is not clearly visible.

To determine the effects of the socialization process on adolescents' perception of happiness and satisfaction, Thompson and Gardner (1969) studied adolescent perceptions of "happy-successful" living. Subjects included delinquent adolescents of both sexes and other adolescents in public and parochial schools. Using an inventory the subjects were required to decide whether some specific behavior is related to the life history of a "happy-successful" person or to an "unhappy-unsuccessful" person. Items included such statements as "To finish any task that he begins" and "To treat other people with kindness and sympathy."

The investigators concluded that youths from all socioeconomic levels wished to behave in ways that would lead to "happy-successful" living. The adolescents in the study saw work and established rules of society as leading to success and happiness. The delinquent subjects showed more inclination toward dominance and aggression, whereas the non-delinquent subjects placed greater emphasis on nurturant and affiliative behavior. The investigators concluded that the goals of their adolescent subjects were generally in keeping with society's goals.

Several years have passed since this study was completed and values in American society, especially the values of young people, are changing extremely rapidly. It seems that more and more youth are rejecting society's standards. Those advocating a change in values away from the main culture have increased their influence on those who were reluctant to change.

Life Styles and Reactions to Stress in the Urban Environment

The search for understanding of the emotions is related to the search for a concept of a state of well-being and *mental health*. This latter term, as well as the terms *emotional* and *mental disorder,* reflects a common conceptual basis for visceral and cognitive processes as they affect overall functioning. Any definition of emotional health or normal psychological condition is usually controversial. Controversy results in part from the fact that "normality" and "deviance" are both relative to cultural values growing out of the role demands and moral expectations of those in the life space (Scott, 1968). Other factors in the definition are dependent upon judgments about the effectiveness of problem-solving behavior or about the causes of ineffective behavior. Such judgments may lead to the conclusion, for example, that a child who cannot learn to read has an emotional disorder that prevents him from mastering the task.

An important factor in the concept of *well-being* is a subjective one: The person must feel that he is living within the expectations of his social group and that his life style brings satisfaction not only to himself but also to those around him. This concept of an emotional state of well-being is dependent not only upon intraorganismic conditions but also upon external conditions in the life space. In recent years more attention has been given to conditions associated with complex factors in urban living, particularly stressful conditions within the city. These stress-inducing conditions have to some extent grown out of the conditions that make the city an attractive place. Many people come to the city because its activities cross the range of human experience, permitting complex esthetic, economic, and recreational life styles; stimulating social interrelationships can be established as individuals traverse common areas in organizational structures.

The city is a place of movement of people, of information, and of material. Activity begins at dawn or earlier, with the noise of trucks, the banging of garbage cans, and the rumble of trains. In a short time, activity reaches an intense level with the inrush of thousands of commuters along the thoroughfares. Desperately seeking favorable positions in the flow of traffic, they move with the realization that they have only a small range of time to reach the center of the city. Because traffic conditions foster aggressive and rule-breaking behavior, many restrictions have been devised that result in a multitude of visual and auditory stimuli that demand careful attention. Enforcers of society's regulations are stationed at frequent intervals, and even patrol the flow itself.

Thousands of people enter the city on trains, buses, subways, and surface cars. The stresses here, although different, are of comparable magnitude. Most forms of such transportation are crowded and ill-kept. For the inexperienced, finding the way is difficult. Courtesy and consideration are disregarded by most people in the pursuit of places to sit or stand. These commuters also move within an allotted time; they must catch a specific train or bus. For these people, anxiety has increased because of criminal activities on all kinds of transportation and at places of departure, transfer, and arrival. Although armed guards accompanied by dogs ride the trains and patrol the corridors of subway stations, apprehension is decreased only a little.

For thousands of people in the city, the day begins, therefore, with a period of stress. As the day advances, other sources of stress emerge from competitive activities in a setting of hurrying people working under time limitations. Added to these sources of stress are conflicts growing out of the activities of groups seeking some redress from grievances, some working advantage, or some change in a policy of an organization. As demonstrations and group activities at times lead to violent behavior, the city worker is wary about getting involved in such group activities.

Because of the close proximity, almost every individual activity necessitates planing and striving to avoid "the rush." This striving becomes a response style—a state of tension and alertness that characterizes most of the day's routine activity. At the end of the day, the mass movement of thousands begins again. The desperate quality of the rush out of the city seems no less marked at the end of the day and the struggle continues, with the lack of personal exchange now further enhanced by fatigue.

While thousands enter and leave the city daily, other thousands live and work within it. Many live in high-rise apartments overlooking parkways and attractive squares, but still more live in deteriorated areas where almost every form of pollution and every hazard to well-being exist. As successful people abandoned the center of the city to become commuters, others, less successful, took up life styles characterized by frustration and despair on both a group and individual basis. Most American cities have vast areas of deteriorating buildings facing refuse-strewn streets, where crime and violence ranging from holdups in neighborhood stores to the depredations of roving bands of hostile adolescents occur daily. Occasionally these gangs rob or kill commuters in the subways or stations.

The city is a place of contrasts. The greatest opportunities for achievement are to be found there; the most successful artists, the most learned men, the wealthiest organizations, and the most far-reaching scientific programs are all found in the city. Because the best opportunities for attainment and accomplishment offered by society are intermingled with many sources of stress, urban life contains bases for substantial conflict in the life styles of everyone. Understanding reaction to the stress of living in such an environment is important in understanding human development.

Stress may be defined as the internal condition that occurs when the individual's mechanisms and capabilities are strained or surpassed by extreme conditions of the life space or environment (Janis and Leventhal, 1968). The definition can be extended to include fearful reactions to conditions about which the individual has feelings of uncertainty. The poorly lighted passageways of the subway through which he must pass to reach his train, for example, may contain no observable cue for danger, but as he walks through them he may experience the stress of fear. Usually no specific response is necessary, because no danger is perceived. But stress arising from such environmental threats results in persistent anxiety and fatigue. The responses to stress will vary considerably among individuals. Because of a range of possible responses, a statistical concept often is used to define stress: conditions are designated as stressful if most people perceive them as threatening and anxiety-producing. Certain results of stress can be expected: abnormal cognitive and visceral conditions continue until environmental conditions are altered; responses are made in order to avoid threatening events; and cognitive processes undergo change. Environmental conditions such as those just described may change conforming behavior to nonconforming behavior. In such instances, conformity to regulations may be perceived as more dangerous than is nonconformity.

IN PERSPECTIVE

The place of emotions in human behavior is ambiguous. First, an adequate definition of emotional behavior is unavailable; second, social values of emotional characteristics are not specific or clearly explained. In regard to the first problem, theory and research have not provided enough knowledge for the understanding of the origin and manifestation of emotional behavior. In fact, available knowledge has increased the complexity of the search for understanding the emotions. As to the second problem, some people believe emotional behavior is an important part of human experience and that such behavior should not only be tolerated but encouraged. Others believe that emotions should be avoided, especially open expression of feeling.

Part of the socialization process has to do with teaching emotional control even though the standards for behavior are unclear. Generally, in this culture, emotions are to be controlled, whether pleasant or unpleasant. In organizations, it is necessary for emotion to be controlled, as overall operation of the organization can be jeopardized if too many people become anxious or disturbed. Further, the "organization man" finds that upward mobility depends upon his ability to avoid the antagonism of others.

In spite of the disadvantages in freedom of emotional expression in social exchange, satisfaction in living depends on the expression of emotions. Interaction with others holds little reward if no emotion is present. Further, the "well-springs" of human accomplishment stem from emotion.

One of the most frequently voiced complaints about modern living in large population concentrations is the lack of emotions in human interaction. That which does occur is usually negative or indifferent. Concern and compassion for others is lost in an infinite number of fleeting exchanges. Train conductors, store clerks, and taxi drivers as well as their customers have neither the time nor desire to show concern in personal contacts. Impersonal, hurried, and impatient, each person demands of the other an expected role performance and then a quick movement onward. All too often impersonality becomes part of a response style, and the urban dweller becomes lonely in a crowd.

REFERENCES

AINSWORTH, M. D. S. Object relations, dependency, and attachment: A theoretical review of the infant-mother relationship. *Child Development,* 1969, 40, 969–1025.

AINSWORTH, M. D. S., & BELL, S. M. Attachment, exploration, and separation: Illustrated by the behavior of one-year-olds in a strange situation. *Child Development,* 1970, 41, 49–67.

ALEXANDER, T. An objective study of psychological factors in ulcerative colitis in children. *The Journal-Lancet,* 1965, 85, 22–24.

ALEXANDER, T., STOYLE, J., ROBERGE, J., & LEAVERTON, P. Developmental characteristics of emotional experience. *Journal of Genetic Psychology,* 1971, 119, 109–117.

BAKWIN, H., & BAKWIN, R. M. *Behavior disorders in children.* Philadelphia: W. B. Saunders, 1972.

BALDWIN, A. L. *Theories of child development.* New York: Wiley, 1967.

BERGMANN, G. The contribution of John B. Watson. In J. M. Scher (Ed.), *Theories of the mind.* New York: Free Press, 1962. Pp. 674–688.

BOLLES, R. C. *Theories of motivation.* New York: Harper & Row, 1967.

BRADY, J. V. Emotion and the sensitivity of psycho-endocrine systems. In D. C. Glass (Ed.), *Neurophysiology and emotion.* New York: The Rockefeller University Press, 1967. Pp. 70–95.

BRONSON, G. W. The development of fear in man and other animals. *Child Development,* 1968, 39, 409–431.

BRONSON, G. W. Fear of visual novelty. *Developmental Psychology,* 1970, 2, 33–40.

BRONSON, W. C. Adult derivatives of emotional expressiveness and reactivity-control: developmental continuities from childhood to adulthood. *Child Development,* 1967, 38, 801–817.

CALDWELL, B. M., HERSHER, L., LIPTON, E. L., RICHMOND, J. B., STERN, G. A.,

EDDY, E., DRACHMAN, R., & ROTHMAN, A. Mother-infant interaction in monomatric and polymatric families. *American Journal of Orthopsychiatry,* 1963, 33, 653–664.

CASLER, L. The effects of extra tactile stimulation on a group of institutionalized infants. *Genetic Psychology Monographs,* 1965, 71, 137–175.

CHAPLIN, J. P., & KRAWIEC, T. S. *Systems and theories of psychology.* (2nd ed.). New York: Holt, Rinehart & Winston, 1968.

COFER, C. N., & APPLEY, M. H. *Motivation: Theory and research.* New York: Wiley, 1964.

COLLARD, R. R. Fear of strangers and play behavior in kittens with varied social experience. *Child Development,* 1967, 38, 877–891.

COX, F. N., & CAMPBELL, D. Young children in a new situation with and without their mothers. *Child Development,* 1968, 39, 123–131.

DELGADO, J. M. R., ROSVOLD, H. E., & LOONEY, E. Evoking conditioned fear by electrical stimulation of subcortical structures in the monkey brain. *Journal of Comparative and Physiological Psychology,* 1956, 49, 373–380.

DENENBERG, V. H. Stimulation in infancy, emotional reactivity, and exploratory behavior. In D. C. Glass (Ed.), *Neurophysiology and emotion.* New York: The Rockefeller University Press, 1967. Pp. 161–190.

DUFFY, E. An explanation of "emotional" phenomena without the use of the concept "emotion." In D. K. Candland (Ed.), *Emotion: Bodily change.* Princeton, N.J.: Van Nostrand, 1962. Pp. 22–34. (Originally 1941.)

FLEENER, D. E., & CAIRNS, R. B. Attachment behaviors in human infants: discriminative vocalization on maternal separation. *Developmental Psychology,* 1970, 2, 215–223.

FLYNN, J. P. The neural basis of aggression in cats In D. C. Glass (Ed.), *Neurophysiology and emotion.* New York: The Rockefeller University Press, 1967. Pp. 40–60.

FREUD, S. (A. A. Brill, Ed.) *The basic writings of Sigmund Freud.* (Translated and edited, with an introduction by A. A. Brill. New York: Modern Library, 1938.

GELHORN, E. *Autonomic imbalance and the hypothalamus.* Minneapolis: University of Minneapolis Press, 1957.

GUARDO, C. J. Personal space in children. *Child Development,* 1969, 40, 143–151.

HALL, E. T. A system for the notation of proxemic behavior. *American Anthropologist,* 1963, 65, 1003–1026.

HARLOW, H. F., & HARLOW, M. Learning to love. *American Scientist,* 1966, 54, 244–272.

HARLOW, H. F., & SUOMI, S. J. Nature of love—simplified. *American Psychologist,* 1970, 25, 161–168.

HEBB, D. O. Drives and C. N. S. (Conceptual nervous system). *Psychological Review,* 1955, 62, 243–254.

HESS, E. H. Imprinting in birds. In N. S. Endler, L. R. Boulter, & H. Osser (Eds.), *Contemporary issues in developmental psychology.* New York: Holt, Rinehart & Winston, 1968. Pp. 163–180.

JACOBSON, J. Emotional brain. In B. A. Curtis, S. Jacobson, & E. M. Marcus (Eds.), *An introduction to the neurosciences.* Philadelphia: W. B. Saunders, 1972. Pp. 429–436.

JANIS, I. L., & LEVENTHAL, H. Human reaction to stress. In E. F. Borgatta & W. W. Lambert (Eds.), *Handbook of personality theory and research*. Chicago: Rand McNally, 1968. Pp. 1041–1085.

KAUFMAN, I. C., & ROSENBLUM, L. A. Depression in infant monkeys separated from their mothers. *Science,* 1967, 155, 1030–1031.

KETY, S. S. Psycho-endocrine systems and emotion: Biological aspects. In D. C. Glass (Ed.), *Neurophysiology and emotion*. New York: The Rockefeller University Press, 1967. Pp. 103–108.

LAZARUS, R. S., AVERILL, J. R., & OPTON, E. M., JR. Towards a cognitive theory of emotion. In M. B. Arnold (Ed.), *Feelings and emotions*. New York: Academic Press, 1970. Pp. 207–232.

LINDSLEY, D. B. *Emotion*. In S. S. Stevens (Ed.), *Handbook of experimental psychology*. New York: Wiley, 1951. Pp. 473–516.

LYKKEN, D. T. Neuropsychology and psychophysiology in personality research. In E. F. Borgatta & W. W. Lambert (Eds.), *Handbook of personality theory and research*. Chicago: Rand McNally, 1968. Pp. 413–509.

MALMO, R. B. Measurement of drive: An unsolved problem. In M. R. Jones (Ed.), *Nebraska symposium on motivation*. Lincoln, Nebraska: University of Nebraska Press, 1958. Pp. 229–265.

McCLELLAND, D. C. Notes for a revised theory of motivation. In D. C. McClelland (Ed.), *Studies in motivation*. New York: Appleton-Century-Crofts, 1955. Pp. 226–234.

MILLON, T. *Modern psychopathology: A biosocial approach to maladaptive learning and functioning*. Philadelphia: W. B. Saunders, 1969.

MIRSKY, A. F. Drive and emotional behavior. In N. B. Talbot, J. Kagan, & L. Eisenberg (Eds.), *Behavioral science in pediatric medicine*. Philadelphia: W. B. Saunders, 1971. Pp. 127–135.

MORGAN, C. T. *Physiological psychology*. New York: McGraw-Hill, 1965.

MUNSINGER, H., KESSEN, W., & KESSEN, M. L. Age and uncertainty: Developmental variation in preference for variability. In N. S. Endler, L. R. Boulter, & H. Osser (Eds.), *Contemporary issues in developmental psychology*. New York: Holt, Rinehart & Winston, 1968. Pp. 319–328.

PLUTCHIK, R. Emotions, evolution, and adaptive processes. In M. B. Arnold (Ed.), *Feelings and emotions*. New York: Academic Press, 1970. Pp. 3–24.

PRIBRAM, K. H. Emotion: Steps toward a neurological theory. In D. C. Glass (Ed.), *Neurophysiology and emotion*. New York: The Rockefeller University Press, 1967. Pp. 3–40.

PROVENCE, S., & LIPTON, R. C. *Infants in institutions*. New York: International Universities Press, 1962.

RHEINGOLD, H. L. The effect of environmental stimulation upon social and exploratory behavior in the human infant. In B. M. Foss (Ed.), *Determinants of infant behavior*. New York: Wiley, 1961. Pp. 143–177.

RHEINGOLD, H. L. The effect of a strange environment on the behavior of infants. In B. M. Foss (Ed.), *Determinants of infant behavior* IV. London: Methuen, 1969. Pp. 137–166.

ROSEN, E., FOX, R. E., & GREGORY, I. *Abnormal psychology*. Philadelphia: W. B. Saunders, 1972.

SARASON, S. B., DAVIDSON, K. S., LIGHTHALL, F. F., WAITE, R. R., & RUEBUSH, B. K. *Anxiety in elementary school children*. New York: Wiley, 1960.

SCHLOSBERG, H. Three dimensions of emotion. *Psychological Review,* 1954, 61, 81–88.

SCOTT, W. A. Conceptions of normality. In E. F. Borgatta & W. W. Lambert (Eds.), *Handbook of personality theory and research.* Chicago: Rand McNally, 1968. Pp. 974–1006.

STEVENSON, H. W., & ODOM, R. D. The relation of anxiety to children's performance on learning and problem-solving tasks. *Child Development,* 1965, 36, 1003–1012.

THOMPSON, G. G., & GARDNER, E. F. Adolescents' perceptions of happy-successful living. *The Journal of Genetic Psychology,* 1969, 115, 107–120.

VAN DEN DAELE, L. D. Modification of infant state by treatment in a rockerbox. *The Journal of Psychology,* 1970, 74, 161–165.

WATSON, G. B. Motor response latency as an indicator of subliminal affective stimulation. *The Journal of General Psychology,* 1970, 82, 139–143.

WATSON, J. B. Psychology from the standpoint of a behaviorist. (3rd ed.). Philadelphia: Lippincott, 1929.

WENGER, M. A., JONES, F. N., & JONES, M. H. *Emotional behavior.* In D. K. Candland (Ed.), *Emotion: Bodily change.* Princeton, N.J.: Van Nostrand, 1962. Pp. 3–10.

WHITE, B. L., & CASTLE, P. W. Visual exploratory behavior following postnatal handling of human infants. *Perceptual and Motor Skills,* 1964, 18, 497–502.

WOOLLEY, D. W. Involvement of the hormone serotonin in emotion and mind. In D. C. Glass (Ed.), *Neurophysiology and emotion.* New York: The Rockefeller University Press, 1967. Pp. 108–116.

YOUNG, P. T. *Motivation and emotion: A survey of the determinants of human and animal activity.* New York: Wiley, 1961.

MOTIVATION AND ACHIEVEMENT IN URBAN SOCIETY AND CULTURE

9

Why do men work at arduous tasks to create a product or strive for long periods of time to attain some position? While the origins of such behavior stem primarily from man's innate characteristics and his learning in family interaction, they also lie in conditions in the society and culture. In the search for understanding man's perseverance toward goals, his basic nature is often questioned. Is man basically "good"—concerned about the welfare of his fellows, unselfish, responsible, cooperative, devoted, emotionally stable, affectionate, insightful, and progressive? Or, is he basically bad—hostile, self-serving, dishonest, emotionally unstable, and destructive? A student of human behavior will be influenced by the point of view he holds. If man is born good, then any problems that arise in development come from the environment and attention must therefore be given to external influences in order to insure that they do not interfere with favorable growth and achievement. If man is believed to be basically bad, control and careful teaching must insure that some badness does not survive. The task of socialization will be much greater if man is naturally bad. If he is born neither good nor bad, experience in his life space will determine his destiny; he must be taught to be a human being and dealing with him is somewhat easier than if he is born bad.

Because man's nature is closely linked to environmental control and influence, a rapidly changing society acts as both a cause and an effect in altering human behavior. Change in society causes change in individuals; and when individuals alter their life styles and goals, the change affects the society. A good society exists only when good individuals comprise it; a bad society cannot exist with a majority of good individuals. Those who characterize a society as "sick" presumably mean that most individuals in it have some degree of psychopathology. They see themselves as exceptions and as capable of making judgments about the pathology of the many. Since a definition of pathology is difficult to formulate and normative behavior is difficult to determine, such an assertion has doubtful validity.

MOTIVATION AND SOCIETAL CHARACTERISTICS

The goals of individuals in society vary because of their biological characteristics and learning experiences, but similarity in goals grows out of the social context, which reflects cultural norms. The accomplishment of tasks leading to the attainment of social goals clearly brings satisfaction to the individual and possibly social rewards and approval. Most individuals place value on achievement in an occupational role, although increasing numbers of youth are rejecting the achievement-oriented society. Some youth do not wish to expend the effort required to prepare for complex and highly technical roles. They voice resentment because competitive effort is expected of them and the difficulties in the attainment of cultural goals have been masked; they are uncertain that their work will bring success. Thus they question the traditional emphasis on the importance of occupational achievement (Williams, 1969).

Values about work and achievement are therefore changing, and those values prevalent during the days of the frontier no longer seem to serve. Performance quality at work and the value of work are questioned, although such values earlier in American history were a part of the moral code. What are some of the forces changing the attitudes toward work? Several hypotheses are possible. First, occupational roles have become diverse, and standards equally applicable to different roles are difficult if not impossible to find. This lack of consistency in standards leads to confusion in the distribution of organizational and social rewards—some workers receive recognition for certain behavior (personal diplomacy, for example) rather than accomplishment in company-assigned tasks. Others, seeing this happen, are less inclined to follow the old values of long and persistent effort toward a distant goal, for example, a responsible and high-paying position.

A second factor in changing values is the new attitude toward money. In the first half of the twentieth century money became the symbol of personal worth; its accumulation was the result of accomplishment, and it came to be desirable in itself, although the manner in which it was acquired became less significant. Money came to mean status in the society. But as money becomes generally available, it has little value as a symbol of high status. American society moved from adherence to the value of work and accomplishment to that of acquisition of money. It seems now to be moving toward values other than money.

A third basis for change lies in organizational activities toward achievement. In the "age of big business" at the beginning of the century, the worker was seen as oppressed, but through organizations (unions) he was given wage increases, better working conditions, and many social safeguards. These were not gained directly by individual or occupational achievement but through negotiation by the group. The individual worker came to feel that his progress and success depended as much on the organization that represented his interests as on his own work.

A fourth factor in change was the development of mass production and the loss of individual fulfillment in the creation of products. As machines became associates in production and as completed products came from the work of many individuals, the workers themselves began to feel like machines, working a certain number of hours and being turned on and off automatically. Less motivation for individual achievement and accomplishment has been the result.

A fifth factor that brought change was the organizational methods of industry. A number of measures designed to insure individual effort and to counteract lack of motivation came into widespread use. One development was the time-clock. By punching a card with the times at which he began and stopped work, the worker provided a record of his effort. This system and method of payment by the hour tied wages to the amount of work done. These controls served as external motivation to work, as absence resulted in less money. The controls, however, lessened the sense of individuality and responsibility for work performance. In order to perform conscientiously under such conditions a worker must be convinced in some other way that he is valued by management and that his interests are the concern of the organization. Unconvinced that management is concerned, he joins others in a united effort to gain desired advantages. Currently, interest in some unions is apparently diminishing, in part because so much progress has been made in obtaining necessary benefits and in part because the worker has directed his search for individuality to other areas within his life space through the pursuit of pleasure and leisure. Many workers feel that their occupation fails to offer opportunities to fulfill social needs and that improvement in the quality of life must be sought elsewhere.

A sixth factor significant in bringing change is a new type of idealism. Not well-enunciated or clear in meaning, it places an emphasis on self-direction—each person must "do his own thing." Because such a value is difficult to hold to in a highly organized and complex society, some young people, particularly those who have never worked in it, have begun to reject the whole system of this society. (They have developed their own informal social organizations to help them cope with the system.) This basic rejection, it should be noted, has its roots in social movements developed earlier in the century; some dissatisfaction in social roles has always been expressed.

A seventh factor in the change of values is the increasing influence of one social structure, the government, on the destiny of the individual. Government has gradually assumed greater control of people's lives. It now takes a substantial part of the rewards of individual effort in exchange for certain benefits; the individual expects to be protected from want, from some of the problems of sickness, and from attack by enemies outside the country. Perhaps the most important aspect of this factor has been the government's demand that young men serve in the military programs. Earlier in American history, military service was considered a moral duty, but now many people hold the reverse view. Because war is immoral (some say), it is immoral to serve in the military organization. This reasoning has had far-reaching effects on American society and to some extent on European and Asian societies. Demands of a powerful social structure have come to be questioned and defied. Although most young people still accept the values related to success and achievement advocated by present social structures, they will very likely derive new definitions of achievement and success in the future.

Social Structures and Individual Achievement

Motivation toward achievement is not innate, in the view of Crandall (1969). Although the initial efforts in walking, grasping objects, and developing speech require motivation, they do not require a cognitive discrimination in reference to the quality of performance. A child must learn during the course of his development to perceive the difference between one level of performance and another. Not only is such perception necessary for achievement, but reasoning about the value of performance levels as a source of satisfaction is important. He must therefore be able to predict not only the characteristics of a higher performance level, but must also predict the characteristics of the emotional experience (satisfaction) that will be associated with the higher performance level. This anticipation of satisfaction has to be learned in exchanges between parent and child. The parents' approval and emotional satisfaction in the child's progress in complexity of performance become part of the child's environmental experience. The parents' satisfaction in the early years is hardly distinguishable from the child's satisfaction. Some investigators believe that a child's experience should not be wholly benign, that definite demands for a higher level of performance should be made on him even though he may not be able to reach that level. In such a view, the frame of reference, or standards for the child, must at least initially be external, that is, standards of behavior must be imposed upon the child. Only in later years, in middle childhood, can the child begin to set his own standards, on the basis of his own striving and his own judgment about levels of performance. Perhaps it is in these years that a significant beginning is made toward change from external to internal in the frame of reference. Movement toward internal standards varies; it may be that only after years of adult experience can a person provide his own standards and claim that his satisfaction is in personal rather than social terms. It does seem reasonable, however, that all the developmental years should contain experiences that will lead to autonomy in setting personal goals.

The development of motivation to set autonomous goals is complex. It may be that an entirely internal frame of reference is impossible, that human accomplishment must be culturally relative in order to be satisfying to the individual. Nevertheless motivation to achieve, to evaluate performance, and to discriminate among levels of performance is learned; persistent motivation to excel is also a learned response style that is personal and first developed in the family.

Because motivation to set up goals within a social system and to work toward them is affected by environmental factors, it follows that the principal structures in society have significant influence on the individual's desires for specific goals. In early life the family begins the development of the individual's drive to achieve; a child's early experience, including imitation of models and specific training in task accomplishment, determines his ultimate response style. During the middle years the school experience continues to develop his desire to complete assigned tasks. In adolescence various social structures of society begin to influence the individual's choice of goals. An adolescent may work part time to buy some article that he wants, or he may seek some opportunity related to vocational interests. Military service with its various training programs may determine a vocational direction for further education. Government programs that provide opportunities to work in poverty areas or in foreign countries may determine aspirations for a particular role in society.

Family Influence on Achievement. The family remains the most significant social structure in the socialization process, and its influence comes at a time in the child's life when basic response patterns are being established. Ambition developed in the family can be of two kinds: It may be primarily directed toward the acquisition of material goods or wealth, or it may be directed toward a particularly satisfying life style in an environment esthetically and intellectually stimulating.

Some evidence from research studies supports the view that child-rearing methods affect ambition and aspiration. Usually these studies are laboratory experiments and therefore represent some artificiality. Because most of the experimenters are strangers to the children an important element is missing—the significant characteristics of a continuing emotional relationship that conditions the child's response to rewards or their lack. The studies suggest trends, however, that can be beneficial to those who have continuing relationships with children in the educational system.

Levels of aspiration in various tasks seem to be affected by the use of rewards. One investigation sought to determine the difference between performance when a reward was withheld and performance when a reward was withdrawn (Ward, 1969). The task was tossing a ball at a target marked on the floor. As it was impossible to make judgments about where the ball had struck, the experimenter could announce whether or not the toss was successful without the child's objection; in this way the rewards could be given, withheld, or withdrawn according to a predetermined schedule.

The experimental situation consisted of four parallel lines 1 foot apart taped on the floor and a target, 6 by 4 feet with taped lines 6 inches apart, located 3 feet from the nearest base line. The children were told that they could win plastic tokens with which they could obtain a prize from a group of toys. Each time a child threw the ball, the experimenter indicated whether or not it was a failure. The child was given one to four tokens, depending upon his choice of lines from which to throw—the line closest to the target would bring one token for a throw declared a success. The subjects were assigned to two groups: one group was designated as the "withholding of rewards" group, that is, for a failure no rewards were given to the child; the second group was the "withdrawing of rewards" group, that is, for each failure tokens were taken back (this group was given 50 tokens to start). After each child had gone through the same success-failure sequence, he was asked to choose a line to stand on for the next trial. The choice of the line or distance from the target was considered to indicate a "level of aspiration." Of 18 children in the "withdrawing of rewards" group, 17 had a "low level" of aspiration on their final choice. In the "withholding of rewards" group, the 18 children were divided between "low" and "high" levels. It seems that "withdrawing" does have an effect on level of aspiration, but that "withholding" for failure does not seem to have much influence.

It may be that withdrawing rewards can be considered punishment or perhaps a fine, but the withholding is also seen as a punishment by some children. The use of rewards also affected the willingness of many children in this group to try more difficult tasks. *Reinforcing* techniques (the rewarding of the child for desirable responses) should be used with caution, especially with some individuals, for withholding a reward may be perceived as punishment and adverse effects may accrue as was seen in this study. Even with the use of rewards, three quarters of the children had a "low level of aspiration."

Further evidence of the influence of child-rearing techniques on motivation techniques can be found in studies of children with various learning disabilities. Children who failed to achieve or who were insufficiently motivated to use their abilities to meet the standards of their school were studied in reference to four factors: the experiencing of *traumatic events* in the first seven years of life (death in the family, life-threatening illness, divorce of parents, hospitalization, separation from a sibling, and an experience of violence or danger); *persistent traumatic conditions* (chronic illness, mental illness, alcoholism of a member of the family, severe financial conditions, marital discord, or parental abuse of the child); *denial of information,* which causes the child to distrust the mother; and *derogation of the child*—negative expressions about the child's ability. By comparing a group of boys seven to nine years old who had difficulties in learning with a group of boys who were learning normally, it was found that the group with learning problems had significantly more traumatic events and problems in the family, that their mothers had withheld more significant information, and that the mothers were significantly more derogatory of their children than was the case with the control group (Brodie and Winterbottom, 1967). Such conditions as were encountered in these children with the learning disabilities not only affected their performance in school but also interfered with their setting of goals and effort to achieve.

The School and the Achievement Motive. Experience in the educational system is secondary only to the family in influence on the development of motivation to achieve. The child's success or failure in academic achievement and the approval or disapproval of teacher and peers have an important effect on his own view of his abilities and on the goals he sets for himself. The influence of the educational system extends beyond its boundaries into the child's surrounding life space to affect his perception of others in other social structures. If the child comes into conflict with the legal system, for example, information about him provided by the educational system may determine decisions about the disposition of the case. Similarly, school information may influence his opportunity for adoption (if he is cared for by an agency). It may influence those in agencies who will make decisions about his future training. If his achievement is high and he expresses aspirations of approved goals, his success and desires may bring him many opportunities from industrial or social organizations and eventually desirable occupational openings.

In the early years, experiences in the family have significant influence on the way the child perceives his school environment and these perceptions affect his social interaction in the classroom; and, in turn, his success or failure in school affects his perception of his place in the family. A study of children in the primary grades is illustrative of this interchange of effects. In this study achievement in a specific subject (arithmetic) was related to perceived relationships with parents based on use of "social schemata" (Rubin, 1969). The subjects were placed in groups on the basis of performance in arithmetic. Information about family relationships was obtained by a specially devised technique. The children were given an envelope containing male and female child figures on 2-inch squares of gum-backed paper and a booklet (8 by 11 inches) containing male and female adult figures placed at the extreme right of each page. The experimenter told the children that the figures were a "mother" and a "father." They were told to pretend the figures in the envelopes were pictures of themselves and to place them wherever they wished. After the children had placed the figures in the booklets, measurements were made between the child figures and the parent figures. The study indicated that the schemata used by the children were both a function of their sex and their achievement. The boys who were performing successfully academically (in arithmetic) placed themselves closer to the mother figure than to the father figure. Achieving girls placed themselves at a greater distance from both figures than did achieving boys. The underachieving girls placed themselves closer to the father than achieving girls did. Such information suggests that family relationships have an interaction effect on the child's perception of himself and his place with his parents. The study indicates that there is some relationship between the child's perception of school success and his perception of his relationship with his parents.

Another study of the influence of the family on ambition provides information about the motivation to achieve of a large number of high school seniors of both sexes who lived in a large city and whose social status ranged from "low" to "high" (Turner, 1969). A "high level of ambition" among the adolescents was found to be associated with a high level of parental education. Boys whose mother's education exceeded the father's tended to have higher ambition than did boys whose parents had equivalent education. The educational level of both parents, however, was an important determinant of the adolescents' ambition. Another important characteristic of the family found to be influential in the development of ambition was that of "family stability." Those adolescents who had lived most of their lives with both parents had a higher level of ambition for educational achievement than did those who had not lived with both parents. This significant relationship of stability to aspiration was not found in adolescents from lower socioeconomic levels. The size of the family also seemed to be a factor in ambition—boys from large families did not have as high aspiration as did boys from small families. This finding did not apply to girls. Adolescents from small families showed more ambition toward educational achievement than toward "material" achievement. Again, this relationship was not found for girls. In general, the information from this study indicated that certain family characteristics are significant in children's motivation to achieve in the educational system and in the goals they set for themselves in society.

Information from a number of research studies indicates that the social and affectional relationships in the family are particularly significant as causative factors in the creation of a high aspiration level. A study of boys in middle childhood (nine, ten, and eleven years of age) who had high levels of need to achieve indicated that their parents wanted them to perform at a high level on any task and expected them to do better than average. The parents of the children in the study responded with definite approval when their children performed well. The influence of the fathers seemed to contribute more to high achievement than did the influence of mothers. The fathers tended to give the children choices and some independence in their effort to solve problems. They also provided behavior to emulate rather than pressure to achieve. As the boys achieved, greater autonomy was granted (Rosen and D'Andrade, 1969). As available evidence indicates that only about one half of the families of children from deteriorated areas of cities have the father present, the absence of a father would be expected to affect the aspiration level of such children.

Other variables which have been studied in reference to school achievement are birth order, genetic make-up, and alienation. First- and second-born siblings (elementary and high school years) were compared on grades and Iowa Basic Skill scores (scores from tests of vocabulary, reading, comprehension, language, work-study, and arithmetic), and the results showed that the first-born children were superior on the basis of both the grades and the test scores (Chittenden, Foan, Aweil, and Smith, 1968). Data about several aspects of motivation such as shown by reaction time to "curiosity stimuli" have indicated that identical twins are more alike in such behavior than are fraternal twins (Scarr, 1966). *Alienation* (nonacceptance of main cultural values as well as unwillingness to take a social role expected by society) has been suggested as a determinant of low achievement among affluent middle-class adolescents. Such individuals who fail to achieve in high school, although of superior mental ability, are seen as rebelling against the educational system by "nonresistance" or by failing to try to meet the standards of the school (Propper and Clark, 1970).

Motivation and Social Stratification

The values of the middle class and lower class differ in the levels of aspiration for social mobility. Motivation to devote effort to long-term goals in spite of disappointment, frustration, and discouragement by others is characteristic of the socialization of the middle class. Motivation for social mobility requires a stability of purpose that maintains some degree of effort through the daily experiences of life. It may well be that an essential factor causing an individual to discontinue effort toward a goal is the interference of forces of daily existence such as the crises of illness, financial deprivation so that obligations cannot be met, job uncertainty, frequent lay-offs, and eviction from housing. These crises divert energy from concerns about goals in the distant future.

The close social relationships of lower-class individuals are not conducive to the development of goals extraneous to the life space. The role behavior in lower social class is often demanding and immediate, so that social mobility by definition is antithetical to the norms of the life space. Encouragement is characteristically in the direction of the role behavior of those close by, and behavior beyond awareness or perceived opportunity is considered illogical. The "kinship system" and social relationships do not sanction abandonment of the community and engagement in behavior outside of that known and understood. Consequently, even though mobility is possible in the "open" society, in reality, the socialization process and role behavior of those in the lower class mitigate against it.

To the lower-class child as he experiences difficulty in the educational system, values associated with educational achievement seem remote and unattainable. The models that symbolize opportunities for mobility are also those which disapprove of the academic performance of the lower-class child. This rejection seems to exclude from realistic perception the possibilities for social mobility. As for such a child a middle-class life style is difficult to perceive, placing value on it as a goal is in reality virtually impossible. The lower-class child is largely unaware of the relationship between educational attainment and middle-class occupational roles. Further, striving toward such goals is not rewarded in his family, nor is a high level of academic achievement and, in fact, efforts in the direction of mobility and accomplishment beyond his own social group are generally disapproved.

Because the behavior patterns in the lower class do not follow life styles which incorporate the values of the main culture, a *culture of poverty* is said to be passed from one generation to the next (Miller and Woock, 1970). Some support for this view comes from the difficulty which the Office of Economic Opportunity encountered in its effort to obtain organized participation by the "poor." The sociocultural organization that does exist in deteriorated urban areas is not one that leads to accomplishment of goals, although it does serve to keep the area separate from the rest of society. The loose organization, life styles, and community cohesion may help members to deal with stress; usually group goals are established only to maintain the current life patterns. An example is provided in the way one community dealt with a policy of the government of a large city. In order to save money, overtime work for garbage workers was prohibited. However, most of the workers were from deteriorated areas of the city and wanted the extra money. The residents of these areas in a unified effort then piled their garbage in the streets for many blocks. Traffic was stopped. As a result, the city government hastily authorized overtime, and the garbage was collected in these areas even to the neglect of other areas. The organized behavior was successful, but the goal was a limited one. The successful venture made life better, but in terms of goals for social mobility or community movement into the mainstream of the larger culture of the society, little was accomplished. A crisis had been dealt with, but the reaction was spontaneous and without much organizational planning. Such experience, however, reinforces the people's perception of the government as arbitrary and their opinion that the government should be dealt with aggressively rather than by reason or persuasion. The middle-class child learns to perceive the government and the police in a positive way and usually feels identification with both. The lower-class child, however, perceives the city government as unsympathetic, hostile, and a threat to safety and well-being. Some understanding of this basic class difference is necessary in the establishment of social programs.

Part of the behavior pattern in achievement characteristic in the lower socioeconomic class exists because of a lack of awareness of possibilities that lie beyond the perceptual field; part of it exists because specific behavior is required to adapt to current realities, and such behavior is in opposition to that which would lead to social mobility; and another part of the pattern stems from anxiety, despair, and hopelessness. There is a basic disbelief that the environment will allow fulfillment of needs or of desires for material gain and that personal capability can improve the life style. With such psychological bases for their life style, the methods brought to the community by the larger society—housing renewal, grants of money, and training programs—do little to alter the conditions of the poor.

Among investigators, agreement is not found on the concept of a *culture of poverty* based on distinctive life styles. Disagreement rests partially on the disparate life styles found in the areas and on the lack of a precise definition of poverty. In a poor area several different kinds of family organization can be found; some have a stable income, with both parents caring for the children, others have a stable income but parental roles and presence are unstable, and others are incomplete (usually only the mother is present) and have financial instability as well. Nevertheless it should be noted that in the face of crises, in all these family variations, some individuals will display personal courage and ability to cope with problems that would be devastating to members of the middle class.

It is sometimes asserted that those in poverty and in lower economic circumstances will make an effort to alter their position in the social strata through education and training if they are only given an opportunity. The problem is more complex, however, as education is a means of mobility and not a causative factor in upward mobility. Some current changes in opportunity in modern society do affect mobility. One change is the widespread demand for technological experts. Industry offers opportunities for lower socioeconomic class members to enter occupational roles that in the past have been perceived as open only to the middle class. And, because of the wide diversity of industry in urban society and also because of the structure of corporations, some decline in a caste system of positions has made possible the attainment by members of the lower socioeconomic class of positions formerly available only to the middle or upper classes. Attainment of these positions requires those of the lower socioeconomic class to learn the techniques and skills characteristic of the middle and upper classes. Such skills consist of the mastery of middle-class language, including appropriate vocabulary and speech inflections, choice of appropriate clothing, recreational activities—skills associated with art and music, and certain social behavior—appropriate conversation in social gatherings, appropriate knowledge in travel, and participation in professional and civic associations (Havighurst, 1966).

Learning the skills and acquiring the necessary knowledge for social mobility are not easy for lower-class children because of certain deficits in their methods of problem-solving. Clues to the nature of some of these deficits are possibly found in studies of their performance on discrimination-learning tasks varied on the basis of size, form, and color. Children (8 years old) of the lower class had greater difficulty than did middle-class children in learning the discrimination tasks provided in the experiment (Scholnick, Osler, and Katzenellenbogen, 1968). This lack of favorable performance of the lower-class children was believed to result in part from their lack of motivation to perform the tasks.

Other factors in addition to motivation to achieve are necessary for an individual to be socially mobile and to move from the lower to the middle class. Among these factors are social effectiveness and the ability to have pleasant and satisfying interaction with others. Some degree of aggressiveness is also important. Favorable opportunities and positions often require effort and some willingness to compete with others. Such effort often must be extended over a period of time, even years, before goals can be reached.

Social Mobility and Individual Goals

A desire to leave the deteriorated environment in which he lives is a basic requirement for mobility for an individual in the lower socio-economic class. It has been assumed by some investigators that an association can be found between lower-class status and a low level of aspiration or motivation to achieve. Several studies support the assumption. For example, in a study of high school seniors, the educational and occupational levels of aspiration were investigated by asking the students if they planned to attend college. Those who indicated that they did plan to go to college were given a rating of "high aspiration." The specific occupation chosen was given a rating according to a "prestige value" schedule. The social status of the families was determined by the prestige value of the parental occupation. The results of the study showed a statistically significant relationship between the status of the student's family and the student's aspiration level (Sewell, Haller, and Straus, 1969). This information suggests that a relationship exists among stratification, occupation, educational level, social interaction, and social mobility. As occupations are ranked in prestige value, they are significant in the establishment of social strata; and as occupations have educational requirements associated with them, educational levels contribute to stratification; and as those with similar strata tend to interact socially, social interaction also contributes to stratification.

Factors significant in social mobility can be summarized as follows: (1) the presence within the perceptual field of the individual of an opportunity for upward movement, that is, the individual must be exposed in some way to the goal and become aware of models living within a stratum before he can respond appropriately; (2) the ability to overcome obstacles and barriers characteristic of the social conditions; (3) the ability to deal with personal inadequacies, physical attributes, and emotions which may interfere with his striving for a higher social status; and (4) the viewing of the new stratum as sufficiently valuable to qualify as a goal toward which to strive. If social mobility is a desirable goal, the educational experience must somehow deal with the effect of those factors that determine the child's aspiration, even if their origin is beyond the sphere of influence of the educational system.

Moving beyond consideration of the origins of motivation toward achievement, attention should be given to the goals of the individual in society and the factors significant in their attainment. Because the rewards of a society are not distributed evenly, variation must be taken into account in the study of motivation and the socialization process. The latter process is important in the determination of the pattern of distribution and in the continuation of the pattern in the culture. The pattern is in reality perpetuated by enculturation and the educational system. The child is taught to accept a specific pattern of distribution associated with the structural organization of society. Although this social determinism seems to be a reality in a complex society, the individual still has considerable choice and can strive toward goals leading to social mobility upward or downward or to goals that can almost remove him from society or from any obligations to it.

Role diversity in some areas of American society has always been possible. Religious groups such as the Amish, Mennonites, and Hutterites have been able, although at times with difficulty, to pursue role patterns and life styles under a social organization quite different from the main culture. The communes of some youth today provide other examples—individuals, while living within the larger culture part of the time (at work or attending college), also establish role patterns and social organizations different from those of the larger society. Some of these differences are found in use of drugs, in sexual relationships without social sanctions, in avoidance of competitive behavior, and in refusal to acquire much of the materiel of modern society.

While a valued social goal in American society has been the "melting pot" of acculturation, separate social worlds have existed in the cities for ethnic groups such as Poles, Puerto Ricans, Italians, and Chinese. In these social worlds, people live close together and to varying extent maintain parts of their native cultures. Some people live out their lives in these settings. Cultural rituals, festivals, and religious observances maintain the values of the native culture and are particularly reinforced by the continuation of the native language. These "spatial segments" are usually little known by others in the city (Strauss, 1970). The goals of the young are affected by cultural experiences within these areas—by the close cultural ties among the residents and by the variance of the life styles from the larger society. For the children, biculturalism is a reality, particularly in their associations in the educational system; yet they continue their lives within their own microculture.

In recent years the melting-pot concept has received less support, while the continuance of cultural group styles has won approval. As a principle, this subject offers considerable opportunity for controversy in a democratic society, for it is immediately apparent that social progress and change may not bring beneficial results to both the cultural enclave and the larger society. Fragmentation into microsocial orders with diverse goals has often been the basis of human conflict. Yet imposition of life styles and aspiration levels on people who do not wish them seems to violate fundamental human rights. Ideally, a society should be created that is so attractive that participation and activity within it are sought without coercion. Apparently fragmentation can inhibit advancement of a civilization. The size necessary for a cohesive society to advance in the modern world would be perhaps impossible to determine; but size does seem to be correlated with complexity, and increasing fragmentation appears to be inimical to advancement.

FOUNDATIONS FOR THE MOTIVATION
OF THE INDIVIDUAL IN URBAN SOCIETY

In the search for understanding of the impelling forces in individual striving in modern society, basic theoretical approaches as well as laboratory studies are contributive. Some investigators and theorists have confined their studies to physiological factors in both emotion and motivation. The laboratory studies of emotion described in Chapter 8 indicate the kinds of information available about motivation. Emotions, as was indicated, are dependent upon the functioning of specific areas of the brain—the hypothalamus, the reticular activating system, and the limbic area. These brain areas have been shown to be related to motivation as well as to emotion. The function of body processes is therefore of importance in understanding activity toward a goal or in accomplishing tasks set by society. Important behavioral mechanisms in these processes are *selection* of stimuli to which to respond and the *continuation* of a response pattern in problem-solving behavior. The level of expenditure of the effort—the extent to which organismic function is committed to reaching a goal—is important in appraising the significance of motivation for the individual or the society.

Although investigators and theorists have tended to concentrate their efforts on either the physiological foundations or the social determinants of motivation, the two bases cannot in reality be separated. Physiological stimuli related to internal conditions always have some influence on behavior, and the two bases for motivation can be related by the use of the concept of needs. If an individual is very hungry (organic need for food), this need may become primary in immediate behavior; however, if the individual has recently eaten, social stimuli from his environment may become the primary factor in determining his behavior.

Motivation has two concepts within its meaning: *activity toward goals* and *goal utilization*. Some prefer to use the terms *instrumental activities* and *consummatory activities*. Expenditure of energy, the intensity of activity, is revealed by the actions of the organism as it strives toward a goal, but once a goal is reached, a reduction in activity occurs. The process of utilizing the goal (actually eating the food when hungry) is still dependent upon a body state (of hunger) and therefore still dependent upon motivation; the goal utilization behavior of eating, however, is certainly different from the goal achievement behavior of hunting food for a meal. To this extent the activities stemming from the same motivating condition vary according to whether the activity is toward achievement of a goal or whether it involves the utilization of the goal.

Some theorists take the view that a hierarchy of motivational activity exists similar to the *hierarchy of needs concept* (Maslow, 1943). According to the concept of needs, the organism, following goal utilization based on one need or motivating factor, turns to another, for example, after eating, a man watches television. Another way of dealing with the same problem is to say that the strongest need or *action tendency* is the basis for action in an organism even though other needs and action tendencies may be present (Birch and Veroff, 1966). This theoretical position does not necessarily assume that the individual is always rational or objective in the decision for a course of activity. In fact, he may not even be aware of the bases for his choice. Not only does the individual select goals on the basis of his own needs and internal conditions, but the decision is also affected by the pulls or "valences" of varying strengths in the life space. In a conflict, the strongest condition or valence determines the goal and the activity directed toward it.

A first condition of *goal-directed* activity is the presence in the life space of a stimulus that can act as a goal or can be perceived as holding possibilities for need fulfillment. If hunger is the primary motivating factor, possible sources of food available in the perceptual field are viewed as promising fulfillment. For goal-directed activity to take place, the expectation of the presence of food is required, and the individual must select the goal he thinks will fulfill his needs. Learned behavioral response patterns and socialization are important determinants in the selection of the specific stimulus to which to respond. When the individual perceives stimuli similar to those which have provided satisfaction in the past, he will tend to respond. Not only is past experience important in selecting the goal or stimulus, it also determines the kind of goal-directed behavior appropriate. If a primitive man is hungry and sees a rabbit, not only is the rabbit perceived as a source of food, but the behavioral patterns necessary to catch the rabbit are recalled. Immediate situational factors are also important: If the rabbit is near its burrow, the man's action will vary from that needed when he sees the rabbit's escape blocked by a cliff. And associated with the valence of the stimulus is the *set* of the individual. If the primitive man particularly likes rabbit to eat, his effort to make the catch is greater than if he does not. Thus, if some behavior in the past has brought satisfaction, an individual will anticipate the repetition of former pleasure, and his activity and effort will tend to be greater.

Another factor in behavior or activity associated with motivation is the consequence of experience with the goal or stimulus. While the primitive man might prefer the rabbit to eat, past experience may have shown him that a rabbit is very difficult to catch and that it would be easier to catch a turtle lying in the sun on the river bank. The probability of success in the goal-directed activity therefore affects selection of the goal as well as behavior toward it. In summary, presence of the stimulus in the perceptual field, past experience with the available stimulus, and the strength of the need for it all determine the course of activity directed toward reaching the goal. The utilization of the goal, the consummatory activity, is also dependent upon the need as well as upon past learning.

As some behavior does not seem to fit into this theoretical framework, other theoretical approaches have been advanced. Consideration of these various approaches contributes to some understanding of motivation and its complexity.

Instinct, Imprinting, and Drive

An *instinct* is defined as a way of acting or behaving toward a goal without knowledge of the goal and without training or experience in how to reach the goal. William McDougall (1914), writing in the early part of the century, believed instincts to be "emotionally toned activities" as well as "inborn reaction tendencies." In human beings instincts were seen as "great primitive drives." The concept of instinct according to Bolles (1967) is used to account for ". . . the apparent intelligence of behavior when it does not seem reasonable to attribute intelligence to the organism." Instincts, in addition to being the basis of wants and desires, were also believed to be accompanied by emotional experience. In McDougall's early thinking, therefore, an instinct meant that the organism attended to a certain stimulus, had certain emotional experience on perceiving it, and then responded to it in a certain way. The use of the term instinct began to decline in the second decade of this century, and this decline was accompanied by the rise of behaviorism, with its emphasis on the view that the only valid data come from observations of the activity of an organism. For several decades *instinct* was a term to be avoided, and the term *drive* was used instead. Later, the term instinct was used again but in a different context and as related to a new theoretical approach, *ethology*. The beginning of this theoretical approach has been attributed to the publication of a work on birds by Konrad Lorenz (1935).

Lorenz took the view that perception of objects differed according to species, that man became aware of several features of an object because of his highly developed brain and sensory capacities, which set him apart from other species of animals. Animals lower in the phylogenetic scale respond to fewer features and in a more restricted way than does man. Response to stimuli is to some extent dependent upon innate behavior patterns; and in reasoning about these innate patterns, Lorenz came to believe that a stimulus released a response from the pattern rather than causing it. Ethologists distinguish between a capacity to be stimulated and the sensitivity of a receptor. The selectivity revealed in responses to only certain stimuli is the essence of a concept of an innate releasing mechanism. In animals both the stimulus that releases the response and the response itself are specific to the species. Such reaction complexes are considered instinctive behaviors. Lorenz described examples of such behavior in geese. The *following response* of a gosling is innate and biologically determined, but the *releaser stimulus* (a stimulus from the environment that sets off a response) is not, as the latter is dependent upon the occurrence of objects in the bird's perceptual field. If at a critical age the bird does not have its own species available, it will follow other objects or animals. If the following behavior is imprinted on the bird because it follows a human being or a mechanical model at the critical period, the behavior will not change even when its own species is encountered. The critical period of imprinting has a very limited duration—perhaps only a few hours. This imprinting is explained as an innate force necessary for the survival of the organism; the force can be altered only during the critical period, by appropriate or inappropriate releaser stimuli.

A number of related behavior patterns depend on a similar "reservoir of behavior"—mating, nest building, and the care of the young (Tinbergen, 1951). The concept of the *reservoir of behavior* also includes the build-up of energy and the need to discharge it. If releaser stimuli are not encountered, then the energy may be eventually discharged in unrelated activities; thus, some instinctive behaviors occur out of context. An example of such behavior is seen when some instinctive behavior is blocked. This behavior, if it occurs in an inappropriate context, is called *displacement activity*.

The instinct and ethological approach has been controversial (Bolles, 1967). Many theorists doubt the value of the concepts of the energy reservoir and of displacement activity. It may be that instinctive behavior is used as an explanation, as Bolles suggests, when behavior cannot be explained in terms of function or structure. Criticism has caused supporters of ethological principles to move from observation of natural behavior to a concern for physiological processes and genetic origins.

The concept of *drive* was developed as an explanation to replace instinct, but it still is related to the concept of instinct. Similarity to the concept of instinct is particularly apparent in the dependence of the drive concept on physiological processes, because understanding a drive is dependent upon information about the physiological conditions within the organism. The drive concept gained considerable support because it seemed to promise eventual revelation of a physiological foundation for motivation growing out of the function of an anatomical structure. At first, drive seemed to have two meanings: the mechanism that controls a pattern of behavior and the energy that sustains activity (Young, 1961). If the second meaning is used, drive can be defined as the chemical energy coming from substances in body tissues, or it can be the stimuli that release the energy. A number of theorists see drive as essentially a persisting stimulus that releases stored energy. Soon after the development of the concept of drive came the idea of multiple drives, although this latter idea was not dependent upon knowledge of the number of drives in existence. But Young sees the idea of the multiplicity of drives as based not so much on the different kinds of energy but on different body mechanisms.

In observation of laboratory animals it can be seen that some of their activity is not directed toward a specific goal, because an animal at times will run about in its cage in a random way. The idea of *general activity* is that such activity does not grow out of external stimulation. Some who take the same view about children's activities believe that children engage in play without basic motivation toward a goal. In this kind of activity, the idea of *intrinsic motivation* has been advanced—the activity itself serves as the motivation. Satisfaction gained in repetitive activity may be considered as the reinforcement or reward feature of it (Hunt, 1961). This view seems to indicate that the activity serves as both motivation and reinforcement; because of the reinforcement aspect, it may then continue at other times as circumstances allow. The instigation of the behavior need not be dependent on either internal or external stimuli. To make the assertion, however, that such activity is simple and uninfluenced by environmental stimuli or stimuli from internal states is open to question. It seems that what is described as general activity can still fit into the concept of the goal-directed and goal-utilization framework described earlier.

Arousal is a concept similar to that of generalized drive. This concept includes the idea that although drive is an "energizer" or a source of power and activity, it is not related to a cue or direction (Young, 1961). Those holding to this view see *perception* as acting like a drive, as in states of being alert or anxious. The excited state serves as the motivation, and the condition need not be linked to a primary drive such as hunger.

Acquired drives, those drives learned in the socialization process, have been a continuing source of controversy. While laboratory experimentation with animals has brought some degree of unanimity about the primary or basic physiological drives of hunger, thirst, sex, or sleep, a generally satisfactory list of social or acquired drives has not been devised. Some agreement has been reached, however, in classifying "fear" as an acquired drive, because it is relatively easy to study in laboratory animals. An illustration of fear behavior as an acquired drive in a laboratory rat is found in experiments using electric shocks. When a rat is given a shock, he is also given an opportunity to learn to press a bar to shut off the current. If, preceding the shock, a light is turned on, the rat will eventually learn to press the bar when he sees the light in order to avoid the shock. Fear, it seems, is transferred from the shock to the light.

Incentives

In dealing with social drives, the concept of incentive systems has been of interest. The definition of an *incentive system* is similar to the one for a physiological need: a condition that can satisfy a need. Seven incentive systems have been suggested: a sensory system, a curiosity system, an achievement system, an affiliative system, an aggressive system, a power system, and an independence system (Birch and Veroff, 1966). The first three of these incentive systems may not be dependent directly on the response of others; thus Birch and Veroff call them "asocial incentive systems." Such a term seems misleading, and the differences between them and the other four do not seem to be sufficiently clear.

Through the body senses or *sensory system* (the first incentive system), body processes are carried on to fulfill needs and sustain life. Food, of course, means more than just a way of sustaining life; associated with food are sensations of taste, touch, and smell and perhaps the feeling of food in the stomach—all of these sensations are considered to be a system. Such sensory incentives cause behavioral variations in activity leading to a goal; and, in attaining a goal such as food, behavior becomes complex because stimuli must be selected and decisions made about how to obtain the food. Negative sensory incentives are those related to an avoidance of failure. The distinction between the choice *to achieve* or *to avoid failure* matters primarily when making a choice about behavior —the possibility of reward as an incentive is much more influential toward achievement than is the mere avoidance of failure. It is also possible that a fear of success can exist. Certain responsibilities may be perceived as the person strives toward a goal, with these responsibilities becoming so frightening that a fear of reaching the goal develops.

A second incentive system, curiosity, consists of perception of *changes in stimulation* or an awareness by a person of a change in the stimulus-pattern in his life space. A man sitting in a park reading the evening paper ignores the city's traffic with its characteristic sounds, but if the sounds suddenly stop, he will be curious about the sudden absence or change of stimuli.

A third incentive system is that of *achievement*. Because achievement behavior has already been dealt with in this chapter, discussion here will be limited. Birch and Veroff see the achievement incentive system as consisting of a desire for improvement in performance and feel that such motivation in a task is in terms of a wish to excel.

A fourth incentive system is *affiliative*. This system includes physical contact, social interaction, and behavior in which anxiety is reduced. A child who feels lonely, for example, will seek the company of a playmate; if frightened, he will go nearer his parent or teacher. If affiliation is deemed of value and a person feels the need to be acceptable to others and to be liked, it would seem obvious that he would engage in behavior acceptable to others, behavior which would make other people feel an affection for him. Such rational behavior does not always occur. One of the characteristics of neurosis is a feeling of isolation and estrangement from others, of being disliked and rejected; yet another characteristic of neurosis is that those with the disorder behave in ways that make them unacceptable and disliked. David was such a person. At nursery school he frequently attacked other children. He would strike with his fists with such force that the other children learned it was safer to avoid him. He usually played in the sand box by himself and glowered at any child who came near. Yet he needed experiences in which he could engage in friendly and cooperative play. He had not learned, however, how to play cooperatively and to obtain the satisfaction possible in friendly exchange with another child. Such a problem can exist at any age. Amelioration of the difficulty requires that someone be sufficiently empathic to continue to offer friendship and affection despite rebuffs and rejection. Usually this behavior is too much to ask of children. Adults who are confident of their own value and who have satisfying personal relationships with at least one other person can help such children by a patient concern and offering of friendship and sympathy.

A fifth incentive system is that of *aggression*. Birch and Veroff see this system as one in which the goal is to injure another person, but a definition of aggression that sees aggressive behavior as directed only toward the injury of others is too limited. One individual can unintentionally injure others in the process of fulfilling his personal needs. A person driving in city traffic in such a way as to serve his own needs may crush someone else's fender, but it is possible that the aggression is not directed in the same way as if he deliberately set out to damage someone's car. The end result, of course, is the same, but the concern here is about the motivational system and its origin. As indicated in the preceding chapter, current research studies have not dispelled all the questions about the origin of aggressive behavior.

The socialization process can directly or indirectly affect aggressive behavior. A child can be taught to be aggressive or to avoid aggressive behavior. Bill Carr continually fought with his fifth-grade classmates. Often on the basketball court he would take the ball and try to keep it from others. If other boys tried to retrieve the ball as it bounced from the backboard, Bill grappled with them and struck them viciously. Frequently a boy would challenge Bill's right to possess the ball. If the ensuing fight came to the attention of a playground supervisor, Bill would be taken to the principal's office. On several occasions, his parents were called to the school. They justified his behavior, however, and saw Bill as only asserting his rights; Bill had behaved according to his parents' training and values. Other parents may teach their child that fighting is improper and that aggression should be avoided. This training may even be done indirectly by teaching that siblings must solve their problems and cope with their differences by means other than fighting. As the child moves out of the family to the school, he employs there the problem-solving approaches which he has learned in the family. It seems a reasonable assumption that aggression is usually channeled into acceptable behavior, but such channeling is learned and becomes quite complex as the child grows older and moves into adulthood. Aggressive behavior patterns are formed first in the family and then influences from the environment come into play during the developmental years.

The sixth incentive system described by Birch and Veroff is that of *power*. They maintain that the motive to control or influence others is a separate incentive system. To differentiate between this incentive system and that of some types of aggression seems to be very difficult, and even these authors suggest the posssibility that the drive for power may not be a separate system. It is clear that, as with aggression, the assertion of power and the need to influence others are learned and are affected by the socialization experience. In a "power system" a person tries to change the behavior of others and also seeks to prevent other persons from influencing him. The power motive stems from conditions of deprivation and to some extent this view is similar to the origin of aggression associated with frustration. Being appointed to a committee as an expert, being appointed or elected to office, or being in a position to coerce others are ways of attaining power. Choices for different types of power grow out of the socialization experience.

The seventh incentive system is that of *independence*. Birch and Veroff define it as "accomplishing an activity without help." Again the possibility of differentiation between this system and others, especially the achievement system, is somewhat difficult. Because independence is relative and always incomplete, particularly in a complex social order, indicating independence as a separate system is of doubtful value.

As these systems have been described, the difficulty encountered over the years in developing categories of *acquired drives* is revealed. This method of classification does provide an organized and analytical attempt to deal with complex behavior. The problem brings into relief the complexity of human behavior growing out of the influences brought to bear on the socialization process.

Unconscious Motivation

Understanding human behavior, according to Freud, depends upon understanding unconscious motivation. The mental processes of nonconsciousness are divided into the *preconscious*—the mental processes that are relatively accessible, that is, those which appear and fade easily—and the *unconscious* ones—those which are difficult to bring into awareness. The latter processes are in the vast majority. Although much of the origin of behavior is unconscious, some behavior is consciously determined and is not left to chance. If such is the case, and man's behavior is in a large part determined by unconscious processes, then he is much less a rational being than he thinks. For Freud, all behavior, to some extent, is unconsciously motivated, and although unconscious factors causing behavior may ultimately be revealed to a person, still the factors often are not realized or accepted. Because of this unawareness, Freud developed a concept of energy that attempted to account for the flow of mental ideation from the unconscious to the conscious. This energy concept was related to innate needs, the bases for activity and motivation. Much human behavior is the result of a struggle to find ways to fulfill the basic needs. Ways to do this, however, are difficult for people to find. Often much energy is misdirected or displaced onto persons and objects that cannot reduce the tensions; as a consequence, elaborate behavioral systems and even social structures are developed (Cofer and Appley, 1964).

Freud divided basic instincts into the life instincts and the death instincts. The *life instincts* are divided into the sexual instincts and the life maintenance instincts, and these two groups of instincts function together under the general life instinct of *Eros*. The *death instincts* were not clearly defined, but their concept grew out of Freud's observations of patients' revelations of conflict within themselves and the antagonisms evident in their behavioral patterns. The life and death instincts are in constant interaction with each other. To understand behavior, Freud believed, a search for motivating circumstances should be made, as well as a search for the identity of counterforces. Although Freud was at first interested in an equilibrium principle, he later maintained that a continuing conflict was present within a person. Repressed motivation and conflict seemed to center around sexual urges; thus Freud came to believe in the importance of sexual wishes as sources of motivation. These wishes usually come into some conflict with concepts of morality and with environmental reality. Such wishes and conflicts are masked; only at times do they come into consciousness.

Differences in interpretation of Freud's ideas have come about through the years. Some theorists see Freud's emphasis on the unconscious as challenging the rationality of man (Bolles, 1967). Others do not emphasize this point but see the unconscious as accounting for the determinants of behavior which the individual cannot bring to awareness (Hall and Lindzey, 1970). Psychoanalytic theory as derived by Freud and his followers has had a profound effect on thought about the origin of man's behavior. Now man is seen as not always acting for the reasons given or those that seem easily apparent. Many now agree with Freud that although man's behavior is determined, it springs from sources unknown to himself and to others. The sources may be revealed in dreams or in descriptions of the circumstances surrounding the behavior, descriptions which can be interpreted only by a skilled observer or clinician. If man's motives are beyond his awareness, then his behavior cannot be the result of objective and careful reasoning—in truth, decisions may be influenced by forces brought into being in years past, perhaps as remote as childhood.

This view has both pessimistic and comforting aspects. Some have despaired of man's rationality because motives explained as objective or altruistic can scarcely be trusted. Further, man is something of a prisoner of the struggle within, and he cannot hope to deal with it successfully. Optimism is possible only through knowing that motives are not what they seem to be and that a search for their actual origin must be made.

Another basis for optimism is that the socialization process can reduce the inner conflict and turmoil that cause irrationality or pathological conditions.

The significance of such a theoretical viewpoint for modern and complex society depends upon two considerations: Can social movements and change be rational—directed toward the common good—or must they grow out of collective inner conflict and represent social pathology? Can man in the necessarily close contacts of day-to-day living show enough control of inner conflict to make social interaction tolerable, that is, is it possible for him to live and work creatively and successfully in close proximity to others?

The answers seem to be equivocal, depending on both an individual and a societal basis. Individuals do seem to be victims of irrational urges and desires as they engage in behavior inimical to their own and society's welfare. But the same individuals at times also engage in behavior that is constructive, rational, and even altruistic. The variation has many causes, both internal and external. Social movements and change can grow out of rational and altruistic planning, but it is apparent that some movements and social organizations are pathological and irrational. Many point to the space program as showing man's rational planning capabilities. Cooperative and rational behavior on the part of a large number of individuals made success possible.

How can more rational behavior be brought about in modern society? Any answer would include attention to the socialization and educational processes. Man can learn to increase rational behavior and find ways to deal with environmental causes of stress that engender irrationality. He also can learn to recognize irrational behavior and can develop systems to deal with it on both an individual and group basis.

The Influence of Urban Society and Culture on Motivation

The influences of the urban environment on individual motivation are difficult to characterize, but geography, ethnicity, and social stratification are essential factors. Geographical mobility has become a part of American life. People who move to urban regions usually advance in their occupations for two reasons: The complexity of social structures offers many opportunities for advancement and diversity in role behavior and the investment of capital in expansion of the social structures has diversified individual opportunity. The situation is cyclic, because as more people with more money are to be found in urban areas, enterprises of many kinds are set up to attract markets in the cities and the neighboring areas, and the investment in turn attracts more people. Exceptions occur, of course, as some industries are locating outside the urban areas and some cities are losing people from their central cores. Still, incentives for motivation are more in evidence in the cities; more positions with higher salaries and more goods of varying qualities and designs are to be had. In the urban areas, accordingly, many rewards provide a basis for individuals to set up their own goals in order to attain what they see others have. The cities with their surroundings contain all that is attainable in the society; the quantity of material on display makes it seem possible that a determined individual can achieve many of these things for himself. As such information becomes available through extended methods of communication and widespread opportunities for travel, people have moved to the urban areas with an expectation of bettering their lot.

Although visible rewards are easily seen and relatively attainable in the cities, for some the cities have not brought opportunity. The migration of black people from the South leaves many with unfulfilled hopes. Because of technological advances and structural complexity, the demand for unskilled labor has dropped, so that while the city offers more rewards than rural areas, the rewards are attainable only by the educated and by those who have the social positions to acquire them.

Another consideration concerning motivation is the freedom to change role behavior. In small ghetto communities or neighborhoods in cities, individuals are known to many, and a change or aspiration for a change in role behavior may be ridiculed or disapproved. In other areas of the urban environment, where social intimacy and community identification are lacking, individuals feel free to experiment and to emulate various kinds of role behavior. This experimentation and emulation can lead to personal growth and use of capacities that might not otherwise develop. Such opportunity for experimentation and emulation itself leads to motivation for extensive change in personal role behavior. Further, because of the reduction in forms of close social interaction in the city, a number of choices for role behavior exist. Hundreds of organizations with a great diversity in activities and purposes can be joined. Many organizations have links to groups in other areas, perhaps even in other countries, so that the sense of identification reaches over large geographical areas. Most organizations, of course, have restrictions in membership. Some are accessible only to those who live in the various ethnic sections of the city, some are accessible only to those who have a background of generations of upper-class affiliation. Urban organization usually follows the social stratification levels of the areas, and acceptance to membership becomes symbolic of success and social status, a reward of individual motivation and achievement. Membership often is impersonal, however, and unlike the kinship systems of folk societies. Because of these impersonal qualities, diversity is possible, and thus shifts in role patterns for individuals occur not only within the organizations but in the choice of dress styles, house or apartment furnishings, food, and entertainment. A banker, for example, who wears conservative suits during the working part of the week may change to colorful and unconventional clothing during leisure hours, and may even risk his money at a racetrack.

Although a lack of social and psychological proximity in the city allows diversity in role behavior, this permissiveness is not necessarily based on personal tolerance, but rather on the fact that control of the behavior of others by the ordinary person is impossible. An indifference to deviation must therefore be cultivated by those living in an urban setting. Indifference is partly a defense and a way of maintaining personal control of emotions. No matter the reason, social indifference allows individuals to experiment and develop role behavior that differs substantially from cultural norms.

Social stratification and ethnic grouping in urban living areas also necessitate flexibility in *overall* cultural requirements. Flexibility comes from the tendency for limits on behavior to be left to the enforcement activities of agencies and institutions of society. As the efforts of the agencies are minimal, many individuals can develop disparate or culturally deviant life styles without encountering trouble, if their behavior is not illegal or too extreme. In terms of motivation, tolerance and opportunity for diversity have both advantages and disadvantages. Tolerance is advantageous because it allows an individual to use his capacity to fulfill his needs in ways suitable to himself and to develop a life style without being hampered by social constraints. It is disadvantageous to the extent that the beneficial influences of a culture are ignored—the influences that contribute to the development of a "good" or "socialized" individual. It is unreasonable to assume that a person becomes "good" only on the basis of his own effort or insight; interaction with others is essential to the process of a socially "good" person.

IN PERSPECTIVE

Motivation is an area of human behavior currently attracting much attention. Why does man undertake difficult tasks and pursue a line of activity over long periods of time? In social interaction, how can the origins of his behavior be explained? Is man innately good or evil? These are fundamental questions for the student of human behavior. Adequate and satisfying answers are not available, although theory and research have recently provided new information and ideas.

Persistence in tasks is certainly greatly influenced by socialization experience, particularly in the family. Characteristics of the life space and the models in it affect the child's perception of his environment and his perception of his capacity to cope with it. Children in the lower socioeconomic class, for example, have experiences which cause their perceptions to be different from children in middle-class families.

Motivation to achieve in our society is undergoing change. Values about work and accomplishment as well as incentives are different in recent years from those existing in the earlier part of the century. Machines, automation, large numbers of people, organizational structures, and financial rewards are all factors in bringing changes in attitudes toward social status and prestigious roles.

Freudian theory, too, has had a profound effect on thinking about motivation in twentieth-century man. Can social movements be rational and can they grow out of a basic human concern, or are they irrational and based on immature and selfish needs? Can man really find satisfaction in modern society? Answers are not clear. Social organizations have a history of conflict, and many examples of irrational behavior are observed in them. Yet many examples of rational and cooperative behavior lead to new attention to the socialization and educational experience during the developmental years. It seems insufficient concern has been given to the effect of these experiences on the emotions of individuals and the development of their motivational goals.

REFERENCES

BIRCH, D., & VEROFF, J. *Motivation: A study of action.* Belmont, Calif.: Brooks/ Cole, 1966.

BOLLES, R. C. *Theory of motivation.* New York: Harper & Row, 1967.

BRODIE, R. D., & WINTERBOTTOM, M. R. Failure in elementary school boys as a function of traumata, secrecy, and derogation. *Child Development,* 1967, 38, 701–711.

CHITTENDEN, E. A., FOAN, M. W., AWEIL, D. M., & SMITH, J. R. School achievement of first- and second-born siblings. *Child Development,* 1968, 39, 1223– 1228.

COFER, C. N., & APPLEY, M. H. *Motivation: Theory and research.* New York: Wiley, 1964.

CRANDALL, V. C. Achievement behavior in young children. In B. C. Rosen, H. J. Crockett, Jr., & C. Z. Nunn (Eds.), *Achievement in American society.* Cambridge, Mass.: Schenkman, 1969. Pp. 95–111.

ELKIND, D., DEBLINGER, J., & ADLER, D. Motivation and creativity: The context effect. *American Educational Research Journal,* 1970, 7, 351–357.

FULLER, J. L. *Motivation: A biological perspective.* New York: Random House, 1962.

HALL, C. S., & LINDZEY, G. *Theories of personality.* (Rev. ed.). New York: Wiley, 1970.

HAVIGHURST, R. J. *Education in metropolitan areas.* Boston: Allyn & Bacon, 1966.

HORROCKS, J. E., & WEINBERG, S. A. Psychological needs and their development during adolescence. *The Journal of Psychology,* 1970, 74, 51–69.

HUNT, J. McV. *Intelligence and experience.* New York: Ronald, 1961.

LORENZ, K. Companionship in bird life. In C. H. Schiller (Ed.), *Instinctive behavior.* New York: International Universities Press, 1957a. Pp. 83–128. (Originally published in 1935.)

LORENZ, K. The nature of instinct: The conception of instinctive behavior. In C. H. Schiller (Ed.), *Instinctive behavior.* New York: International Universities Press, 1957b. Pp. 129–175. (Originally published in 1937.)

LORENZ, K. Comparative study of behavior. In C. H. Schiller (Ed.), *Instinctive behavior.* New York: International Universities Press, 1957c. Pp. 239–263. (Originally reported in 1939.)

MASLOW, A. H. *Motivation and personality.* New York: Harpers, 1954.

MASLOW, A. H. A theory of human motivation. *Psychological Review,* 1943, 50, 370–396.

MAYER, K. B., & BUCKLEY, W. *Class and society.* New York: Random House, 1970.

McDOUGALL, W. On the nature of instinct. In D. Bindra & J. Stewart (Eds.), *Motivation.* Baltimore: Penguin, 1966. Pp. 17–19.

McDOUGALL, W. *An introduction to social psychology.* (8th ed.) Boston: Luce, 1914.

MICHAELIS, W., & EYSENCK, H. J. The determination of personality inventory factor patterns and intercorrelations by changes in real-life motivation. *The Journal of Genetic Psychology,* 1971, 118, 223–234.

MILLER, H. L., & WOOCK, R. R. *Social foundations of urban education.* Hinsdale, Ill.: Dryden, 1970.

MURRAY, E. J. *Motivation and emotion.* Englewood Cliffs, N.J.: Prentice-Hall, 1964.

PROPPER, M. M., & CLARK, E. T. Alienation: Another dimension of underachievement. *The Journal of Psychology,* 1970, 75, 13–18.

ROSEN, B. C., & D'ANDRADE, R. G. The psychosocial origins of achievement motivation. In B. C. Rosen, H. J. Crockett, Jr., & C. Z. Nunn (Eds.), *Achievement in American society.* Cambridge, Mass.: Schenkman, 1969. Pp. 55–84.

RUBIN, D. A comparison of the mother and father schemata of achievers and under-achievers: A study of primary grades and achievement in arithmetic. *The Journal of Social Psychology,* 1969, 78, 295–296.

SCARR, S. Genetic factors in activity motivation. *Child Development,* 1966, 37, 662–673.

SCHOLNICK, E. K., OSLER, S. F., & KATZENELLENBOGEN, R. Discrimination learning and concept identification in disadvantaged and middle-class children. *Child Development,* 1968, 39, 15–25.

SEWELL, W. H., HALLER, A. O., & STRAUS, M. A. Social status and educational and occupational aspiration. In B. C. Rosen, H. J. Crockett, Jr., & C. Z. Nunn (Eds.), *Achievement in American society.* Cambridge, Mass.: Schenkman, 1969. Pp. 183–192.

STRAUSS, A. L. Images of the American city. In F. L. Sweetser (Ed.), *Studies in American urban society.* New York: Crowell, 1970. Pp. 5–44.

TINBERGEN, N. *The study of instinct.* London: Oxford University Press, 1951.

TINBERGEN, N., & KUENEN, D. J. Feeding behavior in young thrushes. In C. H. Schiller (Ed.), *Instinctive behavior.* New York: International Universities Press, 1957. Pp. 209–238.

TURNER, R. H. Some family determinants of ambition. In B. C. Rosen, H. J. Crockett, Jr., & C. Z. Nunn (Eds.), *Achievement in American society.* Cambridge, Mass.: Schenkman, 1969. Pp. 112–128.

WARD, W. D. The withholding and the withdrawing of rewards as related to level of aspiration. *Child Development,* 1969, 40, 591–597.

WHITE, R. W. Motivation reconsidered: The concept of competence. In D. E. Hamachek (Ed.), *Human dynamics in psychology and education.* Boston: Allyn & Bacon, 1968. Pp. 48–91.

WILLIAMS, R. M., JR. Achievement and success as value orientations. In B. C. Rosen, H. J. Crockett, Jr., & C. Z. Nunn (Eds.), *Achievement in American society.* Cambridge, Mass.: Schenkman, 1969. Pp. 13–17.

YOUNG, P. T. *Motivation and emotion.* New York: Wiley, 1961.

THE INDIVIDUAL AND SOCIETY— ADOLESCENCE AND EARLY ADULTHOOD

V

In this section an effort is made to see the place of the individual in modern society. The emphasis is on a view of the *transition years* in development, those of late adolescence and early adulthood. After the study of development in the periods of early childhood, middle childhood, and most of adolescence, such questions are asked as: What are the areas of success and of failure of the socialization process? What are some of the conditions in society that assist or inhibit the individual's destiny in modern society?

An effort is made to see the individual in society from the standpoint of individual needs and capacities as well as to see the societal conditions as they are or how they ought to be. Thus, interest is continued in both process and context. Included also is some examination of the views of those now living in the transition years of both themselves and their society.

Basic issues involved in the realities of authority, autonomy, power, and conflict in the urban age are taken into account. These issues are believed to be an important part of the study of human development; unless some perspective is gained of the panorama of human development in which an interpretation of the transition years is included, an incomplete understanding will result. This totality of perspective is now receiving much more emphasis as a result of youth's dissatisfaction with many conditions in the modern world.

INTERNAL AND EXTERNAL CONTROL

10

In every society on earth some conformity among members is necessary. Each day, whether individuals awake with a sunrise over a lonely lagoon in the South Seas or with a clatter of traffic under a smoke-filled sky, there is already a charted and culturally established program of activities waiting. This program is an organized system of customs, rules, ideals, and requirements which gives shape not only to the life styles of men therein but to the society and culture on which they are dependent. Without this program, life for the individual has little meaning. Of course, no society would exist without it, because only through behavior in expected and predictable ways do human understanding and accomplishment become real. A man who works in the city must be able to predict that his train will run, that his colleagues will be at his business location, and so on; predictions and expectations are a part of social living. Man is dependent, from the beginning of his life through its entire span, upon the cooperation of others; the more complex his role, the more dependent he is. With each step he takes toward achievement and successful role behavior, the more dependent he becomes. He must have association and approval, and therefore his satisfaction in society is a tenuous one; because of this awesome dependence, it is obvious that a lack of approval and cooperation becomes threatening. The seeking of approval or at least cooperation becomes, accordingly, a powerful socializing influence on the behavior of everyone.

One important goal of the socialization process is to insure that individuals develop behavior in accord with what is expected and predicted by others. Aside from basic organismic capacity and the motivation to achieve, such behavior is attained through the complex process of perception. Because response styles are dependent upon the appropriate response to stimuli in the life space, the selection and interpretation of stimuli from the environment form the basis for uniformity in individual life styles. The individual must learn to select the stimuli valued by the society and the culture and to exclude and devalue those that will lead to inappropriate behavior. This selection and valuation process is part of a life style. The life style is developed through learning and through a process of adapting individual abilities and needs to behavioral processes culturally proscribed. Although an individual may not find it fulfilling in the beginning to adapt his behavior to that demanded by the culture (the young child often finds the effort frustrating), his destiny, if it is to be satisfying, requires considerable conformity to cultural proscriptions.

The duties and responsibilities imposed by organizations and the structures of society come to be accepted, even to be sought so that satisfaction and approval can be obtained. Human beings can fulfill needs only in interaction with others, but the control of impulses that interfere with social acceptance and opportunities for fulfillment in a social context is neither simple nor easy. Individuals need the help of others in achieving control; therefore, both external and internal control accounts for the socialized behavior of man.

THE INTERNALIZATION OF CONTROL

A man driving alone on a deserted city street at night, with no one in sight in any direction, comes to an intersection and as the traffic light turns red, he brings his car to a stop and waits until the light turns green before continuing down the street. This man has *internalized* a rule of the social order, and the conformity to the rule has become part of his response style; he needs no external control to enforce the rule. Someone else driving toward the intersection could safely predict that the man had internalized the traffic rule. As conformity to the rule has moral significance—to cross the red light might endanger another person—conformity is therefore part of the moral system of society. The basis for this internalization of rules and its development is a complex phenomenon in human behavior and is another species-specific capability. Impulses, needs, and emotions come to be channeled and controlled so that in spite of needs or impulses an individual will conform to society's regulations. Reasons for nonconformity are few, and approved exceptions are difficult to find.

The Process of Internalization

The internalization of cultural rules is part of the socialization process. Socialization is a broader concept (see Chapter 3) than is internalization, in that socialization not only includes the learning of society's expectations but also allows acquisition of unique and individualized response styles. Internalization refers only to the acquisition of a behavioral system of rules prescribed by society.

Because much human behavior is learned, the *internalization process* as well as the content of what is internalized is learned. It follows, then, that what was said earlier about cognitive development applies to the internalization process. The process includes the selection of appropriate content and the establishment of a response system that can be recalled or "set off" by stimuli similar to those selected in earlier experience. In socialization and internalization, the child must learn that whenever a specific stimulus situation is encountered, a specific response system is to be associated with it. Because such acquired behavior is at first beyond the understanding of the child, external control has to be exercised in the beginning by the parent or by another agent of society. The means whereby internalization is attained can be left to the individual child and his parents. The child's learning pattern and his emotion about the end result are of little concern to the social order; conformity to the rule is of primary concern.

Although human beings generally can accomplish the transformation from external to internal control, a problem arises in some individuals from the effect of the process on their efforts to obtain satisfaction and on the use of their potential for living in society. In such instances, internal controls have so much influence that the life style of an individual is impaired.

In reality, the transformation process should be of concern to society, as a resentful and grudging conformity will eventually affect society adversely. Hence, the general use of some benign system of internalization by parents and the educational system is very important.

A crucial question is: How can the individual be taught to internalize the rules of society so that social values are cherished and socialized behavior is achieved without his behavior being based on fear? Further, how can the content of what is to be internalized be systematically altered to accomplish social change without undue sacrifice for the individual or destruction of the social order? If the internalization is to be effective for society and satisfying for the individual, it seems that the process should contain a minimum of dissatisfaction or pain; that is, a process producing too much discomfort, dissatisfaction, and resentment would seem to interfere with a willingness to follow the internalized code, once the threat of external control is removed. A code introduced under a system of pleasure and reward can be expected to continue longer as a valued code after external control is removed than one internalized under conditions of dissatisfaction and negative emotion (Lana, 1969). A conscience cannot be brought into existence by fear, as the individual conforms under such conditions only so long as there is the presence of threat. If the cultural codes have been enforced under conditions that engender hostility and negativism, rejection of the codes will occur when an enforcing agent is no longer present.

The concept of internalization of cultural codes of behavior can be expressed in terms quite similar to those of psychoanalytic theory. According to that theory, the impulses of the *id* are controlled during the course of development by the *ego,* a reality-related aspect of the personality. The ego allows the individual to fulfill needs and to behave in any way possible as long as well-being is not jeopardized (Freud, 1938). But the *superego,* or conscience, acts as the controlling force within the individual that prevents his doing things he has been taught are wrong. By behaving according to his conscience, the individual may deny one set of needs or desires while fulfilling other needs by behaving in socially approved ways. Although the superego may be described as an entity, the internal control of behavior can also be seen as a response system that the individual has learned to use in appropriate stimulus situations.

Principles of learning may be applied to the process of internalization. The concept of stimulus generalization, for example, is useful, as, obviously, enough rules could not be learned for all situations encountered, whereas through reasoning and generalization the principles of the rules can be applied by the individual when he meets a new situation.

Conditions for the Process. The process of internalization has several basic steps in the course of development. First, beginning in infancy, there is exploration of the life space. The infant's exploration is limited by the immaturity of his sensory abilities, his perceptual capabilities, and his psychoneurological levels of development. As he develops, his environment develops: maturation and learning take place so that he can perceive and respond to more stimuli; thus, an increase in capability is accompanied by environmental expansion. Consequently, as cognitive capability grows, an increase in environmental complexity occurs.

Deprivation of stimulus complexity occurs for some children, as has been indicated in Chapter 2. In order to learn about the culture and to learn to internalize behavioral controls, experience and stimulus situations common to the majority of those in the culture must be available in order that internalization of the code for control may take place. The essential aspects of the culture must be experienced. The child cannot internalize a code with which he has had no experience. Although experience cannot and need not be complete because of such principles as stimulus generalization or concept formation, enough of the culture must be experienced so that response patterns of appropriate complexity can be learned.

An illustration of this point is found in language development—vocabulary must be acquired to the extent necessary to permit the individual to interact and deal with the culture. It should be remembered that vocabulary increase is developmental and that cultural expectations exist for each age level. If developmental expectations are not achieved, the child is handicapped in further development and interaction. Not only in language but in general cultural learning, it is possible that morphological changes result from exercise, so that delayed learning experience is not so effective as that which comes at appropriate developmental times. This means that part of the internalization of control needs to be age-graded and to be a part of the child's experience as he develops. Appropriate stimuli are needed to insure that as the child matures, the learning experience will be available when he is ready for it.

This use of the environment is ordinarily a natural process. When the culture surrounds the child, he uses it as he becomes capable; if it is not there, he is deprived, and his future development is impaired. Introduction of the culture at some later time by an educational system is unsatisfactory, partly because of individual differences and partly because not enough is known about the essential content of the developmental experience that was missed. A better approach lies in providing characteristic cultural stimuli during all the developmental years. When the child's individual capacities develop, the cultural stimuli can be utilized.

Emotional Characteristics. Exploration of the environment, as has been indicated in Chapters 8 and 9, is enhanced by certain emotional relationships and interchanges with one person and by the presence of certain persons. Internalization of the code for control is further complicated by a necessity for certain characteristics in emotional relationships. In order that the child may experiment with ways to learn difficult response patterns, he must have a positive emotion about himself. Unfavorable experience and a lack of positive affect will interfere with new exploration and effort toward behavioral change. Anxiety about capability has an effect similar to that of cultural deprivation, as the child's self-imposed deprivation increases his fear of new experiences. An example is afforded by school phobia. A child afraid to go to school deprives himself of experience needed to cope with his culture. If he is forced to go when frightened or is punished for fleeing from the school, he is not helped to attain the new level of complexity in behavior; his fear and incompetence are only increased, as illustrated by the problems of Robert Kendall.

Robert had lived in a row house in the city all of his life. Before he was old enough to go to school, he would sit on the steps in front of his door and watch the neighborhood children go past on the way to school. As some of his older playmates went off to school, he looked forward to the time when he would be five and could also go to kindergarten.

Robert's father had shift work at a large steel mill, and Robert seldom saw him. Even when his father was at home, he spent little time with Robert. He preferred to watch sports on television while drinking more than his wife liked. Robert's mother worked days in a nearby cigar factory, and a neighbor was paid a small amount each week to "look after" Robert. This arrangement meant that he could play with the neighbor's child and go back and forth between his home and the neighbor's.

When the first day of school came, the neighbor took Robert and her daughter to the school several blocks away. He had looked forward to school, but he became anxious when he found himself in a strange place with no one he knew. As the morning passed, he did not feel any less anxious; there were so many children that the teacher had little time for him. At the end of the school day he walked home with the others and complied with the orders of the children on guard at the street intersections. Next day he did not want to go to school, but, as the neighbor insisted, he went. On the way home, several older boys approached Robert; one took his tablet and pencil. He protested, but the boy shoved him against the playground fence and struck him sharply. Robert cried and ran home.

The next morning he protested vehemently about going to school. The neighbor took him by the arm and forced him to go. Although Robert was crying when he came into the school room, the teacher did not have time to attend to his grief. He sat unhappily at one side of the room, refusing to participate in school activities. Later when the group was taken to the playground, Robert left school and went home. The teacher missed him and called his mother at work. The next morning his mother delayed going to work in order to take Robert to school. Again, the boy had to be forced to go and cried bitterly when his mother left to go on to work. It was only a short time until Robert ran home again.

The following day at school time Robert vomited and complained of a stomachache. He said he was too sick to go, but his mother took him anyway. As the teacher stood by the door, he had no choice but to remain. Robert discovered that he had to learn to conform and to internalize many new rules that he had never before encountered. For him the process was not benign; he was expected to learn the rules whether he felt he could do so or not. From such circumstances it is easy to see how the anxiety and hostility of a small boy can smolder and perhaps be fanned into the flaming emotions of the adolescent in later years. If the "system" is unsympathetic to a child of five, can it be expected to be sympathetic to one of fifteen?

The emotions accompanying the abandonment of formerly successful and age-appropriate behavior for new ways of behaving include uncertainty, fear, and anxiety. These feelings are a part of the maturation process and, to some extent, a normal conflict of development. In the developmental process, behavior that brought approval and satisfaction at an earlier age level is discarded. At first new patterns of required behavior cause dissatisfaction because of the difficulties in learning them. Therefore, the importance of emotional support for the child in his effort to change at succeeding age levels is apparent. Although variations in the developmental sequence occur, the process of acquisition and discard is a continuing one, in which the child needs an emotional alliance with parents and others around him. Maturity is achieved when the individual has sufficient confidence in himself to abandon old response systems and to acquire new ones. In many ways the individual continues to need the emotional support experienced as a child, as the process of discard and acquisition continues throughout the life span (Hamachek, 1971). Emotional alliance and the affectionate concern of parents are more important in childhood than later because, if the child has support then and learns the complexities of human emotional relationships, he can establish alliance for himself in his adult years. But if he is emotionally deprived in childhood, he is unlikely to learn ways to find support in adulthood. Because emotional relationships and cultural experience are never continually favorable to development, difficulties occur in the process. Both the individual and society suffer from the consequence.

Individualization

Although similarities in the internalization process are expected, individual differences of both a genetic and a learned nature cause variability. The internalization process thus differs among individuals—it takes place more efficiently at one time in the life of an individual than at another time, and individuals even in similar environments vary in their transformation from external to internal control. Complete success is never attained; all that can be hoped for is some satisfaction on the part of the individual and society.

In recent years, as the young have entered adolescence, they have rejected some degree of the cultural code as well as some of the process used by society to bring about internalization. Conflict occurs because: (1) the individual's desires are at times so strong that fear of disapproval and personal reluctance at breaking rules are overcome; (2) individuals cannot avoid breaking rules if events are beyond their capacity to cope with the situation or if events are beyond comprehension; (3) some stimulus conditions contain conflicts that make it impossible to respond to one without being thrown in jeopardy by the others; (4) earlier teaching is in conflict with current standards brought about by social change; and (5) some insight has revealed error in the worth of conformity to the current code.

As a result of these conflicts, incomplete internalization occurs. As the code is not internalized, difficulties in social interaction arise. Some of the difficulties are intrapersonal—a person's refusal to conform causes feelings of guilt; he feels he should have conformed and so views himself as unworthy or incapable. Guilt causes a lack of confidence in meeting new situations as well as an increase in generalized anxiety.

Society often imposes sanctions on individuals who respond inadequately (London, 1969). These range from punishment to a mere disapproval. Mutual rejection, however, also occurs. An individual rejects society because of failure; he may even leave his own society to go to another, or he may seek an isolated place to live. Society enforces its sanctions in a number of ways: by exclusion from positions, scholarships, employment, travel to other countries, and opportunities for rewards. This rejection is basically disadvantageous, both to the individual and to the society. If an adolescent is rejected, his opportunities in society to fulfill his needs and to utilize all his potential for development are lessened (Rogers, 1969). With his opportunities lessened, he will have some basis for feeling resentful and negative, and such emotions will not contribute to creative and insightful interaction with the environment. A lack of success thus causes the individual to question his own worth and ability, as it is easier to doubt his own value when social rejection is encountered. Society is the loser, because a good society is dependent upon the generally positive response of its members. If a sufficient number of people reject the society, it will disintegrate. Such rejection need not come from a majority of the people; often a small number can hinder or alter progress toward social change or growth.

Origins of Difficulties. It hardly seems necessary to advocate study of the causes of people's difficulties in the internalization process, as such difficulties are of so much consequence to the person and society (Henry, Sims, and Spray, 1971). But in the past, societies have rejected attention to the causes. Historically, those who could not conform to cultural codes were not only rejected but were punished indiscriminately. Concern for individuals who cannot internalize the code and adopt behavioral patterns in accord with cultural norms has occurred only in the recent history of social orders. In fact, until the eighteenth century, the most advanced societies were intolerant of deviation from expected norms. Even if an individual's problems were obviously from some constitutional impairment, he would be considered liable to punishment. Sometimes those who failed to conform were taken to the edge of the city and driven off to wander about the countryside. Some were whipped publicly, some were placed in dungeons, and others were burned or hanged. In America, one of the advances in dealing with deviation came in 1752 with the establishment of the Pennsylvania Hospital for those with various incapacities, but even in this place conditions were far from good. It is only in recent years that rehabilitative measures have become of substantial significance (Alexander, 1962).

The usual evidence of difficulties in internalization of the code is the emotional reaction of either the individual himself or of those around him (Ahlstrom and Havighurst, 1971; Weiner, 1970). A basic problem is that of antagonistic emotions—of the individual and of society. Conflict develops easily. Even withdrawal—a relatively nonthreatening reaction to society—causes society to take measures against the individual. For example, action will be taken against a young adolescent who stays at home and refuses to go to school. If overt resentment is expressed, limits are placed on behavior.

In modern society, particularly in recent years, much more tolerance for deviant behavior has been evident. Public denouncement of political leaders, forceful occupation of the offices of administrators, destruction and defacement of property, and illegal use of drugs, while not approved, have at times been overlooked. Usually such behavior must occur in groups—one person will not be allowed to behave in such ways. Wide behavioral latitude is now permitted to groups, and increasingly the boundaries of the cultural code are being expanded. Some disapproval is still shown, and these societal reactions will be covered under the discussion of external controls.

The essential concern here is the difficulty in internalization. It should be readily apparent that separation of internal and external control is not absolute because the person may fear disapproval even though he escapes its actual expression. Fear of disapproval is internalized. And as has been indicated, interaction with the environment is impaired by anxieties about personal capacity, hostility toward the self and those in the life space, distortion or exclusion of essential environmental stimuli, displaced aggression, and emotional overreaction.

In dealing with the difficulties of internalization, it is possible to place too much emphasis on physical adequacy. Few individuals have perfectly functioning constitutions; most people must meet society's demands in spite of various physical limitations. In fact, one of the characteristics of mental disorder is a preoccupation with physiological functioning that creates a cyclic effect (Quay, 1972). For example, the stress and conflict initially causing a headache are increased by the pain, the physical discomfort makes coping with the conflict more difficult, and thus the headache worsens. One of the effects of successful socialization and training is that one can relate to environmental situations with some holistic perspective. An attribute of the successful person in society is the attainment of a response system that enables him to deal with the environment under conditions of constitutional limitations.

Aside from constitutional difficulties, most individuals must face problems associated with conflicts growing out of the internalization process. Inadequate as well as adequate response styles are learned, and not all the instruction and experience provided by the culture is appropriate. Some of it is not only inappropriate, but also harmful to the process of developing adequate response patterns. Part of the maturation process, consequently, consists of acquisition of sufficient knowledge to evaluate cultural teaching adverse to personal welfare and development (Cohen, 1971). This, of course, presents new difficulty, as the teaching usually occurs in a completely value-laden context. Rejection of cultural teaching (even though the content is harmful) is usually disapproved by society and its agents; stress-producing behavior (behavior that is no longer useful) thus is passed on from one generation to the next. Warnings about such possibilities are rarely made, as cultural agents (parents and teachers) believe that all they teach is valuable.

In addition to adverse content in the cultural code, other conditions in the life space bring the individual difficulty. Some of the most important of such conditions are abnormalities in family relationships: conflict between parents, rejection, physical abuse, extreme poverty, traumatic or extremely frightening experiences, excessive parental absence, prolonged illness, violent behavior of family members, parental inflexibility in training demands, severe criticism, lack of affection, and ridicule. All the sources of difficulty in the life space cannot be described, but in general the main sources are emotional conflict or emotional deprivation in the family, denial of opportunity to learn about the culture, and the teaching of inadequate response patterns. Although individuals react to such influences differently, anxiety, a low level of self-confidence, and distortion of reality usually result.

The concept of critical periods can be applied to the period of adolescence, which is somewhat analogous to the period of birth, the first critical time. At birth the infant must begin to function independently by initiating his own processes of respiration, digestion, and excretion. In adolescence, the individual must again take a crucial step toward independence. At this time it is the shift from an emotional dependence on parents to independence in fulfilling his emotional needs in relationships with others.

Adolescence is a critical period for two basic reasons: first, the adolescent usually must seek emotional support from peers who, themselves, need support; and second, the techniques the adolescent can use in obtaining such support are inadequately learned in the family. An adolescent who has had insufficient emotional exchange with parents during development or who has been treated harshly or with insensitivity is ill-equipped to fulfill his emotional needs in interaction with others or to function well with only the tenuous support of age-mates. Adolescents who have had problems in family relationships may irrationally demand support from or take advantage of peers. The mutual exchange necessary for adult satisfaction does not occur. The problem of emotional deprivation becomes cyclic: the greater the dissatisfaction, the more disturbed the adolescent becomes. Hostility usually develops, which is directed either outward at others or inward toward themselves. The young adolescent cannot turn to his parents, as maturation forces him to turn to others—yet his needs are often inadequately fulfilled in his social relationships. In such a situation lie the origins of extreme emotional behavior, irrationality, and displaced hostility (Wolfgang, 1970; Blanco, 1972).

Other manifestations of difficulties can be observed in restless and aimless activity, risk-taking behavior of an almost infinite variety, and activities in cliques, gangs, communes, and informal meeting places such as parking lots, streets, and entertainment establishments. Many feel set apart from parents and society, and their dress, music, and behavior are unmistakable manifestations of the separation. An increasingly common behavioral reaction, symptomatic of alienation, is the use of drugs. Almost any drug may be used in early experimentation. Drugs serve the desire for risk-taking opportunities and are often used in a shared experience with others. With them, the efforts of society and parents can be thwarted; through their use, independence and adult status can be explored. Much risk-taking behavior in adolescence is on the borderline between behavior that may be termed psychopathic and behavior common to adolescence.

Society's Reactions. Society vacillates in its methods in dealing with problems of adolescence. Standard approaches of law enforcement and psychotherapeutic problems, although often tried, have not brought generally satisfying solutions. Most psychotherapeutic methods now used involve peer groups. Some effort is directed toward parents, but if the adolescent is seldom at home and has turned to peers, work with parents, although of much-needed assistance to them, will be unlikely to provide a solution to the problems of the adolescents themselves.

Basic problems of adolescence lie in the internalization of behavior expected or desired by society. The adolescent does not conform to social norms because he sees conformity as dissatisfying. Part of the obvious origin of adolescents' problems is that parental life styles and child-rearing methods have not brought desired results. If the methods of the parents and the educational system are examined, some faults are apparent. Often the parents have personal problems, sometimes stemming from relationships with their own parents; they may experience dissension in their marriage; or they may have difficulty in making their way in a complex social order. Such incapacities and inadequacies often are passed on to children.

In a study of adolescents, Ahlstrom and Havighurst (1971) found that parents listed a number of common sources of their sons' difficulties. Poor work in school and the influence of bad companions were among the usual reasons given for the basis of their delinquency.

Although repeated efforts are made to provide adolescents with information about the social codes of society, information about an effective system for teaching children before they reach adolescence is not readily available to parents. Even if an adequate system were available, the difficulties and role behavior of the parents in society probably would not contribute to its use. Because the roles of family members are changing and the length of time that parents and children are together is decreasing, parental methods for dealing with the problems of socialization will probably be even less effective in the future. To further complicate the efforts toward solution, the educational system has increasingly sought to avoid a parental role. Overcrowding in the schools, effort to reform working conditions, and the search for adequate financial support have left little opportunity for concern about the emotional needs of individual children.

Society as a whole seems to have some reluctance to attend to the emotional concerns of children. For example, in some large cities where children in the center city schools have failed to learn to read by the fifth or sixth grade, commercial firms are employed to work with the children to improve reading test scores. The basic difficulties which prevented the children from progressing in the educational system, however, are not attended to. Ignored are such factors as fragmentation of the family, poverty, the children's lack of safety, filth in the living space, and the inculcation of hostility toward the social order. Improvement in reading scores, even if change can be satisfactorily demonstrated, is of little value if the other conditions are left untouched. All too often society, and particularly the educational system, has looked for solutions in teaching methods and techniques without attention to the basic foundation of learning—the child's emotional relationships within the family.

Individual Reactions. A common result of failure to meet social expectations is *aggression and hostility* (Johnson, 1972). As discussed earlier in Chapter 8, aggressive behavior has many variations, ranging from physical abuse of others to influencing others' behavior for one's own benefit. Hostility is similar to aggression, but a persistent negative emotion causes the hostile individual to see others as unfriendly or threatening. Aggression is a difficult concept to describe in conjunction with a concept of normative behavior. Some aggressive behavior is encouraged, in fact demanded, by society, while in other instances it is disapproved or punished. One kind of behavior may be approved in one social role but disapproved in another. Thus, aggression, both as a concept and as behavior governed by social codes, appears in a context of conflict.

Aggression is often approved if it is exerted in behalf of members of one group against another. Such approval is found frequently in primitive societies—if a stranger is encountered on a jungle trail, he is to be killed, because he may be an enemy. In a similar way in the city, an unknown adolescent may cross the "turf" of a gang and be beaten or perhaps killed because he does not belong to the group. Aggressive behavior in such instances is approved both on an individual and group basis.

Aggressive behavior in the urban environment can be characterized as an element of a life style because it is so much a part of behavior in social interaction (Milgram, 1970). In city traffic, aggressive driving is usually within the pattern of rules and laws, even though there are many instances in which rules and laws are broken. In other forms of transportation, an aggressive struggle to get aboard a vehicle and to find a seat is part of expected behavior. In department stores, customers are often aggressive, and salesmen brusquely demand information and impatiently wait for answers. Courtesy, tact, and patience are the exception in the rush of city life.

As discussed elsewhere, as the behavior of groups in modern society has become increasingly aggressive, violence has become a social problem. No social structure in modern society is immune to violence, and in recent years all have experienced some form of it. Part of the difficulty probably comes from the fact that codes for aggressive behavior, provided by the family and the educational and religious institutions, are ambiguous. Approval of aggression varies not only because of varying contexts but also because guides for the amount and intensity of aggression are lacking. Only the disapproval of extreme aggression is clearly delineated. In such extremes, the pathological limits are usually set in urban societies at the outlawing of physical abuse and injury. Those who cause physical injury are institutionalized, sometimes in institutions for the mentally disordered and sometimes in penal institutions.

The frustrations of those who live in the deprived areas of the cities cause hostility and aggressive behavior of a generalized type (Gold, 1970). These negative emotions have resulted in so much hostility that behavior against other people is carried out without direct provocation. On the campus of an urban university one evening, three adolescents from the nearby ghetto came upon a student entering his car. Because they had earlier vowed to kill someone, they spontaneously chose him as the victim, but at that moment a police car appeared on the street. While the car passed, the student entered his car and drove away, unaware of the danger. The boys remained on the corner, and in a few minutes another student approached his car. This time one of the boys pulled a pistol from his pocket and killed the student. The three boys fled, but not before they had been seen by a number of people. Caught by the police in a very short time, they revealed under questioning their youth, hostility, and deprived backgrounds.

The urban environment contains so many sources of stress that some individuals feel overwhelmed to the extent of trying to withdraw from as many contacts as possible. Degrees of withdrawal are associated with individual difficulty. Some people avoid certain parts of the environment —crowds in the subway, on the concourse of an airport, or in a sports arena. Some try to avoid enclosed spaces so that they will not be in close proximity to others. Others seek to avoid places where they feel dependent or inadequate, for example, in the strange part of the city where they do not know their way. Because of the varied sources of stress, all parts of the city are avoided by some segments of the population. Because most urban living involves threatening aspects, most city dwellers engage in some avoidance and withdrawal as an adaptive device. Because of the generality of such behavior, symptoms of withdrawal considered to be indicative of pathology have to be extreme. Whether or not the overall trends of urban living are contributing to more or less withdrawal behavior is difficult to determine, as evidence can be cited of trends in either direction. Improved communication and swift transportation have increased the opportunity for mobility in the city and thus counteract withdrawal. Opposed to such a view are trends toward a rising number of "incidents" in which residents of the city are pitted against each other and toward a rising number of crimes—both of these trends having an adverse effect on mobility and social exchange.

Another problem related to internalization is *negativistic* behavior. This is usually first evident between the ages of three and five, a period when much is demanded of the young child. He must learn control of excretory processes, how to dress himself, intricacies of language, respect for property, routines of cleanliness, tolerance of separation from his parents for periods of time, cooperation in play, and the rudiments of a morality code. Many children feel oppressed by so many demands and try to decrease the influence of external stimuli and control by adults by responding negatively to efforts to secure their cooperation. Even though a new experience may prove satisfying and pleasurable, a negativistic child will refuse to participate. In the extreme, negativism becomes a response style. This behavior differs from aggression, although some aggression may be expressed in blocking the actions of others or refusing to cooperate with them. Some negativistic behavior continues throughout the childhood period and into the adult years. As with other reactions to the internalization of a cultural code, problems can become extreme and pathological.

Asocial behavior is another problem that sometimes results from the process of internalization. This term is applied to behavior directed against society. It consists of defiance of the rules and norms of society and indicates that an individual has internalized very little of the culture's standards for behavior. If everyone were asocial and behaved without regard for social custom and standards, no society would exist. The asocial person shows little concern for standard behavior and acts, in Freudian terms, with little observable influence from the super-ego. The range of asocial behavior covers a large number of violations of social standards, but the most frequent violations are acts against property (stealing) and against the social standards for sex behavior. The asocial person steals when the opportunity permits, often without regard for others or himself. Shoplifting and automobile thefts are common manifestations. Even though the individual is caught and punished by imprisonment, he repeats the same behavior after release. Because it shows an irrational antagonism to society's codes of behavior, asocial behavior is considered pathological. Knowledge of the laws and of the punishment that will be likely to follow disobedience does not deter the pathological person from engaging in such behavior. Some persons who steal seem compelled to continue; neither punishment nor teaching about the importance of a moral code changes the pattern. Similarly, behavior not in accord with society's sexual customs is often repeated. A girl who becomes pregnant without marriage and goes through pregnancy, birth, and placement of the infant will require again the same care and help for other pregnancies. Some welfare officials lose hope for a change in such individuals and seek to have them sterilized. The causes of such behavior are complex; teaching about society's code has little effect, although the individual may profess willingness or determination to change. Investigation of the background and early experience almost always reveals factors that account for the development of asocial behavior.

Problems of body function often accompany the behavioral problems resulting from difficulties in the internalization process. (The relationship of body function to other response patterns was discussed in reference to the emotions.) It is not surprising that at times some alteration of body function takes place when an individual experiences the disappointment of failure. Usually, if not inevitably, some anxiety accompanies frustration and failure, and with anxiety some bodily manifestations occur, as was discussed in Chapter 8. A lack of success in meeting society's demands for conformity to a behavioral code may thus be accompanied by problems of body function. A child who fails to adjust to school or who cannot face leaving home to go to school often develops a headache or a stomachache. Failure to achieve in school, however, is usually symptomatic of other difficulties, although the school failure does become part of a cycle. Anxiety about the failure affects the child's physical functioning, and then his performance becomes even more inadequate. Failure to meet society's standards of behavior increases anxiety, and then the problem of poor performance worsens.

Emotional upset is believed to be related to body functioning in such instances as enuresis in children. Kidney function is affected, and the child's urine volume becomes greater than normal; the greater volume in turn contributes to the enuretic problem. Sleep disturbances, speech disorders, and many other problems associated with anxiety accompany the failure to meet society's standards.

THE CONTROLS OF SOCIETY
AND CULTURE

The channeling and control of individual behavior come about in two ways: through the internal controls—the efforts of the individual himself—and through the controls of the structures of society. Throughout history it has been recognized that internalization of a behavioral code is always incomplete. Man never can be fully trusted to conform. Hence, rules, laws, and means of compelling him to conform have been established. In childhood, considerable effort by the family, the educational system, and religious organizations is made in the socialization process to achieve internal controls, but in adolescence and in adulthood the effort is essentially lessened, and society comes to depend on external controls to deal with failures of internal controls. It is important to examine the function of the social structures in enforcing controls and the effect of the controls on individual behavior and development.

Control of Behavior by Social Structures

The family continues some form of external control through the affiliative bonds established during the developmental years. In some families and for some individuals, this control remains a powerful influence throughout life. For others, from families in which affiliative factors were never strong, influence and control become nonexistent. Society at present still expects the family to exercise control through the adolescent years.

The time when family control is no longer expected is unclear, just as society's expectation about the age at which youth reaches adult status is in doubt. It seems, however, that there is now a tendency to view an adolescent as an adult earlier than in the past. It should be remembered that primitive people generally set the beginning of adulthood at a much earlier age than does modern society. A child or adolescent who violates the law is often "released into the custody" of the parents by the legal system, which indicates that society expects those parents to help protect society's interests by controlling their child. In reality, the parents are unable to control the child—the fact that he is in trouble indicates that the parents have lost control.

In the years between 13 and 18, it is generally agreed that control and responsibility still rest with the parents and that society's agents are expected not to interfere with this control. Yet it is especially in these years that failure of the internalization process becomes evident to others outside the family. It is in these years that the young person begins to move out of the family and to establish relationships which replace the family. And it is during this time that the young are expected to begin to engage in independent behavior, to make choices about activities, and to develop heterosexual interests and relationships (Blos, 1970). Apparently it is expected that this time of exploration and experimentation is to be supervised and limited by parental control. Socialization and internalization, especially in the area of heterosexuality, must in reality await these years; therefore, as adolescents experiment and learn, external control is expected, as internal controls are yet to be firmly fixed.

It is not, however, as if the young person has no guides or as if some behavioral response patterns have not already been established. Adolescent boys who are harsh or cruel in sexual relationships with girls will be found to behave in similar ways in other than sexual relationships; and those who are generally considerate in interpersonal exchange will be found to be considerate in sexual relationships. Principles for human relationships taught in the very early years are the basis for heterosexual relationships. Further, the behavior of models or parents also has powerful effect on adolescent sexual behavior. Because the affectional system experienced in the family becomes a foundation for the affectional relationships with peers, the principles for human relationships and affectional patterns possible in them are ordinarily learned before the adolescent years. If the parents have not produced in their children behavior in accordance with society's code, demands that the parents change and retrain their adolescent are more than can reasonably be expected of them. If the parents cannot be expected to deal with the problems of the adolescents in conflict with society, what alternatives are possible?

Social Action Goals. Two courses of action are necessary. First, one of society's goals should be to provide assistance for parents who need help with their children during the early years. This is a complex goal, as it is necessary then to be concerned about parental life styles and the fulfillment of their needs in society. Second, in cases where parents have not been able to prepare their children adequately for roles in modern social settings, society must have alternate or supportive systems for external control. This approach, involving social agents either participating or engaging autonomously in control programs, has certain philosophical conflicts. Because society becomes a part of the process only after problems or difficulties arise and when the internalization has been recognized as inadequate (it is expected that society will use different methods and set different goals than have the parents), this change implies criticism of the parents' earlier methods and goals. Such an unavoidable implication means that parental support for society's methods will be tenuous. A further consideration is that often both parental and social approaches to external control contain elements of punishment and disapproval. The child is trained in a pattern later seen as undesirable; then in adolescence he resents punishment for behavior specifically taught to him earlier. Why, he asks, should he be punished for behaving in the way in which he was trained or in the way he perceived his parents as behaving? If society is to help the adolescent to become a satisfactory member of society, internalization of the cultural code must be accomplished, even though belatedly, but punishment is unlikely to secure the cooperation and effort of the adolescent in the process.

Several conditions for society's efforts are apparent. Leaving the adolescent in the family situation where the failure took place has unreasonable aspects, and punishment for behavior that failed to achieve conformity to society should not be part of the new training. New concepts for society's efforts therefore are needed, but the efforts should be in some educational framework, as the young adolescent's education is inadequate as a basis for coping with his modern and complex society.

Independent and socially satisfying behavior should be the goal of the program. Many youth are frustrated by the lack of satisfying opportunities within the educational system; they face social control in their lives without access to the rewards that ought to be available for conformity. Opportunities to earn money, to feel independent and free to pursue interests, and to set adult goals are often lacking. Some opportunities are supplied by some colleges and universities, but favorable conditions need to be available several years earlier. It seems that there is a trend for society to assume an increasing responsibility for establishment of educational programs that will take over some of the family's responsibility for early training. This trend is evident in the widespread demand for programs for youth that suggests that the socialization process is going to be much more a part of society's effort than it has been in the past.

Any program set up by society, as has been indicated, will have failures and therefore some necessary external control will have to be used. The need for external control will range from a minimum to complete control, and society will need a graded system of institutions.

To some extent one exists now, but a much more complex system must be devised. In future planning, the philosophical concept of punishment will need to be revised. Primary emphasis within the institutions must be placed on *control* and *prevention*. If the institutional system can be made to function adequately, punishment will not be a major problem. As the individual needs control, it will be supplied by society. Fear of punishment or external control will not be emphasized, and society will not rely upon them to bring about conformity.

The Problem of Punishment. The problems of external control and punishment are as old as social orders. Many humane and learned people are opposed as to methods, but they do agree that modern society is confused and irrational in its current approaches to deviant behavior. Punishment is generally used in the socialization process even with very young children, and few in modern society maintain that this is not a significant principle in child training even into the adolescent years. That is, if internal controls are ineffective or yet to be achieved, punishment is to be used. It is difficult, if not impossible, to separate punishment from the concept of external control, as imposed control necessarily contains an element of deprivation—the person cannot pursue the goals or use the methods of his own choosing.

Some even advocate "discipline" for children as essential to the socialization and internalization process; it is held to be "good" for the child, and it will insure adherence to the cultural code in the future. This view that punishment is of value in the socialization process is increasingly questioned and, logically, the questioning about its value in control of adult behavior has occurred. Before adolescence, punishment is seen as less of an issue because external controls can be forced on a young child much more easily than on an adolescent. In adolescence, the means and principles of punishment used at earlier age levels are easily recognized as inappropriate and ineffective. In this period it is considered important to "reason" with the adolescent.

Obviously, reasoning is much more effective if it has been often used and both parent and child have come to depend on such an approach. But *reasoning* is difficult to define practically—perhaps it means that the parent persuades the adolescent that the cultural code is the reasonable way of behaving and that it is in his best interest to behave in prescribed and parentally approved ways. In the reasoning process, however, is the parent prepared to concede that the adolescent's reasoning is correct and that his own is fallacious? Or, is the adolescent prepared to see the merit of the parent's view and concede that his reasoning is faulty and that he should therefore alter his goal? Either of these outcomes seems improbable.

The internalization process during the earlier years must include a different approach; in fact, the necessary elements are there some of the time. The child internalizes much of the code without reasoning or being upset about it (some reasoning is beyond his interest or capability); the parent need explain only to the extent that "it is the custom." The child conforms in order to achieve other goals—parental approval and affection and perhaps permission to engage in other activities. But later, the adolescent questions the code and may refuse to abide by it if it blocks his desires.

The question of external controls becomes not only one of selectivity but also one of quantity. Perhaps the adolescent will be allowed a different hair style, but will not be allowed to appropriate the property of others. Society would thus allow some deviation but also enforce some of the code regardless of the desires of the adolescent. The code will be enforced even if the adolescent maintains that it is unreasonable. If the custom is the law, the adolescent is made to conform. It is on this issue that a basic conflict arises. At what point does the individual or society concede to the "reasoning of the other"?

If external control and society's will must prevail, how will the "punishment be made to fit the crime" if the person does not conform? And, should punishment be eschewed, what other courses of action are possible? Could methods be devised which would help the individual to adopt the code? Adoption of course is possible, as in earlier years the code is adopted to some extent by the child in order to achieve other goals. If some goals valued by the adolescent are met, would he in turn be willing to adopt society's code? If he believed that there was an affectionate concern for his happiness, would he in turn show an affectionate concern for the happiness of his parent or the agents of society?

Often in the city, particularly in the black ghettos, youth have few or no opportunities to find work or a way into the society. No one cares about them. They are not admitted to desirable opportunities in society, but nevertheless respect for society's code is demanded of them. They are expected to be bound by the code even though society does not help them to obtain the rewards of the system. If they transgress, harsh external controls are imposed, and little or no enculturation or education is supplied to them. Punishment for "wrongdoing" is the theme of society's philosophy. But why is not internalization a part of the program? Why is the problem not approached on the basis that the socialization process has failed and that the individual should be helped to find a satisfying place in society? Incarceration (punishment) followed by the return of a deprived adolescent to the ghetto is hardly a reasoned approach to his problems. Most juvenile delinquency could be dealt with on the basis of a socialization program and an inculcation of the knowledge that society is concerned about individual destiny.

A much more difficult problem is encountered in instances similar to the one described earlier in which a student was killed by three adolescents. It has been advocated by some (Menninger, 1963) that all punishment be avoided and that prisons be turned into rehabilitation centers. It is advocated that society reject the concept of punishment either as revenge or as a deterrent. Others (Barzun, 1963) believe that the death penalty should be continued and that those who kill should be killed by society, that the death penalty signifies a forfeiture of rights in society and is, in fact, more humane than imprisonment. Others believe that research and experimental programs could be undertaken to determine methods of rehabilitation in institutions other than prison. Currently many are concerned about conditions in prisons and society's lack of effort to experiment in developing meaningful rehabilitation programs.

Significant factors in present-day concern about the effectiveness of controls are technical advances in society and the changes in the cultural code. Even if little change takes place in society's system of external control, still the cultural code will change, and thus confusion about the code will inevitably worsen. Maintenance of an unchanging code may be even more dangerous to society than experimentation in new approaches, in that defiance of the code and general dissatisfaction can become so great that the code will become unenforceable. Signs of such difficulty are already at hand; for example, rules in some universities have been unenforceable because of the action of a large number of students. But this is, of course, the history of revolution (see Chapter 2). In a revolution, a large number of people decide to defy the social order's function and bring about governmental overthrow.

It is obvious that the goal of an enlightened society should be to minimize external control, for if much control is necessary, the socialization system has failed in some way. Ideally, the socialization process should lessen external control during the developmental years and make the necessary effort to help all individuals internalize essential aspects of the cultural code. Further, the code should be limited and should consist of only what is basic and fundamental in order to insure survival of the social order. As some conflict is inevitable, adjudication of differences is necessary, as well as some imposition of external control on dissident groups. At the same time, means to seek change and redress should be provided. It seems clear a social order cannot be entirely equal in its external control, but it should allow freedom to pursue life styles of a wide variety.

Because of past failures in the socialization and internalization process, external control seems to be necessary for a long time in the future. The amount can be lessened, however, and punishment can be reduced or devalued as a concept. For the violent crimes against people, punishment should be continued as a relief for society and the injured individuals, but its lack of value as a deterrent should be recognized. Capital punishment is unlikely to be continued, partly because no one in modern society will want to carry it out. Life imprisonment seems to be replacing it. Punishment for violent crimes, however, will not be a main issue in spite of the fact that such crimes are on the increase. Changes in thought about punishment are occurring even in less urbanized societies. For example, in one society thieves are now to have a hand cut off by a surgeon instead of by an unskilled man with a hatchet, and adulterous women are to be shot instead of stoned (Bazelon, 1963). Concern for internalization of rules will increase in modern societies, but respect for diversity will also become much more widespread. Disorder and dissension will also increase as more minority groups seek equalization of opportunities and some of the wealth of the society.

External Controls and Social Change

Perhaps one of the most significant aspects of social change in the latter half of the twentieth century is the change in viewpoint about the place of external controls in the lives of people in modern and urban society. The control of the state or society over man's affairs has changed steadily since the writing of the Magna Carta, but the changes in recent years have become more personal, intimate, and complex. It is not possible, however, to make comparisons as to whether man is more or less "free" than he was a century or two ago, because in part his definition of freedom has changed. A century or so ago, he saw freedom perhaps as escape from tenancy on a nobleman's estate to ownership of his own land. Today he may view freedom as time to watch a football game on Saturday afternoon without having to push a hand mower over his lawn.

Considerable emphasis today is on freedom to make decisions about places to work, to live, and to send children to school. Demands also are made for a voice in decisions about company policy, about wages, about use of land adjacent to personal property, and the content of the educational system's curriculum. Although leisure time has increased, even more such time is desired for such activities as sports, travel, and other recreational pursuits. Increased discretionary income has allowed many more people to make choices about recreation. In these activities, external control is seemingly less marked than in work areas, but as more people pursue recreation, regulations increase rapidly. Because the trend in recreational activities is toward more control, freedom will probably be sought in other sources and patterns of activities.

Control and Privacy. Much external control currently comes from the activity of government in the lives of people; but in almost any social cause, the financial support of government is sought even though it means regulation. Some advocate more local effort as in reality items can be bought directly by cash or credit. The individual in either case must pay for them himself. The private "store" from which purchases can be made is still larger than the public (government) store, and this means more freedom (Wallich, 1963). If services and functions are to be obtained from the public source, taxes as a form of external control, as well as regulation, leave little direct choice for the individual in his life style.

In modern and urban societies many new and subtle means of external control are to be found in the rapidly multiplying means of monitoring individual activities and in the gathering of information about individual life styles. A vast accumulation of information and storage of personal information about many in urban society is now held in "secret" files. Usually the secrecy applies only to the individual concerned; although it is almost impossible for him to see the information, it may be for sale to a large number of organizations or individuals. In addition, the individual himself has no opportunity to verify the information or to be assured that it is up to date. People have become inured to the prying operations and questions and have even come to accept peremptory demands for it. The individual has little opportunity to review a vast collection of information, to contribute items to the file which he believes to be important, or to correct the errors contained in it. One cannot assume that one pattern for obtaining information appropriate for thousands of people will be appropriate for specific individuals. Facts and information which are "individualized," however, are not included nor will they be included by personal request. Changes in activities, accomplishments, and life styles take place over the life span; therefore, judgments about information in the files should be periodically changed. The personal file of an individual follows him wherever he goes in society. If he makes application for credit or for a position in a distant city, information can be requested or bought by those who will make judgments about him. These judgments will be made on the basis of information about which he has no knowledge. The subjective statements of numbers of interviewers continue in his file all his life. Some of the information in the file is of little value—for example, the place of birth is continually recorded and yet no one can justify its inclusion.

With the increase in the collection of information growing out of technological advances, safeguards for the individual must be devised; and as society changes an individual should have an opportunity to make decisions about the content of the information collected. Because urban life styles demand the use of credit to buy a house, to rent an apartment, to buy or rent a car, or even to enter a hospital, the information in a man's file must be viewed as of consequence. Yet, because of technological developments in information processing, the anonymity of collection, and the "confidentiality" of processing and use, the significance of these external controls over the lives of the individual in modern society has been overlooked.

New developments for surveillance have been increasing at a rapid rate. Many a city dweller leaves a commercial establishment where he has been anonymously watched on closed circuit television, drives his car under radar surveillance (in some instances closed-circuit television) to another establishment where the clerk "calls the office" for details about him as well as feeding into the file information from his driver's license, then returns to his apartment to find that a "maintenance man" has entered at the order of the manager.

This kind of surveillance is quite different from the shared knowledge about individuals in folk societies. In those societies, knowledge was largely verbal and consequently revision or contradiction was possible. The individual also had an opportunity to learn about those surrounding him who influenced his affairs. In modern society, much of the information-gathering is anonymous. Although a commercial establishment gathers and demands information about a customer, the customer can gather little of consequence about the establishment or its management. If the goods fail in some way or prove to be not what was expected, the seller refers the customer to a distant manufacturer for recourse and assumes no responsibility. This impersonal and anonymous quality will be an increasing problem in urban society, and all the consequences for the individual are not now predictable. New technologies can be utilized with secrecy, and decisions can be made by powerful social structures currently beyond individual influence.

New means of external control will come from the planning activities of large social structures and organizations such as the military structure, federal agencies, city governments, special commissions, and large industries. New problems will arise because of the anonymity of some of the activities of these large organizations and because of their power to overcome opposition or restraints (Hallett, 1967).

The *psychological* consequence of external controls is significant. When a social problem develops, clamor rises for some social agency, usually the government, to deal with the problem. A case in point is that of air piracy. Because of the great danger for increasingly larger numbers of people, the government cooperated with industry in bringing about increased surveillance of passengers as they board. Passengers, by submitting to either electronic search or personal inspection, are expected to contribute to the solution of a serious social problem. The solution requires relinquishing the privacy of persons and belongings, although most passengers agree to the value of such procedures and admit readily that they believe the search is for their own good. But regardless of the worthiness of the goal, the agents of the state or industry require submission of personal affairs to an impersonal authority. Such policies provide foundations for the extension of external controls. If inspection is necessary for aircraft, why not search people on entering a department store or a public building? Step by step it is possible to justify extensive control for the common good.

The Functioning of Controls. Two basic difficulties lie in the use of external controls: they tend to increase, and they are difficult to remove. Removal is difficult, because persons come to depend on them; if external controls solve the problem, then individuals need not accept responsibility for the origin of the difficulty. Although a very young child must have external controls because he has not matured sufficiently to develop internal controls, he is expected to depend on them less as he grows older. A principle of socialization thus can be stated: The more a person or society depends upon external control, the less socialized is the person and the less civilized the society.

Although the goal of external control is to prevent adverse conditions for society, the method is a hazardous one. If personal searches of passengers and armed guards on board are effective in preventing air piracy, it might be concluded that society is well served and a social goal is reached. But if antisocial individuals (potential aircraft pirates) turn to holding high government officials for ransom, then society must turn to other restrictive measures. (It should be remembered that the real burden of external controls falls on the innocent.) If, however, causes of the creation of antisocial behavior are sought and general measures are undertaken to deal with the usually tragic conditions that create antisocial persons, then the difficulties and necessity for external controls will be greatly reduced. When origins of social problems are dealt with, not only is a better society created with more satisfied people in it, but the restrictive social controls on the majority of people in the society are lessened. Thus, by placing emphasis on the reduction of external controls and on a search for causes of the antisocial behavior which makes them necessary, members of society become aware of adverse social conditions.

During the first half of the twentieth century many cities built up external controls and increased agencies to enforce them. At the same time, vast areas in cities were allowed to deteriorate, thereby creating conditions that required more controls in order to deal with the antisocial behavior of the inhabitants. One large eastern city more than doubled the budget for the police department in one year, but little progress was made that same year in alleviating the distressing conditions in block after block of deteriorated and unfit housing.

Disadvantages of Controls. If external controls solve the problems without general social awareness of the original social problems, then the problems are not likely to receive attention. This does not mean that external controls are wrong, or that they are unnecessary, but that they can become ends that ultimately will destroy society. They should be looked upon as temporary measures, and the basic causes of the malady must be sought. A compassionate and mature social order will endeavor to reduce external controls and will understand that controls are indicative of its failure rather than of its success.

In the first place, controls inhibit growth toward more mature behavior. Because their removal demands public effort and planning, considerable resistance to removal of controls is usually encountered. Yet, resistance to the continuance of the controls ultimately develops. This paradox will be discussed in a later chapter.

In the second place, although external controls may provide a successful structuring of behavior in the early period of their use, they decline in value after an initial period. This early effectiveness and subsequent inhibition of effective individual behavior is illustrated in a study of adolescents who engaged in delinquent behavior while they were part of a training program. The study was done in a residence unit of an urban Job Corps training center. Different kinds of leadership for three groups were devised. The leader of one group set up a system of external controls and a definite structure of standards and goals; a second leader asked his group to work at several tasks without expecting a report of plans or information about results of the group's effort; while a third leader sought to assist in group solutions of problems, to involve group members in assuming responsibility for standards of behavior, and for the establishment of work goals. Personal records of members of the three groups furnished information about infraction of rules as well as the accomplishment of tasks.

The first group, in which the leader exerted the most control, had the greatest success in an initial period of several weeks—the group had fewer rule infractions and greater accomplishment in performance than the other two groups had. But after the initial period, the third group, the one with minimal controls and with members encouraged to set their own standards, surpassed the group with external controls. The group in which the leader neither provided control nor encouraged individual responsibility was the least successful (MacDonald, 1967).

The study suggests a deterioration in socializing accomplishments under external controls. The results also suggest, however, that the greatest control was not an unsuccessful method to use with these adolescents. It might be argued that they had not had sufficient opportunity to learn the use of internal controls in their earlier years and thus external controls were expected and needed. Similarly, those in the group who received encouragement toward the assumption of individual responsibility also needed time to make progress in the development of internal controls. The inferior performance of the group with little leadership suggests that there is indeed a need for a model of appropriate behavior and, certainly, if appropriate behavior has not been learned, some external controls, at least in the form of a code or structure, are a necessity. If the conditions described in these experimental groups are representative of various experiences in society, then it must be concluded that inadequate and even antisocial behavior can be altered by the provision of certain types of leadership and group conditions.

The Significance of Early Training. It seems reasonable to expect that previous learning and experience with external control are of consequence in determining the effectiveness of various conditions of group structures. Individuals who have already learned to depend on external controls find it difficult to make progress on their own when controls are not present and, as in the experiment just described, a period of learning must take place. Individuals who are dependent on controls and who are in situations where they are provided seem to be able to make only limited progress in the development of internal controls; they may expend excessive energy in emotional reaction to the controls rather than in development of responsible and effective behavior.

These principles provide some guides for the early experience of children in the educational system. Even for the other social structures of society, attention to such principles is worth while. "Age-grading" is not only necessary in the opportunities provided for learning of the use of internal controls; when controls are necessary in learning experiences at later ages, a gradual lessening of control will result in more effective and satisfying behavior. Although giving up behavior that was useful in the past is a difficult learning experience, the effort on the part of those who provide the experience, as well as of those who learn, is much more likely to bring ultimate satisfaction in the levels of achievement than continued dependence on external controls.

IN PERSPECTIVE

In human interaction, some control of behavior by the individual himself is necessary. A man, for example, wishes to keep his family intact, to hold on to some of his possessions, and to have a measure of privacy. For these desires to be fulfilled, other people must learn to respect his claims and to exercise control over their impulses to intrude or destroy. Consequently, argument against the need for internal controls seems unreasonable.

Problems about controls arise in modern society in respect to several subjects: (1) the manner of teaching internal controls, (2) the selection of controls to be internalized, (3) the recourse that society should have if the individual does not internalize appropriate controls, and (4) the determination of the type of action the individual should take if society insists on controls inimical to his personal welfare.

Early in the developmental years, external controls are imposed on the child because he is incapable of internalizing complicated principles of behavior. For example, in reference to safety in crossing a street, the child must be forced into certain behavior by restraint, that is, external control must be imposed.

If a person accepts external controls imposed by society without question or evaluation, social change is unlikely, and those in power roles tend to take advantage of such acceptance.

Because some individuals are unable to internalize rules about behavior, society must protect itself from the consequences of their behavior. External controls are set up to compel such people to behave in required ways. This society, as all modern societies, insists that individuals internalize the rules and codes for behavior or face the consequences, usually punitive action. Although all societies see this demand as justified, there is of course a long history of misuses of social power to compel certain behavior.

In the course of enforcing cultural requirements all demands are not applied with equal justice, in part because people in power in a modern society cannot attend to individual problems arising from general demands. Therefore, individuals will have to make decisions to avoid or reject internalization of some demands. Some societies provide ways for this to be done, and in them some measure of success in rejection may be achieved through legal means, political effort, or counterdemands that exceptions be made. No society is entirely fair, nor are all expectations of social agents reasonable; therefore, some means of recourse for the individual ought to be provided. In modern and complex society, unfortunately, recourse becomes increasingly difficult to achieve.

REFERENCES

AHLSTROM, W. M., & HAVIGHURST, R. J. *400 losers.* San Francisco: Jossey-Bass, 1971.

ALEXANDER, T. What is mental retardation? *Clinical Pediatrics,* 1962, I, 161–165.

BARZUN, J. In favor of capital punishment. In H. K. Girvetz (Ed.), *Contemporary moral issues.* Belmont, Calif.: Wadsworth, 1963. Pp. 105–112.

BAZELON, D. L. The dilemma of punishment. In H. K. Girvetz (Ed.), *Contemporary moral issues.* Belmont, Calif.: Wadsworth, 1963. Pp. 83–94.

BLANCO, R. F. *Prescriptions for children with learning and adjustment problems.* Springfield, Ill.: Charles C Thomas, 1972.

BLOS, P. *The young adolescent: Clinical studies.* New York: Free Press, 1970.

COHEN, Y. A. The shaping of men's minds: Adaptations to the imperatives of culture. In M. L. Wax, S. Diamond, & F. O. Gearing (Eds.), *Anthropological perspectives on education.* New York: Basic Books, 1971. Pp. 19–50.

FREUD, S. (A. A. Brill, Ed.) *The basic writings of Sigmund Freud.* (Translated and edited, with an introduction by A. A. Brill). New York: Modern Library, 1938.

GOLD, M. *Delinquent behavior in an American city.* Belmont, Calif.: Brooks/Cole, 1970.

HALLETT, S. J. Planning, politics, and ethics. In W. R. Ewald (Ed.), *Environment for man.* Bloomington, Ind.: Indiana University Press, 1967. Pp. 232–252.

HAMACHEK, D. E. *Encounters with the self.* New York: Holt, Rinehart & Winston, 1971.

HENRY, W. E., SIMS, J. H., & SPRAY, S. L. *The fifth profession.* San Francisco: Jossey-Bass, 1971.

JOHNSON, R. N. *Aggression: In man and animals.* Philadelphia: W. B. Saunders, 1972.

LANA, R. E. *Assumptions of social psychology.* New York: Appleton-Century-Crofts, 1969.

LONDON, P. *Behavior control.* New York: Harper & Row, 1969.

MACDONALD, W. S. Social structure and behavior modification in job corps training. *Perceptual and Motor Skills,* 1967, 24, 142.

MENNINGER, K. Therapy, not punishment. In H. K. Girvetz (Ed.), *Contemporary moral issues.* Belmont, Calif.: Wadsworth, 1963. Pp. 94–97.

MILGRAM, S. The experience of living in cities: A psychological analysis. In F. F. Korten, S. W. Cook, & J. I. Lacey (Eds.), *Psychology and the problems of society.* Washington, D.C.: American Psychological Association, 1970. Pp. 152–173.

QUAY, H. C. Patterns of aggression, withdrawal, and immaturity. In H. C. Quay & J. S. Werry (Eds.), *Psychopathological disorders of childhood.* New York: Wiley, 1972. Pp. 1–29.

ROGERS, C. R. *Freedom to learn.* Columbus, Ohio: Charles E. Merrill, 1969.

WALLICH, H. E. Private vs. public. In H. K. Girvetz (Ed.), *Contemporary moral issues.* Belmont, Calif.: Wadsworth, 1963. Pp. 161–168.

WEINER, I. B. *Psychological disturbance in adolescence.* New York: Wiley-Interscience, 1970.

WOLFGANG, M. E. Violence and human behavior. In F. F. Korten, S. W. Cook, & J. I. Lacey (Eds.), *Psychology and the problems of society.* Washington, D.C.: American Psychological Association, 1970. Pp. 309–326.

THE
INDIVIDUAL
IN CONFLICT WITH
MODERN AND
URBAN SOCIETY

11

A new society came into being in the latter part of the eighteenth century. Although it grew out of the old societies of Europe, it represented the most radical political beliefs then known. The bold assertions of the Americans that all men are born free and equal, that freedom is not something to be attained or granted by someone else, that the right to seek one's own destiny is for the many rather than the few, and that gradations and classifications of men in society according to prestige and influence are not to be tolerated—all these ideas led many throughout the world to see hope for their own struggle to bring basic changes in their lives. As the original colonies were established mainly by dissenters and by those who wished to better their lot, the opportunities in the New World continued to attract all who were dissatisfied with their outlook in the old social orders of Europe. The new society offered them a chance to make their fortunes regardless of their social position. The rights of an individual were so far extended that even the most radical reformer of today can find no quarrel with the Declaration of Independence or with the Bill of Rights. The long struggle up from the Dark Ages thus had culminated in the establishment of a society and order that held hope for all those who sought a life better than that of their fathers. An added advantage of the new society was that, if social conditions seemed to become oppressive, it was possible to move westward where rewards depended mainly on individual effort, energy, and courage.

Despite the society's advantages, in little more than a half century disaffection for the new order appeared. By then some of the conditions which had driven people to flee from the Old World had recurred in the New. The development of privilege for a few in disregard of the poverty of many, the lack of humanitarian principles in the acquisition of fortunes and property, and the increasing control of industrial management over workers caused a number of dissenting voices. In addition, moral, political, and economic divisions over slavery were sweeping the society. Soon the early voices for social reform and humanitarian causes were lost in the tragedy of civil strife.

After the Civil War, towns and cities grew at an extremely rapid rate. During this time many small property owners and businessmen became dependent on larger organizations. Growth of the society was so rapid that any general concern about inequities in the system of social organization was obscured by the surging struggle to take advantage of the opportunities for wealth. By the end of the nineteenth century, great fortunes had been amassed, and preoccupation with economic growth had greatly reduced attention to the humanitarian principles avowed at the society's beginning. Although the last decade of the eighteenth century saw widespread social exuberance (the Gay Nineties), there were already rumblings of substantial discontent—notably the voices of those in the labor movement who called attention to the long hours and dangerous working conditions of the low-paid factory workers.

Some ideological themes came to light in the cries of the dissenters and in their despair of and antagonism to the existing social conditions characterized by disparities of class and social stratification. Since the "classless society" seemed to be a myth in the early years of the twentieth century, the labor movement became not only a significant factor in social change, but an identification group for men of varying ideologies.

As the twentieth century advanced, however, labor made rapid progress in achieving its goals. And, despite the social upheavals caused by World War I, the Great Depression, World War II, and subsequent smaller wars, the standard of living of Americans surpassed that of any other nation on earth. The society came to be characterized as the "Affluent Society"—the American dream of a good life seemed within reach. But in the second half of the twentieth century, a swiftly rising tide of discordant voices indicated that many still were oppressed—that there was another America that was not affluent, that all were not born free and equal, and that the destiny in society of some seemed indeed to be grim. A small war in Indochina became a raging moral issue as well as a political one. Various groups began to point not only to social inequities and the continuing failure of the society to provide equal opportunity for all, but to hypocrisy and a loss of idealism.

After the passing of a century since "freedom," black people began to demand that immediate attention be given to their lack of progress in reaching the mainstream of American life. Although those in the civil-rights struggle sought justice within the framework of a policy of non-violence, violence was associated with the movement from the beginning, as civil-rights activities aroused antagonism from entrenched elements of various social structures. Closely following and sometimes associated with the civil-rights movement were other movements largely composed of students. Their demands were less clear than the earlier demands of labor or those identified with movements for civil rights, but in many instances they were no less insistent. Militant groups began to appear both in the civil-rights movement and in the universities and violence became a theme. And so it was that after two hundred years, conditions in the society in the latter part of the twentieth century turned out to be no less tumultuous than those in the eighteenth that accompanied the beginning of the society. In fact, some dissenters proclaimed a new revolution and joined with emerging nations in a vision of a Third World.

While a few proclaimed a policy of violent overthrow of the social order, others spoke of a different type of revolution and change (Forster, 1968). Though dissent was common, little unity could be found among the voices expressing it. The society was divided not only on the underlying issues of dissent, but also because the society could not be characterized as totally bad. Indeed the society endeavored to make some response to the major issues. Those who opposed criticism of the society could marshal evidence that some progress was being made toward the change desired. Broad paradoxes therefore stood out in sharp relief: Although the dread specters of mass destruction or mass poisoning were clearly visible, the technology underlying these destructive forces held promise for a much better life than ever before. While power to annihilate life on the earth was at hand, this same power made possible a much easier way of life for millions. Though the population increase threatened to strip the earth of its resources, new means for population control and new processes for producing food seemed possible. Though the conditions of the great urban areas had spawned burnings, riots, and looting, plans to eliminate poverty for the first time from any society, to build new cities, to alleviate illness and its expense, and to guarantee an adequate subsistence income for all were being implemented. Many of the adverse conditions in the centers of cities were recognized as resulting from a lack of planning, and thus new multimillion-dollar plans for "model cities" were developed. Apparently in the urban areas of the nation—most of the nation—the latter part of the twentieth century seemed to be the worst of times and the best of times; the broad social paradoxes were there for everyone to see. Every social structure had come to be challenged in its function. Principles for the foundation of marriage and the family, the tenets of the church, the intentions of government, and the dedication of members of the educational system were questioned.

SOCIAL ISSUES IN URBAN SOCIETY

Societies, and particularly social structures within them, seek to maintain customs much as an individual tends to hold onto established habit patterns of behavior. Conflict in society stems both from the limitations of perceptual awareness of persons in power and from the difficulty in discontinuing old behavior patterns and acquiring new ones. As the socialization process is generally successful in the inculcation of values, society has difficulty in perceiving irrelevant or detrimental parts of its organization and demands.

In urban and modern society, some conflicts are created that seem extremely difficult to avoid. In part, difficulty comes from interrelationships; individuals forged the society and, in turn, the society has forged the individuals in it. Alteration of conditions means basic alteration in the foundations of individual behavior as well as in the evolving complexity of social structures. As difficult as such alterations may be, consideration of the necessity for meeting the essential needs of individuals is required if life is to improve in quality and satisfaction. If attention is not given to the quality of urban life, serious consequences seem inevitable.

Solutions to current problems require much reorientation and continued effort for many years to come. The conflicts considered here transcend the physical conditions of the environment and the plight of many in the city; they are related to basic relationships of man to society.

The New Radicalism

An understanding of modern social conditions in urban society and how they affect the place and opportunity of the individual in the modern world requires a historical perspective. This perspective is necessary because the radical thought and criticism of some youth are aimed at the fundamental bases of society created in the past. In effect, the New Radicals are social critics. Whether one considers the criticism an evil to be combatted or a means of social progress, its complexity cannot be understood without knowledge of the significant trends in the development of the society.

Social criticism has occurred in generational cycles in the twentieth century—in the first decade, in the 1930s, and in the 1960s (Bottomore, 1969). In the first two periods, economic and social-class issues were emphasized, but in the later period, the issues were less clear. In the first few years of the century, the rising economic and political power of both industry and labor was given further impetus by World War I. After that war, during the "Roaring Twenties," many of the voices of society reflected shallow concerns. But then came the Great Depression. It was during the gloom of these years that criticism of society became deep and widespread. It was plain to see that the social order did not work for millions of people. Again, however, social reform and criticism were lost in the years during World War II.

American society emerged from this war only to be confronted immediately with an intense rivalry with the Soviet Union. A backdrop for the drama of the struggle between the two world powers was the awesome possibility of world destruction with nuclear weapons. The fear of complete devastation lingered in the minds of many, and even the President cautioned that a "prudent man" would build a bomb shelter in his basement, even though survival seemed unlikely or even undesirable after a nuclear attack. Ominous markings on buildings began to appear, designating them as shelters. Radio programs were frequently interrupted by tests of "emergency" broadcast systems. Accompanying this pervasive anxiety was a developing suspicion that there were forces leading to destruction from within the society. These forces were thought to be ready to bring destruction following some signal from an external enemy (usually seen as the Soviet Union or possibly China). This suspicion undergirded a drive against "subversive elements."

Although the effect of the rivalry with the Soviet Union was reflected in many areas of American society, it was particularly evident in education. Large sums from the federal government were made available by Congress to the elementary and secondary educational systems with the justification that the appropriations were based not so much on a desire for social progress as on defense against a Russian society which threatened to "bury" American society. In the early 1960s, considerable preoccupation with the "Soviet problem" and Communism led to the Bay of Pigs invasion of Cuba and subsequently to the intervention in Vietnam. It was the latter that turned out to be the fulcrum of deep controversy. But other trends were significant, although their importance was often overshadowed by the social issues growing out of the war. The basic structure of American society came to be challenged, not as some had feared by Communists aided by a sinister foreign power, but by Americans disaffected by the inequities of the social order.

Three elements were part of the new criticism of society. First, beginning in the late 1950s with Martin Luther King's bus boycott in Montgomery, a rising tide of dissent in urban society centered around civil rights. This criticism of society, at least at first, was basically not a new ideology, nor did it demand a restructuring of the existing order; rather, blacks demanded more opportunity in society and elimination of discrimination. The force of the movement in the early days stemmed largely from the church; ministers led the demonstrations and the churches provided refuge when groups were under attack. The educational system became involved when the goal of equality was extended to integration of the schools in both South and North. From the very beginning, many white university students and faculty joined in the movement. Generally, whites traveled from the northern universities to southern states to participate.

The second element of social criticism grew out of opposition to the Vietnam War. Students and educators expressed disillusionment about the war, but concern about it was in part displaced—many in society became more troubled by the depressed mien of youth than by the war. Concern about the war, it ultimately became clear, was symptomatic of a deeper feeling of dissatisfaction with life in general in contemporary society. Controversy about the war was accompanied by a fundamental change in attitude toward Communism and the Soviet Union. A turning point in the attitudinal change had begun with the Cuban Missile Crisis of 1963. When the American warships prepared to intercept the Soviet vessels near Cuba, the Russian government recalled their ships— an act of reason in an emotionally unstable world. Next, American success in space reduced the fear of Soviet technology. Still another factor was the increased information about life in the Soviet system—it was revealed that the system had many imperfections. And, finally at the end of the 1960s came the capstone—the men who first walked on the moon were Americans! As the entire world expressed admiration, fear in America of outside enemies was reduced to an even lower level. As a consequence, the basic reason for the Vietnam War given earlier in the decade no longer seemed valid.

It is important to see, in perspective, that a generally acceptable basis for the war disappeared concomitantly with the rise of student opposition. It seems reasonable that if society felt no strong commitment to the war, its youths would certainly not want to risk their lives. In other wars an idealistic theme had provided a vehicle for commitment; in the Revolution, "independence"; in the Civil War, "abolition" and "preservation of the Union"; in World War I, "democracy"; and in World War II, eradication of "totalitarianism." During the Korean War, Americans were still caught up in the fear of the spread of Communism. But in the 1960s, no ideological base survived for the Vietnam War—if Communists were no longer an urgent threat, the war was an anachronism. War, in general, came to be examined. Added to a general concern about the "immorality of war" was the fact that the enemy country in no way posed a threat to the United States.

While the nation was shocked by the refusal of many youths to serve in the military forces, no national emergency could be found to support the contention that they should go. The conflict intensified the differences between parents and children—parents had been part of the united effort of the society in World War II and defiance of their country's government deeply disturbed them. But the angry and bitter sadness of their young was even more disturbing. Parents were appalled at the alienation of their children from society and dismayed as they saw the structures of the society attacked. The wave of dissent swelled and became another element in twentieth-century social criticism.

The third element of social criticism was alienation. None of the virtues formerly valued by society escaped ridicule or debasement; sexual mores, religious practice, patriotism, work, study, military preparedness, ambition—all were declared out of date. Interest in drugs, music in gatherings of thousands, and a new kind of social interaction further separated the generations.

To an observer of the New Radicalism, no ideology, no political theory, no charismatic theoretician, no hero, no place, and no specific theme were clearly visible. Accordingly, no dogmatism about social ideals and no program for social reform were identifiable for discussion. The lack of a reasoning approach to problems widened the generation gap. Some articulation, however, indicated a humanism—a brotherhood of man, although vague and certainly excluding some agents and members of the establishment.

The new radicals obviously had many issues, both social and personal, which encompassed contemporary society. They rejected the capitalistic and competitive system with its practice of planned obsolescence, its lack of concern for public welfare if a profit could be made, its slowness in righting obvious social wrongs, its tolerance for hypocrisy, and its past failures to reach a brotherhood of man. For some, a deep depression accompanied the alienation—withdrawal from an immoral system became a moral obligation. This alienation precluded effort to make plans for the reorganization of the existing social order or to use society's resources, its technology, and its talented people in the achievement of reform. Many of the radicals were united in "alienation," but not in a plan for social reform. Reform for some was considered hopeless, it was better to drop out; and so for them the means—the withdrawal, the alienation—became, in the end, the goal.

As many believe that there is at least some justification for social criticism, modern society needs to be examined and some basic sources of the individual's conflict with it ought to be determined. This determination is particularly needed if the hopelessness of some disaffected youth is to be ameliorated.

Youth and the Institutions of Society

While much of the disaffection of some youth originates in their early relationships in the family, none can claim that modern society is without some fault in the process of their socialization. If their parents were unable to provide a socializing experience that would help them enter society's mainstream, social conditions must have had an influence in the creation of the parents' deficiencies in training. The role of society's policies in causing their alienation must be carefully weighed. It is recognized that the disaffection cannot be laid at the door of young people alone, for they are a product of American society.

So far, the usual recommendations for dealing with the problems of these youth have depended on dismissal from the educational system or on tightening control. Those universities that responded with patience and tolerance have been criticized as being "soft" and contributing to society's problems with the radicals. Universities, as well as other social institutions, were not prepared to deal with the strong emotions and sometimes irrational and reprehensible behavior of some of the troubled youth. Problems with them, however, were easily recognized as tragic. When universities are called upon to expel the "troublemakers," whither are these youth to be expelled? Where in society are their needs more likely to be met or their problems solved? It is possible that, as some charge, the universities may become huge treatment centers for psychological disturbance. Yet, to some extent treatment has always been part of the task of the educational structure, as its essential purpose is to deal sympathetically with youth's fears, anxieties, doubts, and perplexities and at the same time provide a program of learning for life in society.

If universities are to deal with youth's problems, the effort must be made in a social context. Solutions must be related to social conditions as well as to the psychological stance of society about youth problems. The effort cannot be isolated within the educational system. Progress toward solution, begun within the educational system, must be continued as the young emerge into society. Certain trends, however, indicate some misunderstanding on the part of the public as to society's responsibility to youth.

The university must clearly endeavor to maintain idealistic and humanistic principles even though it is accused of lacking idealism. It must seek through understanding and patience to educate the young. It must present a model of forbearance in what too often has been for troubled people a harsh and rejecting world. If the young are lacking in courtesy and tolerance, the university must nevertheless maintain its integrity and tolerance. If society is to stress rehabilitation rather than punishment for its members, the university must provide an example. Further, a good society must be built upon the cooperation of its members and therefore the university must seek and obtain the cooperation of students and the members of the society at large. Not only does the university need to examine its own actions and goals, but it obviously must examine and understand conditions and trends in society as they relate to it. The rapid growth and extensive change in urban society have greatly affected higher education. More than half of the students in American society now attend universities in cities. As technological progress has come to characterize much of the social change in American society, demand for training in new occupations as well as continuing education has increased. Universities in general have grown enormously, but they have grown especially large in the cities.

In the urban university, all the problems of the city affect the students to varying degrees. Crises in human relations, transportation, financial planning, and government all require some adjustment by universities; the students cannot be sheltered from society's problems. They are particularly aware of the problems of the city and of life in a mass society. In addition they must cope with the established demands of the large impersonal educational structure.

The commuter students coming for only a short time during the day or evening can attend classes and then scatter through the city, to its boundaries, and beyond. Many finish a day's work, then make their way through rush hour traffic to class without the opportunity for an evening meal. Urban universities, although having large numbers of such students, have made little effort to understand their problems or to alleviate the strain of their educational programs. Food, for example, is only available at class breaks in vending machines in stairwells or from trucks on the street, but there is no time for a relaxed meal within their study program. Although there are lounges, there are no places for quiet study; there is an "advising system," but little time is available in the evening for consultation. Although there are many advantages as the result of the presence in the city of cultural activities—museums, orchestras, and theaters—little utilization of these resources has been possible; and although there are many opportunities to relate students' work experience to the educational program, little progress has been made in working out relationships. Activities on the campus fail to touch the lives of many. Field trips into the community and musical or theater events are poorly attended. The urban university student in the midst of "plenty" often remains "malnourished" educationally in comparison to potential benefits from the experience. It is not surprising that the large urban university has become the center of much student dissatisfaction.

Conflicts in Urban Society

⌈One significant conflict for man in modern society is *accelerating social change*. As societies emerged from the Dark Ages into the Renaissance and the Age of Science and Discovery, changes occurred within shortened time spans. Technological advances and new discoveries led to the hope that a better life would result from social change, but it is now being recognized that many people do not have more favorable feelings about themselves or their society than did the men of times past. It is obvious that many live out their lives in dissatisfaction with modern society and their own place in it, even if the position is taken that they have a better life than was possible a century ago.⌋In the past, social change spawned conflicts in an infinite variety of combinations and the individual has been both aided and impaired by change. Advantage is offset by disadvantage so that evaluation of his changed condition is virtually impossible. Now it is not only social change such as has occurred in the past but accelerating change that is a serious problem for modern urban man. Increasingly rapid social change is particularly stressful when response styles that require skill and knowledge suddenly become of little value or even inimical to the welfare of the individual. It can be assumed, consequently, that for many in society rapidly increasing change can be expected to bring traumatic or cataclysmic sequelae to a way of life achieved through discipline and sacrifice.

Positive expressions about social change indicate that change is generally viewed as favorable. Apparently the effects of the resulting stress and dislocation in lives are well masked or repressed. Perhaps, because of the necessity of adapting to increasingly rapid change, cultural teachings have reiterated the favorable aspects of change. Perhaps much of this favorable response to change has come because of the visibility of technological developments—substitution of the motor for the sail, the telephone for the messenger, the automobile for the horse, and medicaments for magic. Because these advances have altered man's way of life and on occasion seemed to have made it less difficult and hazardous, technological change has been perceived as beneficent.

American society was established with the idea that the order should be different from that of Europe and should thereby better meet the needs of man. Change from the beginning has been perceived as a favorable factor in American civilization. The society at first had few vested interests and no feudalistic hierarchy of social structure—it was open to change. The long period of the open frontier gave continuing opportunities for individuals to change their way of life.

The fundamental consequences of social change on the psychological make-up of the individual have not been given much attention, however. Even now, in the urban setting, psychological implications of displacement are overshadowed by concern over finding homes for those displaced by an expressway or by urban renewal projects, and the personal and holistic significance of change is not of concern. A changing society, however, is not a problem alone because of technological and environmental alteration but also because of emotions about life processes.

Man's life is always uncertain, and control of coming events seems as tenuous today as it must have seemed centuries ago. In other societies, connections with the past have helped in strengthening the precarious hold on the present and lessened doubt about the future. Expectations for the future appear more certain in a society where events are linked to the past. But modern man has rejected the past, although fear of dread events and hope for a beneficent future seem to be even more intense in the modern world than they were in the past. Even with modern housing, transportation, and medical knowledge, assurances about the beneficence of the future seem no greater. While many individuals feel free to achieve within modern society, they perceive little linkage with the past, nor do they depend on age-old verities to help them with predictions about coming events. A continuing conflict for the individual, therefore, is anxiety about the awesome change in his social environment. He learns very early in life that a "good" destiny in modern society cannot be assured and that cultural discontinuities have cut him off from the past. He remains seemingly suspended in time with neither a firm hold on the past nor a clear vision of the future.

This dependence on the present has heightened the emphasis on living for the moment. The old adage can be changed a little and still apply: "Eat, drink, and be merry," as neither tomorrow nor the past are relevant. The preoccupation of some youth with feelings of the moment is in part a reflection of those of others. One cannot count on tomorrow

—one's job, home, or savings may be of no value. Hence, it should be understood that preoccupation with the present is not characteristic only of some youth—the preoccupation has come to characterize many in urban America.

A second major conflict in modern society is *interactional discontinuity*. The discontinuity is both cultural and individual. It is cultural in that in some instances the culture does not provide a normative code that contains certainty of belief over a long period of time. Some individuals are particularly affected by discontinuity in role behavior learned in the family. Only portions of the parents' life styles can be appropriately adopted, but decisions about what to reject and what to maintain are difficult to make. Although much of the sex-role behavior, for example, is learned in the family, changes in sex mores make former patterns impractical or impossible. Many parents have provided insufficient emotional support for their children, yet opportunities for the young to find emotional support outside the family in the educational system or in other settings are rarely possible.

This lack of emotional support in turn leads to a third type of conflict in the urban environment—*cultural depersonalization*. The individual in the urban setting becomes an object standing in the way of someone else. A general lack of humane qualities results in social interaction that is not characterized by courtesy or a consideration for the welfare of others. The egocentrism of childhood reappears in the urban environment, and mature qualities of behavior tend to disappear. Accordingly, there is much inconsiderate behavior not only in haste to move ahead of others, but in direct action to take advantage of others. This direct action is found in confidence rackets and in many activities to trap the unwary in situations such as charging high interest on installment loans, offering spurious bargains, and selling training courses of little value. All these and more cause those who live in cities to be distrustful, secretive, and irascible in social interaction.

Depersonalization also results from another problem. Overstimulation by emotionally unrewarding contacts with people cause an *interaction satiation*. A kind of emotional starvation continues in the midst of a wide diversity of human interaction. The city dweller, however, is unaware of such emotional malnutrition that, like neurosis, becomes a cyclic condition. The longer the dissatisfaction continues, the more the individual seeks to keep at a distance those people with whom he could find satisfaction.

Implicit in American culture is a concern for the unfortunate—a basic humanitarianism which is not only of secular origin, but also comes from religious beliefs. Many in society are taught that a man is his brother's keeper and that the welfare of others is an important value in human interaction. But in the modern city such a principle often interferes with successful environmental adaptation and raises a moral conflict because it is not always clear when to look after one's own welfare and when to be considerate of others. The large number of persons with whom one individual must interact prevents practical application of the principle of concern. In many instances the residents of the city find it unsafe to become "involved" in the affairs or problems of others.

THE INDIVIDUAL AND
PSYCHOLOGICAL COMMUNITY

What is the meaning for an individual to be a part of a city—to be a Chicagoan, a Philadelphian, or a New Yorker? Man in the past found satisfaction in identification with a city. It was of both psychological and social significance to be a Roman or an Athenian. Does the modern urban environment contribute to a cohesive life style and hence to a practical self-identification?

In earlier societies, especially agrarian ones, life styles had some unity. Work, religion, and family life were inseparable from community activity and goals. Individuals were known, and they had a significant role in interaction with others. Interdependence made their opinions of consequence, and their views made contributions to community life. Early in this country, a Sioux or a Cheyenne had an identity as a "warrior of the plains." A fusion of the role of warrior, tribesman, and person was possible. Another tribesman was a "brother," and his welfare mattered. In urban society many have become separated from their *community*. As social change has accelerated, so has separation from identification groups. Thus, "belonging" possibilities have disintegrated.

The Individual and Community Organizations

For a significant number of people in the urban environment, clubs, lodges, religious organizations, professional societies, and unions no longer supply sufficient opportunities for identity.

Within an urban community a large number of organizations make demands on the individual for some expenditure of energy. Thus, society's complexity accounts for this fragmentation of the individual's capacity to respond. A person who works in a city must divide his day into time segments which determine his activities—the commuter train, the walk from the station, the elevator to the appropriate floor, desk activities, coffee-break, lunch hour, elevator, and again train—all before he reaches home after sundown. His role activity is thus broken into fragments with little possibility of alteration. This fragmentation provides scant opportunity for emotional commitment to the organization, and reverence and loyalty are not given or expected. It also fosters considerable anxiety about opportunities for advancement in a context of possible failure. The individual moves between two worlds—the world of work with its impersonal characteristics and its demands for role conformity and the world of his family and its expectations. If the individual turns to the family for primary identification and satisfaction, he finds that many of its processes go on without him because many of his commitments of energy and time are outside its sphere of activity. Under such circumstances it is difficult, if not impossible, to obtain from the family a fulfillment of emotional needs when the major commitment of energy is made to another organization. This fragmentation of time contributes not only to a lack of unity in commitment but to a lack of need-fulfillment in either the work or family role.

Most urban people belong to a number of organizations; multiple membership seems to reflect a search for an organization that can offer some emotional fulfillment. But these expectations turn out to be illusions for several reasons. Some of the interfering factors originate in the individual himself and others come from characteristics of the organizations. The individual, because of his already fragmented life style, is wary about obligation to an organization to which he can devote only a fraction of his energy and emotion. The organization has found that in order to function with fragments of commitment it can give members only fragments of opportunity for satisfaction and activity. The urban dweller finds that in reality he is without a community, and perhaps for the first time in the world's history millions of people lack a real place in the society of man. As a result of fragmentation in commitment to persons and places, dissociation occurs among the potentially integrating factors in a life style. The individual's emotions especially lack unity and coherence with everyday experience.

The Emphasis on Cognitive Modes

As a result of complex role requirements and lack of commitment, modern man in the city emphasizes cognitive modes in his response repertoire. Emotion and feeling are subordinated to objectivity, practicality, empiricism, and measurement. Solutions to many problems with workers in industry, for example, entail careful attention to sampling and objective procedures of obtaining personal information. The methodology is as close as possible to that of the physical sciences. Analysis of the data with appropriate statistical methods is an important requirement. The information gathered must therefore be in "bits" or units small enough to be processed in formulae and machines. This approach is a reflection of the values of a technological society that emphasizes techniques in dealing with the environment. Hence many of the decisions of management are based on the results of studies designed to obtain fragments of information.

This preoccupation with technology in American society is reflected in the curriculum content of the educational system. Even in classes for very young children cognitive development is emphasized. Experiences deemed necessary are those which assist in the development of such skills as number concepts and reading readiness. This latter condition of readiness may be fostered by requiring children to learn to perceive similarities and differences between geometric forms as well as to extend the understanding of words by the use of pictures. Society's emphasis on cognitive development rather than on emotional and social development is apparent, however, not only in early childhood but throughout the developmental years.

The importance placed on cognitive modes of behavior in a technological society is associated with a general dependence on machines and techniques for solving problems. An example of an important problem so pursued is the exploitation of the resources of the environment—this activity is particularly furthered by various kinds of technology and quantitative measures.

The development of quantitative techniques is seen as indicative of progress in the acquisition of knowledge. With mechanical techniques decisions presumably can be made objectively without feeling and in the best interest of all concerned. In many instances the data-gathering process becomes the decision-making process. The "decision-makers" gather around a machine that provides a print-out of the facts—any decision reached is thereby automatically objective and unbiased. In these and other ways emotions and feelings are subordinated in the workaday world. Accomplishment lies in the objective realm of scientifically obtained information, and man functions as if technological equipment were an extension of himself. Little room is left for affect, a quality seen as a threat to rational activity. Hence, modern man has become distrustful of decisions other than the most objective ones. He has come to believe that the only reliable decisions are those made after all the facts have been carefully weighed.

The extent of the illusion of man's dependence on technology in decision-making is difficult to determine. It is possible, however, that some of the dependence on technology is as primitive as is the practice of the Trobriand Islander's consultation with the spirits of the nearby jungle before he does his planting. In both primitive and urban instances reassurance is obtained that the correct procedures have been followed in order to obtain success. Over against the "objectivity" of modern man is the view that man's factual decisions are as subjective as they ever were—that the elaborate technological processes carried out prior to reaching a decision are ritualistic and for the sake of reassurance, just as were primitive man's.

It seems reasonable to conclude that the emphasis on objectivity in modern society has contributed to alienation because an individual feels he has little influence on decisions about his life. The machine makes the decisions. The present system is seen as not having a "heart"; therefore it cannot be merciful or human. Not only does the impersonal system operate in a nonhuman way but its goals also are nonhuman. If the system is nonhuman, no compunction need be shown in rebellion against it. No commitment need be given to it since commitment involves "feeling." And, does not the system itself eschew feeling? A sense of community and belonging therefore cannot be fostered by a social system which operates on facts and impersonal processes. So modern rationality, long sought and greatly valued in the scientific age, is a paradox in man's search for ways to find a good life and satisfaction in society. Rationality in modern times, although responsible for unprecedented technological accomplishment, has created an impersonal basis for living in urban society. It has contributed to a depersonalization and a sense of rootlessness that have become an anathema to many. The current emphasis on empiricism and the fragmentation of role behavior contribute to the stresses now characteristic of life in the urban setting.

The great dependence on cognitive modes of behavior and impersonal actions has influenced man to become primarily practical. But more than that, to continue to function effectively, he finds he must acquire increasingly complex skills, greater emotional control, more persistence in long-range projects, more assimilation of information, and more accommodation to rapid change in environmental conditions than ever before. As a result, in today's complex society, many do not have the experience or capacity for the role activity required. The mainstream of society is now quite difficult to enter without enormous amounts of preparation through the developmental years. Thus, environmental deprivation may become in the future even more difficult to overcome than it is today. Specific experience directed toward the development of effective cognitive functioning in society in the future is likely to be even more essential to performance than it is now.

Social Structures and New Directions

The emphasis on quantitative data and technological methods over man's emotional life are indeed a paradox, as much of the way of life in the urban environment would not be possible if it were not for quantitative technology. So much knowledge and control of the environment have been accomplished that none could wish present achievements to be denigrated. But as man has created complex techniques to extend his capacities, his relationship to the techniques has been difficult to hold in a humanistic perspective. That perspective for some has gone awry is clearly evident. The alienated experiencing dire conflict in modern society and disaffection for the "system" are products of this society and, obviously, things for some are out of joint. The onus for disaffection cannot be placed on them alone. The alienated cannot only be told to "shape up," and to fit in. Present difficulties require long-term planning directed toward preventive efforts for those now in their developmental years, as well as alleviation of the stress of those who are presently alienated.

Society needs some members who have a capacity for mature judgment, a tolerant mien, and an ability to take an historical perspective of the long struggle to cope with the difficulties encountered in the creation of a good society. Somehow it is necessary to lessen the inequities, heartlessness, hypocrisy, and inhumanity in social structures. A weighing of the consequences of social change must take place in order to forestall the rejection of society.

The two social structures most closely related to the nurture and training of the young, the family and the educational system, are the ones most responsive to society's adverse conditions. Certain activities by society's other structures, particularly governments, should not be antithetical to their well-being. For example, welfare policies that make it necessary for parents to separate to obtain adequate income for their children ought not be followed, and neither should economic readjustment policies that cause unemployment with its deleterious effect on families. Nor should the educational system be expected to function adequately with meager financial support, antiquated facilities, and minimum social and financial rewards for those who work in it. A new perspective must be gained of the disparate levels of wealth in an affluent society. The deprived will not indefinitely support a social system that allows some to have so much when others have so little. The quality of "humanness" can only come in society from the family. But it must be realized that the fulfillment of the basic needs of those in the developmental years depends upon the fulfillment of the needs of society's members. Thus, society must be so structured that man can find a "psychological community" within it.

IN PERSPECTIVE

In recent years, a number of critics of society have called attention to problems in society that interfere with their satisfaction, but often the critics' reactions and behavior reveal problems in their own lives. Nevertheless, the socialization process should contribute to an individual's capacity to deal with his own and society's problems in an effective way.

Developmental experience should prepare the individual to establish satisfying emotional relationships with others. And, modern society should provide opportunities for individuals to develop a sense of community—a feeling of satisfaction in organized groups of people. The stress of urban life, however, all too often interferes with the attainment of satisfaction in relationships with others.

REFERENCES

ARON, R. The anarchical order of power. In S. Hoffman (Ed.), Conditions of world order. Boston: Houghton Mifflin, 1968. Pp. 25–48.

BITTNER, E. Radicalism and the organization of radical movements. In B. McLaughlin (Ed.), Studies in social movements. New York: Free Press, 1969. Pp. 290–310.

BLUMER, H. Social movements. In B. McLaughlin (Ed.), Studies in social movements. New York: Free Press, 1969. Pp. 8–29.

BOTTOMORE, T. B. Critics of society. New York: Vintage, 1969.

COLEMAN, J. S. Resources for social change. New York: Wiley, 1971.

COMMAGER, H. S. The American mind. New Haven: Yale University Press, 1950.

DAVIES, J. C. Toward a theory of revolution. In B. McLaughlin (Ed.), *Studies in social movements*. New York: Free Press, 1969. Pp. 85–108.

FORSTER, A. Violence on the fanatical left and right. In J. A. Winter, J. Rabow, & M. Chesler (Eds.), *Vital problems in American society*. New York: Random House, 1968. Pp. 229–238.

FRIEDRICH, C. J. Loyalty and authority. In H. M. Ruitenbeek (Ed.), *The dilemma of organizational society*. New York: E. P. Dutton, 1963. Pp. 49–58.

HEIST, P. Activist students challenge the social scientists. In F. F. Korten, S. W. Cook, & J. I. Lacey (Eds.), *Psychology and the problems of society*. Washington, D.C.: American Psychological Association, 1970. Pp. 395–405.

KENISTON, K. *The uncommitted*. New York: Dell, 1965.

KENISTON, K. *Young radicals*. New York: Harcourt, Brace & World, 1968.

KOBRIN, S. The impact of cultural factors on selected problems of adolescent development in middle and lower class. In E. T. Keach, Jr., R. Fulton, & W. E. Gardner (Eds.), *Education and social crisis*. New York: Wiley, 1967. Pp. 66–69.

LEINWAND, G. *The city as a community*. New York: Washington Square Press, 1970.

MANNHEIM, K. The sociological problems of generations. In B. McLaughlin (Ed.), *Studies in social movements*. New York: Free Press, 1969. Pp. 352–369.

MANUEL, F. E. Toward a psychological history of utopias. In B. McLaughlin (Ed.), *Studies in social movements*. New York: Free Press, 1969. Pp. 370–399.

MARTINDALE, D. *Institutions, organizations, and mass society*. Boston: Houghton Mifflin, 1966.

McCORMACK, T. H. The motivation of radicals. In B. McLaughlin (Ed.), *Studies in social movements*. New York: Free Press, 1969. Pp. 73–84.

NEFF, F. C. "Let them eat cake." In A. Kerber & B. Bommarito (Eds.), *The schools and the urban crisis*. New York: Holt, Rinehart & Winston, 1965. Pp. 147–156.

RIESMAN, D. The college student in an age of organization. In H. M. Ruitenbeek (Ed.), *The dilemma of organizational society*. New York: E. P. Dutton, 1963. Pp. 99–117.

SCHLESINGER, A. M., JR. The revolt against revolt. In B. McLaughlin (Ed.), *Studies in social movements*. New York: Free Press, 1969. Pp. 199–202.

SIMMONS, J. L. On maintaining deviant belief systems: A case study. In B. McLaughlin (Ed.), *Studies in social movements*. New York: Free Press, 1969. Pp. 189–198.

TURNER, R. H. Collective behavior and conflict: New theoretical frameworks. In B. McLaughlin (Ed.), *Studies in social movements*. New York: Free Press, 1969. Pp. 63–68.

VAN DOORN, J. A. A. Conflict in formal organizations. In A. deReuck & J. Knight (Eds.), *Conflict in society*. Boston: Little, Brown, 1966. Pp. 111–132.

WEISS, R. F. Defection from social movements and subsequent recruitment to new movements. In B. McLaughlin (Ed.), *Studies in social movements*. New York: Free Press, 1969. Pp. 328–348.

ZALD, M. N., & ASH, R. Social movement organizations: Growth, decay and change. In B. McLaughlin (Ed.), *Studies in social movements*. New York: Free Press, 1969. Pp. 461–485.

INDIVIDUAL AUTONOMY IN URBAN SOCIETY

12

Autonomy should be viewed as relative, limited, and changing throughout life. It is relative in that it varies with social situations. It is limited in that man is always dependent to some extent on others. Complete autonomy does not exist, and autonomy as an end-state can never be reached. For each individual, autonomy changes not only with age but also with alterations in social roles and social conditions. The task of understanding autonomy in social interactions is therefore complex and requires specific knowledge about the intricacies of human behavior in relation to the function of social structures in modern society. The life-long paradoxical effort of the individual to attain independence is of renewed interest to modern social scientists.

The background of modern interest in individual freedom can be found in the writings of Rousseau, Tocqueville, Marx, Freud, and Watson. These writers have sought to define man's relationship to society and to the influences of those around him in the determination of his destiny. How much, it has been asked, does man control his destiny? What are the optimum conditions in terms of external control from society? Although concern about these questions of autonomy of the individual in society is not new in history, it seems that more people today are expressing concern about personal autonomy than ever before. While early in the century it seemed that the voices of the labor movement were most vehement, now they scarcely can be heard among the voices demanding racial equality, participation in governance of universities, and equality for women. All social institutions are faced with demands for more autonomy by their members. Educational institutions, especially, have been rent by actions for autonomy not only by students but by faculty. Staid professional organizations, such as those of medicine and law, have seen rebellious factions seek to force a change in the power structure; people on welfare have stormed state capitols to demand control in administrative matters; prisoners have rioted and sought institutional reform in order to gain an improvement in prison conditions; high school students have taken over offices of principals to enforce their demands for greater freedom from supervision; stockholders have tried to wrest control from disfavored corporation managers in order to increase their responsiveness; and military personnel have demanded that superiors consult them about their welfare. Even the Congress at times is apparently paralyzed by cacophonous voices. The conflicting conditions in reference to control in current institutions seem to mirror the conflicts in the lives of individuals in the society at large.

Historically, a struggle for autonomy similar to that of individual man is seen in the achievement of parliamentary forms of government. Present forms represent hundreds of years of shifting social trends as men searched for favorable organizational restrictions. The struggle was not only against the evolutionary bonds of social constraints but against those related to the physical conditions in the environment. Centuries ago, at the beginning of the modern age, exploration of lands remote from Europe was difficult not only because of technological limitations but also because of the limitations of ignorance and superstition. These limitations were compounded by general resistance to social change. As efforts to achieve independence and social change met with some success, however, a reaction occurred, resulting in even more constraints to individual freedom. Associated with the struggle toward an autonomous life style, consequently, came a conflict about responsibility to conform to expectations of the established order.

Resolution of such a conflict is difficult because membership in society means some surrender of autonomy; the more complex the society, the more subtle and intricate the web of social responsibility for the individual in it. As man is dependent on others, he cannot escape this social matrix of demands to engage in completely self-serving behavior. Achieving a balance between autonomy and social responsibility is now more difficult than ever. Today in modern and urban society, vision of a desirable balance seems to be obscured by the tangled complexity of an infinite number of responsibilities.

Autonomy is difficult to define, and a psychological definition is accordingly imprecise. The term means generally the ability of the individual to make choices among the stimulus-situations in his life space and to choose his own response style, not necessarily to accept one within a social or cultural framework. Such a definition does not mean, however, that the individual must reject all conformity to culture or society. He may choose in many circumstances to make responses which are in accord with the culture (Goodman, 1967). The definition does emphasize the importance of selectivity, reasoning, and innovation in behavior that may or may not be in conformance with social custom.

It should be remembered that in the discussion of internal and external controls (Chapter 10) it was pointed out that so much of the culture can be internalized that little behavior remains self-directed. Under such conditions of overcontrol the individual does not realize that he himself was the origin of his conformity.

Autonomy, as has been indicated, is not the antithesis of conformity. It is a capability to go beyond conformity to cultural expectations and yet it represents a capability to abide by cultural mandates if circumstances indicate that such behavior is reasonable. Thus, autonomy implies ability either to detach the self from the ordinary or to conform if critical judgment so dictates. Autonomy in this sense indicates behavior according to reason exercised in idiosyncratic response patterns but still within the boundaries of cultural expectations. In some instances the individual can conform by setting a culturally acceptable goal, with the behavior to reach the goal being personally devised. Autonomous behavior also can lie beyond the culturally expected behavior, both in the determination of the goal and in the means chosen to reach it. As used here, autonomy is a highly individual quality—a "state of mind," a learned response pattern, which acts as a wellspring for individual expression. Although no change may be wrought in society or in the life space and no recognition may come from those about him, attainment of a goal can be a highly personalized and satisfying experience. An autonomous individual's life style is therefore relative to a culture and a society but not necessarily in conformity with it. Autonomy can exist only in relation to a society, and as society can be based only on the social responsibility of its members, responsibility is part of autonomy.

SOCIAL PROBLEMS AND
INDIVIDUAL AUTONOMY

Several generalizations can be made about the problem of the autonomy-responsibility continuum (Olsen, 1968). At present no condition can be described that is idealistically satisfactory for man or society. Social change brought about by technological development and new knowledge, as well as changing values brought about by social evolution, does not permit an adequate description of an end-state in which individuals are ideally autonomous. And no condition can be equally satisfying to everyone in a complex society. Accordingly, as far as one can see into the future, inequalities in opportunities for individual satisfaction will be found in any society, as no one way seems likely to be devised that will satisfy members equally. Man can seek only to discover ways to reach some compromise.

Neither complete autonomy nor complete social responsibility is possible or desirable. Complete autonomy would mean that the individual serves only himself and owes nothing to others. Such a view obviously destroys the concept of a society, as man cannot live and develop under such a condition. No one can really "do his own thing." The other extreme is equally untenable. A man cannot live under conditions of serving only society. He must at least have food and shelter for himself, and some of his psychological needs must be met. Over the ages, conflicts and issues among men have centered on where the line is to be drawn between individual needs and social responsibility. The problem of autonomy and the giving of personal service and goods to the social order is part of the complexity of human life. In today's urban society, it seems that resolution of the age-old conflict is as far away as ever. Today's youth, however, believe that personal autonomy is a major issue in man's life in urban society.

The path to attainment for many youths appears to lie in an adversary situation—that is, change toward more autonomy must be demanded and it must be granted by the authorities. Autonomy is perceived as being attained by overcoming an enemy that is external and personified by a hostile society. In one way this parallels the development of the child: in order to achieve independence, the child must rebel against society and culture, as personified by his parents. The young child, in struggling to put on his own shoe, may peremptorily brush away any parental assistance with an insistent cry, "Self"! Part of his learning inevitably is that "one must demand one's rights." The adversary system has its beginning accordingly within the family when the parent reaches out to steady the child in his first steps and the child refuses the offered assistance. It is only a few more steps, figuratively, to the adolescent's acknowledgment of a "generation gap" and his assertion that the values of the preceding generation are to be rejected.

The concept of the adversary system has been challenged periodically through the ages, and perception of the welfare of one's neighbor in other than an adversary perspective has been a social value for a long time. Perhaps here, too, no complete resolution is in sight. One cannot completely avoid the concept of an adversary either for the young child or for the adult in society. Yet, perceiving society only as an adversary may be disastrous.

Some believe that by increasing autonomy it is possible to increase social responsibility or by increasing social responsibility to increase autonomy (Olsen, 1968). The two achievements can be mutually reinforcing. An individual can improve his lot through his contribution to society. For example, by contributing to a system of parliamentary representation, he can increase his own autonomy. In essense, this hope of improving one's opportunities through assumption of social responsibility provides the motivation for man to struggle; through effort he hopes his life can be improved. Easily apparent also is the possibility that some individuals can seize an opportunity to advance themselves and engage in little socially responsible behavior. Others seeing such success may become cynical and reduce their socially responsible behavior. If this occurs in widespread fashion, society then must increase its social constraints in order to insure that responsible behavior does occur.

In considering the relationship of man to society and his need for autonomy, earlier discussion of the meaning of society and the significance of its social structures, particularly in Chapter 2, should be recalled. Social structures are units in which members have relationships that directly affect the behavior patterns of members. Some direct control over members is exercised. Rules and regulations reflecting the norms of the society are established, and membership in the unit requires general conformity to these rules. As the structure provides external controls, rules, or laws which the individual must obey, his autonomy is thus limited. The structure seeks, partly in order to survive, to achieve some success in developing internal controls in individual members. This process begins in early childhood and continues through the developmental years with gradual reduction of external control in the adolescent years. By then much internalization of cultural expectations is supposedly achieved. Through internalization and education, the social unit and the society achieve control over individual behavior. The individual learns social responsibility—conformity to the expectations of the society and culture. In a complex and urban society the process is far from simple; many difficulties occur both naturally and artificially in the system.

Socialization and Difficulties in Autonomous Role Behavior

Even in the simplest societies social roles become specialized. Part of the socialization process thus becomes specialized, too, often unconsciously —the farmer teaches his son to be a farmer without awareness on the part of either that role specialization is being achieved.

As societies become more complex and as vast numbers of people congregate in urban centers, specialization increases and in many instances is formalized. Groups begin to certify specialization. Training and preparation for specialized roles extend in duration and competency is difficult to achieve. Furthermore, admission to specialized roles is limited and barriers are set up so that social status and resources are required even before one can pass through the door to preparation. Not only are admissions to professional roles limited, but they are also regulated in the crafts and trades. For the highly complex roles, extended training has become necessary, but many colleges have enrollment limitations so that only those with certain backgrounds and resources can enter. One of the recent changes in urban society has been development of significant steps toward "open admissions" to higher education. Such policies require change in the educational structure and ultimately in the social structures comprising society. Open admissions in universities will not suffice to bring equality of opportunity in society unless the principle is applied to the admission policies of other social organizations.

Role Requirements and Constraints. Some specialized roles have such complex requirements that the training for them must begin in early childhood. In truth, for some roles, if early experiences are inappropriate, needed characteristics are virtually impossible to acquire later. But for the child who grows up in an upper-class home with many enriching experiences, preparation for admission to a prestigious educational institution has effectively been achieved. Very early in life such a child is almost guaranteed success in a specialized and advantaged social role. Such inevitability of success in social role specialization has been in existence for many centuries, as some individuals are better prepared than others for roles involving power, wealth, and prestige. Prestigious opportunities have thus appeared to be inherited and passed from one generation to the next according to blood relationships. Perpetuation of position and privilege was assured, and as acquisition seemed to parallel genetic patterns, genetic factors were assumed to be of significance. Controversy about the significance of genetic factors as opposed to environmental factors continues today, however.

Associated with role specialization is a multitude of constraints upon the individual, so that role behavior is proscribed by the culture from one generation to the next. In modern society all role behavior is becoming more complex. It is generally conceded, for example, that little opportunity for satisfying work remains for those in the "unskilled" labor force. Many years of education are necessary for entrance into the mainstream of society and participation in it. Even outside the urban societies of the world, demands for sophisticated machinery and technological methods develop rapidly. Underdeveloped societies seek assistance from advanced societies, often on the basis of political expediency. They endeavor to become rapidly complex by fashioning their organizations and technology after the advanced ones. Advanced urban and technological societies therefore seem to be the desired pattern in spite of their apparent difficulties and the many criticisms made of them. Actually, all societies on earth are evolving toward an ever-increasing complexity necessitating more and more constraints on individual behavior. This evolution toward complexity results in a threat to individual autonomy.

Bureaucracy and Rules. The term *bureaucracy* refers to complex rules and processes in organizations. Bureaucracy seems to be increasing in societies throughout the world. From this standpoint, concern about individual autonomy is indeed justified. Any society requires the relinquishment by the individual of some control over his own actions and the more complex the society, the greater the number of restrictions that are placed on individual behavior. Because society dictates certain behavior, the socialization process must include a conditioning of the young to accept cultural rules. Perceptual sets characteristic of the culture are established in the young. Thus through many learning experiences role conditioning is achieved as part of the socialization process.

Such a system is not of recent origin, but is part of the history of social organizations. The medieval serf was conditioned to accept his lowly status and the principle of respect for his "betters." He was considered not good enough to aspire to a higher status; hence his world was cast in such a way that he was excluded from prestige roles. The serf accepted his lowly destiny even though it was one of deprivation. Similarly, the elite perceived their destiny as one of privilege. Because such principles were inculcated in children from the earliest days of their lives, they saw no other way as proper. The task of society and its members was to perpetuate itself, and so its structure was effectively taught. Social determinism was therefore a common and logical philosophy. According to general belief and subscription, individual destiny was determined by the family condition. At birth rewards and life opportunities were already determined, as the child was destined for a social role in accord with family position in the society's hierarchy. In modern and urban society, the bureaucracy operates in a similar way. Current society is too complex to be really open. Individuals must be trained to accept available roles and tasks appropriate to these roles.

Such reasoning has led some social scientists to perceive modern society as still ruled by an "advantaged" class (Domhoff, 1967). General acceptance of elite rule is gained by the assertion that an elite group can best determine the trends and role assignments necessary for the welfare of all members. It is possible to view the rule of a bureaucracy as having little difference from the rule of an elite class or group. In a bureaucracy, assignment of roles is made on the basis of technical qualifications. Assurance that a person is qualified is accomplished by examinations and by the submission of resumes or detailed application blanks. These are deemed to be impersonal and thus insure that the organization is an "equal opportunity employer."

Professions, too, for many years have had examinations that a candidate must pass in order to be admitted to practice. In recent years these examinations have been challenged on the basis of sex and race discrimination. This criticism of professional examinations developed because individuals, although certified by a public university as competent or qualified for role specialization, still had to overcome the barriers of examinations set up by the professional organizations. While these examinations allegedly exist for the protection of the public, they may also serve as controls to admission on other than avowed professional qualifications. This criticism of professional admission policy indicates the complexity of role specialization in modern society.

Inside bureaucratic structures a hierarchy of authority and privilege is maintained. The organization, as Etzioni (1964) has pointed out, relies to a degree on its power to secure cooperation of members. Activities in the organization follow clearly defined patterns of behavior, often in regulations published in manuals. Because the officials of the organization are appointed as a result of being "qualified," tacit responsiveness to society is achieved by the establishment of an elected group as a board of directors or regents who are supraordinate to the organization. Although public announcements indicate that overall policy is set by the board, the goals of the organization are the responsibility of the technical or qualified personnel.

The benefits of such an organization with a board are seen as residing in a capacity for precision and continuity in efficient functioning and in the maximum use of resources. Policies of bureaucratic officials are established by the company so that only impersonal relationships are fostered within the organization. Decisions about members must be dependable, reliable, and objective. Details and information about technical operations carried on in the organization are not made known to the public. Such information about internal operations is made available only in a public announcement. A special unit of the organization is usually assigned to deal with the task of informing the public.

The success of the bureaucratic organization lies in a socialization process whereby the members develop specific perceptual sets toward the organization. These sets are reinforced over a period of time so that members believe they see the advantages of the rules and techniques in operation. A fusion of motives occurs, and the individual then has the same goals for himself that the organization has for him. His personal autonomy then becomes functional as his goals merge with those of the organization.

Bureaucratic organizations are so similar in structure and operation that individuals can transfer membership from one to another with relative ease. The socialization and role specialization thus contribute to some degree of mobility and even provide the opportunity to bargain for a better position. If goals cannot be achieved in one organization, a move can be made to another. But there is also some disadvantage. Conflict or difficulty in one organization may prevent the acquisition of a new position if the new organization investigates the individual's background. This is often done surreptitiously so that the individual seeking the new position is never informed about the search into his background. Similarly, within an organization, the individual may wish to move from one position to another but the move may be blocked for a number of reasons. If the member is valued by those in his present section, he can be held; if he is not valued, those in the new section may block his transfer. Under such circumstances the individual has little opportunity to reach his own goals.

A bureaucratic organization, through its operations and the influence of its directors, may become so powerful in a society that public regulation or control of it is impossible. Such an organization can influence the bureaucratic structures of government and secure favorable advantages. One or several bureaucratic organizations can dominate socioeconomic conditions in society, political affairs, even foreign policy. The organization and its affiliates may thus attain enough power to rule as would an elite person or group.

An elite group or bureaucratic organization can attain dictatorial or totalitarian control. In either form, individual autonomy in the society is effectively reduced. The main characteristic of such a controlling group or organization is the absolute control it has over its members. Further, it seems that complex societies develop so many controls over individual behavior that it matters little whether or not the control is centralized in one organization—the effects on the individual's behavior are the same. Totalitarianism under either type of control can be diffuse, that is, spread to many organizations. The effects on individual autonomy will be similar. Diffusion of control among a number of organizations, however, would appear to offer more opportunity for society's members to alter conditions and increase autonomy than would be possible if only one organization had control.

Acceptance of the many requirements for role behavior in modern society is opposed to a natural disposition toward independent behavior. The imposition of an ever-increasing number of demands on the developing individual is basically detrimental to the individual's feeling about opportunities for achievement. Conflict is thus inevitably a part of the socialization content.

If it is agreed that the individual cannot assimilate all the demands made in a complex society, which demands shall he select for rejection? Decisions about rejection are so difficult, particularly for youth who have little experience in the system, that it is easier to reject the system in its entirety than it is to work with insufficient information toward a sifting of a reasonable degree of conformity.

The problems of youth are compounded by large numbers of people and the probability of being alone in the crowd. Attainment of personal autonomy is thus further complicated by mass society.

Innominate Individuals in Urban Society

Modern man in the great cities has the difficulty of establishing purpose and meaning in his life. Some cannot find a sense of community in the locality where they live or in organizations to which they belong. Consequently they cannot attain a feeling of security. The complexity of life in the city threatens a basic sense of individuality. Characteristically, in a mass society individuals become insignificant parts of the whole and come to feel that their problems stem from the complexity of their life space. Problems of living are attributed to an anonymous "they"—an unidentifiable conglomerate which they feel provides more of a threat to individual autonomy than would a clearly visible authority. Although such difficulties have been recognized for a long time, as shown by Riesman's (1950) description of the problems of man in mass society, the problems have recently been compounded. In current mass society, the individual feels distinctly separated from the source of controls over his daily life. His participation in his life space seems little related to the overall goals of the huge organizations around him. Even the architecture of the cities overpowers him as he stands in the canyons of concrete, glass, and steel. To add to his difficulty, his senses are assailed by the deafening roar of traffic; by a gray instead of a blue patch of sky; and by loss of even his sense of direction and orientation in space in his underground transit. In the modern urban setting he cannot escape the ever-present sensation of being overwhelmed by the bureaucratic organizations of the city. His fare on the subway, for example, can be raised without his understanding or approval by a social structure called a "public authority," set up, he is told, to guard his interests. By living beyond an invisible line (the limits of the city), he is disenfranchised and thus denied an opportunity to change the conditions under which he works. The performance of city officials, mayor, councilmen, and others is beyond his influence. This separation occurs even though he is financially involved through the large sum withheld from his pay check each month as a wage tax to run the city.

As the city worker leaves his commuter train and walks through the murky interior of the concourse toward the crowded station lobby and to the escalators leading to the street, he feels chilled, not alone by the cold of the huge building, but by his isolation from those who step in front of him or brush by him as they hurry by without a glance. Modern man in the urban-industrial complex of the city accordingly feels an estrangement and a personal loss of ability to deal with significant forces in his life space. He feels alienated from a value system, from his work, and from the people around him. He doubts his own capacity to cope with the forces pressing upon him.

Mass Society. While individual feelings may be described, an explicit concept of mass society is difficult to develop. Nevertheless as the individual is perceived as an anonymous face in a crowd of people moving in mass conformity, certain forces and trends can be seen. Wilensky (1967) believes that it is important to attend to the interplay of social structures, high culture, and mass culture. *High culture* is that which depends upon a cultural elite who determine values and standards and who serve as models for others in the society. *Mass culture* has to do with cultural products developed for use in a mass market and the behavior in the use of such products. Mass cultural characteristics are standardized because they please the average person; thus common standards create the mass culture.

An important influence of mass culture is its creation of mass behavior. Something of a paradox is taking place in modern society, Wilensky asserts, a trend toward cultural conformity and the development of mass behavior in conjunction with social differentiation. This differentiation results from the increasing development of role specialization in modern society. As urban society grows, it becomes more complex and dependent upon an increasing number of social roles related to occupational activities. Although many complex demands and pressures are placed on professional groups in our society, freedom to organize activities in these roles continues. Certain groups with a high degree of specialization and long training function in ways that enhance autonomy. For example, certain legal groups within local bar associations have been formed to help the poor obtain justice.

While this trend toward specialized group autonomy is apparent, nevertheless increasing demands for conformity to mass culture are also apparent, and a standardization of cultural behavior and beliefs is taking place (Bonjean, 1967). This standardization results from mass education, mobility in the population, nationwide markets, and mass communication. Wilensky sees television as especially significant in the development of a mass culture. Many people watch television several hours daily, but the precise significance of the large amount of time spent in watching is difficult to determine. Whatever the effect, it is widespread in that those over the entire age span are involved. Conditioning in the early years of watching television contributes effectively to the continuing influence of the medium in modern society. Because of television's extended influence through all social groupings, it will undoubtedly have a standardizing effect. One troublesome result is that those in the high culture will have their creative and versatile productivity reduced. For example, those in the universities have reduced their exposure to quality communication media. Differentiation in role behavior within the culture therefore seems to be decreasing in spite of demands for complex role specialization. It is likely that forces within society will further reduce differentiation tendencies in the future, even though the trend toward standardization contributes to the anonymity of all individuals and heightens identity loss.

Not all of the causes of anonymity stem directly from social conditions; individuals themselves contribute to their own isolation. Because of the plethora of social stimuli, part of the adaptive skill of the urban dweller consists of avoidance behavior. Thus each individual, surrounded by thousands of others, must develop avoidance measures in order to deal with this large number of potential social contacts. Further, not all are benign sources of satisfaction—some pose a definite threat even to life itself. The total range of stimuli may also pose a threat just as an overload of stimuli (Milgram, 1970).

Reflexive Social Interaction. Dealing with social stimuli requires cognitive modes involving sensory, perceptual, and reasoning sequences. First, behavioral mechanisms must become virtually reflexive, as otherwise too much energy is lost in repeated analysis of successive situations. Time and energy in interpersonal transactions must be reduced; for example, the actions of buying a ticket, asking a fellow commuter to move over in a seat, handing the conductor a ticket, buying a paper, all must be carried out in an almost reflexive and noninvolved way, else energy for vital and complex behavioral efficiency will be reduced. Second, part of the defense against too much stimulation is to shift the burden of response to others as much as possible. Urban social filters can be set up both for individuals and for organizations. Those seeking contacts, for example, can be given box numbers to write to, application blanks to complete, assistants to see, or vague suggestions as to others who may be contacted. These methods and many more are used by individuals as means of protection. It is clear, of course, that this creates anonymity for those seeking the contacts as well as the person who is sought. It puts social interaction on an object basis. The situation becomes quite complex as ingenuity is developed by those who wish to set up filters and by those who wish to avoid being filtered out. While such a social milieu appears to be hopelessly discouraging, those seeking contacts have the hope that one break will provide a great reward and an opportunity for achievement in securing a position or a desired contract.

Other aspects of the overload in the urban social milieu are of considerable significance in the development of individual and group behavior. Excessive social stimuli cause individual interaction to be callous and cause social concern for others to be considered irrelevant or nonadaptive. Such lack, of course, is similar to that of a worker at an assembly line conveyor—he performs a sequence of actions with objects involving no affect. Similarly, in the many brief social contacts, little attention is given the possibility that the person has needs, a capacity to fulfill needs, or that he indeed poses some threat—all possibilities are ignored.

A basic problem encountered in social interaction in the city is lack of *nurturant behavior*. Most social scientists believe that some nurturant qualities, the helping of others, should be part of all social interaction. The urban dweller, however, through his adaptive behavior seeks to eliminate this quality. He does this first because of physical and social danger and second because of excessive social contacts. The urban setting is known to contain a larger number of sociopathic and psychopathic individuals than does a rural setting. Hence, the urban dweller must be constantly alert that he does not become a victim; if he is accosted on the corner and asked for directions, it may be a genuine plea for help, or it may be a ruse to catch him off guard in order to rob him. So it is considered wise to ignore the plea for assistance. If a fight occurs, it is better to move quickly away; a shoot-out is dangerous to bystanders. Nurturance is repressed as a safety precaution, and strangers seeking assistance in the city are generally distrusted. This distrust of unknown persons in the city is primitive; it limits and ultimately endangers autonomous and creative interaction with the environment. Furthermore, it harms those who seek assistance; they come to characterize their environment as harsh and unfeeling.

Urban Norms. The many problems besetting social interaction in the urban setting have brought about certain social norms, not necessarily desirable, but nevertheless adaptive. These norms for behavior are expectations of the city dweller, and departure from them arouses suspicion and hostility. If a man offers a woman his seat on a commuter train, she may take it without acknowledgement or she may prefer to ignore the offer. Such offers are outside behavioral norms of the city and thus are suspect. Even though a person is lonely and yearns for social contacts, prudence and social convention require that the greeting on the apartment elevator be brushed aside. Social interchange must be confined to those known, and all others must be distrusted. Because of these conditions of social interaction, some effort has been made to characterize behavioral norms of the world's great cities. Milgram suggests, for example, that people tend to characterize New York in reference to "physical qualities" while London is characterized on the basis of "favorable response" to strangers by its inhabitants. Within a city, therefore, social interaction seems to contribute to the development of characteristic normative behavior. A prosperous economy, adequate housing, esthetic physical attributes, conscientious government, efficient transportation, availability of cultural and leisure activities may all contribute to the development of social norms which cause people to react to strangers with less distrust and more nurturant behavior. Little research effort or governmental attention have been given to the problems of anonymity and sense of powerlessness of the urban dweller. At the present time, thousands of people feel little sense of autonomy and little hope for change in the fundamental problems of those who live in the city.

AUTONOMY AND SOCIAL CONTROL

As societies in the world evolve toward greater complexity, will the individual inevitably be overwhelmed by social restrictions of a complex social order? Some social scientists see a trend toward increased control and point to a number of signs leading to such an eventuality.

First is the fact that an increasing number (almost all) of the developmental years are spent within the educational structure. Many children two and three years of age are no longer trained with the family alone but within governmental or private organizations. The federal government is increasingly becoming involved in greater commitments for care of very young children of working mothers. Some industries in Europe now provide infant care while mothers work. In some areas of this country and abroad, cooperative groups have taken over the child-rearing responsibility from parents. Parents visit only at specified intervals of a week or month. The dormitories where infants and young children live are designated as schools. Such mass rearing of children by specially trained people, some assert, assures the learning of behavior in accord with norms fostered and approved by the organization.

Second, the extension of governmental knowledge about individual affairs and life styles is seen as a trend that eventually will preclude autonomous actions. Information, as has been discussed earlier, is gathered and processed by machines. Surveillance by government is constantly being increased so that even some political candidates, it has been alleged, are watched by government agencies. The federal government is asking for more and more information about individual preferences and activities. Family planning, for example, is now becoming a subject of government interest.

Third, governmental controls are evident in many areas of the individual's activity. The government creates occupations and also abolishes them. The space program created the occupation of "space engineer" and many highly trained people devoted years to this occupation. When national goals were changed the engineers were dismissed and faced the necessity of changing their occupation. Governmental control of individual income is increasing at every level; larger and larger portions of personal income are taken by local, state, and federal governments.

Fourth, the way in which the physical environment is utilized seems beyond individual influence. Industries add a variety of substances to the water, air, and food; they advertise their products with such vigor that their wares become a necessity; and, often without supervision, they use vast quantities of the earth's resources. All of these actions and more are carried on without the individual's participation in the decisions although they may vitally affect his well-being.

In addition to these problems, conditions in other parts of the world also affect life within this society. Powerful societies in other countries with different ideologies and varying degrees of distrust and hostility affect individual goals in diverse ways. Other societies pursue policies which have the avowed purpose of undermining this society and its goals. Relations with those societies which may affect the destiny of members in this one are seemingly beyond the control of most individuals and at times apparently beyond that of their elected representatives. The world outside our own society is often characterized as a dangerous place. Aggressive actions still are censured only by those societies that seem to have a self-interest in the issue. No man has ever lived in a city or national group under any form of protection other than might. Today an incomprehensible amount of energy and materiel are devoted to defense systems because no supraordinate social structure exists with a capacity to protect one society from aggression by another. Consequently, should one society be able to accomplish some favorable organization that provides optimum internal conditions for individual autonomy, much would still need to be accomplished in other societies before assurance of security or autonomy would be possible. Yet, some progress has been made in this century and most nations in the world subscribe to the principle of some "control organization" supraordinate to national sovereignty. There is hope that international responsibility safeguarding national autonomy can someday be achieved.

The intention here is to explore the problems of the individual in the achievement of autonomy and the social conditions necessary for it. Further, attention will also be given to the individual's responsibility to maintain and change the society of which he is a part.

Individual Behavior and Attainment of Autonomy

The attainment of autonomy is not dependent alone upon conditions in society but on the development of the individual—his physical capacity and learned ability to interact with the environment. Autonomy depends on physical development because, after learning to walk or talk, the child behaves in a much more independent way. Just as physical development is of consequence, so are cognitive abilities. These include sensory awareness, perceptual accuracy, complex reasoning, and memory. All these innate and learned characteristics are part of the individual's capacity to respond. (Some of the principles covered in Chapters 5 and 6 should be applied here in reference to autonomy.) Beyond these capabilities are the emotional and motivational characteristics (Chapters 8 and 9) appropriate for the individual's role and social status (Chapters 2, 3, and 4). Also needed are capacities for creative behavior to find new ways of solving problems and new factors necessary for a satisfying life style.

Cognitive functions are of special significance in highly technological societies, and these must be developed if a high degree of personal autonomy is to be achieved. Selection of stimuli, appropriate use of past experience in association with perceptual processes, assimilation, synthesis, and differentiation—the same functions that are carried out in all problem-solving must be a part of accomplishment. Further, experience must be organized and responses coordinated so that energy and activity will be effective. This kind of behavior can be considered in theoretical terms (for example, in accordance with psychoanalytic theory).

To be autonomous, adequate strength of ego functioning must be acquired. This strength is necessary in order that the individual's behavior will be adaptive, rational, and efficient. The individual must utilize and efficiently control impulses and motives so that they assist in efforts directed toward the fulfillment of needs. Control implies utilization of impulses and motives, not the denial or stifling of them. Some constraints must be applied, however, so that learned capacities can be developed to perceive and to respond within cultural expectations and norms. Skills and competencies must develop which direct motivation and emotional needs not only within normative channels but within channels which provide satisfaction and a basis for further striving toward new goals. Capabilities for seeking new solutions and new ways of responding in the rapidly changing society of today must be cultivated. Emotions must be expressed and controlled in ways which avoid excessive conflict and at the same time fulfill needs not only for one's self but for others. All these capabilities are essential in the individual's attainment of autonomy. They are essential, too, in the attainment of identity and maturity. From such a standpoint, autonomy and identity are conditions of functioning that require effort and accomplishment by the individual—they cannot be transferred, made available, or conferred by social structures such as a university. The individual, therefore, has responsibility in the attainment of autonomy; no matter how favorable his environment may be, an individual must accept responsibility for his personal accomplishment in order to obtain a favorable condition of autonomy.

An even more complex thesis about autonomy is possible. As has been indicated, social interaction helps an individual increase the complexity of response patterns and this implies that the environment can contribute to development. Yet, conditions must be favorable in society so that the individual is able to develop qualities of independent behavior. For satisfactory environmental conditions to exist, individuals must obviously contribute to the environment.

What are the means of individual contribution? First, the individual contributes as a *model*. An individual, acting independently and courageously so that conflicts are not defeating, serves not only as a guide or model but as reinforcement for others in their search for an autonomous and satisfying life style.

Second, the individual can provide information gained from experience. In social structures information must be contributed, if the organization is to continue as an effective unit.

Third, the individual can carry to completion within the expected time the tasks required by the organization. That is, as the individual depends on the organization, he in turn is dependable. This responsibility to the organization is part of a value system and represents an essential element of individual development. In order for human relations to be satisfying, nurturance, concern for group welfare, and fulfillment of obligations must be part of each individual's value system. Growth toward psychological and social maturity is dependent upon the eventual recognition by the individual of his social obligations. Some of the most valued social institutions, as pointed out earlier, are fragile, and a lack of individual concern for their viability can be destructive. Ultimately a lack of concern for fulfillment of social obligations is self-destructive. Part of independence therefore is an ability to conceptualize the necessity for giving in return for what one takes from the organization. For such a value to exist, it obviously must be a part of the socialization process and a part of the psychological maturing process. The infant has no awareness of his mother's lack of sleep as he cries to be fed. As he grows older he must become aware of the giving of others and in turn must learn to give in order to be a part of the web of social interaction.

How does such awareness develop? In part, it evolves in affective interaction in the family. Emotion must be associated with receiving and giving. It is easily recognized that a person who does not contribute to the well-being of others is perceived as an unfeeling person. Sensitive awareness must be a part of the socialization process. Perhaps such awareness can only be learned in the early years of childhood. Deprived of affection in early experience, a person becomes distrustful, hostile, and perhaps hopeless. These negative feelings result in the tragic consequences of alienation; the alienated person loses empathy with others and develops an unwillingness to give to society while receiving benefits from its system. The development of this essential capacity of awareness should therefore be a significant part of the socialization and educational experience. Direct attention to it is often lost in the effort to reach informational and skill requirements.

Of concern particularly, is the question about whether or not the group programs for child rearing now expanding so rapidly in societies throughout the world will provide this sensitivity. Children, it is asserted, will become *institutionalized* if the danger is not recognized. Institutionalized individuals are those who cannot give or show nurturant behavior. They are in reality arrested in development and a burden to those with whom they interact. As adults they cannot fulfill the needs of others, of husband, wife, or children. In social organizations they demand fulfillment of their own needs but do not or cannot perceive the needs of others or the welfare of the group. An interaction effect is set up: as they grasp without giving, others lacking reinforcement of nurturant behavior in their own struggle will also grasp without giving. The efficiency and morale of the organization then becomes adversely affected. This interaction effect is similar in a family, an office, or a religious organization. In essence, man's autonomy grows out of his dependence. As his dependency needs are fulfilled, he can be more independent. The more individuals contribute to a social structure, the more it can contribute to them. Such a situation will not necessarily occur, however, as a social organization can take without giving in return, just as individuals can.

Still another condition of autonomy is one related to fantasy. The individual must believe himself to be secure enough to engage in fantasy and to roam in his own thoughts; in psychoanalytic terms "to free his ego," to remove the self from some cognitive demands, and to circumvent some of the constraints imposed by society. In doing so, the ego or controlling aspects of the individual must limit and integrate this personal freedom with social conditions and with the normative behavior required by the society. He must care about the society while caring about himself. It is possible, of course, for cognitive controls and work to remain too much in control of the person and interfere with feeling in reference to himself and to society.

Some conditions in modern society interfere with a reduction of cognitive controls. Intense competition and the excessive overload of demands require so much time and energy that the individual becomes conditioned to reacting "cognitively" with little feeling. Working with complex machines and systems taxes the individual's ability to keep up with the machines' tireless pace and the collective input from large numbers of people. Work and its role demands accordingly become uppermost in the life of the individual while the emotional area of social interaction becomes subordinate and secondary. This self-denial, while on first examination appearing a mature response, actually becomes a regressive one, as it leads the individual to interact on a nonfeeling basis. When feeling and emotional exchange are devalued, autonomy is really lessened because the individual is preoccupied with the control of the cognitive demands of his particular area of activity and distracted from feelings about needs for autonomy. A narrowing and limiting of the individual's potential for fulfillment and growth take place. While much cognitive control may bring some success in an occupational setting, it often is disastrous for interpersonal relationships: As progress is made in a career, family life deteriorates and the individual finds himself isolated from sources of emotional support. His emotional needs may go unrecognized as cognitive demands increase with occupational success and progress. Many modern occupations require individuals to function at a very high level of efficiency. In order to meet competition and to use technological skills and abilities, a man's occupational effort absorbs most of his capacity for emotional interaction. Little desire or energy remains for fulfillment beyond the cognitive functioning required by an occupational role.

This kind of absorption in work has become a social problem in that many youth reject a society that makes such role demands. Their rejection may also be associated with the fact that industry is encountering increasing difficulty in securing employee commitment to work. Many employees endeavor to devise ways of reducing the time spent in the organization's tasks. In the city, for example, the accepted lunch hour has increased so much that the work day is substantially shortened. To meet urban role demands, certain essential behavior patterns such as the following must be learned during the developmental years: *to work persistently at tasks for a long time with no assurance that the reward will be forthcoming; to resume work at a task after a period of cessation of effort; to control feelings about the procedures and demands associated with prolonged tasks; to attend carefully to instructions for a complex behavioral sequence; to memorize facts and methods; and to conceptualize and communicate verbally in reference to complex processes.*

Middle-class parents who teach their children to strive for long-term and remote goals and who urge their children toward autonomous behavior in problem-solving prepare them for the behavior required in the educational system and in an occupational role beyond. In contrast, difficult is the road ahead for the child who enters the educational system without experience in long-term tasks, who has a limited vocabulary, who has not had an opportunity to conceptualize and to communicate in protracted verbal exchange, and who has not learned to listen to and understand instructions. As he goes on, he is likely to fall farther behind children who have had such experience. In fact, a deprived child often never overcomes the deficit in experience. To some extent autonomy or independence in a life style grows out of the developmental experiences in the early years. Although some demand that autonomy be given them, it cannot in reality be given but must be learned over a long period of time. In fact, the ability to interact with the environment on an autonomous basis is difficult or impossible to acquire in later years.

Role behavior in a highly complex society (because of rapid social change and technological advances) requires longer and longer preparation as well as more and more devotion of energy. Today some youth reject the lengthy preparation for society's highly specialized roles, as their childhood experience did not equip them with the strength and motivation to strive for delayed rewards. It is apparent that permissiveness without requirements for acquisition of cognitive skills and without strong emotional relationships within the family will not enable the young to meet the expectations of modern society.

Although this society now makes many demands on those who seek to enter its mainstream, the socialization experiences of some youth, not only in the middle class but in the lower class, have not equipped them for the struggle. Some feel constrained, confused about identity, and hopeless about achievement. In anger and frustration they turn away from the effort to find a way into the system. In seeking a solution for those who cannot meet society's requirements for the achievement of autonomy and for those who do not choose to do so, it is necessary to examine not only the characteristics of the individual and the socialization process, but also the conditions in society that prevent autonomous behavior.

Individual Autonomy and Urban Social Conditions

Just as essential commitments and capacities are necessary on the part of the individual for development toward autonomy, conditions within society also need to be of such a nature that autonomous behavior will be fostered. Conceptualizing the relationship of individual autonomy to social conditions is difficult, because the individual *is* society. While this argument holds, the aggregatory effects of individuals working together can be a relatively unified force. It is possible, therefore, that the sum of the effect is more significant than the total of the parts. This seems a reasonable conclusion if the effects of their actions become a cultural norm. Such reasoning leads to the view that *society* stands for forces growing out of the aggregate behavior of many people; it embodies a framework of constraints, requirements, and rewarding conditions that mold human development and individual behavior. Autonomy is a worthwhile concept of a human condition insofar as it refers to activity and role behavior designed to obtain satisfaction and fulfillment of human needs and desires.

Favorable Conditions for Autonomy. The primary concern here is to describe favorable conditions in society that foster the development of autonomous behavior. The following suggestions reflect in part the ideas of Olsen (1968). First, there must be *opportunities for goals of choice.* The individual must be relatively free of restraint on his activities and he must be encouraged to believe that he can reach the goals he values. This provision of a basis for hope means that not only must the individual be able to set his own goals, but he must be allowed to engage in kinds of behavior which he sees as leading to attainment of his goals. Possibly the conceptualization of this principle should also include social reinforcement and valuing by others. Accordingly, for the attainment of autonomy the society must approve the choice of goals, the behavior pattern selected, and the final reaching of the goals. If the individual's effort is directed toward the creation of a product—a painting or musical composition—he needs to have his product accepted and his effort rewarded. Rejection of this sequence by the society will ultimately be stultifying not only to an individual but to others who wish to pursue similar goals. Problems can arise at various points in the sequence of behavior required of the individual in goal-seeking behavior. For example, the society might not actually disapprove of the individual's choice or the means used, but it might be indifferent to the individual's needs for assistance in meeting his goals. As was discussed earlier (Chapter 10), *reinforcement* is a complex condition—the withholding of reinforcing conditions (indifference to the individual's efforts) can be interpreted by the individual as punishment. In such instances, indifference may be devastating in its effect on the pursuit of goals requiring autonomy. In fact, modern youth react to an institution's indifference to their concerns with more negative emotion than they show when they are openly opposed.

A second condition in society important for the development of individual autonomy is that of *order*. Order here means that the society's functioning, laws, and services will provide bases for predicting events. With order, plans can be made for personal goals. If a house is built or a business firm established, the individual must be able to count on opportunities for role behavior appropriate to the creation, reasonable taxation, and protection from usurpation. A lack of order on the part of society in such a situation obviously would be devastating to the individual.

A third condition in society necessary for autonomy is *role diversity*. Wide diversity, of course, is possible only in a complex society. In primitive societies, only a few roles were possible. In modern and urban society, diversity allows those with varying capacities to take roles in which they can find satisfaction. In the city the range is great even within role categories—an artist may teach, work in advertising, sell his own work, or act as an agent for other artists.

Satisfaction in a role is not a simple attainment for an individual, as satisfaction involves the fulfillment of his unrecognized needs as well as those recognized. It is also dependent upon the *interaction effect* of the individual with society's dictated values. Human satisfaction is quite difficult to separate from concordance with social values. An individual's satisfaction in the creation of a product is much enhanced by social approval, and his satisfaction cannot therefore be completely separated from the satisfaction of others in his life space.

While current urban society has a wide diversity of roles, not all permit easy access; if the individual is not permitted a role in accord with his interest, motivation, and values, the society, at least for him, lacks significant opportunity for autonomy. Many people, particularly minority groups, are aware of the diversity of roles in the urban setting, but if they cannot secure the necessary education or overcome other barriers, the existence of diversity makes no contribution to their autonomy. Consequently, an openness to assistance and training for the various roles must be society's concern. To insure this openness, however, is dif-

ficult in today's modern urban areas. Powerful social structures and
work organizations are sometimes too inflexible; forcing or persuading
organizations to become open is an enormous task for governmental
agencies. Some social organizations can change on their own. Such is the
case when universities offer "open admissions." For many years, colleges
that limited opportunities to those who could profit by higher education
on the basis of test scores and past educational history prevented many
potentially able people from gaining admission. Openness and diversity
are products of a value system and a complex, affluent society.

A fourth condition is that of *structural differentiation* in social institutions. It follows that if the society is to have a diversity of social
roles, there will have to be a diversity within the major social structures.
Solutions to the problems of minority groups and social deprivation
must begin during early childhood and extend beyond the college years.
In the educational structure many kinds of educational opportunities
must be made available in addition to the usual public school programs.
Opportunities for education should be extended in trade organizations,
union apprenticeships, industrial training programs, art schools, and
music schools; and in higher education in junior colleges, technical
schools, religious schools, colleges, and universities.

It is obvious that the student's educational experience has a significant role in the development of a concept of autonomy as he looks
forward to a place in society. The student in the future will not be
educated in an *authoritarian* system for an *autonomous* adult role. The
meager concern shown for the problem in the past has largely grown
out of the idea that close control and a highly structured educational
experience will cause the person to behave in adulthood in accordance
with his training. Such a course can be relatively successful in a slowly
changing society. In a rapidly changing society the educational experience and conditioned response patterns learned originally must be
altered drastically as the individual is forced in later years to change
career objectives and life-space adjustment. *Education for specific response patterns, specific values, and patterned life styles cannot serve
the individual in the urban society of the future.* Although education
must emphasize information gathering, assimilation, and decision processes, the student should have much autonomy in the pursuit of knowledge. It is only reasonable that the educational experience be aligned
with role experience in society much more than it has been in the past.
The individual who is trained through the developmental years for one
approach to environmental interaction cannot be expected to change
suddenly on becoming an adult. Thus, the educative process should
provide *learning in relation to commitment to tasks, flexibility in the
utilization of problem-solving approaches, training in the reconstruction
of perceptual sets, and experience in the reorganization of a value system.*
For successful role adaptability, capabilities in the urban age will have
to be learned over a long period of time and cannot, for example, be
taught or learned only in the college years.

Changes in the educational structure and its place in society must be considerable even though controversy inevitably accompanies alteration in the structure's programs. In recent years education has been involved in controversy more than at any other time in history. The great changes required in the future are likely to be disparate, with some institutions and local programs changing much more than others. Support and resources can be expected to change, too, in an uneven way. Controversy is likely to increase about the extent of control and the influence of government at federal, state, and local levels. Varying trends in control tend to develop and fade, as do different methods and types of facilities. In some localities in the future, parts of the educational system will be largely dominated by community control while others will be at the opposite extreme, under federal control.

Much more attention must be given to education in early childhood because many more children will begin their educational experience at two years of age, less than is currently the case. Although there is a trend for early education to consist of programmed experience aimed at the development of language and numerical concepts—a trend reflecting much concern about cognitive development, a countertrend is also visible toward individual goals and an "open" type of experience.

In the future many more students will be allowed to progress at individual rates so that education is not tied closely to chronological age or to grade. For superior students, programs designed according to personal characteristics will allow many kinds of choices of pace and content. Programmed instruction and team teaching will permit a "systems" approach to a vast range of experience. Machine-related education used at first as a system to facilitate an extension of factual knowledge will eventually develop more sophisticated programs in order to include concept formation and theorizing.

Issues are likely to be clouded in a system of much flexibility in programs and choices. Differences between students and faculty will be at the extremes; that is, beginning students will find choice of curriculum but will be able to influence their life space in the institution in only a limited way. More advanced students, however, will participate in the program of the university in teaching and research. At the other extreme will be faculty members who contribute to the institution but have contact with only a few specific students—those well on their way to professional status.

Many different programs designed for specific needs will be available: these will include tutorial, remedial, and social assistance. Facilities and expert assistance will be obtainable for a wide variety of problems so that anger, disappointment, and hostility can be dealt with in a framework designed to fulfill individual needs. This is not to say, of course, that deprivation during the developmental years will be easily or completely offset.

Information, long a basic part of education, will be systematized much more than is currently true. Student frustration at inaccessibility of information and materials will be essentially avoided through the use of machines and new methods of reproduction. Students, for example, will be able to have personal copies of all general information useful in a course. The information will not be limited to the student's own university library but will come from worldwide sources and to an increasing extent from television. Thus, the machines of the future will free information from limitations of place, and the student's energy will be devoted to utilization instead of search.

A closer relationship between the student role and the adult role will be possible. Participation in a career role can begin long before so-called graduation. Through participation, students will not feel insulated from the system but will be able to learn in it and influence it at the same time. Many opportunities for financial autonomy will be achieved through this interchange, and distinctions between the campus and the city will disappear. In fact, communities far removed from the campus will be part of the experience: for example, the subjects of architecture or archeology may be taught in remote areas of the world.

Great flexibility in programs will be the rule. Education will be less dependent on "degree programs"; that is, higher education will consist of two-, three-, or four-year programs not necessarily tied to the standard bachelor's degree. Society in general, and particularly industry, will become more flexible in educational requirements for hiring as their own educational programs are developed. Industry and the institutions of higher education will cooperate and share in curricular and experiential planning, and the separation between the activity of large companies and the large urban universities will become much less distinct. It can be noted that in recent years industry has been increasing its educational activity; a closer relationship between university and company educational programs will benefit both types of training.

Because the complexity of society will rapidly increase in the urban age, education will be perceived even more than is true today as a key to finding satisfaction in society. As the educational system's offerings become more related to capabilities required in the adult years, young people who turn their backs on the system will be fewer, as they will be able to find sufficient flexibility for their needs. The opportunities will be much greater in the educational system than can be found anywhere else in society.

Choice for occupational roles will be so diverse that reasonable conflict with the system will be difficult. Differences in values will not be an issue. It seems that, in the future, society's affairs and governmental policies for the major social structures will be dominated by specialists who will be perceived by some as an elite corps. Nevertheless, a major difference from the governing elites of the past will be that the governing group of the future will not be the only one in society with a good life or social status. Further, if one wishes to devote the effort to obtain status in the governing elite, the opportunity will be available. In essence, variance in the social roles and life styles in the society will be so diverse that membership in the elite and governing group will not stand out as the only satisfying status. It is possible this will be a new achievement in the societies of man and will provide a significant contribution to the meaning of autonomy for the individual.

A fifth condition of concern in the provision of opportunities for the development of individual autonomy is that of *functionalism*. This means that society should be so organized and its members so motivated that its structures will adapt to the functional processes of society. Under such a condition, the form of society's organizations and the function of its social structures contribute to individual autonomy. Basic activities of society, it should be recalled, are utilization of natural resources, distribution of processed products, education of the young, promulgation of a value system, maintenance of order, and protection of members from internal and external hostile action.

Modern society in its processes provides some freedom for pursuit of individual goals by its distribution of roles. In a complex society, individual effort is lessened because of the availability and cooperative effort of many people with diverse skills. In some primitive societies much activity over the entire lifetime is devoted to procurement of food and shelter, but by contrast in modern society only a small part of income and little direct effort is devoted to providing food and shelter. Scarcely anyone builds his own house and grows all his own food. As a result, many in society can set personalized goals for much of their activity. Cooperative endeavor through routinization of tasks allows members of a complex society to choose their activities. In a society with a high degree of technology, this freedom of choice is usually widely distributed. In medieval and feudal society, groups having freedom in choice of activity obtained that freedom through the work of others who maintained them. In such a society, opportunities for autonomy were limited to only a few.

In terms of functionalism, choices of activities resulting from role assignments and technological advances can be the basis for problems as well as benefits. Although functionalism refers to society's service to its members, it is conceivable that a large number of people in their choice of activities can act adversely toward the social order that provides the "free" conditions. They can, for example, use the opportunity for anti-social behavior—behavior that is destructive to the society as well as to individuals. A question thus arises: Can people in the mass be given opportunity to pursue their own goals and will their choices bring about a good life for others as well as for themselves? Will they contribute to the creation of a good society? Or must the social order routinize *free activity* as it has done in organizational activities to insure that energy be channeled into socially constructive and self-fulfilling activities? If so, must society still be served in "free time"? Or, does autonomy mean that the individual can, if he so chooses, spend time in ultimately self-destructive ways or in ways which impair the society? If there is to be social evolution and, in fact, personal development, should not the society exert some influence—perhaps control—of leisure activity?

A possible alternative to such a choice would be to bring about internal control through conditioning and training during the developmental years. Through training it might be that in the adult years the individual would choose socially constructive and personally enhancing activities. These considerations provide basic questions for modern society and particularly for the educational structure. Any decision about the function of society must be supported by a widely accepted value system. This system must be a guide for individual members and organizations. It would, of course, be internalized to varying degrees. A so-called perfect society, that is, one in which all members have internalized the value system, is unlikely to come about; and if it did, it would be difficult to include in the concept the social evolution of the value system itself. In urban society, as free time is lengthened through the reduction of time devoted to work, difficult decisions about social control of leisure activity will have to be made. In reference to the autonomy—social responsibility continuum, it should be remembered that the more autonomy is available, the greater is the demand for social responsibility.

Work in Modern and Urban Society. In considering the meaning of autonomy, attention must be given to the meaning of toil. The drudgery of work is not a new problem; it has only received greater emphasis since the industrial revolution. Man, toiling for long hours at highly repetitive jobs, has brought great productivity and a new way of life to many; but for others, wages have barely covered subsistence needs and have done little to enhance the quality of life. As machines have eased man's toil they also have routinized much of his waking day, decreased his opportunities for decisions, inhibited the development of new skills, and reduced dependence on his thought processes. Difficulties growing out of the Industrial Revolution have long been the subject for debate. Youths today express a distaste for an industrial system which demands that they take a place in a bureaucracy and work at tasks which do not allow personal development. Indeed, some have returned to the simpler way of life in a rural setting to devote most of their energies to the acquisition of food and shelter.

Many problems in finding satisfaction in living result from "social imbalance" (Galbraith, 1968). Among societies of the past, only a few have had satisfying life styles; in an affluent society most people can examine their lives and question the quality of their experience. In some societies in the world today, however, the struggle for existence, the socialization experience, and the value system do not permit a questioning of the quality of life. The pursuit of happiness is not an issue—only the pursuit of food and shelter and conformity to a rigid system of duty are perceived. In societies since the beginning of civilization, particularly in the Renaissance, some groups have pursued happiness and have shown concern for the quality of life. In recent times, the number of people who can pursue happiness and who can afford to be concerned with quality in their life styles has grown. Now new emphasis is being given to a definition of individual welfare—a definition of needs for leisure and contentment (Winter, Rabow, and Chesler, 1968).

The consideration of such issues as autonomy, individual destiny, and welfare in society have not been given much attention in the past by research workers in the area of developmental psychology. Rather, their energy has been devoted to such areas as the learning process, the acquisition of language, and the measurement of intelligence. Considerable emphasis, however, should be placed on socialization and preparation of the individual for a satisfying role in society. Research effort should include concern for the ultimate goal of the processes of development—satisfaction in a living style basically dependent on the emotional quality of interaction with others. Emphasis on only cognitive experience in preparation for adulthood is being reordered. Concern is now turning toward the relationship of developmental experience to social conditions and goals. Perhaps the former lack of concern for the destiny of the individual in society accounts in part for the failure of society with so many of today's youth.

An essential issue for many youth is the link between *job* and *sustaining income.* Modern society seeks to provide individuals with at least a minimum standard of living while reducing the effort and time at work. Associated with this purpose is one to distribute the products and material of the society to its members on some basis of equality. As Theobald (1968) maintains, modern societies have depended on the principle that a proper distribution results automatically from conditions of supply and demand. The supposition is that each individual will seek to obtain through work the necessary sustenance, material, and security for himself and his family. This formula for human destiny grew out of a moral concept that man should work for and deserve whatever amount of goods, security, and prestige he obtains. If he does not achieve enough of these things, the fault is his own; it is not the malfunction of the system. If a man is successful he should be recognized as a good citizen without much critical attention to the methods used to achieve his goals.

In the past, work itself was perceived as moral. The poverty one suffered was punishment for a lack of diligence and farsighted planning. Many implications are evident in such a concept of morality. It is implied, for example, that work in itself is good no matter what it is. Another implication is that the rewards of work will be appropriate to the individual's diligence and competency. If a man is thrown out of work, it is in some way his fault, not that of the system. A still further implication is that work contributes to the total welfare of society and to a man's own personal development. None of these implications is necessarily wrong. The belief in the system of supply and demand as capable of regulating itself has brought a higher level of living to Americans than to any other society on earth. The system has not worked, however, for a large number of people, and therefore it needs some examination, as does the morality system implied in the work-income formula.

It should be clear, of course, that the questioning of the system is not new. The economic measures taken by the government during the Great Depression were not based on economic principles of the past but on social and humanitarian exigencies growing out of widespread suffering and social unrest. The so-called economic measures were really psychosocial measures undertaken because of the system's malfunction.

Later evidence of psychosocial concern transcending economic concern was the passage of the Employment Act of 1946 which supported the principle of full employment: that man has a right to work (Michael, 1968). This act was not based on an economic principle but on a psychosocial one, that employment was to be maintained at any cost, even that of deficit spending. This is a principle followed today: Governments can and should spend beyond their income for the welfare of the individuals in the society. An added part of this principle is that the government is committed to guarantee the income of those who are too old, too young, or too ill to work. Therefore the principle that government should guarantee the income of members of society is already well established. What remains in controversy is: How many people shall receive this guarantee? What shall be the conditions which determine that they deserve it? How much shall they receive? These questions are not just economic; they depend also on concepts of the autonomy of the individual in society and on the concepts of the goals of a good society.

A further concern in reference to the morality of work is: How much should an individual work? If a man must work to deserve an income, how long and how hard is enough? It should be noted that one of man's goals in living is to avoid toil. The primitive man who constructed a canoe so that he would not have to swim behaved in a similar way to the suburbanite who removes the snow from his sidewalk with a snow-blower instead of a shovel. Something of a paradox in values exists in modern society, in that work is supposed to be moral and self-enhancing and yet effort to reduce toil is approved. In industry, for example, automation has generally been approved as a way to lessen toil and increase efficiency. Aside from efficiency and direct economic benefits, machines are better workers. They require no rest periods, make no demands for a wage increase, and offer no criticism of management. In industrial plants in the future, machines are expected to do much of the work. Society is confronted with a movement to reduce work and at the same time with the contention that an individual can be a deserving citizen only if he works.

In a complex society, what kind of overall design will insure the fair and appropriate distribution of work after machines have taken over much of it? On what basis will role and work assignments be made? Are the displaced individuals to be held responsible when great governmental projects are discontinued or when new technological advances eradicate needs for people? Can an increasingly complex economic system be expected to operate fairly for a majority of its citizens without some kind of overall control? Theobald does not believe that periodic governmental manipulation will keep the system in balance so that massive unemployment can be avoided. If this prediction is correct, it means some change is necessary in the conception of social role, in the idea of the morality of work, and in the idea of individual responsibility to find work.

Some steps toward a change in concept are visible although they are now disguised by labels. For example, social security benefits are periodically increased, but actuarily the payments exceed individual contributions. The principle is that those who through their work contributed to the success of the American economy in the past are entitled in retirement to some safeguard for the remainder of their lives. Another step already taken is in unemployment insurance. It is conceded that those who are displaced by shifts in the economy and in society's goals ought not to be punished or suffer too much social stigma by a disastrous reduction in income.

Can enough meaningful work be provided? If work opportunities are reduced, should everyone be expected to work, and is income to be provided only on the basis of work? If it is maintained that man must work, employment in bureaucratic structures will hardly enhance individual development in the society of the future, as man will only be a partner to a machine. With improved education and new insights into socialization and education, the citizen of the future will be unlikely to find satisfaction in highly structured work situations associated with machines. Further, there will simply not be enough desirable work for an increasing and highly educated population.

Accordingly, social goals and the morality-of-work concept must be changed. Socialization and education will have to assist individuals to enhance their own development and to contribute to their own quality of life as well as to the quality of the society without holding a job. Hence the income and wealth of society must be distributed in some other way than by a work principle, perhaps on some dimension of the contribution to self and society. Criteria for this change will have to be derived on the basis of psychosocial issues rather than on moral or economic issues. It may be that individuals with freedom from work at a job they detest can contribute creatively to society, perhaps not. If they cannot, society will have to develop activities for them which are not income-related. Education and family training may, however, produce people who will have sufficient motivation to develop their potential and contribute to society without direct control. In the future, society will not demand that an individual find a job to maintain himself. The individual of the future will have enough money to live within the standards of the culture, and society will demand only that he develop his potential and contribute to the quality of life in society. This concept is one of a truly "brave new world" and can promise life styles long sought after by man on earth. Under such circumstances man possibly can become "good" and so can his society. In such a society, autonomy may have a meaning not only in terms of the individual's social responsibility but in terms of the society's responsibility to the individual.

IN PERSPECTIVE

A basic consideration in reference to autonomy is the place of "work" in modern society. Today, concepts of work are changing in significant ways. In the past, work was considered a moral and social obligation as well as a source of personal fulfillment. Societies have long punished people who do not work, as idleness is considered immoral and damaging both to the individual and to the social order. Social structures, understandably, maintain that only through work can satisfaction in society be achieved. Work and rewards for it are not usually commensurate, however. In fact, distribution of society's goods and wealth has never been closely related to the amount of work performed. Most men work diligently only to find the rewards distributed to them both meager and unequal. In modern society more and more questions are being asked about the *meaning* of work. Doubt is now expressed about the value of the rewards for conscientious toil. Further, the axiom that work fulfills the basic desires of man is also being doubted as a result of the effects of assembly lines and the break-up of tasks formerly performed by one man. Work broken into bits and segments reduces meaning for the individual in terms of a holistic sense of personal accomplishment. As a result, organizations have used work incentives other than job satisfaction and wages.

Not only production jobs but also service jobs have changed; service occupations now bring less satisfaction than was the case earlier in the century. As customer and worker have only hasty and casual contacts, a "good job" is not appreciated.

Work in modern society holds less and less satisfaction. Thus, autonomy and satisfaction in a life style are not seen as being enhanced by work. In addition, the meaning of autonomy is changing—a definition applicable to conditions in modern society is difficult to find.

REFERENCES

AHLSTROM, W. M., & HAVIGHURST, R. J. *400 losers.* San Francisco: Jossey-Bass, 1971.

ARENSBERG, C. M., & NIEHOFF, A. H. *Introducing social change.* Chicago: Aldine, 1964.

ARGYRIS, C. Individual actualization in complex organizations. In G. D. Bell (Ed.), *Organizations and human behavior*. Englewood Cliffs, N.J.: Prentice-Hall, 1967. Pp. 208–217.

BELL, G. D. Formality versus flexibility in complex organizations. In G. D. Bell (Ed.), *Organizations and human behavior*. Englewood Cliffs, N.J.: Prentice-Hall, 1967. Pp. 97–106.

BLOS, P. *The young adolescent: Clinical studies*. New York: Free Press, 1970.

BONJEAN, C. M. Mass class and the industrial community. In G. D. Bell (Ed.), *Organizations and human behavior*. Englewood Cliffs, N.J.: Prentice-Hall, 1967. Pp. 60–73.

COHEN, Y. A. The shaping of men's minds: Adaptations to the imperatives of culture. In M. L. Wax, S. Diamond, & F. O. Gearing (Eds.), *Anthropological perspectives on education*. New York: Basic Books, 1971. Pp. 19–50.

COOK, T. I. Individual liberty today: Challenge and prospect. In M. Berger, T. Abel, & C. H. Page (Eds.), *Freedom and control in modern society*. New York: Octagon, 1964. Pp. 177–191.

DOMHOFF, G. W. *Who rules America?* Englewood Cliffs, N.J.: Prentice-Hall, 1967.

DURKHEIM, E. The division of labor in society. In G. D. Bell (Ed.), *Organizations and human behavior*. Englewood Cliffs, N.J.: Prentice-Hall, 1967. Pp. 33–41.

ETZIONI, A. *Modern organizations*. Englewood Cliffs, N.J.: Prentice-Hall, 1964.

FROMM, E. Man is not a thing. In H. M. Ruitenbeek (Ed.), *The dilemma of organizational society*. New York: E. P. Dutton, 1963. Pp. 59–66.

GALBRAITH, J. K. The social balance and the investment balance. In J. A. Winter, J. Rabow, & M. Chesler (Eds.), *Vital problems for American society*. New York: Random House, 1968. Pp. 328–340.

GALBRAITH, J. K. The theory of social balance. In H. K. Girvetz (Ed.), *Contemporary moral issues*. Belmont, Calif.: Wadsworth, 1963. Pp. 151–160.

GERTH, H., & MILLS, C. W. *Character and social structure: The psychology of social institutions*. New York: Harcourt, Brace & World, 1964.

GOODMAN, M. E. *The individual and culture*. Homewood, Ill.: Dorsey, 1967.

GROSS, B. M. The city of man: A social systems reckoning. In W. R. Ewald (Ed.), *Environment for man*. Bloomington: Indiana University Press, 1967. Pp. 136–156.

HARRINGTON, M. *The accidental century*. Baltimore: Penguin, 1965.

HAVIGHURST, R. J., & NEUGARTEN, B. L. *Society and education*. Boston: Allyn and Bacon, 1962.

HENRI, COMTE DE SAINT-SIMON. On social organization. In H. M. Ruitenbeek (Ed.), *Varieties of classic social theory*. New York: E. P. Dutton, 1963. Pp. 23–29.

JOHNSON, R. N. *Aggression: In man and animals*. Philadelphia: W. B. Saunders, 1972.

KERBER, A., & BOMMARITO, B. (Eds.), *The schools and the urban crises*. New York: Holt, Rinehart & Winston, 1966.

KNELLER, G. Education and cultural values. In E. T. Keach, R. Fulton, & W. E. Gardner (Eds.), *Education and social crisis*. New York: Wiley, 1967. Pp. 9–22.

LEMERT, E. M. *Human deviance, social problems, and social control.* Englewood Cliffs, N.J.: Prentice-Hall, 1967.

LONDON, P. *Behavior control.* New York: Harper & Row, 1969.

MALEK, I. World order and the responsibility of scientists: A functional as opposed to an institutional approach. In S. Hoffman (Ed.), *Conditions of world order.* Boston: Houghton Mifflin, 1968. Pp. 236–257.

MANUEL, F. E. Toward a psychological history of utopias. In B. McLaughlin (Ed.), *Studies in social movements: A social psychological perspective.* New York: Free Press, 1969. Pp. 370–399.

MARTINDALE, D. *Institutions, organizations, and mass society.* Boston: Houghton Mifflin, 1966.

MEAD, M. The pattern of leisure in contemporary American culture. In H. M. Ruitenbeek (Ed.), *The dilemma of organizational society.* New York: E. P. Dutton, 1963. Pp. 177–185.

MERTON, R. K. Bureaucratic structure and personality. In H. M. Ruitenbeek (Ed.), *The dilemma of organizational society.* New York: E. P. Dutton, 1963. Pp. 119–131.

MICHAEL, D. N. Education in the next generation. In J. A. Winter, J. Rabow, & M. Chesler (Eds.), *Vital problems for American society.* New York: Random House, 1968. Pp. 445–461.

MILGRAM, S. The experience of living in cities: A psychological analysis. In F. F. Korten, S. W. Cook, & J. I. Lacey (Eds.), *Psychology and the problems of society.* Washington, D.C.: American Psychological Assn., 1970. Pp. 152–173.

MOORE, W. E. *Order and change.* New York: Wiley, 1967.

MURPHY, G. The internalization of social controls. In M. Berger, T. Abel, & C. H. Page (Eds.), *Freedom and control in modern society.* New York: Octagon, 1964. Pp. 3–17.

OLSEN, M. E. The mature society: Personal autonomy and social responsibility. In J. A. Winter, J. Rabow, & M. Chesler (Eds.), *Vital problems for American society.* New York: Random House, 1968. Pp. 417–435.

POTTER, D. M. American individualism in the twentieth century. In G. H. Mills (Ed.), *Innocence and power: Individualism in twentieth-century America.* Austin: University of Texas Press, 1965. Pp. 92–112.

RIESMAN, D. *The lonely crowd.* New Haven: Yale University Press, 1950.

RIESMAN, D. The college student in an age of organization. In H. M. Ruitenbeek (Ed.), *The dilemma of organizational society.* New York: E. P. Dutton, 1963. Pp. 99–117.

ROVERE, R. H. The invasion of privacy: Technology and the claims of community. In H. M. Ruitenbeek (Ed.), *The dilemma of organizational society.* New York: E. P. Dutton, 1963. Pp. 67–76.

SMITH, M. B. Competence and socialization. In J. A. Clansen (Ed.), *Socialization and society.* Boston: Little, Brown, 1968. P. 270.

SOLOMON, B. P. The person alone. In H. M. Ruitenbeek (Ed.), *The dilemma of organizational society.* New York: E. P. Dutton, 1963. Pp. 93–97.

SOMMER, R. *Personal space.* Englewood Cliffs, N.J.: Prentice-Hall, 1969.

SUMNER, W. G. Some natural rights. In S. Persons (Ed.), *Social Darwinism: Se-*

lected essays of William Graham Sumner. Englewood Cliffs, N.J.: Prentice-Hall, 1963. Pp. 65–69.

THEOBALD, R. The background to the guaranteed-income concept. In J. A. Winter, J. Rabow, & M. Chesler (Eds.), *Vital problems for American society.* New York: Random House, 1968. Pp. 341–351.

WADDINGTON, C. H. The desire for material progress as a world ordering system. In S. Hoffman (Ed.), *Conditions of world order.* Boston: Houghton Mifflin, 1968. Pp. 228–235.

WALTERS, R. H. The effects of social isolation and social interaction on learning and performance in social situations. In D. C. Glass (Ed.), *Environmental influences.* New York: Rockefeller University Press, 1968. Pp. 155–184.

WEBER, M. The ideal bureaucracy. In G. D. Bell (Ed.), *Organizations and human behavior.* Englewood Cliffs, N.J.: Prentice-Hall, 1967. Pp. 86–90.

WHITE, L. A. Individuality and individualism: A culturological interpretation. In G. H. Mills (Ed.), *Innocence and power: Individualism in twentieth-century America.* Austin: University of Texas Press, 1965. Pp. 3–35.

WHYTE, W. H. Individualism in suburbia. In H. M. Ruitenbeek (Ed.), *The dilemma of organizational society.* New York: E. P. Dutton, 1963. Pp. 21–34.

WILENSKY, H. Mass society and mass culture. In G. D. Bell, *Organizations and human behavior.* Englewood Cliffs, N.J.: Prentice-Hall, 1967, Pp. 41–60.

WINTER, J. A., RABOW, J., & CHESLER, M. (Eds.). To promote the general welfare. In J. A. Winter, J. Rabow, & M. Chesler (Eds.), *Vital problems for American society.* New York: Random House, 1968. Pp. 320–327.

YOUNG, W. M. Desegregation: What impact on the urban scene. In J. L. Berry & J. Meltzer (Eds.), *Goals for urban America.* Englewood Cliffs, N.J.: Prentice-Hall, 1967. Pp. 99–111.

SOCIAL POWER AND SOCIAL LEARNING   13

The twentieth century saw a basic change in child training and socialization. Child training heretofore was characterized by control, direction, and demands for strict adherence to rules. Obedience and conformity to rules were, in part, accomplished by a system of rewards and punishment. And discipline, ostensibly the means, sometimes became an end.

Up until the latter part of the nineteenth century, children stood in the presence of adults and ate at separate tables. Their conversation was not considered acceptable in adult society. Many parents believed in the adage "Spare the rod and spoil the child." Even in school, children's learning was viewed as best accomplished by holding over them the threat of corporal punishment as a consequence of both academic failure and indecorous behavior. Some parents considered it proper to tell their children: "If you are punished at school, you will also be punished at home." Support for punishment and absolute authority of parents and educators also came from the church.

Although such principles as freedom of speech and discussion of alternatives in social interaction were adult values, these principles did not apply in interaction between children and adults. Generally, the view was that the best training for participation in a democratic society was for the child to have strict control and training; later, when given opportunity for making decisions in adulthood, the individual could then be depended upon to make decisions consonant with his early training. Much of this control was achieved not only by the threat of pain but by its actual infliction. The basic approach to child training, accordingly, was control. By control the child was believed to be prepared for participation in a democratic society. But with the changing of society in the twentieth century, the structure of the family and its concepts of authority and power in reference to the rights of the individual in society changed drastically (Conger, 1971).

Today some believe that the behavior of youth and their forceful protests against society's structures are a result of these changes. They assert that both the family and the educational system should return to the control manifest in the training characteristic of the latter part of the past century. Currently this issue is a subject for debate by those in power in society, particularly, in government. They easily perceive that people who are nonconformists and who refuse to comply with institutional mandates are indeed difficult to govern.

The debate reveals a basic philosophical and psychological issue represented by the following question: How should an individual be trained to fit into society? In approaching such a question it is of course necessary to determine the conditions of society into which the individual must fit. That is, is the society democratic in its functioning? Will the individual be expected to make decisions about the destiny of society and its goals? Will he have some measure of power in determining the actions and goals of the social structures?

If the society is considered to be a democracy, what is the real nature and meaning of a democratic society? Is an individual better prepared for life in a democratic society by experiencing strict control in his social learning during the developmental years, or is he better prepared for life in a democracy by experiencing democratic conditions during the preparatory years?

In approaching answers to these fundamental questions, it is necessary to deal with the bases for satisfaction for life in a society. Is human satisfaction more likely to be obtained in a democratic society? If so, what are the theoretical and practical characteristics of democracy? And why do some members of society have more satisfaction than do others?

PSYCHOSOCIAL FOUNDATIONS FOR
SOCIAL ROLES IN SOCIETY

Many people perceive wrongs in modern society and believe that they must take action to right these wrongs. The social structures, such people believe, should be responsive to the voices of the community. In fact, a general belief in the need for responsive social organizations seems to have become prevalent. This view is now especially apparent in the urban setting. In the past, people in large areas of the city where the poor and minority groups live seemed voiceless. Now the situation has changed. In poor areas of the city where some organizational progress has been achieved, representatives from the black community frequently attend a wide variety of meetings from which they were formerly excluded. Many a staid urban organization or rubber-stamp committee has begun a standard and routine meeting only to be interrupted by someone striding forward to present demands as a representative of the community. Committees and representative organizations of schools, churches, and government have been interrupted and even taken over by such emissaries. In general the organizations have responded with some acceptance of the rights asserted. Only a short time ago, such behavior would not have been tolerated, but now the view prevails that such voices should be heard and responded to.

The interruptions are often dramatic. One committee preparing for a governmental conference met in a large room of a high school in a center city where even through the brick walls the steady noise of traffic penetrated. Above the continuous noise, an occasional siren proclaimed an emergency. Two co-chairmen at the front of the room, one black and one white, presided. After the meeting had continued for a time in a rather lethargic discussion, a commotion from the hallway consisting of heavy steps and loud voices came to the attention of the audience. In a moment several black men in leather jackets strode to the front of the room. The discussion stopped and the audience watched in silence. One intruder remained standing, while the others sat on the front row. A small child, about four years of age and also black, entered and sat at the edge of the platform near the standing man. That man now raised his fist and shook it at the audience. Without waiting for an invitation, he began to speak. His language contained obscenities and colloquialisms as he listed the "black community's" needs in a strident voice. He spoke for nearly a quarter of an hour before taking a seat at the front. The meeting continued in a much more spirited fashion after the black chairman expressed his satisfaction in hearing from the "community" and "our black brother." Although the intruder's actions had been hostile and challenging, he was willingly received by the group. The discussion then centered directly on the problems of children in the black areas of the city and continued with enthusiasm for several hours.

Many other meetings have similar interruptions. Even church services are disrupted by such entries. Usually the interruptions find support from the audience on the basis that people have a right to be heard and that the challenges grow out of society's failures to be fair or to provide opportunities for equality in the past.

Most people would agree that those in the black community of large cities have not been heard nor have they had a voice in the goals of the society. As concern about conditions in the city developed, recognition has come belatedly that in order for programs to be successful, action must be initiated by the people themselves. But some still ask: If programs are devised for the poor and those at the poverty level, should the goals be set by the power structures for the powerless or should the poor be allowed to set their own goals and use public funds in the ways they see fit? Others believe that a compromise should be worked out so that agents of the government and the people can work together to establish goals and the methods to achieve them. Approaches to the problems of the city remain controversial. Ignorance and a lack of information are charges made both by agencies and by community groups. At times domineering attitudes characterize each group. At this action level, a psychosocial issue is illustrated. How does democracy function? Should only the agents of the government be allowed to set the goals? Or should only the representatives of the community set goals for themselves?

This social conflict is a major one. It is significant particularly in the social programs of this society. Although many people advocate "revenue-sharing" and local administration of social programs, others believe past history indicates that local administration and control means inefficiency and waste. Some believe trained experts of the federal government, an elite, are best able to plan and carry out the needed programs, while community control means that essential knowledge about the complexity of the problems will be lacking. The difference in viewpoints seems to be analogous to the differences covering the advantages of a governing elite versus the advantages of proletariat power.

The argument about whether or not social programs should be under central or local control is closely related to arguments about how a democratic society should function. These issues are in turn related to concern about equality in the power of individuals or groups in society. If agents of a central government are to carry out social programs, inequality in power necessarily results. If local control is to prevail, how will the control actually take place? Will the poor, for example, actually be in control, or will some among them seek power for their own advancement so that in the end the majority of the poor will be as powerless as they might be under federal administration?

These issues are basic to the individual's satisfaction in society. Description of the basic principles of a democratic society and of the necessary conditions for some measure of equality in power and influence needs therefore to precede conclusions about socialization principles in relation to power.

Theoretical Perspectives of Democracy

Democracy as a practical approach in the organization of social structures is a development of the twentieth century. While partially democratic societies existed in earlier times, democracy is mainly a current concept. A significant movement toward democracy in government began with the American and French revolutions, although a precise tracing of the development of democratic thought would lead back through the development of the democracy in English government. In ancient times Aristotle saw "constitutional government" as government by the poor and usually directed toward their own benefit. At present, democratic organizations are believed to contribute to the general welfare and hence have as an important goal the welfare of the many. It should not be overlooked that practical democracy came to be a reality at the same time that significant changes took place in the structure of the American family.

Two categories of meanings of democracy are possible: *classical democratic theory* and *organizational realities* (Schulz, 1966). According to the classical theory of democracy, members of an organization influence policies through representatives responsible to the members of the organization who reflect their will. Problems of such a definition are easily apparent. For example, the number of members who must favor a policy in order for the representatives to carry it out is difficult to agree upon. A majority of one could theoretically determine the organization's policy. In the second definition of democracy, *functional* realities are paramount. In this definition, reflecting organizational realities, competition is an essential factor. Members must compete with other members not only to elect representatives but to persuade others to join in support of a specific policy. Conflict and a struggle to overcome rivals are inevitable in the process of competition.

As part of the functioning of a democratic organization, leaders must struggle for support and at the same time must seek to mold the responses of the members. Even in a democratic society, it must be recognized that disappointment and a lack of opportunity for participation occur for a large number of people. When a group and its leadership loses in an expression of will, for them the democracy of the organization is not functional and their life styles must be altered in ways they consider undesirable. In fact, for those losing the competitive struggle, an authoritarian system can be said to exist, as policies which they disapprove will control their behavior. A basic difference between democratic rule and authoritarian rule therefore is in one sense merely quantitative. In a democracy, policies are carried out according to the wishes of a *majority*. In an authoritarian organization, policies are carried out by a *minority*. Yet, theoretically the difference between democracy and authoritarianism might rest on a very few people.

A theoretical corollary of democracy in organizations is the principle of equality in influence. "One man—one vote" is a common slogan. Theoretically, each man's influence or input into the system of a democratic social order should have the same effect—each member's vote should carry the same weight. This implies that all members of an organization are equal and each individual's contribution to the determination of goals has the same value. Weighted voting (in which some persons' votes count for more than others) is viewed as undemocratic and as a violation of democratic principles.

As Sumner (1963) observed, democracy is a political form in which power comes from the *demos*, the people; but never has a state existed in which the *mass* could express its will. In American society discrimination among voters has been and still is a principle. Those under age, recently moved, unnaturalized, felons, mentally disordered, and so on are legally excluded. Others are illegally excluded. And for much of the world's history, women have had little influence in government. Practical extension of the principle of equality in influencing the system has not worked and does not work. Again, it is a matter of quantity—democracy is approached as a principle only in terms of some quantity. As all societies are hierarchical in the sense that some persons are excluded from influencing policies, democracy as a functional principle is relative and always incomplete.

This view of a theoretical limitation on democracy is of consequence in the socialization process. Limitations on the pursuit of individual goals can realistically be learned in the family. If the development of individual potentiality is valued, variance in the process of socialization must be accepted. It is obviously of no value to a child for the parents to subscribe to democratic conditions in the family and at the same time direct the formation of the child's goals or the means he selects to reach his own goals. A dilemma is clear. If the child is not given choices in his activities and goals, how can he participate in and contribute to a democratic society? If he is permitted to make his own choices about his behavior, how can he be socialized?

Two answers seem possible. First, a person can contribute to society only by some originative behavior. It will not serve society if all individuals merely follow rules and customs already in existence. And, as originative behavior can take place only in a democratic setting, the family must provide opportunity for choices of behavior and must encourage the setting of goals. Second, the child's goals are likely to exist within the framework of society, because his experience and his models are found mainly within the framework of his culture. Hence, if the child is not driven by irrational and unfavorable conditions, he will develop according to cultural expectations. Freedom available to him in the family will allow some variation in goals, but most of his behavior will be within cultural limits, limits he will willingly observe himself.

It is reasonable to believe that development of individual potential is probable when participation in the establishment of the society's goals is possible. As the individual is molded in interaction with a social order, his sense of identity as a person is enhanced if he can have some part in the construction of his life space. Motivation to develop knowledge and skills is also dependent upon an opportunity to use them, and their use is certainly affected by the goals of the social order in which the individual lives. It is thus imperative that if an individual is to develop skills and knowledge in keeping with his capacity, he must be allowed to create conditions under which development of his capacities will flourish. Hence, a close relationship between human development and democracy in organizations is realistic.

The "wrongs" pointed to by some youth in modern social organizations (such as a university or the agencies of the federal government) are not easily righted. Under any system, real functional democracy is always beyond the reach of some members. One of the problems of socialization, consequently, is to teach children to value democracy, knowing at the same time that in many, if not most, organizations in modern society opportunities for influence will be minimal for most people.

As strange as it may seem, distinction between democratic principles and authoritarian principles of government is not always easy. Autocratic government may be considered oligarchical and irresponsible if the few who govern serve their own ends and disregard the welfare of most of the people. Democracy is supposed to be desirable because the *general welfare* is theoretically more likely to be secure under a democratic government than under an autocratic one. Democracy is expected to allow participation of many in mass society; it is perceived as a way for the noninfluential to become influential. In reality, democracy is similar to happiness in that it is an abstraction—a goal to strive for but unlikely to be attained.

Equality and Inequality in Society

Security in urban society is partly determined by economic factors. As a society changes from simple to complex, the economic security of its members decreases. A native in New Guinea can survive indefinitely in his jungle village by his own effort. The situation of a resident of a modern city such as New York is different, however. Here a resident could survive only briefly without the work of a great many people. An urban dweller would not be able to plant and harvest a food crop, to hunt for game, or to prepare flour for bread (Heilbroner, 1967). Dependence on the complex distribution system and many machines means dependence on many other people. Hence, the more complex the society, the more dependent are the individuals in it. In American society certain groups of workers are essential for its vital processes. A strike by the teamsters, for example, can stop the flow of food to an entire city, and disastrous consequences can occur in a day or two. Those who work in a power plant can instantaneously paralyze activity in a region. Thus, an increase in vulnerability to tragic consequences is incurred by those who choose to live in a city. Their affluence, and even life itself, depends upon the willingness of thousands of people to carry out their work roles. Fulfillment of needs and ease of living are attained only in an aggregate,

The Well-being of Individuals. Individual well-being grows out of the bonds holding the social order in balance and in an ordered functioning. While there must be some willingness on the part of workers for such cooperative endeavor, forces of varied sorts have been set up by society to insure compliance in necessary role behavior. The foundation for struggle and conflict in such a system is apparent: The welfare of the individual depends on formalized and functional behavior in roles to maintain the order, but in much of this behavior the individual is compelled to conform. A job will be lost if the individual does not perform required tasks; in some cases failure to conform may mean imprisonment. In spite of the forces keeping them at their tasks, individuals seek to influence society so that it functions for their benefit. In a complex society, however, the checks and balances are so numerous that harmonious and advantageous operation for all seems impossible. The delicate relationships are too easily disrupted.

Economic growth and progress are desirable goals for society but they result in greater complexity. This greater complexity in turn means that the individual's well-being is made even more precarious. Upon examination it can easily be seen that any city, in spite of its abundance of goods, exists on a fragile network of interdependent life styles.

Although the well-being of those in the city stands apart from the vagaries of the basic processes of nature, many other factors operate to cause difficulty. Production of goods depends upon the functioning of social institutions that make possible the utilization of human capacities for work. Complex societies generate complex needs for their members; the needs of those in the city far transcend basic needs for shelter and food. The needs of the urban dweller therefore contribute to and are influenced by the social order's technological accomplishments. Consequently, the needs of those in the city are much greater than if life styles were closer to nature. Hence, man in the city may feel he must hear a symphonic orchestra periodically, see certain plays, or attend some athletic event; and his residence may require many items to meet his living standards. "Needs" in the city therefore grow out of the city's activities and offerings.

Economic growth and stability, essential conditions for the urban dweller's life style, increasingly move further from nature and become more dependent on man's decisions. If malfunction occurs in the operation of the society, it is believed to be because of man's interference with the delicate balancing. Government can decide, for example, in order to reduce inflation, to engage in certain restrictive monetary policies, but the restriction may throw thousands out of work. No society, however, has been able to keep at work all of its members that want work. While thousands are out of work in any large city, things that need to be done for better housing, transportation, or education remain. The tasks to be done are easily recognized and people are available to do them, but the organization and means to do them are lacking.

As a result of this situation it is reasonable to conclude that allocation of roles, labor, and products is not as much dependent on impersonal forces as it is on man himself. The system of allocation of roles and the functioning of society are at fault. Human suffering in complex society stems basically from human behavior. Certain monetary policies devised by men may curb inflation by causing the economy to go through an "adjustment period," but during such an adjustment period some suffer at the hands of their government while others prosper. Theoretically, the good of the majority is served. But in principle that type of function of the social order is similar to older autocratic forms of government. On the basis of the labor of the serfs on the medieval estate, the few in the castle enjoyed a luxurious life style.

Societies with grievous faults exist and in fact have so developed over the centuries. Political confusion, unrest, wars, and revolutions have occurred through the years because of man's inability to distribute in some reasonable fashion his products and status roles. Even today, the fundamental issue in the urban setting is the inequality of distribution of what the city has to offer. In block after block in every city, thousands live outside the mainstream of distribution of products and satisfying role opportunities. In spite of vast efforts at welfare and attempts of many governmental agencies, the problem continues from generation to generation. Man cannot or will not evenly distribute his material and life style possibilities.

The Distribution of Goods. Societies in the world today depend essentially on three systems of control to distribute goods in a society: an historically derived system maintained by law and cultural beliefs, an economic command system, and a marketing system (Heilbroner, 1967). All have some disadvantages. American society is a mixture of these three systems.

The *historically derived* way of distribution has characterized many societies on the earth. In this type of order, the distribution system of products and roles takes place according to custom. A son takes his father's occupational role, social status, and outlook for a share of the products of his society. In this way sanctions and custom keep the order so that inequality is accepted as being in the nature of things. Such a system insures stability, and the great cycle of civilization stays on course through the centuries. But such stability has built-in hazards.

This stability requires that change will take place slowly and within the format provided by the culture and the organizational system. The entrenched elements of power will resist any change that threatens displacement or alteration of their influence. No systematic methods can realistically be applied to alter inequality, and those with inferior status are not allowed to acquire enough power to change their position in the hierarchy. Cultural teaching and socialization specifically insure that effort is not made to change the inequality of roles and power. Under such circumstances democracy is not part of the socialization process; at least, the individual is not to influence the system for his own benefit. In fact, the desire for change is not expected even to occur to him. In this way socialization insures that the power structure remains intact from generation to generation. If democracy exists to some extent, the influence of the people is channeled in directions considered safe for the group in power.

In a society where power is unequally distributed, the distribution of products and advantageous roles will be uneven also. This uneven distribution is a source of potential agitation for change. Those with less power seek to gain allies and to organize so that they can increase the importance of their efforts and change their place in the hierarchy. But as they endeavor to increase their power, so do those in the hierarchy above them. As a result of the agitation and organization of the less powerful, those in power tend to increase their defenses (Wolfe, 1972).

A society undergoing rapid change is, of course, unstable. Alteration of values, by anomie, and a destruction of social norms occur. The basis of power or authority is therefore questioned, and social activity of groups or individuals is difficult to characterize as either legitimate or illegitimate. Charismatic figures appear and describe possible ideal conditions once the existing power structure is replaced (Schermerhorn, 1961). For the replacement of the power structure to be accomplished, beliefs of the people must be changed so that they conform to the new program. This change in perceptual reality brings cultural change and subsequent change in the enculturation of children. Socialization and enculturation are thus related directly to social conditions. For the young to fit into society, their training must be appropriate to social conditions.

In American cities and society today, large groups of the disadvantaged are seeking to alter the traditional power structure. Also, an increasing number of youth are defying the traditional system of authority. As indicated earlier, the disadvantaged, largely blacks of the cities, are better organized than are the youth, and their demands are more clearly articulated. Both, however, have organizations which seek to bring change through legitimate channels and groups which favor violent force in a direct challenge to the power structures of the society.

A second system of control, that of *economic command*, also has a traditional base. As Heilbroner sees it, this system of control represents the only way a democratic society can operate effectively in emergencies of war or national disaster. In such instances the power structure takes over individual rights and resources in order to achieve a certain goal. It should be noted that social change can be rapidly effected under authoritarian policies. Wage and price controls can be enforced or certain industries such as the railroads can be taken over. These latter methods may be undertaken within a representative as well as an authoritarian form of government. For some individuals the results remain the same. Although authoritarian methods of control can be used under either a democratic or authoritarian system of government, theoretically, the difference for individuals lies in the hope that in the democratic system their influence can replace the group in power or force them to alter their methods.

In urban society, it seems that democracy in all areas is an impossibility. Government must engage in such complex activities that decisions cannot be made by individuals in any direct fashion. At times, in order to better the people's overall condition, authoritarian methods to which they object must be imposed. An example would be wage controls. In any event, no modern society is without its "commands."

A third system of control of roles and distribution of goods is that of *market organization*. This system depends upon the activity in the society itself. Under this system neither tradition nor command are depended upon. The principle of this method is that each person makes his own role assignment. A distribution occurs automatically because people see the advantage offered by opportunity in roles remaining unfilled. They can, for example, demand their own price if not enough people are available for the role.

The problem of the market organization system is basically psychological. It is that man is not free to make choices because he is inexorably bound by tradition and cultural prerogatives. He lacks freedom of choice for two basic reasons. First, because of the socialization process—although he perceives himself as capable of making a free choice, actually he has been conditioned by his training to make certain selections. Therefore, in a way, the culture has made his choice for him. The second block to his freedom results from the cultural web of social expectations—he will be influenced in any choice by "what people think" and by the emotional ties he has with those close to him in his life space. Consequently, a market system does not, in reality, work as a system of free choice as it appears to. Man is entangled in the complex socialization experience provided by society. To a degree, a person can act under the illusion that he makes a free choice, but in reality his choice is one that his culture would have predicted he would make, given his past socialization experience. Indeed, "culture" and "society" for the individual mean that his behavior is predictable. An individual, then, according to his cultural experience, deliberately chooses a role (and a share of his society's products) that places some above him in status and opportunity; yet he willingly accepts this inequality because he was trained to do so. Freedom of choice and equality are therefore culturally relative.

THE PSYCHOLOGY OF POWER

Man's psychological development as related to *power* is of much concern in modern society, especially since youth's protests about power have struck a responsive chord in many adults. Those in the black community also would agree that man's relationship to power and authority is a basic theme in human development and behavior in the urban setting. While some maintain that the interplay of emotional and motivational factors determines response styles that lay the foundation for power, cognitive experience also determines perceptual sets of the place of power in modern society. Training in the family and experience with educational models also are significant in the development of feelings about the power of the structures of society.

Although the issues currently voiced about power have historical roots, with American society now generally committed to individual welfare, the understanding of the origin of the issues and the psychological factors forming behavior toward power is of more consequence than ever before in history. With some individuals demanding power and others protesting its lack, one can only reasonably conclude that the issue of who is to have power is basic and thematic in modern society.

As one considers the problem in almost any city, the cry of a protest group streaming toward city hall can be heard: "Down with the power in City Hall." The urgency of the issue is particularly apparent when a protest group is revealed to be teachers, the principal socializing agents in modern society. The cries and slogans are similar, however, whether the group is composed of teachers, police, industrial workers, welfare recipients, or students.

In the urban setting an increasing number of voices now seem to echo the old cry of "Down with the Bastille": predominant voices are those of Mexicans, Indians, and blacks. They demand equality of opportunity and an end to cultural discrimination. The most urgent cries are those of the blacks. Never having found the promised land of Reconstruction days in the South, these people have migrated in vast numbers in recent years. The great cities and industrial centers of the North have received many thousands. At the same time, the way of life in the cities was changed, and the substantial old homes of the nineteenth century no longer served the middle class. Large migrations of whites left simultaneously for the periphery of the cities. The blacks, with little education and few of the skills needed for the new industrial complexity, had little choice but to occupy the old houses. A great part of the cities of America became black.

The rate of deterioration rapidly increased and large sections of the cities became areas of blight, crime, degradation, and despair. Because of this despair leaders in the communities sought to rally the spirit of the blacks with the concept of "black power." Some were revolutionaries whose leaders advocated violence and revenge for their plight. Thus guerilla warfare threatened the cities. In many areas the streets became unsafe even for those who were armed. The years of neglect had led to a problem that now seemed beyond solution.

The cities' financial conditions rapidly became precarious and qualities of most of the services declined. Schools became all black, a change accompanied by a deterioration of facilities and the quality of education. Juvenile behavior caused great concern. Teachers were intimidated and some even were killed by their pupils. Adolescent gangs killed members of rival gangs on the way to school. Not only social control of government, but even civilization itself began to be questioned.

At the same time, questions about the system came from youth in the universities. They challenged the basic social structure, particularly, because the cities were ruled by privileged groups. The views of these new youthful critics were linked to views of some earlier critics of society. Both raised basic issues about the "rulers" of society.

Social Control and Elitism

Youth in common with the blacks decried the power of the establishment and their own powerlessness. Dissatisfaction with the rulers of society has occurred, however, throughout man's social history. In the past the people having power have been referred to as the *elite,* the *group in power,* and the *capitalists.* Most of the people have been called the *masses,* the *people,* and the *proletariat.* Today, when a politician is frustrated with his colleagues' blocking his policy in government, he threatens to take the issue to the people in order to obtain support. His colleagues in the elite or group in power, on hearing his threat, weigh the consequences of such action because theoretically in a democratic society the *people* can remove the elite from power if they become sufficiently dissatisfied. As a matter of fact the people (the proletariat) have at times through the course of civilization thrown out all forms of government.

The opposition of youth today to an administration policy is frequently voiced as opposition to "inflexible power." They see their opposition to the rulers of society as idealistic, and they see their identification with groups lacking power as idealistic. They perceive their idealism as a *new* idealism as compared with views of parents and others. Conflict with rulers is, however, not new, but has occupied men's thoughts for probably as long as human society has existed. Plato in ancient Greece did not like the basic structure of his society. In his work, *The Republic,* he took the view that private property should be abolished and that all ownership should be communal. But he did not object to the principle of social inequality or to a ruling elite.

Recent thinkers believe that the definition of democracy includes the understanding that an elite group will rule. It is, of course, apparent that all cannot participate equally in government and therefore the ruling group will be a minority. Such a group always seeks to perpetuate itself in power, but this is as it should be, else the society will always be ruled by those with no experience. Although the American Constitution developed from democratic principles and the basic rights of men, American society and government from the very beginning provided for government by a few. The founders of the republic recognized that in order for the government to function practically that government would have to consist of a minority composed of people with special interests. In essence, those who set up the American government agreed that in any society, no matter its place in history of the modern world, conditions of people are of two kinds: the rulers—the powerful—and the ruled—the powerless. These groups are never equal—the rulers are always in the minority.

At the time of the founding of the republic, concern was nevertheless expressed about elitism and equality, particularly in reference to private property. Those planning the government were likely influenced by some writers of the time who believed that private property was the source of inequality and the basis for conflict in human interaction. Rousseau, for example, believed that society was the source of evil because it could not exist without depending upon the principle of private property. The issue about the equality of men centered on the possession of wealth; thus the destiny of men in society depended upon the holding or acquisition of property.

In American history the election of Andrew Jackson in 1828 to the Presidency was hailed as the "Rise of the Common Man" because of his identification with the backwoodsmen and those of low socioeconomic status. Few voices were raised against the dogmatic views of "popular democracy." As a result, Jackson, as one of the common people, enjoyed immense popularity. He was seen as a leader opposed to a wealthy elite and a stratified society. Today in the twentieth century some youth also object to the importance assigned to property and goods in our society. They frequently express opposition to the cultural tendency to equate social status with acquisition of property and material goods. Hence, two centuries after the beginning of American government and nearly twenty-five centuries since Plato, the place of property in the value system continues to be a source of debate.

Various forms of economic philosophy for the last two hundred years have tried to deal specifically with the problem of property in society. Marx, for example, believed that *products* were the motivating factors in human behavior and development. He, as well as others, asserted that man is in a struggle against nature, and that the good life comes with material plenty and an absence of rulers or an elite group. He believed that the elite characteristically exploited the common worker. Marx's assertion, however, that profit is synonymous with theft is not an original idea, as a number of social critics have taken this view. Critics of Marxian philosophy suggest that Marx's faith in the wisdom and ideals of the workers as opposed to the ideals of an elite was unjustified.

In most societies, the rulers are not only the ones with the most power but generally are the ones who have the highest incomes in the society. Such a distribution of income is found no matter what the nature of the social system. The wealth of the elite group helps the members of that group as they seek to remain in power. Sometimes the power and wealth are used dishonestly, particularly in the control of information about methods used to obtain goals. A modern term for a failure to provide information to the public is that of "credibility gap."

Motivation to stay in power, it should be recognized, must be maintained at a high level. Those in power who do not wish to maintain motivation at such a level are soon replaced. Widely differing factors cause variance in motivation and capacity to obtain or maintain power (Lipset and Dobson, 1972). Factors growing out of genetic differences, physical development before and subsequent to birth, and culture all contribute to differences in response style in a struggle for power. The demands of society's roles also are sources of a wide range in behavior to secure a position of power.

Philosophical approaches to the meaning of power are based on the view that it is an abstract and imprecise term. One meaning, for example, includes only the *capacity* to take action. In this meaning those in power have the necessary force but never actually use it. In another meaning, however, *activity* toward a goal is added to the capacity for action. In the first instance, a governor may have the power to call out the National Guard but never does—yet a power "in being" exists which may influence events and behavior of individuals and groups. In this concept of power, a passive one, its mere existence affects social interaction and behavioral processes in the society. The active concept of power refers not only to the existence of a force but also to its use. In using the example of the National Guard, not only would the Guard exist as a power in being, but it would be active in carrying out policies affecting events when the governor thought it necessary. In either type, events would be controlled or influenced in some direction by the "power." The intensity or effectiveness of the power does not necessarily depend on whether or not the power is active.

In philosophy, the nature of man and variance in power have been subjects for discussion for a long time. Some believe that a desire for power and the opportunity to control others is basic and innate in human nature. A biological basis for power came out of the ideas of Darwin, Sereno (1968) believes, as Darwin thought that only the powerful survive. According to this idea, the essential purpose in life is a struggle for power and survival. It could be argued, if one took this view, that the elite and the rulers are those most capable in a society and that biological selection is an important force in the acquisition of their position of power. The fact that power is universally wanted or that it is a basic need, however, would be quite difficult to establish. The struggle for power is a subjective idea. Behavior directed toward the acquisition of power results from the socialization experience rather than from a genetic trait. Power therefore should not be viewed as a generalized or as a unitary drive within individuals. It is clear that in some instances an individual seeks to direct events while in others he does not choose to be active.

The question of the concept of a drive for power is an important one for those concerned about the socialization process, particularly in view of youth's angry voices against power and their lament about their powerlessness. Yet, if rule is always by an elite and no other type of society is practical or possible, their anger against such a reality can only be disturbing and fruitless. Youth must learn to see power and its place in the affairs of man in its proper perspective. If it is necessary to have government and rule, then emotional upset about this necessity is unrealistic. Socialization must provide some experience or training in how to live with power and rule. Power must not be perceived as an inevitable evil. Nor must a position of power be seen as the only way "quality" in life can be attained.

Because of the generalized nature of the socialization experience, rule by an elite, from one point of view, will not cause dysfunctional conditions in society. In making decisions, the elite are necessarily influenced by those who have some kinship or some association with them, and they will be swayed by those who were significant models in childhood or adolescence. Decisions of the elite may therefore seem to be made independently and on the basis of information and facts available, but the ramifications for the basis of the decisions reach out into the cultural enclaves and to people remote from the center of power. In such a concept, the rule of the elite is not separate and removed from the desires of the rest of the society or from the "masses." In this sense the tendrils of human relationships affect the role of behavior of the rulers as much as those who are ruled. The elite thus are not entirely removed from the people—cultural norms, long since internalized, affect their decisions and role behavior. In essence this is the concept of *cultural determinism*.

Those in power, consequently, really do not make immediate and independent decisions; rather, their behavior is an outgrowth of past learning and socialization experience. A realistic and functional distinction between the rulers and the ruled becomes much less clear. It is possible to postulate that the elite are indeed prisoners of their culture and are no more free as rulers than are those who are ruled. Hence, most decisions and policies are, in reality, culturally determined over a long period of time. The elite seek only to perpetuate the social order as they perpetuate themselves in power. Although their roles and life styles vary from those of the masses, they still are in accord with the social conditioning and controls generally approved in the society—their values are similar to those of the people whom they rule.

Powerlessness in Society

One night in the slum area of the city, a policeman in a squad car stopped two adolescent boys on the street. He rolled the window down to ask the boys for names and addresses. As he rested his notebook on the steering wheel and wrote, one youth only fifteen years of age pulled a pistol from his pocket and shot the policeman twice. The boys ran as the policeman lay dying across the steering wheel.

The net of the city's law enforcement organization soon identified the boy. As dawn came to the wintry and polluted skies above the ghetto, the boy and his companion were arrested. Both were found to have a history of school problems and frequent arrests for stealing. The fifteen-year-old attended a school for the mentally retarded.

Culturally, the boys were almost a world apart from those in the city's power structure, since both the mayor and the head of the school board were millionaires. The boys came from the powerless—those at the very bottom of the society. They had turned to violence against the representatives of the elite (the police). Many of those on their social level saw the act as only part of a crusade against repression and the awful despair of the ghetto. While the action was deplored by the boys' community, the conditions under which the powerless lived and which brought about the despair and hate were perceived as the responsibility of society.

American society now has wide extremes. Equalitarianism, the dream of the men of colonial times, has not come to pass. Programs have yet to make an inroad on the extensive erosion of the cities. Yet the filth and the pollution are no match for the despair and hate often directed by the powerless toward society's established elite.

It is not that some in the elite do not hear the cries of the powerless, and they have tried to better the city's conditions. Although governmental agencies of the city, state, and nation sometimes see promising programs lose their momentum and vast sums, too huge to visualize, are needed, plans are underway to deal with housing, transportation, health, and welfare. But the blacks see the plight of the cities coming from a lack of "will." If the society willed to solve their problems, they would be solved, their leaders assert. The problems are basically social and psychological, not economic, they say.

A valued approach to these problems reflects society's belief in education. Some programs were designed to help very young children when they enter school. Realization soon came, however, that a "head start" would not offset the cumulative effects of the ghetto conditions of continuing poverty and the adverse conditions of a slum school. The enthusiasm and considerable effort devoted to Head Start and other early childhood programs lessened. It was concluded that separation of the problems of housing, employment opportunities, and psychosocial attitudes from the programs for early childhood is impossible. With the beginning of the decade of the 1970s discouragement about the Vietnam War, generally depressed economic conditions, the demands of various minorities, the divisiveness of religious groups, unrest in the universities, and the financial plight of the cities and states—all led to a "social depression" for many in society. Crises in social institutions come almost to be accepted as daily occurrences.

But other problems characterize city life in the new decade. Civilized man has begun to threaten his environment. The very air has become so dangerous at times that pollution alerts commensurate with alerts reserved for nuclear disaster are common. Not alone air, but water, too, has become a threat to survival. Waste threatens not only to devastate the esthetic character of the land and the seas but to engulf man himself.

Food too has become a problem. Additives of all kinds are so common that few people try to determine what they eat; some additives, although used widely, have been found to endanger health. Fish, a food staple for man since he was first on the earth, threatens to become a poison because of pollution.

Despite the struggle of centuries, justice has become hard to attain, especially for the powerless. Some estimate that half the inmates of prisons in the country have not been tried. Conditions in many prisons are so bad that they cause despairing men to revolt, even at the cost of their lives. Society's confidence in the system of justice, too, has been reduced. Men are arrested and released many times without coming to trial. And the time lag for legal adjudication stretches over an increasing number of years. So, today the powerless in the cities remain malnourished, poverty-stricken, beset by health hazards, threatened by crime, and cut off from justice or a voice in their government.

An even greater problem looms. Although a better distribution of goods may be achieved in American society, what of the millions across the world who will still be in need? Philosophical questions, hence, arise about the powerless and the elite in American society: Can even a highly advanced society solve problems on so vast a scale? Should material division be made now so that the world can progress in a much more even manner? The problems of modern and urban society reflect not only historical questions of the past but, in microcosm, the problems of the planet. Emerging nations of the world are scarcely less demanding than the minority groups in our society, nor are their pleas any less just. Perhaps a new social concern will spur man to exceed his reach and take new giant steps on earth, but the problems loom large.

The view of the powerless that society lacks the will to face its problems is an important one for social scientists. In a highly competitive and increasingly complex society, the energy of the elite is easily absorbed in their role tasks. How much of their energy can or should be diverted to the problems of the powerless in the world?

The view of those who advocate a reordering of values and a reduction of the drive for more material goods as a goal for man also must be considered. A man in New Guinea paddling a dugout canoe might arrive at his destination in a shorter time if he had an outboard motor. He would, however, soon pollute his river and erase the sound of the birds in the jungle above his head. Further, after the motor he would desire a boat of fiberglass that would plane over the water instead of gracefully cutting through it. The artistic quality of his own construction would disappear. Perhaps materialism is not the source of man's happiness or equality of property a proper goal.

Power and powerlessness become less of an issue when materialism is no longer a primary goal. Perhaps man can learn to view equality differently. The man in the dugout on an unpolluted river has rewards that a man in the city can never have. But the man in the city also has special rewards from his environment: He can hear the sounds of a great orchestra or he can contemplate art of the ages. Both men thus have satisfying life experiences—of a different order, of course, without the possibility of equation. Neither man should exalt or denigrate himself by designation as a "have" or a "have not." Approaches to equality lie more with man's emotions about himself and his world than in either his technology or his possessions.

IN PERSPECTIVE

The individual's capacities to interact with power and control in modern society are determined by the developmental experience. Learning about power and personal capacity to influence it or to achieve it should be a part of the socialization experience. Further, beliefs about distribution or centralization of power affect participation in and contribution to society. Some of the inevitable attributes of power and social organizations need to be learned. If youth rejects all power, as some now do, they need knowledge of the results of such rejection.

Experience with appropriate models in the family and in the educational system is significant in learning about power and the purpose of social organizations. It is clear that the experience of many youth today has not fitted them for coping with the problems of finding a place within this society. All too often realization of the limitations of the principles of democracy and of the effectiveness of social organizations comes belatedly. If youth are to find satisfaction in adult roles, the limitations as well as the values of social organizations need to be understood. Further, if social change and a better society are to be accomplished, attention to means and methods of bringing about social change is of much importance. Human developmental experience cannot rationally be an area of study that is separate from the society and culture in which that development takes place.

REFERENCES

ARENSBERG, C., & NIEHOFF, A. H. *Introducing social change.* Chicago: Aldine, 1964.

BERLE, A. A. Of statist and non-statist economic power. In J. A. Winter, J. Rabow, & M. Chesler. *Vital problems for American society.* New York: Random House, 1968. Pp. 123–126.

BIERSTEDT, R. The problem of authority. In M. Berger, T. Abel, & C. H. Page (Eds.), *Freedom and control in modern society.* New York: Octagon, 1964. Pp. 67–81.

CHEIN, I. The concept of power. In F. F. Korten, S. W. Cook, & J. I. Lacey (Eds.), *Psychology and the problems of society.* Washington, D.C.: American Psychological Association, 1970. Pp. 327–343.

COMTE, A. The science of society. In H. M. Ruitenbeek (Ed.), *Varieties of classic social theory.* New York: E. P. Dutton, 1963. Pp. 30–74.

CONGER, J. J. A world they never knew: The family and social change. *Daedalus, Journal of the American Academy of Arts and Sciences,* Fall, 1971, 1105–1138.

COOK, T. I. Individual liberty today: Challenge and prospect. In M. Berger, T. Abel, & C. H. Page (Eds.), *Freedom and control in modern society.* New York: Octagon, 1964. Pp. 177–191.

DAVIS, K. The demographic foundations of national power. In M. Berger, T. Abel, & C. H. Page (Eds.), *Freedom and control in modern society.* New York: Octagon, 1964. Pp. 206–242.

DODSON, D. W. *Education and the powerless.* In E. T. Keach, R. Fulton, & W. E. Gardner (Eds.), *Education and social crisis.* New York: Wiley, 1967. Pp. 311–320.

DURKHEIM, E. Society and anomie. In H. M. Ruitenbeek (Ed.), *Varieties of classic social theory.* New York: E. P. Dutton, 1963. Pp. 320–364.

GERTH, H., & MILLS, C. W. *Character and social structure.* New York: Harcourt, Brace & World, 1964.

HEILBRONER, R. L. The making of economic society. In G. D. Bell, *Organizations and human behavior.* Englewood Cliffs, N.J.: Prentice-Hall, 1967. Pp. 15–24.

LENSKI, G. *Power and privilege.* New York: McGraw-Hill, 1966.

LEVIN, H. Psychologist to the powerless. In F. F. Korten, S. W. Cook, & J. I. Lacey (Eds.), *Psychology and the problems of society.* Washington, D.C.: American Psychological Association, 1970. Pp. 121–127.

LIPSET, S. M., & DOBSON, R. B. The intellectual as critic and rebel: With special reference to the United States and the Soviet Union. *Daedalus, Journal of the American Academy of Arts and Sciences,* Summer, 1972, 137–198.

MARX, L. An analysis of class. In H. M. Ruitenbeek (Ed.), *Varieties of classic social theory.* New York: E. P. Dutton, 1963. Pp. 75–97.

MOSCA, G. *The ruling class.* New York: McGraw-Hill, 1939.

OWEN, D. Urbanization in the developing world. In B. J. L. Berry & J. Meltzer (Eds.), *Goals for urban America.* Englewood Cliffs, N.J.: Prentice-Hall, 1967. Pp. 22–37.

SCHERMERHORN, R. A. *Society and power.* Random House, 1961.

SCHULZ, E. B. *Democracy.* Woodbury, N.Y.: Barron's, 1966.

SERENO, R. *The rulers.* New York: Harper & Row, 1968.

SISTRUNK, F., CLEMENT, D. E., & ULMAN, J. D. Effect of reinforcement magnitude on nonconformity. *The Journal of Social Psychology,* 1972, 86, 11–22.

SUMNER, W. G. Democracy and plutocracy. In S. Persons (Ed.), *Social Darwinism: Selected essays of William Graham Sumner.* Englewood Cliffs, N.J.: Prentice-Hall, 1963. Pp. 136–149.

WADDINGTON, C. H. The desire for material progress as a world ordering system. In S. Hoffman (Ed.), *Conditions of world order.* Boston: Houghton Mifflin, 1968. Pp. 228–235.

WHITE, L. A. Individuality and individualism. In G. H. Mills (Ed.), *Innocence and power.* Austin: University of Texas Press, 1965. Pp. 3–35.

WILSON, C. E. Toward a new social order. In F. F. Korten, S. W. Cook, & J. I. Lacey (Eds.), *Psychology and the problems of society.* Washington, D.C.: American Psychological Association, 1970. Pp. 268–274.

WOLFE, R. N. Effects of economic threat on anomia and perceived locus of control. *The Journal of Social Psychology,* 1972, 86, 233–240.

INDEX

Y

Young, Paul Thomas, 169-70
Youth, 291, 305 (*see also* Adolescents)
  achievement motivation and, 198
  in American society, 47
  and autonomy, 275-76, 289-90

Youth (*cont.*)
  idealism of, 199
  and mass society, 280
  and power, 315, 322
  social change, 36, 112
  and social control, 243
  socialization of, 47-49, 61-62
  and work, 296-300